UNDERSTANDING INSTITUTIONAL DIVERSITY

UNDERSTANDING INSTITUTIONAL DIVERSITY

Elinor Ostrom

PRINCETON UNIVERSITY PRESS   PRINCETON AND OXFORD

Library of Congress Cataloging-in-Publication Data

Ostrom, Elinor.
Understanding institutional diversity / Elinor Ostrom.
p.   cm.
Includes bibliographical references and index.
ISBN-13: 978-0-691-12207-6 (cloth : alk. paper)
ISBN-10: 0-691-12207-5 (cloth : alk. paper)
ISBN-13: 978-0-691-12238-0 (pbk. : alk. paper)
ISBN-10: 0-691-12238-5 (pbk. : alk. paper)
1. Diversity in the workplace. 2. Multiculturalism. 3. Interpersonal
relations. 4. Organizational behavior. 5. Social norms. I. Title.
HF5549.5.M5O88   2005
302.3'5—dc22   2004065772

British Library Cataloging-in-Publication Data is available

This book has been composed in Sabon

Printed on acid-free paper. ∞

pup.princeton.edu

Printed in the United States of America

10   9   8   7   6   5   4   3   2

To the fabulous colleagues, students, visiting scholars, and staff who have made scholarship at the Workshop over the past thirty years highly productive, challenging, and rewarding

Contents

Illustrations _____

Figures

Tables

Acknowledgments

ANY BOOK DRAWING on unpublished and published papers that an author has drafted and thought about for multiple decades requires many acknowledgments. As I mention in several places in the volume, sections of this book were started in the 1980s when I was a research scholar at the Center for Interdisciplinary Research at Bielefeld University in Germany. I was fortunate enough to visit Bielefeld during 1982 and again in 1988. The opportunity to express some of my early thinking about nested sets of rules and action situations with colleagues participating in both Bielefeld groups is deeply appreciated and helped me immensely. I can remember the puzzlement of several colleagues when I decided to entitle a lecture given at Bielefeld in 1982 "The Hidden Structure behind the Structure." In some respects, one may think of this book as my effort to uncover that hidden structure and to answer their many questions.

My major home base throughout this entire period, of course, has been the Workshop in Political Theory and Policy Analysis at Indiana University, Bloomington. Many earlier draft sections of what is now in this book have been presented at our colloquiums, at miniconference sessions, and in various working group meetings (e.g., the CPR Rules Coding Group, the Evolutionary Theory Working Group) at the Workshop. It has been an intellectual home for me where one could present radical ideas and get them taken seriously at the same time as they are being challenged and debated. The support of the Workshop by Indiana University is deeply appreciated.

Vincent Ostrom cofounded the Workshop with me more than thirty years ago, and his ideas permeate all that we do at the Workshop. None of us could have achieved what we have done without his inspiration, criticism, encouragement, and help, and there is no way of really adequately thanking him for years of lively discussions about the theoretical issues discussed in this book.

Throughout this period, we have been fortunate to receive funding from the National Science Foundation (SES-8619498; SES-8921888; SBR-9521918; SES-0083511), the Ford Foundation (950–1160–1), and the MacArthur Foundation (00–63798-GSS). Work with colleagues in the Resilience Alliance (supported by the McDonnell Foundation) has proved important during recent years and has helped to stimulate work on the last sections of the book. I was fortunate to spend a month with colleagues at the Max Planck Center for the Study of Common Goods in Bonn, Germany, during 2001. The staff there was very helpful and as-

sisted me in getting a number of notes that had been written in the 1980s
into text form.

In recent years, I have given a number of seminars at different universities on various sections of this book. These include: the Sanford School
of Public Policy at Duke University in November 2001; the Department
of Political Science, University of California, San Diego, in March 2002;
as part of the Walker-Ames Lecture Series at the University of Washington
in April 2002; Kathmandu University in April 2002; the Department of
Economics and the Complex Systems Group at the University of Michigan in November 2002; the Max Planck Institute in Jena, Germany, in
June 2003; Purdue University in October 2004; Cornell University in November 2004; Case Western University in January 2005; and at the Workshop itself on October 18, 2004, as well as in my seminar during the fall
semesters of 2003 and 2004.

During the many years that colleagues and I have been trying to understand institutions, the occasion to write a number of papers and chapters
have enabled coauthors and me to develop initial versions of many of the
arguments in this volume. Thus, there are partial sections of earlier papers
that are drawn on in multiple chapters of this volume, including:

Chapters 1 and 2: Elinor Ostrom, "Institutional Rational Choice: An
Assessment of the Institutional Analysis and Development Framework,"
in *Theories of the Policy Process*, ed. Paul A. Sabatier (Boulder, CO: Westview Press, 1999), pp. 35–71; and Elinor Ostrom, "Doing Institutional
Analysis: Digging Deeper Than Markets and Hierarchies," in the *Handbook of New Institutional Economics*, ed. Claude Ménard and Mary Shirley (Dordrecht, the Netherlands: Springer, 2005), pp. 797–926.

Chapter 4: Elinor Ostrom, "Collective Action and the Evolution of Social Norms," *Journal of Economic Perspectives* 14 (3) (2000): 137–58.

Chapter 5: Sue E. S. Crawford and Elinor Ostrom, "A Grammar of Institutions," *American Political Science Review* 89 (3) (September 1995): 582–600. (Reprinted with the permission of Cambridge University Press.) Reprinted in *Polycentric Games and Institutions: Readings from the Workshop in Political Theory and Policy Analysis*, ed. Michael McGinnis (Ann
Arbor: University of Michigan Press, 2000), pp. 114–55. Figures and tables
reprinted with the permission of the University of Michigan Press.

Chapter 8: Elinor Ostrom, "Reformulating the Commons," in *Protecting the Commons: A Framework for Resource Management in the
Americas*, ed. Joanna Burger, Elinor Ostrom, Richard B. Norgaard, David
Policansky, and Bernard D. Goldstein (Washington, D.C.: Island Press,
2001), pp. 17–41.

Chapters 8 and 9: Elinor Ostrom, "Coping with Tragedies of the Commons," *Annual Review of Political Science* 2 (1999): 493–535. (Reprinted with permission of the *Annual Review of Political Science*.)

Chapter 9: Elinor Ostrom, "Institutional Analysis, Design Principles, and Threats to Sustainable Community Governance and Management of Commons," in *Law and the Governance of Renewable Resources: Studies from Northern Europe and Africa*, ed. Erling Berge and Nils Christian Stenseth (Oakland, CA: ICS Press, 1998), pp. 27–53.

As I work on this book, I am deeply appreciative of the long conversations that I have had with colleagues about the Institutional Analysis and Development (IAD) framework, which many of us have had a direct role in creating. The many conversations and memos shared with Larry Kiser and Sue Crawford are particularly important in affecting my own thinking, and working with Roy Gardner and James Walker to model these ideas using game theory and build experimental games to test our predictions has been invaluable. Roger Parks has repeatedly given me extensive comments on earlier manuscripts that have challenged me to work still harder to explain the concepts. Marco Janssen and Mike McGinnis have both read and commented extensively on sections of this manuscript. Working with T. K. Ahn on multiple papers has also added to my understanding. Chuck Myers at Princeton University Press has given me many useful suggestions and has been extremely helpful through the final year of moving an amorphous manuscript toward being a real book. Cindy Crumrine, who copyedited this book for Princeton University Press, did an outstanding job. The anonymous reviewers for Princeton University Press also provided useful advice. Eric Coleman has read through the final draft with a critical and useful eye and developed the index for this book. Without Patty Lezotte's excellent editing skills, thoughtful insights, and cheerful help under high stress, I do not know how I could have finished this book.

In addition, there have been a number of people who have given one or more chapters a very serious read and given me comments. These include: Ryan Adams, Arun Agrawal, Alexander Alexeev, Marty Anderies, Krister Andersson, Ed Araral, Robert Axelrod, Brian Bartels, Avner Benner, Robert Bish, Juan-Camilo Cardenas, Robert Christensen, Daniel Cole, Eric Coleman, Meritxell Costeja, Shanon Donnelly, Ginger Elliot, Ernst Fehr, Susan Fitzpatrick, Bruno Frey, Norman Frohlich, Jessica Gerrity, Gerd Gigerenzer, Werner Güth, Tobias Haller, Grant Hemphill, Pamela Jagger, Kenneth Koford, Kudan Kumar, Wai Fung Lam, Joe Oppenheimer, Mike Radcliffe, Eric Rasmusen, Bo Rothstein, Fritz Scharpf, John Schiemann, Edella Schlager, Ganesh Shivakoti, Shui Yan Tang, Ingela Ternstrom, Catherine Tucker, Frank Van Laerhoven, Tommaso Vitale, James Wilson, Lihau Yang, and Eric Zeemering.

Part I

AN OVERVIEW OF THE INSTITUTIONAL
ANALYSIS AND DEVELOPMENT (IAD)
FRAMEWORK

One

Understanding the Diversity of Structured Human Interactions

TO UNDERSTAND institutions one needs to know what they are, how and why they are crafted and sustained, and what consequences they generate in diverse settings. Understanding anything is a process of learning what it does, how and why it works, how to create or modify it, and eventually how to convey that knowledge to others. Broadly defined, institutions are the prescriptions that humans use to organize all forms of repetitive and structured interactions including those within families, neighborhoods, markets, firms, sports leagues, churches, private associations, and governments at all scales. Individuals interacting within rule-structured situations face choices regarding the actions and strategies they take, leading to consequences for themselves and for others.

The opportunities and constraints individuals face in any particular situation, the information they obtain, the benefits they obtain or are excluded from, and how they reason about the situation are all affected by the rules or absence of rules that structure the situation. Further, the rules affecting one situation are themselves crafted by individuals interacting in deeper-level situations. For example, the rules we use when driving to work every day were themselves crafted by officials acting within the collective-choice rules used to structure their deliberations and decisions. If the individuals who are crafting and modifying rules do not understand how particular combinations of rules affect actions and outcomes in a particular ecological and cultural environment, rule changes may produce unexpected and, at times, disastrous outcomes.

Thus, understanding institutions is a serious endeavor. It is an endeavor that colleagues and I at the Workshop in Political Theory and Policy Analysis have been struggling with for at least three decades.[1] After designing multiple research projects; writing numerous articles; developing ideas in the classroom; learning from eminent scholars in the field, from students, and from colleagues; and making diverse attacks on this problem, it is time to try to put thoughts on this subject together within the covers of a book, even though I am still not fully satisfied with my own understanding. Consider this a progress report on a long-term project that will be continued, I hope, by many others into the future.

Diversity: A Core Problem in Understanding Institutions

A major problem in understanding institutions relates to the diversity of situations of contemporary life. As we go about our everyday life, we interact in a wide diversity of complex situations. Many of us face a morning and evening commute where we expect that others, who are traveling at great speeds, will observe the rules of the road. Our very lives depend on these expectations. Others depend on our own driving behavior conforming in general to locally enforced rules about speeding, changing lanes, and turn-taking behavior at intersections. Those of us who work in large organizations—universities, research centers, business firms, government offices—participate in a variety of team efforts. In order to do our own work well, we are dependent on others to do their work creatively, energetically, and predictably, and vice versa. Many of us play sports at noontime, in the early evening, or on the weekends. Here again, we need to learn the basic rules of each of the games we play as well as find colleagues with whom we can repeatedly engage in this activity. During the average week, we will undertake activities in various types of market settings—ranging from buying our everyday food and necessities to investing funds in various types of financial instruments. And we will spend some hours each week with family and friends in a variety of activities that may involve worship, helping children with homework, taking care of our homes and gardens, and a long list of other activities undertaken with family and friends.

Somehow as individuals we implicitly make sense of most of these diverse and complex situations. We do so even today, with all of the new opportunities and risks that were not even conceivable a few generations ago. We now expect to watch the Olympic games and other international competitions as they happen, no matter where they are located or where we are in the world. We have become accustomed to buying bananas, oranges, and kiwi fruit at any time of the year in almost any market we enter around the globe. Not only do millions of us drive to work regularly, many of us also fly to other parts of the globe on a regular basis, trusting our lives to the knowledge and skills of pilots to know and utilize the many do's and don'ts of flying airplanes.

If we are considered to be adults and sane, we are expected to be able to reason about, learn, and eventually know what to do in many diverse situations that we confront in today's world. We know that when we are shopping in a supermarket that we can take a huge variety of goods off the shelf and put them in a pushcart. Before we put these same goods in our car, however, we need to line up at a counter and arrange to pay for them using cash or a credit card (something else that was not so widely available a few years ago). When we are shopping in an open bazaar in

Asia or Africa, however, the do's and don'ts differ. If we go at the end of the market day, we may bargain over the price of the fruit that is left on the stand—something we could never do in a supermarket where fruit will be refrigerated overnight. If we are in the household goods section of the bazaar, vendors would be astounded if we did not make several counteroffers before we purchased an item. Try that in a furniture store in a commercial district of a Western country, and you would find yourself politely (or not so politely) told to leave the establishment. Thus, there are many subtle (and not so subtle) changes from one situation to another even though many variables are the same.

These institutional and cultural factors affect our expectations of the behavior of others and their expectations of our behavior (Allen 2005). For example, once we learn the technical skills associated with driving a car, driving in Los Angeles—where everyone drives fast but generally follows traffic rules—is quite a different experience from driving in Rome, Rio, and even in Washington, D.C., where drivers appear to be playing a bluffing game with one another at intersections rather than following traffic rules. When playing racquetball with a colleague, it is usually okay to be aggressive and to win by using all of one's skills, but when teaching a young family member how to play a ball game, the challenge is how to let them have fun when they are first starting to learn a new skill. Being too aggressive in this setting—or in many other seemingly competitive situations—may be counterproductive. A "well-adjusted and productive" adult adjusts expectations and ways of interacting with others in situations that occur in diverse times and spaces.

Our implicit knowledge of the expected do's and don'ts in this variety of situations is extensive. Frequently, we are not even conscious of all of the rules, norms, and strategies we follow. Nor have the social sciences developed adequate theoretical tools to help us translate our implicit knowledge into a consistent explicit theory of complex human behavior. When taking most university courses in anthropology, economics, geography, organization theory, political science, psychology, or sociology, we learn separate languages that do not help us identify the common work parts of all this buzzing confusion that surrounds our lives. Students frequently complain—and justifiably so—that they have a sense of being in a Tower of Babel. Scholars also see the same problem (V. Ostrom 1997, 156).

Is There an Underlying Set of Universal Building Blocks?

The core questions asked in this book are: Can we dig below the immense diversity of regularized social interactions in markets, hierarchies, families, sports, legislatures, elections, and other situations to identify universal building blocks used in crafting all such structured situations? If so, what are the underlying component parts that can be used to build useful theories of human behavior in the diverse range of situations in which humans interact? Can we use the same components to build an explanation for behavior in a commodity market as we would use to explain behavior in a university, a religious order, a transportation system, or an urban public economy? Can we identify the multiple levels of analysis needed to explain the regularities in human behavior that we observe? Is there any way that the analyses of local problem solving, such as the efforts of Maine lobster fishers for the last eighty years to regulate their fisheries (see Acheson 1988, 2003; Wilson 1990), can be analyzed using a similar set of tools as problem solving at a national level (Gellar 2005; McGinnis forthcoming; Sawyer 2005) or at an international level (Gibson, Anderson, et al. 2005; O. Young 1997, 2002)?

My answer to these questions is yes. This answer is, of course, a conjecture and can be challenged. Asserting that there is an underlying unity is easy. Convincing others of this is more difficult. I welcome exchanges with others concerning the fundamental building blocks of organized human interactions.

Many Components in Many Layers

The diversity of regularized social behavior that we observe at multiple scales is constructed, I will argue, from universal components organized in many layers. In other words, whenever interdependent individuals are thought to be acting in an organized fashion, several layers of universal components create the structure that affects their behavior and the outcomes they achieve. I give a positive answer to these questions based on years of work with colleagues developing and applying the Institutional Analysis and Development (IAD) framework.[2]

Helping others to see the usefulness of developing a multilevel taxonomy of the underlying components of the situations human actors face is the challenge that I undertake in this volume. Scholars familiar with the working parts used by mathematical game theorists to describe a game will not be surprised by the positive answer. To analyze a game, the theorist must answer a series of questions regarding universal components of a game, including the number of players, what moves they can take, what outcomes are available, the order of decisions, and how they value moves and outcomes.

On the other hand, game theorists will be surprised at the extremely large number of components identified in this book that create the context within which a game is played. Further, if one drops the use of a universal, simplified model of the individual, the number of options that a theorist must self-consciously make is even larger than experienced in the past. While the usefulness of a universal *model* of rational behavior is challenged in chapter 4, the assumption of a universal *framework* composed of nested sets of components within components for explaining human behavior is retained throughout the book.

Building a Framework

Game-theoretical analysis is drawn on and expanded in this book in several ways. First, I do not confine analysis to those situations that are simple enough to be analyzed as formal games. The core concept of an action situation (discussed in chapters 2 and 3) can be formalized as a mathematical game to represent many simple and important situations. Many other significant situations—particularly where rules are the object of choice— are too complex to be modeled as a simple game. (Agent-based models and simulations of diverse types will provide the modeling tools we need to capture patterns of interaction and outcomes in many of these more complex settings [Janssen 2003].)

Second, I dig further to develop a consistent method for overtly analyzing the deeper structures that constitute any particular action situation. For some game theorists, this deeper structure is irrelevant once the structure of a game itself is made explicit. Third, the narrow model of human behavior used in game theory is viewed as one end of a continuum of models of human behavior appropriate for institutional analysis. The three basic assumptions of that model are used as a foundation for specifying the type of assumptions that a theorist needs to make when animating an institutional analysis.

The challenge for institutional theorists—as I discuss in chapter 4—is to know enough about the structure of a situation to select the appropriate assumptions about human behavior that fit the type of situation under analysis. Thus, the approach presented here encompasses contemporary game theory as one of the theories that is consistent with the IAD framework. Also included, as discussed in chapter 4, are broader theories that assume individuals are fallible learners trying to do the best they can in the long term by using norms and heuristics in making their immediate decisions.

As a scholar committed to understanding underlying universal components of all social systems, I do not introduce complexity lightly. I view scientific explanation as requiring just enough variables to enable one to explain, understand, and predict outcomes in relevant settings. Thus, for many questions of interest to social scientists, one does not need to dig down through nested layers of rules that are examined in the last half of this book. One can develop a good analysis of the situation (chapters 2 and 3), decide what assumptions to make about participants (chapter 4), and predict outcomes. If the predictions are supported empirically, that may be all that is needed.[3]

If the predictions are not supported, however, as is the case with much contemporary work on social dilemmas and settings involving trust and reciprocity, one has to dig under the surface to begin to understand why. And if one wants to improve the outcomes achieved over time, one is faced with the need to understand the deeper structure in the grammar of institutions discussed in chapter 5 and the types of rules used to create structure as discussed in chapters 7 and 8. This volume can be viewed as presenting a series of nested conceptual maps of the explanatory space that social scientists can use in trying to understand and explain the diversity of human patterns of behavior. Learning to use a set of conceptual maps and determining the right amount of detail to use is, however, itself a skill that takes some time to acquire just as it does with geographic maps (see Levi 1997b).

Frameworks and Conceptual Maps

For example, if I want to know the quickest route from Providence Bay to Gore Bay on the Manitoulin Island, where Vincent Ostrom and I spend summers writing at our cabin on the shores of Lake Huron, I need a very detailed map of the interior of the island itself. If I want to explain where the Manitoulin Island is to a colleague—who wants to know where we spend our summers—I need a less detailed and larger map that shows its location on the northern shores of Lake Huron, one of the Great Lakes of the North American continent. If I try to use a map of the entire Western Hemisphere, however, the Great Lakes are all so small that locating the Manitoulin Island itself may be a challenge. I may only be able to point to the Province of Ontario in Canada, where it is located, or to the entire set of the Great Lakes. The advantage of a good set of geographic maps is that after centuries of hard work, multiple levels of detailed maps of most places are available and are nested in a consistent manner within one another. Most of us recognize that there is not one optimal map that can be used for all purposes. Each level of detail is useful for different purposes.

The "map" that I will elucidate in this volume is a conceptual framework called, as mentioned above, the Institutional Analysis and Development (IAD) framework. The publication of "The Three Worlds of Action: A Metatheoretical Synthesis of Institutional Approaches" (Kiser and Ostrom 1982) represented the initial published attempt to describe the IAD framework. Our goal was to help integrate work undertaken by political scientists, economists, anthropologists, lawyers, sociologists, psychologists, and others interested in how institutions affect the incentives confronting individuals and their resultant behavior.[4] During the time since this publication, the framework has been developed further[5] and applied to analyze a diversity of empirical settings. These include:

- the study of land boards in Botswana (Wynne 1989);
- the impact of institutions on creating effective monitoring and evaluations in government development projects (Gordillo and Andersson 2004);
- the incentives of operators and state government regarding coal roads in Kentucky (Oakerson 1981);
- the evolution of coffee cooperatives in Cameroon (Walker 1998);
- the causes and effects of property-right changes among the Maasai of Kenya (Mwangi 2003);
- the performance of housing condominiums in Korea (J. Choe 1992);
- the regulation of the phone industry in the United States (Schaaf 1989);
- the effect of rules on the outcomes of common-pool resource settings throughout the world (Oakerson 1992; Blomquist 1992; E. Ostrom 1990, 1992b; Agrawal 1999; Schlager 1994, 2004; Tang 1992; E. Ostrom, Gardner, and Walker 1994; Lam 1998; de Castro 2000; Dolšak 2000; Futemma 2000; Yandle 2001; Gibson, McKean, and Ostrom 2000);
- a comparison of nonprofit, for profit, and government day-care centers (Bushouse 1999);
- the impact of decentralization on forest governance in Bolivia (Andersson 2002, 2004);
- the evolution of banking reform in the United States (Polski 2003); and
- the effect of incentives on donor and recipient behavior related to international aid (Gibson, Anderson et al. 2005).

Our confidence in the usefulness of the IAD framework has grown steadily in light of the wide diversity of empirical settings where it has helped colleagues identify the key variables to undertake a systematic analysis of the structure of the situations that individuals faced and how rules, the nature of the events involved, and community affected these situations over time. What is certainly true is that the number of specific variables involved in each of these empirical studies is very large. The specific values of variables involved in any one study (or one location in a study) differ from the specific values of variables involved in another study.

The problem of many variables, and potentially few instances of any one combination of these variables, has been recognized by other scholars as one of the perplexing problems haunting systematic empirical testing of social science theories. James Coleman (1964, 516–19) referred to the development and testing of "sometimes true theories," by which he meant that explanations were likely to hold under specific conditions and not under others. If a small number of conditions were identified, sometimes true theories would not present a major problem for the social sciences.

Rigorous analysis of many important questions, however, does eventually require examining a large number of variables. Viewing macropolitical orders in developed Western societies, for example, Fritz Scharpf (1997, 22) points out that the national institutional settings "known to affect policy processes can be described as being either unitary or federal, parliamentary or presidential, have two- or multi-party systems in which interactions are competitive or consociational, and with pluralist or neo-corporatist systems of interest intermediation." Each one of the five variables can exist in one or the other "setting" independently of the other four variables. And, to make it worse, there may be variables related to the particular policy area—such as banking, environmental policy, or education—that may also change. "For comparative policy research, this means that the potential number of different constellations of situational and institutional factors will be extremely large—so large, in fact, that it is rather unlikely that exactly the same factor combination will appear in many empirical cases" (23). A similar level of complexity exists when analyzing factors affecting the performance of city-county consolidation efforts (Carr and Feiock 2004).

Hammond and Butler (2003) have illustrated this problem clearly in their critique of the work of some institutional theorists who have made overly strong claims for the overarching differences between parliamentary and presidential systems. Presidential systems—according to Burns (1963), Sundquist (1968), and Valenzuela (1993)—are thought to slow, if not halt, policy change and lead to obstruction, frustration, and deadlock interspersed with occasional bursts of change when a president faces both houses of Congress dominated by his own party. Hammond and Butler carefully analyze the interaction between rules and the preference profiles that may exist in five variations of institutional rules. They conclude "that considering institutional rules alone provides an inadequate guide to the behavior of any system" (Hammond and Butler 2003, 183).

As Marwell and Oliver (1993, 25) put it, the "predictions that we can validly generate must be complex, interactive and conditional." And, we can hope that some changes in a component are neutral—or have no impact on outcomes—in at least some settings (as biologists are now learning about in regard to genotypes; see Gavrilets 2003). While verifying the empirical warrantability of precise predictions has been the guiding standard for much of the work in political economy, we may have to be satisfied with an understanding of the complexity of structures and a capacity to expect a broad pattern of outcomes from a structure rather than a precise point prediction. An outcome consistent with a pattern may be the best verification we can achieve in settings of substantial complexity (Crutchfield and Schuster 2003).

Thus, the many relevant variables, the immense number of combinations of these variables that exist, and their organization into multiple levels of analysis make understanding organized social life a complex endeavor. If every social science discipline or subdiscipline uses a different language for key terms and focuses on different levels of explanation as the "proper" way to understand behavior and outcomes, one can understand why discourse may resemble a Tower of Babel rather than a cumulative body of knowledge. This book is devoted to the task of building on the efforts of many scholars to develop a conceptual approach that hopefully has a higher chance of cumulation than many of the separate paths currently in vogue in contemporary social sciences.

Holons: Nested Part-Whole Units of Analysis

Like good geographic maps, the IAD framework can be presented at scales ranging from exceedingly fine-grained to extremely broad-grained. Human decision making is the result of many layers of internal processing starting with the biophysical structure, but with layers upon layers of cognitive structure on top of the biophysical components (Hofstadter 1979). Further, many of the values pursued by individuals are intrinsic values that may not be represented by external material objects, and their presence and strength are important parts of the individual to be examined. Building on top of the single individual are structures composed of multiple individuals—families, firms, industries, nations, and many other units—themselves composed of many parts and, in turn, parts of still larger structures. What is a *whole* system at one level is a part of a system at another level.

Arthur Koestler (1973) refers to such nested subassemblies of part-whole units in complex adaptive systems as *holons*. "The term holon may be applied to any stable sub-whole in an organismic or social hierarchy, which displays rule-governed behaviour and/or structural Gestalt constancy" (291). Christopher Alexander (1964) earlier conceptualized all components of social arrangements as having a pattern and being a unit. Units have subunits and are themselves parts of larger units that fit together as a pattern. Koestler asserts that a "hierarchically organized whole cannot be 'reduced' to its elementary parts; but it can be 'dissected' into its constituent branches on which the holons represent the nodes of the tree, and the lines connecting them the channels of communication, control or transportation, as the case may be" (1973, 291). Thus, much of the analysis presented in this book will be a form of "dissecting" complex systems into composite holons that are then dissected further. Explanations occur at multiple levels and different spatial and temporal scales.

Because explanations occur at multiple levels and different spatial and temporal scales, the relevant theoretical concepts needed to understand phenomena at one level do not necessarily scale up or down. One of the core puzzles facing the field of landscape ecology, for example, is the problem of identifying the scale at which a process or phenomenon occurs. According to Pickett and Cadenasso (1995, 333), "The basic question about scale in ecology consists of determining whether a given phenomenon appears or applies across a broad range of scales, or whether it is limited to a narrow range of scales" (see also S. Levin 1992).

The parts used to construct a holon are frequently not descriptive of the holon they have created. A house is constructed out of floor joists, roof beams, lumber, roofing material, nails, and so forth. When one wants to talk about the house itself, one usually talks about the number of rooms, the style of the house, the number of stories, rather than the number of nails used in construction—even though a contractor and a hardware salesperson may try to estimate exactly this variable at some point during construction. When one wants to talk about the street on which the house is located, one uses terms such as the size of the lots, the width of the road, the complementarity or lack of complementarity of the building style, and the like. Descriptions of a neighborhood will use still different concepts, as will a description of an urban or rural political jurisdiction in which a neighborhood is located. On the other hand, some concepts can be used to dissect holons operating at different scales of analysis.

Consequently, the institutional analyst faces a major challenge in identifying the appropriate level of analysis relevant to addressing a particular puzzle and learning an appropriate language for understanding at least that focal level and one or two levels above and below that focal level. It is not only social scientists who face this problem. At a meeting of the global change scientists held in Bonn in March of 2001, Peter Lemke of the World Climate Research Project indicated that the earlier emphasis in climate research was all on global weather forecasts. This has proved to be a myth and a delusion. Now they recognize that to do good weather forecasting, one has to have detailed local models supplemented by global weather models. Both local and global are needed. They are complementary rather than competitive. Physical scientists are trying now in their global models to integrate some of the more localized conditions, but that turns out to be very difficult.

Ecologists have struggled with understanding ecological systems composed of communities, modular units within communities, subunits within these, and attributes of the species in a community (such as diver-

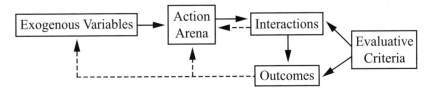

Figure 1.1 The focal level of analysis—an action arena.

sity) or of individual species (such as trophic level) (see Tilman 1999; Tilman, Lehman, and Bristow 1998). Extensive field research, analytical modeling, and simulations now enable ecologists to make relatively strong predictions about some of these interactions. "Increasing species diversity is likely associated with more complex community structure, as species with unique ecological roles are added. The introduction of new ecological roles may be stabilizing or destabilizing, depending on how species function within the community. For example, the addition of a third trophic level to an otherwise stable community with only prey and predators could potentially destabilize the system" (Ives, Klug, and Goss 2000, 409). Social scientists are slowly gaining greater capabilities for understanding multilevel complex systems, but until we develop the appropriate theoretical language for analyzing these systems, we will continue to condemn all complex communities of interacting human organizations as chaotic, as was the dominant view of urban scholars during the last half-century (see, for example, Hawley and Zimmer 1970).

Action Arenas as Focal Units of Analysis

The focal level for this book is the holon called an action arena in which two holons—participants and an action situation—interact as they are affected by exogenous variables (at least at the time of analysis at this level) and produce outcomes that in turn affect the participants and the action situation. Action arenas exist in the home; in the neighborhood; in local, regional, national, and international councils; in firms and markets; and in the interactions among all of these arenas with others. The simplest and most aggregated way of representing any of these arenas when they are the focal level of analysis is shown in figure 1.1, where exogenous variables affect the structure of an action arena, generating interactions that produce outcomes. Evaluative criteria are used to judge the performance of the system by examining the patterns of interactions and outcomes.

Outcomes feed back onto the participants and the situation and may transform both over time. Over time, outcomes may also slowly affect some of the exogenous variables. In undertaking an analysis, however, one treats the exogenous variables as fixed—at least for the purpose of the analysis. When the interactions yielding outcomes are productive for those involved, the participants may increase their commitment to maintaining the structure of the situation as it is, so as to continue to receive positive outcomes. When participants view interactions as unfair or otherwise inappropriate, they may change their strategies even when they are receiving positive outcomes from the situation (Fehr and Gächter 2000b). When outcomes are perceived by those involved (or others) as less valued than other outcomes that might be obtained, some will raise questions about trying to change the structure of the situations by moving to a different level and changing the exogenous variables themselves. Or, if the procedures were viewed as unfair, motivation to change the structure may exist (Frey, Benz, and Stutzer 2004).

Similar efforts to identify a core unit of analysis, such as the action arena, that is contained in many diverse environments have a long history. Core units of analyses identified by other scholars include:

- collective structures (Allport 1962);
- events (Appleyard 1987; Heise 1979);
- frames (Goffman 1974);
- social action and interaction settings (Burns and Flam 1987);
- logic of the situation (Farr 1985; Popper 1961, 1976);
- problematic social situations (Raub and Voss 1986);
- scripts (Schank and Abelson 1977);
- transactions (Commons [1924] 1968); and
- units of meaning (Barwise and Perry 1983; Raiffa 1982).

Because the IAD framework is a multitier conceptual map, the simplest schematic representation of an action arena shown in figure 1.1 will be unpacked—and then further unpacked and unpacked throughout the initial chapters of this book. Action arenas include two holons: an *action situation* and the *participant* in that situation (see figure 1.2). An action situation can, in turn, be characterized using seven clusters of variables: (1) participants (who may be either single individuals or corporate actors), (2) positions, (3) potential outcomes, (4) action-outcome linkages, (5) the control that participants exercise, (6) types of information generated, and (7) the costs and benefits assigned to actions and outcomes (see figure 2.1 in the next chapter). Thus, an action situation refers to the social space where participants with diverse preferences interact, exchange goods and services, solve problems, dominate one another, or fight (among the many things that individuals do in action arenas). In chapter 2, we will zoom in and unpack the action situation as a focal unit of analysis. We will illustrate the working parts of an action situation in

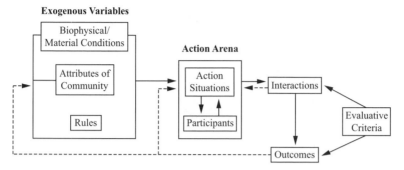

Figure 1.2 A framework for institutional analysis. *Source*: Adapted from E. Ostrom, Gardner, and Walker 1994, 37.

chapter 3, showing how this holon can be operationalized in an experimental laboratory. In chapter 4, we will zoom in to unpack the concept of a participant and discuss the puzzles and possibilities available to animate the actor. But first, let's use zoom out to examine the variables that are treated as exogenous when examining an action arena (but may themselves be an outcome of another action arena). Let's look at a broader overview of the IAD conceptual map.

Zooming Out to an Overview of the IAD Framework

An institutional analyst can take two additional steps after an effort is made to understand the initial structure of an action arena leading to a particular pattern of interactions and outcomes. One step moves outward and inquires into the exogenous factors that affect the structure of an action arena. From this vantage point, any particular action arena is now viewed as a set of dependent variables. The factors affecting the structure of an action arena include three clusters of variables: (1) the *rules* used by participants to order their relationships, (2) the attributes of the *biophysical world* that are acted upon in these arenas, and (3) the structure of the more general *community* within which any particular arena is placed (see Kiser and Ostrom 1982). The next section of this chapter provides a brief introduction to this first step (see the left side of figure 1.2). How rules influence the action arena will then be discussed in much more depth in chapters 5, 6, and 7.

The second step also moves outward—but to the "other side" of a particular action arena—to look at how action arenas are linked together either sequentially or simultaneously. This step will be discussed in the last section of chapter 2 after discussion of the components of action situations.

Viewing Action Arenas as Dependent Variables

Underlying the way analysts conceptualize action situations and the participants that interact in them are implicit assumptions about the *rules* participants use to order their relationships, about attributes of the *biophysical world*, and about the *nature of the community* within which the arena occurs. Some analysts are not interested in the role of these underlying variables and focus only on a particular arena whose structure is given. On the other hand, institutional analysts may be more interested in one factor affecting the structure of arenas than they are interested in others. Anthropologists and sociologists tend to be more interested in how shared or divisive value systems in a community affect the ways humans organize their relationships with one another. Environmentalists tend to focus on various ways that physical and biological systems interact and create opportunities or constraints on the situations human beings face. Political scientists tend to focus on how specific combinations of rules affect incentives. Rules, the biophysical and material world, and the nature of the community all jointly affect the types of actions that individuals can take, the benefits and costs of these actions and potential outcomes, and the likely outcomes achieved.

The Concept of Rules

The concept of rules is central to the analysis of institutions (Hodgson 2004a). The term *rules*, however, is used by scholars to refer to many concepts with quite diverse meanings. In an important philosophical treatment of rules, Max Black (1962) identified four different usages of the term in everyday conversations. According to Black, the word *rule* is used to denote regulations, instructions, precepts, and principles. When used in its *regulation* sense, rules refer to something "laid down by an authority (a legislature, judge, magistrate, board of directors, university president, parent) as required of certain persons (or, alternatively, forbidden or permitted)" (115). The example of a rule in the regulation sense that Black uses is: "The dealer at bridge must bid first." When using rule in its regulation sense, one can meaningfully refer to activities such as the rule "being announced, put into effect, enforced (energetically, strictly, laxly, invariably, occasionally), disobeyed, broken, rescinded, changed, revoked, reinstated" (109).

When the term *rule* is used to denote an *instruction*, it is closer in meaning to an effective strategy for how to solve a problem. An example of this usage is, "In solving quartic equations, first eliminate the cubic term" (110). When speaking about a rule in this sense, one would not talk about a rule being enforced, rescinded, reinstated, or any of the other activities relevant to regulation. When rule denotes a *precept*, the term is being used as a maxim for prudential or moral behavior. An example would be: "A good rule is: to put charity ahead of justice" (111). Again, one would not speak of enforcing, rescinding, or reinstating a rule in the precept sense.

The fourth sense in which the term *rule* is used in everyday language is to describe a law or principle. An example of this usage is: "Cyclones rotate clockwise, anticyclones anticlockwise" (113). Principles or physical laws are subject to empirical test, and as such truth values can be ascribed to them. But physical laws are not put into effect, broken, or rescinded.

Social scientists employ all four of the uses of the term *rule* that Black identifies—and others as well (see discussion in chapter 5). Scholars engaged in institutional analysis frequently use the term to denote a regulation. The definition of rules used in this book is close to what Black identified as the regulation sense. Rules can be thought of as the set of instructions for creating an action situation in a particular environment. In some ways, rules have an analogous role to that of genes. Genes combine to build a phenotype. Rules combine to build the structure of an action situation. The property rights that participants hold in diverse settings are a result of the underlying set of rules-in-use (Libecap 1989).

Rules, in the instruction sense, can be thought of as the strategies adopted by participants within ongoing situations. I will consistently use the term *strategy* rather than *rule* for individual plans of action. Rules in the precept sense are part of the generally accepted moral fabric of a community (Allen 2005). We refer to these cultural prescriptions as norms. Rules in the principle sense are physical laws.

Until recently, rules have not been a central focus of most of the social sciences. Even in game theory where "the rules of the game" seem to play an important role, there has not been much interest in examining where rules come from or how they change. Game-theoretical rules include all physical laws that constrain a situation as well as rules devised by humans to structure a situation. The rules of the game—including both physical and institutional factors—structure the game itself, but have been irrelevant to many game theorists once a game can be unambiguously represented. An influential contributor to the development of game theory, Anatol Rapoport (1966, 18) stated this distinction very clearly: "Rules are important only to the extent that they allow the outcomes resulting from the choices of participants to be unambiguously specified. . . . Any other game with possibly quite different rules but leading to the same relations among the choices and the outcomes is considered equivalent to the game in question. In short, game theory is concerned with rules only to the extent that the rules help define the choice situation and the outcomes associated with the choices. Otherwise the rules of games play no part in game theory." So long as the game theorist has adequately represented this focal level of analysis, the theorist interested primarily in finding the solution to a game has no need to dig into the rules, attributes of a community, and physical laws that create the structure of the situation. As institutional analysts asked to diagnose why perverse outcomes occur and to propose ways to improve the outcomes of many action situations, on the other hand, we have to dig below and learn how rules create the set being analyzed. One cannot improve outcomes without knowing how the structure is itself produced (Eggertsson 2005).

As will be discussed in more depth in chapter 5, rules as used in this book are defined to be shared understandings by participants about *enforced* prescriptions concerning what actions (or outcomes) are *required, prohibited,* or *permitted* (Ganz 1971; V. Ostrom 1980; Commons 1968). All rules are the result of implicit or explicit efforts to achieve order and predictability among humans by creating classes of persons (positions) who are then required, permitted, or forbidden to take classes of actions in relation to required, permitted, or forbidden outcomes or face the likelihood of being monitored and sanctioned in a predictable fashion (V. Ostrom 1991).

Well-understood and enforced rules operate so as to *rule out* some actions and to *rule in* others. In a well-ordered human enterprise, some behaviors are rarely observed because individuals following rules do not normally engage in that activity in the given setting. It is rare to observe, for example, that one driver on a public freeway within the United States will race another driver on that freeway at a speed exceeding one hundred miles per hour. State highway patrols invest substantial sums in an attempt to enforce highway speeding laws and to rule out excessive speeds on freeways.

At a racing track, however, one can observe speeds of well over one hundred miles per hour and drivers directly racing one another in a determined manner. The rules of a racing track *rule in* some activities that are *ruled out* on a freeway. Anyone driving on a freeway will observe a range of speeds rather than the single maximum speed mentioned in the speed limit law. Speed limits illustrate rules that authorize a range of activities rather than requiring one particular action. Further, enforcement patterns differ regarding the range of speed in excess of the official upper limit that will be tolerated, once observed, before a sanction is issued.

It is also important to recognize that rules need not be written. Nor do they need to result from formal legal procedures. Institutional rules are often self-consciously crafted by individuals to change the structure of repetitive situations that they themselves face in an attempt to improve the outcomes that they achieve.

ON THE ORIGIN OF RULES

When one is interested in understanding the processes of governance, one needs to ask where the rules that individuals use in action situations originate. In an open and democratic governance system, many sources exist of the rules used by individuals in everyday life. It is not considered illegal or improper for individuals to self-organize and craft their own rules if the activities they engage in are legal. In addition to the legislation and regulations of a formal central government, there are apt to be laws passed by regional and local governments. Within private firms and voluntary associations, individuals are authorized to adopt many different rules determining who is a member of the firm or association, how profits (benefits) are to be shared, and how decisions will be made. Each family constitutes its own rule-making body.

When individuals genuinely participate in the crafting of multiple layers of rules, some of that crafting will occur using pen and paper. Much of it, however, will occur as problem-solving individuals interact trying to figure out how to do a better job in the future than they have done in the past. Colleagues in a work team are crafting their own rules when they might say to one another, "How about if you do A in the future, and I will do B, and before we ever make a decision about C again, we both discuss it and make a joint decision?" In a democratic society, problem-solving individuals do this all the time. They also participate in more structured decision-making arrangements, including elections to select legislators.

WORKING RULES

Thus, when we do a deeper institutional analysis, we attempt first to understand the working rules that individuals use in making decisions. Working rules are the set of rules to which participants would make reference if asked to explain and justify their actions to fellow participants. While following a rule may become a "social habit," it is possible to make participants consciously aware of the rules they use to order their relationships. Individuals can consciously decide to adopt a different rule and change their behavior to conform to such a decision. Over time, behavior in conformance with a new rule may itself become habitual (see Shimanoff 1980; Toulmin 1974; Harré 1974). The capacity of humans to use complex cognitive systems to order their own behavior at a relatively subconscious level makes it difficult at times for empirical researchers to ascertain what the working rules for an ongoing action arena may actually be in practice. It is the task of an institutional analyst, however, to dig under surface behavior to obtain a good understanding of what rules participants in a situation are following.[6]

Once we understand the working rules, then, we attempt to understand where those rules come from. In an open society governed by a "rule of law," the general legal framework in use will have its source in actions taken in constitutional, legislative, and administrative settings augmented by rule-making decisions taken by individuals in many different particular settings. In other words, the rules-in-form are consistent with the rules-in-use (Sproule-Jones 1993). In a system that is not governed by a "rule of law," there may be central laws and considerable effort made to enforce them, but individuals generally attempt to evade rather than obey the law.

THE PREDICTABILITY OF RULES

Rule following or conforming actions are not as predictable as biological or physical behavior explained by scientific laws. All rules are formulated in human language. As such, rules share problems of lack of clarity, misunderstanding, and change that typify any language-based phenomenon (V. Ostrom 1980, 1997). Words are always simpler than the phenomenon to which they refer. In many office jobs, for example, the rules require an employee to work a specified number of hours per week. If a staff member is physically at their desk for the required number of hours, is daydreaming about a future vacation or preparing a grocery list for a shopping trip on the way home within the rules? Interpreting rules is more challenging than writing them down.

The stability of rule-ordered actions is dependent upon the shared meaning assigned to words used to formulate a set of rules. If no shared meaning exists when a rule is formulated, confusion will exist about what actions are required, permitted, or forbidden. Regularities in actions cannot result if those who must repeatedly interpret the meaning of a rule within action situations arrive at multiple interpretations. Because "rules are not self-formulating, self-determining, or self-enforcing" (V. Ostrom 1980, 342), it is human agents who formulate them, apply them in particular situations, and attempt to enforce performance consistent with them. Even if shared meaning exists at the time of the acceptance of a rule, transformations in technology, in shared norms, and in circumstances more generally change the events to which rules apply. "Applying language to changing configurations of development increases the ambiguities and threatens the shared criteria of choice with an erosion of their appropriate meaning" (342).

The stability of rule-ordered relationships is also dependent upon enforcement. According to Commons ([1924] 1968, 138), rules "simply say what individuals must, must not, may, can, and cannot do, if the authoritative agency that decides disputes brings the collective power of the community to bear upon the said individuals." Breaking rules is an option that is always available to participants in an action situation (as contrasted to players in a formal game-theoretic model), but associated with breaking rules is a risk of being monitored and sanctioned. If the risk is low, the predictability and stability of a situation are reduced. And instability can grow over time. If one person can cheat without fear of being caught, others can also cheat with impunity. If the risk of exposure and sanctioning is high, participants can expect that others will make choices from within the set of permitted and required actions. The acceptance of rules represents a type of Faustian bargain (V. Ostrom 1996). Someone is given authority to use coercion to increase benefits for others—hopefully, for most others.

The simplifying assumption is frequently made in analytical theories that individuals in an action situation will take only those actions that are lawful given the rules that apply. For many purposes, this simplifying assumption helps the analyst proceed to examine important theoretical questions not related to how well the rules are enforced. Highly complicated games, such as football, can indeed be explained with more ease because of the presence of active and aggressive on-site referees who constantly monitor the behavior of the players and assign penalties for infraction of rules.[7] And these monitors face real incentives for monitoring consistently and for applying fair and accepted penalties. Both the fans and the managers of the relevant sports teams pay a lot of attention to what the monitors are doing and the fairness of their judgments. In settings where a heavy investment is *not* made in monitoring the ongoing actions of participants, however, considerable difference between predicted and actual behavior can occur as a result of the lack of congruence between a model of lawful behavior and the illegal actions that individuals frequently take in such situations.

This is not to imply that the only reason individuals follow rules is because they are enforced. If individuals voluntarily participate in a situation, they must share some general sense that most of the rules governing the situation are appropriate. Otherwise, the cost of enforcement within voluntary activities becomes high enough that it is difficult, if not impossible, to maintain predictability in an ongoing voluntary activity. (One can expect that it is always difficult to maintain predictability in an ongoing activity where participants do not have the freedom to enter and leave the situation.)

WHAT ARE THE IMPORTANT RULES?

What rules are important for institutional analysis? For some institutional scholars, the important difference among rules has to do with the system of property rights in use. At a very general level, it is sometimes useful to know whether the rules related to a situation can be broadly classed as government property, private property, community property, or no property which is an open-access setting (Bromley et al. 1992). Scholars in the legal pluralist tradition have strongly criticized these categories as not being precise enough to understand the incentives facing participants and thus are inadequate as a foundation for public policy (Benda-Beckmann 2001). They argue that an analyst needs to learn more about particular property rights that specify particular bundles of rights (such as the right to enter a state park versus the right to hunt deer in the same park) in much more detail than those broad categories of rights (Benda-Beckmann 1995, 1997).

A myriad of specific rules are used in structuring complex action arenas. Scholars have been trapped into endless cataloging of rules not related to a method of classification most useful for theoretical explanations. But classification is a necessary step in developing a science. Anyone attempting to define a useful typology of rules must be concerned that the classification is more than a method for imposing superficial order onto an extremely large set of seemingly disparate rules. The way we have tackled this problem using the IAD framework is to classify rules according to their direct impact on the working parts of an action situation (as will be discussed in chapters 6 and 7).

Biophysical and Material Conditions

While a rule configuration affects all of the elements of an action situation, some of the variables of an action situation (and thus the overall set of incentives facing individuals in a situation) are also affected by attributes of the biophysical and material world being acted upon or transformed. What actions are physically possible, what outcomes can be produced, how actions are linked to outcomes, and what is contained in the actors' information sets are affected by the world being acted upon in a situation. The same set of rules may yield entirely different types of action situations depending upon the types of events in the world being acted upon by participants. These "events" are frequently referred to by political economists as the "goods and services" being produced, consumed, and allocated in a situation as well as the technology available for these processes.

The attributes of the biophysical and material conditions and their transformation are explicitly examined when the analyst self-consciously asks a series of questions about how the world being acted upon in a situation affects the outcome, action sets, action-outcome linkages, and information sets in that situation. The relative importance of the rule configuration and biophysical conditions structuring an action situation varies dramatically across different types of settings. The rule configuration almost totally constitutes some games, like chess, where physical attributes are relatively unimportant. The relative importance of working rules to biophysical attributes also varies dramatically within action situations considered to be part of the public sector. Rules define and constrain voting behavior inside a legislature more than attributes of the biophysical world. Voting can be accomplished by raising hands, by paper ballots, by calling for the ayes and nays, by marching before an official counter, or by installing computer terminals for each legislator on which votes are registered. In regard to communication within a legislature, however, attributes of the biophysical world strongly affect the available options. The principle that only one person can be heard and understood at a time in any one forum strongly affects the capacity of legislators to communicate effectively with one another (see V. Ostrom 1987).

Considerable academic literature has focused on the effect of attributes of goods on the results obtained within action situations. A key assumption made in the analysis of a competitive market is that the outcomes of an exchange are highly excludable, easily divisible and transferable, and internalized by those who participate in the exchange. Markets are predicted to fail as effective decision mechanisms when they are the only arena available for producing, consuming, or allocating a wide variety of goods that do not meet the criteria of excludability, divisibility, and transferability. Market failure means that the incentives facing individuals in a situation, where the rules are those of a competitive market but the goods do not have the characteristics of "private goods," are insufficient to motivate individuals to produce, allocate, and consume these goods at an optimal level.

Let us briefly consider two attributes that are frequently used to distinguish among four basic goods and services: exclusion and subtractability of use. Exclusion relates to the difficulty of restricting those who benefit from the provision of a good or a service. Subtractability refers to the extent to which one individual's use subtracts from the availability of a good or service for consumption by others. Both of these two attributes can range from low to high. When these attributes are dichotomized and arrayed as shown in figure 1.3, they can be used as the defining attributes of four basic types of goods: toll goods (sometimes referred to as club goods), private goods, public goods, and common-pool resources. Goods that are generally considered to be "public goods" yield nonsubtractive benefits that can be enjoyed jointly by many people who are hard to exclude from obtaining these benefits. Peace is a public good, as my enjoyment of peace does not subtract from the enjoyment of others. Common-pool resources yield benefits where beneficiaries are hard to exclude but each person's use of a resource system subtracts units of that resource

		Subtractability of use	
		Low	*High*
Difficulty of excluding potential beneficiaries	*Low*	Toll goods	Private goods
	High	Public goods	Common-pool resources

Figure 1.3 Four basic types of goods. *Source*: Adapted from V. Ostrom and E. Ostrom 1977, 12.

from a finite total amount available for harvesting (E. Ostrom, Gardner, and Walker 1994; Aggarwal and Dupont 1999). When a fisher harvests a ton of fish, those fish are not available to any other fisher.

EXCLUDABILITY AND THE FREE-RIDER PROBLEM

When the benefits of a good are available to a group, whether or not members of the group contribute to the provision of the good, that good is characterized by problems of excludability. Where exclusion is costly, those wishing to provide a good or service face a potential free-rider or collective-action problem (Olson 1965). Individuals who gain from the maintenance of an irrigation system, for example, may not wish to contribute labor or taxes to maintenance activities, hoping that others will bear the burden. This is not to say that all individuals will free-ride whenever they can. A strong incentive exists to be a free-rider in all situations where potential beneficiaries cannot easily be excluded for failing to contribute to the provision of a good or service.

When it is costly to exclude individuals from enjoying benefits from an investment, private, profit-seeking entrepreneurs, who must recoup their investments through quid pro quo exchanges, have few incentives to provide such services on their own initiative. Excludability problems can thus lead to the problem of free-riding, which in turn leads to underinvestment in capital and its maintenance.

Public sector provision of common-pool resources or infrastructure facilities raises additional problems in determining preferences and organizing finances. When exclusion is low cost to the supplier, preferences are revealed as a result of many quid pro quo transactions. Producers learn about preferences through the consumers' willingness to pay for various goods offered for sale. Where exclusion is difficult, designing mechanisms that honestly reflect beneficiaries' preferences and their willingness to pay is challenging, regardless of whether the providing unit is organized in the public or the private sphere. In very small groups, those affected are usually able to discuss their preferences and constraints on a face-to-face basis and to reach a rough consensus. In larger groups, decisions about infrastructure are apt to be made through mechanisms such as voting or the delegation of authority to public officials. The extensive literature on voting systems demonstrates how difficult it is to translate individual preferences into collective choices that adequately reflect individual views (Arrow 1951; Monroe forthcoming).

Another attribute of some goods with excludability problems is that once they are provided, consumers may have no choice whatsoever as to whether they will consume. An example is the public spraying of insects. If an individual does not want this public service to be provided, there are even stronger incentives not to comply with a general tax levy. Thus, compliance with a broad financing instrument may, in turn, depend upon the legitimacy of the public-choice mechanism used to make provision decisions.

SUBTRACTABILITY

Goods and facilities can generate a flow of services that range from being fully subtractable upon consumption by one user to another extreme where consumption by one does not subtract from the flow of services available to others. The withdrawal of a quantity of water from an irrigation canal by one farmer means that there is that much less water for anyone else to use. Most agricultural uses of water are fully subtractive, whereas many other uses of water—such as for power generation or navigation—are not. Most of the water that passes through a turbine to generate power, for instance, can be used again downstream. When the use of a flow of services by one individual subtracts from what is available to others and when the flow is scarce relative to demand, users will be tempted to try to obtain as much as they can of the flow for fear that it will not be available later.

Effective rules are required if scarce, fully subtractive service flows are to be allocated in a productive way (E. Ostrom, Gardner, and Walker 1994). Charging prices for subtractive services obviously constitutes one such allocation mechanism. Sometimes, however, it is not feasible to price services. In these instances, some individuals will be able to grab considerably more of the subtractive services than others, thereby leading to noneconomic uses of the flow and high levels of conflict among users.

Allocation rules also affect the incentives of users to maintain a system. Farmers located at the tail end of an irrigation system that lacks effective allocation rules have little motivation to contribute to the maintenance of that system because they only occasionally receive their share of water. Similarly, farmers located at the head end of such a system are not motivated to provide maintenance services voluntarily because they will receive disproportionate shares of the water whether or not the system is well-maintained (E. Ostrom 1996).

ADDITIONAL ATTRIBUTES

In addition to exclusion and subtractability, the structure of action situations is also affected by a diversity of other attributes that affect how rules combine with physical and material conditions to generate positive or negative incentives. The number of attributes that may affect the structure of a situation is extraordinarily large, and I do not want even to start a list in this volume. The crucial point for the institutional analyst is that rules that help produce incentives leading to productive outcomes in one setting may fail drastically when the biophysical world differs. As our extensive studies of common-pool resources have shown, for example, effective rules depend on the size of the resource; the mobility of its resource units (e.g., water, wildlife, or trees); the presence of storage in the system; the amount and distribution of rainfall, soils, slope, and elevation; and many other factors (see E. Ostrom, Gardner, and Walker 1994).

These additional attributes are slowly being integrated into a body of coherent theory about the impact of physical and material conditions on the structure of the situations that individuals face and their resulting incentives and behavior. Analysts diagnosing policy problems need to be sensitive to the very large difference among settings and the need to tailor rules to diverse combinations of attributes rather than some assumed uniformity across all situations in a particular sector within a country.

Attributes of the Community

A third set of variables that affect the structure of an action arena relate to the concept of the community within which any focal action arena is located. The concept of community is again one that has many definitions and meanings across and within the social sciences. Given the breadth of what I already plan to tackle, I do not plan to focus in detail on how various attributes of community affect the structure of situations within a community (see Agrawal and Gibson 2001 for an excellent overall review of the concept of community). The attributes of a community that are important in affecting action arenas include: the values of behavior generally accepted in the community; the level of common understanding that potential participants share (or do not share) about the structure of particular types of action arenas; the extent of homogeneity in the preferences of those living in a community; the size and composition of the relevant community; and the extent of inequality of basic assets among those affected.

The term *culture* is frequently applied to the values shared within a community. Culture affects the mental models that participants in a situation may share. Cultures evolve over time faster than our underlying genetic endowment can evolve. Cultures have in turn affected how the human brain itself has evolved (Boyd and Richerson 1985; Richerson and Boyd 2002). The history of experience with governance institutions at multiple levels affects the way local participants understand, implement, modify, or ignore rules written by external officials (Medard and Geheb 2001).

For example, when all participants share a common set of values and interact with one another in a multiplex set of arrangements within a small community, the probabilities of their developing adequate rules and norms to govern repetitive relationships are much greater (Taylor 1987). The importance of building a reputation for keeping one's word is important in such a community, and the cost of developing monitoring and sanctioning mechanisms is relatively low. If the participants in a situation come from many different cultures, speak different languages, and are distrustful of one another, the costs of devising and sustaining effective rules are substantially increased.

Whether individuals use a written vernacular language to express their ideas, develop common understanding, share learning, and explain the foundation of their social order is also a crucial variable of relevance to institutional analysis (V. Ostrom 1997). Without a written vernacular language, individuals face considerably more difficulties in accumulating their own learning in a usable form to transmit from one generation to the next.

Institutional Frameworks, Theories, and Models

So far in this chapter, I have provided a brief overview of the IAD framework without telling the reader what I mean by a framework. The terms— *framework*, *theory*, and *model*—are all used almost interchangeably by diverse social scientists. This leads to considerable confusion as to what they mean.[8] Frequently, what one scholar calls a framework others call a model or a theory.[9] In this book, I will use these concepts to mean a nested set of theoretical concepts—which range from the most general to the most detailed types of assumptions made by the analyst. Analyses conducted at each level provide different degrees of specificity related to a particular problem (Schlager 1999).

The development and use of a general *framework* helps to identify the elements (and the relationships among these elements) that one needs to consider for institutional analysis. Frameworks organize diagnostic and prescriptive inquiry. They provide the most general set of variables that should be used to analyze all types of settings relevant for the framework. Frameworks provide a metatheoretic language that is necessary to talk about theories and that can be used to compare theories. They attempt to identify the *universal* elements that any relevant theory would need to include. Many differences in surface reality can result from the way these variables combine with or interact with one another. Thus, the elements contained in a framework help the analyst generate the questions that need to be addressed when first conducting an analysis.

The development and use of *theories* enable the analyst to specify which components of a framework are relevant for certain kinds of questions and to make broad working assumptions about these elements. Thus, theories focus on parts of a framework and make specific assumptions that are necessary for an analyst to diagnose a phenomenon, explain its processes, and predict outcomes. To conduct empirical research, a scholar needs to select one or more theories to use in generating predictions about expected patterns of relationships. Several theories are usually compatible with any framework. Empirical research should narrow the range of applicable theories over time by showing the superiority of the remaining theories to explain data. Microeconomic theory, game theory, transaction cost theory, social choice theory, public choice, constitutional and covenantal theory, and theories of public goods and common-pool resources are all compatible with the IAD framework discussed in this book.

The development and use of *models* make precise assumptions about a limited set of parameters and variables. Logic, mathematics, game theory models, experimentation and simulation, and other means are used to explore the consequences of these assumptions systematically on a limited set of outcomes. Multiple models are compatible with most theories. In an effort to understand the strategic structure of the games that irrigators play in differently organized irrigation systems, for example, Weissing and Ostrom (1991a, 1991b) developed four families of models to explore the likely consequences of different institutional and physical combinations relevant to understanding how successful farmer organizations arranged for monitoring and sanctioning activities. These models enabled us to analyze in a precise manner a subpart of the theory of common-pool resources and thus also one combination of the components of the IAD framework. Models are extensively used in contemporary policy analysis by officials working with the World Bank, national governments, as well as state and local governments.

For policy makers and scholars interested in issues related to how different governance systems enable individuals to solve problems democratically by modifying rules at various levels, the IAD framework helps to organize diagnostic, analytical, and prescriptive capabilities. It is similar in structure and intent to the "Actor-Centered Institutionalism" framework developed by Renate Mayntz and Fritz Scharpf (1995) and applied to several national policy settings by Fritz Scharpf (1997). It also aids in the accumulation of knowledge from empirical studies and in the assessment of past efforts at reforms.

Without the capacity to undertake systematic, comparative institutional assessments, recommendations of reform may be based on naive ideas about which kinds of institutions are "good" or "bad" and not on an analysis of performance. Some policy analysts tend to recommend private property as a way of solving any and all problems involving overuse of a resource. While private property works effectively in some environments, it is naive to presume it will work well in all (see Tietenberg 2002; Rose 2002). One needs a common framework and family of theories in order to address questions of reforms and transitions. Particular models then help the analyst to deduce specific predictions about likely outcomes of highly simplified structures. Models are useful in policy analysis when they are well-tailored to the particular problem at hand. Models are used inappropriately when applied to the study of problematic situations that do not closely fit the assumptions of the model (see E. Ostrom 1990 for a critique of the overreliance on open access models of common-pool resources regardless of whether users had created their own rules to cope with overharvesting or not).

The Limited Frame of This Book

Several times in the past, I have participated with colleagues in efforts to outline a book that examined how rule configurations, attributes of goods, and attributes of the community all affected the structure of action situations, individual choices, outcomes, and the evaluation of outcomes.[10] Each time, the projected volume mushroomed in size and overcame our capacity to organize it. Thus in this book, I have tried to focus primarily on how rules affect the structure of action situations instead of trying to work out the details of the entire framework. The focus on the components of institutions in this volume should not be interpreted to mean that I feel that institutions are the *only* factor affecting outcomes in all action situations.

Institutions are only one of a large number of elements that affect behavior in any particular situation at a particular time and place. No single cause exists for human behavior. To live, one needs oxygen, water, and nutrition. All are key parts of the explanation of life. Life itself operates at multiple levels. Genes underlie phenotypic structures in a manner that is broadly analogous to the way that rules underlie action situations. But neither genes nor rules fully determine behavior of the phenotypes that they help to create. Selection processes on genes operate largely at the individual level, but rules—as well as other cultural "memes"—are likely to be selected at multiple levels (see Hammerstein 2003). When one steps back, however, for all of the complexity and multiple levels, there is a large amount of similarity of underlying factors. In the biological world, it is somewhat amazing that there is only a small proportion of the genes that differ between an elephant and a mouse. As we develop the logic of institutions further, we will see that many situations that have the surface appearance of being vastly different have similar underlying parts. Thus, our task is to identify the working parts, the grammar, the alphabet of the phenotype of human social behavior as well as the underlying factors of rules, biophysical laws, and community.

Thus, the focus of this book reflects my sense that the concept of institutions, the diversity of institutions and their resilience, and the question of how institutions structure action situations require major attention. This volume is, thus, an effort to take an in-depth look at one major part of what is needed to develop fuller theories of social organization. In this volume, I will try to articulate in more detail than has been possible before what I think the components of institutions are and how they can be used to generate explanations of human behavior in diverse situations. The focus on institutions should not be interpreted, however, as a position that rules are always the most important factor affecting interactions and outcomes. In the midst of a hurricane, rules may diminish greatly in their importance in affecting individual behavior.

This volume should be thought of as part of a general effort to understand institutions so as to provide a better formulation for improving their performance. Our book *Rules, Games, and Common-Pool Resources* (E. Ostrom, Gardner, and Walker 1994) provides one focused application of the IAD framework. Michael McGinnis has recently edited three volumes (1999a, 1999b, 2000) that present earlier elucidations of the IAD framework and empirical studies that are closely related. Kenneth Bickers and John Williams (2001) and Michael McGinnis and John Williams (2001) clearly elucidate important aspects of the general approach.

I am writing this book from the perspective of a policy analyst. Without the careful development of a rigorous and empirically verifiable set of theories of social organization, we cannot do a very good job of fixing problems through institutional change. And, if we cannot link the theoretical results into a coherent overall approach, we cannot cumulate knowledge. All too often, major policy initiatives lead to counterintentional results. We need to understand institutions in order to improve their performance over time (North 2005).

As I demonstrate in chapter 8, however, the option of optimal design is not available to mere mortals. The number of combinations of specific rules that are used to create action situations is far larger than any set that analysts could ever analyze even with space-age computer assistance. This impossibility does not, however, leave me discouraged or hopeless. It does, however, lead me to have great respect for robust institutions that have generated substantial benefits over long periods of time (see Shepsle 1989; E. Ostrom 1990). None have been designed in one single step. Rather, accrued learning and knowledge have led those with good information about participants, strategies, ecological conditions, and changes in technology and economic relationships over time to craft sustainable institutions, even though no one will ever know if they are optimal. Thus, in chapter 9, I dig into the process of learning, adaptation, and evolution as processes that enable polycentric institutional arrangements to utilize very general design principles in the dynamic processes of trying to improve human welfare over time. It is also necessary to discuss the threats that can destroy the resilience of complex social systems.

Two

Zooming In and Linking Action Situations

An Action Situation as a Focal Unit of Analysis

Whenever two or more individuals are faced with a set of potential actions that jointly produce outcomes, these individuals can be said to be "in" an action situation. Typical action situations include:

- buyers and sellers exchanging goods in a market;
- legislators making legislative decisions about future laws;
- powerful politicians bargaining over the allocation of public support;
- users of a common-pool resource withdrawing resource units (such as fish, water, or timber);
- heads of state negotiating an international treaty.

The structure of all of these situations—and many more—can be described and analyzed by using a common set of variables. These are: (1) the set of participants, (2) the positions to be filled by participants, (3) the potential outcomes, (4) the set of allowable actions and the function that maps actions into realized outcomes, (5) the control that an individual has in regard to this function, (6) the information available to participants about actions and outcomes and their linkages, and (7) the costs and benefits—which serve as incentives and deterrents—assigned to actions and outcomes. The internal structure of an action situation can be represented as shown in figure 2.1. In addition to the internal structure, whether a situation will occur once, a known and finite number of times, or indefinitely affects the strategies of individuals.

The number of participants and positions in a situation may vary, but there must always be participants in positions for one to talk about an action situation. Similarly, there must be potential actions that participants can take. The set of available actions represents the means that participants have to achieve particular outcomes in that situation. Information about the situation may vary, but all participants must have access to some common information about the situation for an analyst to even state that the participants are *in* the same situation. The costs and benefits assigned to actions and outcomes can be thought of as the external incentives and deterrents in a situation. How these affect the choice of participants regarding specific actions, and thus the cumulation of results, de-

Exogenous Variables

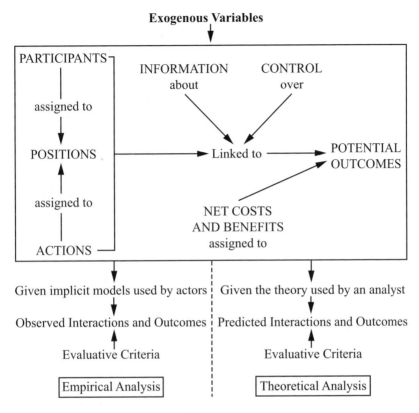

Figure 2.1 The internal structure of an action situation.

pends also on the initial resources and valuation patterns held by the participants. In some action situations, the standing of participants is grossly unequal, allowing some to have substantial power over others and the relative benefits they can achieve.

When doing analysis at a focal level of analysis, these working parts are the "givens" of a situation. For the purposes of analyzing the likely human behavior and outcomes within a particular structure, one assumes that the structure of the situation is fixed for the short run. *Within* a particular situation, individuals can attempt to choose only in light of their beliefs about the opportunities and constraints of that situation. In an open society, individuals may be able eventually to affect the structure of action situations in which they repeatedly find themselves by changing the rule configurations affecting the structure of these situations. To do so, they move to deeper analytical levels (collective-choice or constitutional-choice action situations) where the outcomes generated are changes in the rules of other action situations. In a closed society, individuals at an operational level may have little opportunity to change rules at any level and may find themselves in highly exploitative situations. We discuss shifting to a higher level in the last half of this chapter.

The working parts of an action situation are both necessary and sufficient to describe the structure of an action situation. They are similar to the elements identified by game theorists to construct formal game models (see Gardner 2003; Gintis 2000b). A formal description of a game is thus one way of describing a subset of all action situations and will soon be used to illustrate the concept of a simple action situation.[1]

The mathematical tools of game theory are powerful and enlightening. They can only be used, however, to elucidate the structure of relatively simple action situations. The full game tree for a highly structured game, such as chess, cannot be fully articulated. In chess, for example, the first player can open with any of twenty actions and the second player can respond with twenty as well. Thus, after the first two moves, there are already four hundred branches to specify if one wanted to try to represent chess as a formal game. "It has been estimated that the total number of possible moves in chess is on the order of 10^{120}, or a 'one' with 120 zeros after it. . . . A supercomputer a thousand times faster than your PC, making a billion calculations a second, would need approximately 3×10^{103} years to check out all of these moves" (Dixit and Skeath 1999, 66).

In addition to using the elements of an action situation to analyze a formal game, the elements can also be used to describe the structure of more complex action situations in a nonmathematical form. One strategy is to represent key parts of complex chains of action situations as a game without trying to represent the entire structure as one game (McGinnis forthcoming). The basic elements of an action situation have also been used in empirical studies of complex action situations in the field.

Scholars associated with the Workshop in Political Theory and Policy Analysis have developed three large databases that measured as many aspects as we could regarding the structure of action situations facing appropriators from common-pool resources: inshore fisheries (see Schlager 1990, 1994, 2004; Schlager and Ostrom 1992, 1993); irrigation systems (see Tang 1992; Lam 1998); and forests (see Gibson, McKean, and Ostrom 2000; Moran and Ostrom 2005; Poteete and Ostrom 2004). These efforts to measure the structure and the realized outcomes of various property regimes as they relate to diverse common-pool resources led us to realize both how difficult it is to measure these concepts in field settings as well as the substantial scientific benefits achieved by so doing. Specific sets of questions on our coding forms were our way of operationalizing the basic working parts of operational-level action situations.

A carefully crafted case study is another method for analyzing more complex action situations and their linkages (Yandle 2001). Analytical narratives are an important technique for examining the structure of complex action-outcome linkages and their consequences (Bates et al. 1998, 2000). So long as theorists use a consistent language to describe their structure, much can be learned from single case studies over time or comparative case studies of action situations that are not presented in formal language (see Theesfeld 2004; Yandle and Dewees 2003).

Computer programs have been written as ways of representing the actions of players. An IBM team, for example, put years of effort into a chess-playing program—Deep Blue—to try to beat a world champion chess player. The IBM team succeeded in beating Gary Kasparov, the then world champion chess player in 1997, only after many years of trying.[2] Agent-based computational models are currently used by some analysts to examine a variety of action situations that are too complex to be analyzed completely using mathematical models (see Axelrod 1997; Tesfatsion 2002; Janssen 2003; Janssen and Ostrom forthcoming a; Parker et al. 2003; Hodgson and Knudsen 2004). The method of institutional analysis described here can thus be implemented using a wide variety of analytical tools.

Example of a Simple Action Situation

Before turning to a discussion of the individual working parts of a situation, let us illustrate the concept of an action situation using the tools of game theory to examine a simple game—the Snatch Game.[3] The Snatch Game characterizes situations where the individuals involved do not share norms or rules. In other words, it is a game in a "state of nature." In this normless and ruleless environment, let us assume there are two farming households who are fully self-reliant. Each produces a different commodity—say, chickens and potatoes. Meals composed of all chicken or all potatoes are not as flavorful or healthy as meals composed of both chicken and potatoes. Both households would thus benefit from finding a way of exchanging some of the chickens and potatoes they produce.

The structure of a Snatch Game in a state of nature is shown in figure 2.2. In this game, Household 1 and Household 2 both have ten comparable units of the commodity they produce. Household 1 has ten chickens and Household 2 has ten sacks of potatoes (each sack of potatoes is considered comparable to one chicken). Both would be better off if they could exchange half of their own commodities for half of those grown by the other farming household. Say, each household valued their own commodity as one. If they could exchange five units of their own production for

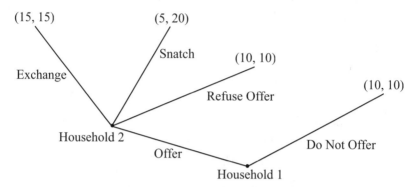

Figure 2.2 The Snatch Game. *Source*: Based on STEAL in Plott and Meyer 1975, 70.

five of the other farming household, the marginal value of the second commodity would give them twice as much value—or a total of fifteen value units each. The problem is how to accomplish an exchange when there are no well-defined property rights.

Household 1 could either offer or not offer to exchange five units with Household 2. If Household 2 gets an offer, then it has three choices. The first is to refuse to exchange. The outcome here would be for both households to retain their original ten units. Second, Household 2 can agree to an exchange and both households would be better off with fifteen value units. A third alternative—especially if Household 2 had several young, strong sons—would be to snatch the five commodities offered by Household 1 and keep their own. This leaves Household 1 with five units. Household 2 then has fifteen commodity units valued at twenty units of value.

Let us assume that both households value only the goods they finally receive. If Household 2 has the physical capability of snatching the goods once they were brought out in this "lawless" situation, no exchange would take place. Given that Household 2 has not developed strong norms against snatching, which affect the value of the outcomes and are also known to Household 1, Household 1 would predict that Household 2 will snatch the goods. And without internal norms against using physical force to take possession of goods, Household 2 would definitely snatch Household 1's goods, if given the opportunity. Given this certainty,

Household 1 would never offer an exchange in the first place. The predicted equilibrium of this game is an inefficient outcome—no exchange.

Readers familiar with game theory will recognize that the Snatch Game is one example of a very broad class of games that has the structure of a one-shot, sequential social dilemma. Social dilemmas are ubiquitous in economic, political, and social life. They occur whenever the private returns to each participant are greater than their share of a joint return no matter what other participants do. If the structure of a one-shot social dilemma game is not changed, and individuals pursue their own immediate, objective outcomes as the only values taken into account, individuals will not achieve outcomes that could leave everyone better off. Asymmetric social dilemmas, similar to the Snatch Game, are sometimes called: the "Trust Game," or the "Investment Game," or even the "Peasant Dictator Game" (Berg, Dickhaut, and McCabe 1995). We will describe findings from a series of experiments on these games in chapter 3.

The pervasiveness of social dilemmas has repeatedly been recognized in the great books of political philosophy. Hobbes described such a setting as a "war of all against all." Rousseau used a stag hunt to illustrate the problem of a group needing to all work together to hunt a large animal but facing the temptation to break up into separate groups when small animals appeared on the scene that were easy to catch. A small group could catch a rabbit, but ruined the chance for the group to obtain a large animal. Many important books of the last several decades have been devoted to an analysis of simultaneous or sequential social dilemmas (Barry and Hardin 1982; Taylor 1987; Schelling 1978). We shall often use social dilemma situations as examples throughout this book, since understanding how individuals act within social dilemma situations constitutes one of the major puzzles facing all contemporary social science disciplines.

We shall return to a discussion of the Snatch Game at different junctures throughout the book—not because we think that all of the interesting action situations are illustrated by simple, two-player games. Rather, simple situations can help us understand the concept of an action situation itself. And these simple situations also illustrate that a large body of important situations—social dilemmas—are at the heart of our discourse about institutions and the diversity of institutions.

The Basic Working Parts of Action Situations

Let us now turn to the elements of an action situation so we can begin to understand these fundamental elements of all interactive situations.

Participants

Participants in an action situation are decision-making entities assigned to a position and capable of selecting actions from a set of alternatives made available at nodes in a decision process. The participants in action situations can also be corporate actors—nations, states in a federal system, private corporations, NGOs, and so forth. Whenever participants are organizations, one treats them "in" the situation as if they were a single individual but one that is linked to a series of additional situations within their own organization. For some purposes, one may ignore the linked situations—especially when the interests of the organization, and thus the strategy it will follow, are very clear and unlikely to change due to an internal challenge. Alternatively, one may self-consciously examine the linked structure (see McGinnis and Williams 1989). Several attributes of participants are relevant when representing and analyzing specific situations. These include (1) the number of participants, (2) their status as individuals or as a team or composite actor, (3) and various individual attributes, such as age, education, gender, and experience.

THE NUMBER OF PARTICIPANTS

Interdependent action situations require at least two participants—such as the two households in the Snatch Game—where the actions of each affect the outcomes for both. Adding a third participant changes the structure of the situation substantially.[4] The dividing line between major types of games, for example, is between two-person and N-person games, where N is defined as any number greater than two. The *specific* number of participants is frequently overtly specified in real-world settings (or in formal theories about these settings) such as legislatures, juries, and most sports. Some descriptions of a situation, however, specify the number of participants in a looser fashion such as a small or large group, or face-to-face relationships versus impersonal relationships. Since many other components of an action situation are affected by the number of participants, this is a particularly important variable in the analysis of any action situation.

THE INDIVIDUAL OR TEAM STATUS OF PARTICIPANTS

Participants in many action situations are individual persons, or they may represent a team or composite actor, such as the households in the Snatch Game. Under specific conditions, a group of individuals may be considered as *one* participant (a team) in a particular action situation. Let us address the conditions that are necessary to treat a group as a participant when they participate individually in at least one other linked situation.

Drawing on the work of Fritz Scharpf (1997), we need first to distinguish between sets of individuals who share many similar characteristics and whose aggregate behavior may be predictable from knowledge acquired about a sample of individuals. In electoral politics, one can discuss "the urban voter," or "veterans," or "the labor vote." These are shorthand terms for a class of individuals who share characteristics that are perceived to be very important in affecting their individual preferences related to some events. These are meaningful concepts. They help the analyst make sense out of many events when a large number of individuals act independently, and it is useful to gain a realistic expectation about their likely actions. They are not, however, acting as a team.

As Scharpf, and Granovetter (1978) before him acknowledge, when individuals who share some key attributes also differ in the strength of some other key variable, aggregate behavior may be characterized by frequency-dependent behavior with strong threshold effects. This has been used in the explanations of street protests or revolutionary actions (Kuran 1989). For example, those who feel the most strongly against a policy may be willing to stage protest marches even if others do not join them. If the number of individuals who have strong views is not sufficiently large, however, other individuals may not be willing to engage in protest actions. On the other hand, depending on the distribution of preferences, it is possible for a strong initial showing to trigger more individuals, whose actions in turn trigger still others, to participate. Such processes can still be explained primarily at the individual level.

For an institutional analyst to consider a set of individuals to be a "composite" actor, one must assume that the individuals intend to participate in a collective action. One needs to assume that "the individuals involved intend to create a joint product or to achieve a common purpose" (Scharpf 1997, 54). Such composite actors—such as a household—will, of course, vary in regard to the type of internal decision-making mechanisms that they will use. Some will depend on very widespread preferences of their members—which Scharpf calls "collective actors." "Corporate actors," on the other hand, are not so dependent on the preferences of their members and beneficiaries, and activities "are carried out by staff members whose own private preferences are supposed to be neutralized by employment contracts" (54).

A fully organized market with well-defined property rights, for example, may include buyers and sellers who are organized as firms as well as individual participants. Firms are composed of many individuals. Each firm in a market is treated as if it were a single participant, but this is a "shorthand" way of viewing the lattice of internal action situations within a particular firm that leads to external decisions to be taken in market settings.

Whether an analyst treats separate individuals as participants or as members of a collective or corporate organization depends upon the concerns and questions of the analyst. The game of bridge, for example, may be represented as having either four participants or two teams, each composed of two individuals. If the analyst is interested in examining communication behavior during bidding, bridge is best represented as involving four participants. For the purpose of explaining how moves lead to a final score, the game may best be represented as involving two teams.

ATTRIBUTES OF PARTICIPANTS

Participants bring a diversity of ascribed or acquired characteristics to any situation. These characteristics may not influence their actions in some situations, while having a major impact on others. Whether drivers passing one another on a busy highway are both of the same social or ethnic background is unlikely to affect their actions. A young, inexperienced driver of any background, however, may approach passing another car with great hesitation and not pass when most adult drivers would do so. The same two adults might hesitate a long time before extending trust and reciprocity to each other if facing an opportunity to enter a long-term contract in a community that has recently faced racial or ethnic conflict. Even the simple Snatch Game is likely to have different outcomes depending on the attributes of Households 1 and 2. The outcomes of many situations depend on the knowledge and skills of the parties. Two chess masters will play a chess tournament differently than two young children just learning the game.

Attributes of participants are also affected by the rules structuring an action situation. The A in the ADICO syntax presented in chapter 5 identifies the attributes of participants as an important element of all rules. Individuals with some ascribed or acquired attributes, such as ethnic background, gender, or education may be enjoined from participation.

Positions

Another element of an action situation is the set of positions or "anonymous slots" into and out of which participants move. Examples of positions include players, voters, judges, buyers, sellers, legislators, police officers, and so forth. Positions and participants are separate elements in a situation even though they may not be clearly so identified in practice. In many formal games, the distinction between a participant and the position that a participant holds is blurred. In the Snatch Game, for example, there are two participants and two positions. The positions are simply labeled as Household 1 and Household 2. The household in the first position has the opportunity to make the first move. While in this instance, given the prediction of no exchange, holding the first position does not give a special advantage. Frequently, however, first mover advantages exist and may give one participant substantial power over the other.

The number of positions is frequently fewer than the number of participants. In legislative committee situations, for example, there are frequently only two positions—chair and member—while there may be five to twenty-five or more participants. When game theorists identify the elements of a game, they rarely mention positions in their definition (see Rapoport 1966; Gintis 2000b). They then tend to name positions in the text describing a game, as I did above, using terms such as Player 1 and Player 2, Principal and Agent, or Agenda Setter and Member.

Depending on the structure of the situation, a participant may simultaneously occupy more than one position. All participants will occupy whatever is the most inclusive position in a situation—member, citizen, employee, and the like. In a private firm, additional positions such as foreman, division manager, or president will be occupied by some participants while they continue to occupy the most inclusive position—that of employee.

Positions are thus the connecting link between participants and actions. In some situations, any participant in any position may be authorized to take any of the allowable actions in that situation. However, in most "organized" situations, the capability to take particular actions is assigned to a specific position and not to all positions. The nature of a position assigned to participants in an action situation defines the "standing" of the participant in that situation. The standing of a position is the set of authorized actions and limits on actions that the holder of the position can take at particular choice sets in the situation. Those who hold the position of a member of a legislative committee are authorized to debate issues and vote on them. The member who holds the position of chair can usually develop the agenda for the order of how issues will be brought before the committee or even whether a proposal will even be discussed. Determining this agenda frequently determines which issue will win in a final vote (Plott and Levine 1978; Weingast 1989).

Action situations vary substantially in the degree to which participants control their own entry into or exit from a position. A defendant in a criminal trial does not control his or her movement into or out of this position. Participants in many formal social dilemma games are treated as if they have no choice regarding entry and exits. When exit is feasible, however, the outcomes of social dilemma situations are likely to be different (Orbell and Dawes 1993). Orbell, Schwarz-Shea, and Simmons (1984) have shown that cooperators, when given the opportunity to exit after playing with a defector, choose the exit option more than defectors.

A participant in a legislature could not be a member of the legislature against his or her will, but could lose this position involuntarily. In some hierarchical situations covered by civil service systems, individuals have to compete vigorously for positions by passing examinations, but once appointed, they may hold their positions for life, subject to their taking legal actions.

Potential Outcomes

In the analysis of formal games, the standard practice is to report the outcomes of joint decisions as the analyst assumes they are ranked in utility to the participants in particular positions. In the Snatch Game, the value of ten is assigned to each of the households for keeping their own chickens and potatoes. A utility value of fifteen is designated for a successful exchange of half of the chickens for half of the potatoes, and the utility value of twenty to Household 2 for keeping its own commodities and snatching five from Household 1. When the purpose of analyzing a situation is focused entirely on understanding the result of a particular structure and the analyst is certain about the ordinal ranking of participants' values over outcomes, then this abbreviated process of representing outcomes in utility space is an effective means of analyzing a situation.

When the analyst wants to understand how rules or attributes of the biophysical world or the community change an action situation, greater precision is obtained by separately analyzing the biophysical outcomes and then the value assigned by participants to outcomes. In the Snatch Game, the physical outcomes are the actual bundles of commodities that exist at each end point. If no offer is made or an offer is rejected, both households end up with ten units of commodities. If Household 2 successfully snatches Household 1's commodities offered for sale, it ends up with fifteen commodity units and Household 1 is left with five units of their own commodity. If they reach a successful exchange, each household now has five sacks of potatoes and five chickens, which is assigned a utility valuation of fifteen units.

As discussed below, external benefits and costs are frequently assigned to outcomes by payoff rules. If there were a market where commodities were exchanged at known prices, one could assign a monetary value to the commodities. If there were taxes imposed on the exchange of commodities (a sales tax), one could represent the outcomes in a monetary unit representing the market price minus the tax. If one wanted to examine the profitability of growing chickens as contrasted to potatoes or other crops, one would represent the outcomes in terms of the monetary value of the realized sales value minus the monetary value of the inputs (land, labor, and other variable inputs).

Combining biophysical outcomes, external payoffs, and participants' internal valuation into one measure is useful for making decisions in a static setting. It does not, however, enable an analyst to identify how specific rules might affect the structure of a situation. The set of physically possible actions and resulting transformations remains the same if payoff rules are the only rules to be changed affecting a situation. What is affected by a change in payoff rules is the net level of benefits or costs assigned to a particular path of actions and physical results. Thus, to examine the effect of rules in a careful and systematic manner, one needs to consider the underlying physical transformations separately from the material rewards assigned a chain of actions and results.

One example of the essential difference is between the amount of *goods* produced during a particular time period and the net *financial sums* assigned to participants in positions (workers, managers, owners, etc.) for that time period. It is also important to consider the internal valuation placed by a participant on the rewards and costs assigned to physical results. Thus, in the approach taken in this volume, there are three components to what individuals value as outcomes: (1) the *physical results* obtained as a result of a chain of actions by participants, (2) the *material rewards* or costs assigned to actions and results by payoff rules, and (3) the *valuation* placed on the combination of the first and second components by the participants. The valuation placed on exchanging potatoes for chickens would be quite different—perhaps even negative—for a vegetarian household, as contrasted to one that enjoyed eating chicken.

The state variables affected by a situation, however measured, are what the participants in an action situation are thought of as affecting. A frequent assumption is made that the participants self-consciously decide to affect particular results or to leave them in as they were in the status quo. Analysts can also include "unintended outcomes" within the set of potential outcomes included in an action situation. Polluters, for example, frequently do not know the full range of physical results generated as a result of their actions.

THE OPPORTUNITY INVOLVED IN AN ACTION SITUATION

The "opportunity" involved in an action situation can be defined as the range of the values of the outcome variables potentially affected in a situation (von Wright 1966, 124; Commons [1924] 1968, 67). If one variable is affected, the opportunity existing in a situation is the difference between the highest and lowest achievable value on that outcome variable. When that variable is dichotomous, its presence or absence is the full range of variation. The range on a quantified variable may be small or great. The level of opportunity in a market exchange, for example, is the difference between the lowest price offered by a potential buyer and the highest price offered by a potential seller. When that range is severely constrained, the market does not offer much opportunity for affecting the price that a buyer obtains or a seller must pay. When the range is large, the market offers considerable opportunity for affecting the price (Commons [1924] 1968, 66–67). When multiple state variables are included as potential outcomes, the concept of opportunity becomes more difficult to measure but involves a cumulative score of the range of all the state variables affected using concepts such as net benefits or utility.

THE STATUS QUO OUTCOME

The status quo is a concept used to describe the relationship between the values of the end-state variables compared to the values of the initial-state variables. If none of the values on any of the state variables has changed, one concludes that the outcome remains the "status quo." In the Snatch Game, the status quo exists under two conditions: (1) if the first player does not make an offer or (2) if the first player does make an offer and the second player refuses it. When one conceptualizes the outcomes of a legislative session as the values of a set of policy variables, the status quo is always included in the set of potential outcomes. Unless there is a minimum winning coalition within those authorized to change particular policy variables, the status quo policy will continue in effect.

As discussed in some detail in the last half of this chapter, the outcome of one action situation may include the possibility or necessity of proceeding to another situation. Thus, the outcome of a committee hearing in the U.S. House of Representatives may be the successful reporting out of proposed legislation. Combined with this success, however, is the necessity to take action on the floor of the House, in a committee of the Senate, on the floor of the Senate, and potentially in a combined Senate-House committee that reports back to both houses that again reconsiders the legislation one more time (Shepsle and Weingast 1984).

If one action situation is not reached until after particular outcomes are achieved in other action situations, the first situation can be considered a "contingent action situation" (Coleman 1973, 64). The internal behavior of participants in most organizations can be analyzed as a complex series of differentially structured action situations linked by a set of procedural rules. When analyzing the "actions" of one organization in a multiorganizational setting, many of these internal situations will not be separately analyzed and some overall method for determining the most likely action to be taken by a particular type of organization in a specific type of action situation will be substituted for the full chain of linked situations. In work on two-level games, McGinnis and Williams (1989) analyze international bargaining situations where they examine both the interaction of nations in a bargaining situation and then the internal structure of relationships within the respective governments.[5]

Actions

Participants assigned to a position in an action situation must choose from a set of actions at any particular stage in a decision process. An action can be thought of as a selection of a setting or a value on a control variable (e.g., a dial or switch) that a participant hopes will affect an outcome variable. In game theory, the set of actions available to a participant at a specific sequence in a game—a decision point—is the available *moves*. The specific action selected by a participant from the set of authorized actions is called a *choice*. In the Snatch Game, the first player has a choice between two moves (offer or not offer) and the second player a choice among three moves (refuse, snatch, or exchange). A complete specification of the moves to be taken in all possible contingencies in a one-shot or repeated game is called a *strategy*.

The types of variables included within the concept of a set of authorized actions are vast. Examples of typical action sets available to participants who hold positions in different types of situations are arrayed in table 2.1. The term "action" thus includes both overt acts as well as the choice not to act in some situations or "forbearances" (von Wright 1966). Both voting for one or another candidate and abstaining from voting are included in a voter's action set, for example. Both can be conceptualized as a setting on a control variable.

Action-Outcome Linkages

A setting on a control variable is considered "linked" to a state variable when it is possible to use that setting to cause the state variable (1) to come into being, (2) to disappear, or (3) to change in degree. A light switch, for example, is a control variable with two positions—on and off. It is linked to some source of light that shines or does not shine. By turning the switch to off, one can make the light disappear. By turning the switch to on, one can produce light. In this situation, the control variable does not change unless a human actor takes a positive action to change it. Since the state variable may also change as a result of some physical process (such as the light bulb burning out), the actor can be said to have some effect on the outcome by knowing the linkage and choosing whether to change the

TABLE 2.1
Action sets assigned to positions in several "typical" action situations

Position to which action set is assigned	Authorized actions included in action set
A voter in an election	Vote for Candidate i, Candidate j, or abstain from voting
A seller in a competitive market	Sell up to X quantity of good Y at the going price; do not sell any of good Y at the going price
A member of a legislature	Submit an amendment to add provisions to an already submitted bill; submit an amendment to delete or change provisions to an already submitted bill; submit no amendments
A chair of a committee	Order the votes on an original bill (B), an amendment (A), and the status quo (Q) in any of the three following ways: (1) A vs. B and then the winner vs. Q (2) A vs. Q and then the winner vs. B (3) B vs. Q and then the winner vs. A

setting (take a positive action) or to retain the old setting (to forbear from taking a positive action).

A state variable may be linked to many control variables. One might think of a situation in which three switches jointly control a light—at least two of them must be in the "on" position for the light to appear. A person authorized to set one of the switches to on or off can potentially affect whether the light is on or off, but cannot totally control the presence or absence of light. If only one other switch is turned on, a person assigned to one of the other two switches can either make the light appear (by turning their switch on) or can produce darkness (by turning their switch off). If one person's switch is already off, the other person can allow darkness to continue by refraining from changing his or her control switch. It is in this sense that a "nonaction" may affect an outcome variable. Since all three light switches are linked to the light, choices to change the switch position or leave it the same are both considered to be an action.

To give some political content to these concepts of action and transformation functions, let us analyze the situation facing the chair of a five-person county council located in a state that authorizes local options regarding the legality of alcohol being sold within the county boundaries. The other four members of the council are divided equally on the issue. On a tie vote, a chair can vote in favor of a law, vote against a law, or abstain. What effect his or her positive action (voting for or against) or

TABLE 2.2
Results if collective-choice rules specify that a tie vote retains the status quo

Selling liquor in the county is	Legislation proposes	Result with tie	Act of chair	Final outcome
Illegal	Illegal	Illegal	Abstain	Illegal
(Forbearing to let a state remain absent)				
Illegal	Legal	Illegal	Vote Yes	Legal
(Acting to make a state come into being)				
Legal	Illegal	Legal	Vote Yes	Illegal
(Acting to make a state disappear)				
Legal	Legal	Legal	Abstain	Legal
(Forbearing to let a state continue)				

TABLE 2.3
Results if collective-choice rules specify that a tie vote leads to a change

Selling liquor in the county is	Legislation proposes	Result with tie	Act of chair	Final outcome
Illegal	Legal	Legal	Vote No	Illegal
(Acting to keep a state from occurring)				
Illegal	Legal	Legal	Abstain	Legal
(Forbearing to let a state come into being)				
Legal	Illegal	Illegal	Abstain	Illegal
(Forbearing to let a state disappear)				
Legal	Illegal	Illegal	Vote No	Legal
(Acting to prevent a state from disappearing)				

forbearance (abstaining) has depends on the rules governing what happens if there is a tie vote, as shown in tables 2.2 and 2.3.

Any specific situation would not have all eight elementary modes of action and forbearance present at once. Which subsets of the eight would be included in an action situation obviously depend on the collective-choice rules of a particular situation regarding what happens with a tie vote. Actions designed to produce a certain state or an outcome are frequently called production functions. Various combinations of materials, time, and effort are used to produce a commodity. Transformation functions are not all as determinate as those presented above. Stochastic transformation functions relate actions to outcomes in a probabilistic manner. Thus, the concepts of certainty, risk, and uncertainty are relevant to considerations of these linkages.

CERTAINTY, RISK, AND UNCERTAINTY

In action situations that are formally analyzed, the linkage of actions to outcomes is usually presumed to be knowable. In such situations, one could represent the chain of actions and results as a tree, as in the Snatch Game. When the full tree or matrix is presumed to be known to the participants, analysts refer to three types of linkage between actions and outcomes: certainty, risk, and uncertainty.

In a certain linkage, every available action is linked directly with one and only one outcome. The perfectly competitive market, as represented in neoclassical economic theory, links actions to outcomes in a certain manner. Neither sellers nor buyers in a perfectly competitive market have any control over price. The price at which alternative quantities of a product can be bought and sold is determined by market forces, and thus certain, in the short run. Offers to buy or sell at the market price lead to one and only one outcome.

The analytical world of certainty is vast and includes much of the formal theory in economics and management science. Efforts to find maxima and minima of functions, feasible regions, production possibility frontiers, and so forth, are all modes of analysis appropriate for situations characterized by certainty. Outside of formally organized large-scale markets, few interactive situations are likely to have one-to-one relationships between actions and outcomes.

Action-outcome linkages that are considered to be risky or uncertain involve one-to-many relationships between actions and outcomes, like both games presented above. In a situation characterized by *risk*, the objective probabilities' relationships between each action and set of outcomes can be known (F. Knight 1921; Cashdan 1990). A classic situation of this type is the urn filled with a known number of red and black balls where the individual must decide upon actions that can lead to one or another outcome depending upon the color of the next ball drawn from the urn. A roulette wheel is an instrument of risk. Insurance firms face a world characterized by risk when they calculate premiums to be charged for different types of insurance policies. Once data about the distribution of past events are available, probabilities can be assigned to different distributions of future events. When the probability that particular actions will lead to particular outcomes is known, a probability matrix can be developed that indicates the probability of each outcome occurring given particular combinations of states of affairs and actions.

An essential indeterminacy of social interactions remains in the context of many action situations. This indeterminacy is called uncertainty (F. Knight 1921). When institutional arrangements leave open wide avenues for choice, and each individual's outcome is dependent upon the actions taken by others, uncertainty will characterize the resulting decision situation. Uncertainty characterizes a situation in which the probabilities of specific actions leading to outcomes are unknowable. The set of actions and the set of outcomes are still assumed to be finite and knowable. The linkages between actions and outcomes are also presumed to be knowable. Most formal games are characterized by uncertainty, as are most situations existing in the political realm. The potential decision of the individual is taken into account in the decision making of the "other." Each individual must decide in the presence of at least one "strategic other" whose decision to act will be contingent upon expectations about the individual's action (Coleman 1973, 42). For situations that can be represented as formal games, the Nash equilibrium and its refinements are a method for predicting the likely action-outcome linkages assuming that all participants view the situation with common knowledge about its structure and the rationality of the other players. Anthropologists and ecologists have delved into a number of fascinating questions related to the presence of substantial risk in the ecology in which humans find themselves (see Kaplan, Hill, and Hurtado 1990; Low 1990). Hawkes, O'Connell, and Blurton Jones (2001), for example, explain the frequently observed relationship that hunted meat from large animals is widely shared, while food obtained from subsistence agriculture is not as related to the difference in the risk of obtaining food from these two activities (see also Kameda, Takezawa, and Hastie 2003 for an excellent synthesis of the debate over explanation).

The distinction presented here among certainty, risk, and uncertainty focuses entirely on structural aspects of the situation (linkage patterns) and not on the level of information that an individual has about the situation. Theorists sometimes blur this distinction. This blurring leads to considerable confusion when they treat the uncertainty in the situation and the lack of information by an individual as the same phenomena. The separation of situational and cognitive aspects of uncertainty draws heavily on the earlier work of F. Knight (1921) and Buchanan and di Pierro (1980), who stress the need to distinguish between the structure of the situation and the cognition of the individual. H. Simon (1955) and Williamson (1975) also distinguish between situational complexity and uncertainty on the one hand and cognitive limitations on the other.

Control

The extent of control over the linkage of the action to outcomes that a participant has varies from absolute to almost none. An individual has total control (omnipotence) over an outcome variable, which we may call o_i in a situation if for each value o_i potentially affected within that situation there is an action a_i, such that the conditional probability of o_i given a_i equals one. For two-dimensional outcomes, an individual has total control if for each combination of outcome variable values o_io_j there is an a_i, such that the conditional probability of o_io_j given a_i equals one (Coleman 1973, 61).

An individual has partial control over a state variable if the conditional probability of a change in the value o_i of the state variable given an action a_i available to the individual is greater than zero and less than one. Partial control can, thus, vary from an extremely small chance of affecting an outcome to a high probability of affecting the outcome. A participant can be said to be impotent with respect to an outcome when he or she has no control over the values of a state variable (see von Wright 1966, 129–31 for a discussion of control that is similar to that of Coleman).

The "power" of an individual in a situation is the value of the opportunity (the range in the outcomes afforded by the situation) times the extent of control. Thus, an individual can have a small degree of power, even though the individual has absolute control if the amount of opportunity in a situation is small. The amount of power may also be small when the opportunity is large, but the individual has only a small degree of control. Action situations may involve differential distributions of control and opportunity to different individuals in the situation. Consequently, individuals may differ in the amount of power they have in the situation. Concepts of opportunity, control, and power are thus defined as situation-dependent. A single individual may have dramatically differing levels of control, opportunity, and power in the different action situations in which they participate. An executive may have more power in regard to those issues where the executive must initiate action than when the executive can only stop action.

Information about the Action Situation

Participants in an action situation may have access to complete or incomplete information. Almost all formal representations of action situations assume that participants have access to complete information by which is meant that each participant could know the number of other participants, the positions, the outcomes, the actions available, how actions are linked to outcomes (and thus the certainty, risk, or uncertainty of the linkage), the information available to other players, and the payoffs of the same. In other words, complete information is an assumption that each participant could know the full structure of an action situation as defined here.

When participants are assumed to have access to complete information, a further distinction is made in formal theory between perfect and imperfect information. When a participant has access to perfect information, they cannot only know all of their own past actions, they can also know the actions of all other players before they make any move. In other words, they can know the exact decision node at which they are making a choice. Household 2 in the Snatch Game has perfect information. Under imperfect but complete information, the individual is assumed to have access to knowledge of the full structure of the situation, but may not have access to knowledge about all the moves that other participants have taken prior to a particular move. The participants could know all the possible nodes at which he or she could be, but is unable to distinguish the exact node for the current move.

When information is less than complete, the question of who knows what at what juncture becomes very important. With incomplete information, how much any one individual contributes to a joint undertaking is often difficult for others to judge. When joint outcomes depend on multiple actors contributing inputs that are costly and difficult to measure, incentives exist for individuals to behave opportunistically (Williamson 1975). Opportunism—deceitful behavior intended to improve one's own welfare at the expense of others—may take many forms, from inconsequential, perhaps unconscious, shirking to a carefully calculated effort to defraud others with whom one is engaged in ongoing relationships. The opportunism of individuals who may say one thing and do something else further compounds the problem of incomplete information.

In many work situations, a boss cannot know exactly what employees are doing and how this adds to or takes away from the accomplishment of a joint output. Developing a contract that motivates them to be highly productive has long been recognized as a challenge (Barnard 1938). In the contemporary economics literature, the problem of a principal negotiating with an agent—when the agent's actions cannot be fully known to the principal—is known as the Principal-Agent problem (Fudenberg, Holmström, and Milgrom 1990; Laffont and Martimort 2002). Asymmetric information problems also occur when individuals try to develop a contract to share risk. An insurance firm can never know the intentions and behavior of those it insures. Thus, all insurance situations involve a moral hazard problem (Arrow 1963).

When action situations are being analyzed in a less formal manner, analysts are more apt to assume that participants have access to incomplete information about the full set of actions available to them, the full set of outcomes, and about how actions are linked to outcomes. This assumption is frequently linked to fundamental assumptions made about the limitations of human cognitive abilities in a model of the individual. However, the usefulness of an assumption of complete or incomplete information also relates to the complexity of the action situation being modeled and the language structure used, the channels of communication, and the type of communication normally assumed to be present in the action situation.

Costs and Benefits

The discussion of outcomes, and of action-outcome linkages presented above, relies on the relationships between control variables and state variables. In addition to the physical actions and outcomes that are involved in a situation, rewards and/or sanctions may be distributed to participants in positions dependent upon the path taken to achieve a particular outcome. Costs and benefits are cumulative. External rewards or sanctions assigned to outcomes include the rewards (financial returns) or sanctions (taxes or fines) assigned to actions taken along a path to an outcome.

For simplicity, it is frequently assumed in theoretical models that acts are costly and outcomes are beneficial. Participants are then viewed as weighing the costs of an action against the benefits of an outcome. Actions may, however, have associated benefits, and outcomes may be "bads" instead of "goods." In the Snatch Game, for example, one of the outcomes is very bad for Household 1 and very good for Household 2. All actions are represented in figure 2.2 as having zero costs. If the place where Households 1 and 2 meet is located some distance away from each of their farms, the cost of traveling to this location could be included in a payoff table. Thus, the final external value assigned to an outcome for a participant in a position is the *net* value of the path taken to an outcome given the choices made by the participant and those of others. The external value to a seller in a fully developed market setting is the profit resulting from the sale of a quantity of goods minus the cost of buying or producing those goods.

In conducting an institutional analysis, a distinction needs to be made between a physical outcome, an external reward or sanction, and the valuation that a participant assigns to the physical transformation and external rewards and/or sanctions. So long as the physical linkage between actions and outcomes remains the same, the outcome remains the same. A firm following a routine production process generates, on average, the same quantity of a product per unit of time. If the price of the commodity increases or decreases substantially, or a new tax is imposed on the sale of the commodity, the net profits obtained differ substantially. The external or extrinsic values are the set of "reward" variables affected by the path of actions and outcomes. Examples of extrinsic rewards include the financial returns assigned a worker in a Principal-Agent contract. The reward may be assigned strictly on action variables (e.g., how many hours the worker clocks in), strictly on outcome variables (e.g., how much of a particular final or intermediate product is produced), or on some combination of action and outcome variables (a wage plus a production bonus). Extrinsic benefits and costs are frequently assigned through the operation of a rule system and thus do not rely only on biophysical processes.

If the primary interest is to predict what will happen in a particular situation, and not how to change the situation, the only value that a researcher needs to use is the net value assigned by participants to the achievement of an outcome. This value is referred to as *utility* in economics and game theory. Utility is a summary measure of all the net values to the individuals of all the benefits and costs of arriving at a particular outcome. Game theorists use utility values in representing an outcome and only rarely decompose this into component costs and benefits. Some individuals may pay attention only to the objective, extrinsic valuation assigned to an action-outcome link. For simplicity, many analysts assume that subjective utility is positively associated with the net value of the external rewards. In economics, theorists normally assume that utility is monotonically associated with profits, for example. As discussed extensively in chapter 4, this assumption is reasonable to make in many but *not* all situations. Individuals may assign either a positive or negative intrinsic value to actions or outcomes. Participants in the same situation may not even assign the same internal valuation to the objective outcome (see Schiemann 2002).

The *intrinsic valuation* attached to an external reward or sanction is the internal value that individuals associate with the components of the objective transformations and rewards (Frey 1997a; Deci 1975). Joy, shame, regret, and guilt are all forms of intrinsic values. If the person evaluates an action as being improper, they may assign a negative intrinsic value. If the person is proud of an action, they may assign it a positive intrinsic value. Measuring intrinsic valuation is extremely challenging. In fact, dissecting the holon referred to as "the participant" in this framework is among the more challenging tasks an institutional analyst faces. Thus, all of chapter 4 is devoted to a beginning elucidation of this process.

The Number of Times the Action Situation Will Be Repeated

In addition to the internal components of an action situation, it is also important to know whether the situation is a one-shot or a repeated interaction. Analysts usually agree, for example, that the outcomes that individuals will obtain in a social dilemma game like a Prisoner's Dilemma or the Snatch Game will depend, among other factors, on whether the participants are engaged in a one-time encounter or over an indefinitely long sequence of plays. The predicted equilibrium in a single-play Snatch

Game (assuming that both players do not know one another and value only the objective outcomes) is that neither participant would trust the other when in the first position. Thus, both players are worse off than they could be if they exchanged commodities. If this game were repeated a finite number of times, most game theorists would predict the same equilibrium as for a single-round game due to backward induction. The last play of this game is similar to the single-round game. Given this, analysts predict that participants will not cooperate on this last round. Once the participants have decided not to cooperate on the last round, they would also decide not to cooperate on the second-to-the-last round, and so forth, back to the first round.

When participants in a social dilemma game are placed into an indefinite series of rounds, however, the disadvantage of continued lack of cooperation can lead them to adopt a conditional cooperative strategy so long as other participants also cooperate. The well-known folk theorem of game theory establishes that full cooperation is one of the feasible equilibria that participants in an infinitely repeated (or even an indefinitely repeated) situation may achieve if they use one of several conditional cooperative strategies (Kreps et al. 1982). It is, however, only one of many equilibria. Thus, participants face a challenging coordination problem in reaching this outcome.

One of the most famous and useful conditional strategies is "Tit for Tat," where players in a repeated, symmetric social dilemma cooperate on their first round and then take whatever action their counterpart took in the last round (Axelrod 1984). If there are only two participants in a repeated, symmetric social dilemma situation, they can monitor and punish one another through future actions. Thus, whenever one of the participants tries to take advantage of the other participants, the second participant can directly punish the first participant on the next round. Once a group is larger than two, simple strategies or heuristics like Tit for Tat are much harder to implement since an error by one person may set the entire group into a never-ending series of retributions.

The possibility of participating in a repeated symmetric situation, then, may be enough to lead small groups of individuals to seek out mutually advantageous strategies when they might not otherwise do so. For asymmetric social dilemmas, however, such as the Snatch Game, there is no single, simple heuristic—like Tit for Tat—that can be successfully employed to reach the higher joint outcome. This is due to the fact that the first player can simply stay with the status quo, and what the second player would do is irrelevant. The second player does not have an easy method for "punishing" the first player in later rounds as there may be no later rounds. Scholars are working on a set of heuristics that are posited to help individuals cope with asymmetric, social dilemma situations where trust and reciprocity are so very important (see Rieskamp and Gigerenzer 2003).

Linking Action Arenas

In addition to analysis that digs deeper into the exogenous factors affecting action arenas, an important development in institutional analysis is the examination of linked arenas. Whereas the concept of a "single" arena may include large numbers of participants and complex chains of action, most of social reality is composed of multiple arenas linked sequentially or simultaneously (see Shubik 1986). Rarely do action situations exist entirely independently of other situations. Political scientists frequently study processes within a legislature where decisions are first made in a committee, then in one house, then in a second house, then in conference committees, then by the chief executive. Decisions inside one unit of a private firm must also go through a sequence of action situations before they are final. Given the importance of repeated interactions to the development of a reputation for reciprocity and the importance of reciprocity for achieving higher levels of outcome over time, individuals have a strong motivation to link situations so as to utilize the capabilities achieved through gaining a reputation in one situation that helps to provide credibility in others.

Action situations are linked in two different and important ways. The first kind is an organizational linkage. Within larger organizations, what happens in the purchasing department affects what happens in the production and sales departments and vice versa. For some purposes, it is useful to isolate a single situation in an organization to try to understand why particular kinds of outcomes are achieved in that situation without embedding the situation of interest in a larger lattice of related situations.

Further, interesting and important institutional arrangements for coordinating complex chains of actions among large numbers of actors involve multiple organizations *competing* with one another according to a set of rules. Markets are the most frequently studied institutional arrangements that achieve coordination by relying primarily on rule-governed, competitive relationships among organizations. Rule-governed competition among two or more political parties is considered by many analysts to be an important requisite for a democratic polity. Less studied, but potentially as important a means for achieving responsiveness and efficiency in producing public goods and services are arrangements that allow rule-ordered competition among two or more potential *producers* of public goods and services (see McGinnis 1999b).

A more fundamental form of linking is shifting levels of analysis from one situation to a deeper rule-changing situation. All action situations where individuals engage in the provision, production, distribution, appropriation, assignment, or consumption of goods and services are classified as operational situations. Operational situations are themselves affected by the biophysical world, the rules affecting the structure of the operational situation, and the attributes of the community in which the situation was embedded. If operational situations were all that is analyzed in this book, we would not need to go further than the presentation of the Institutional Analysis and Development (IAD) framework for a single level of analysis. In this case, the rules analyzed are presumed to be fixed and the linkage between a situation at one level (where rules are assumed to be fixed and unchanging) and another level (where rules are themselves the outcomes produced) is unnecessary.

We do, however, want to understand how operational situations are linked to a deeper situation where the rules of the operational situation are made or modified. Not only are there two levels of analysis; one can dig deeper into where the rules come from in a collective-choice situation to examine constitutional-choice situations. For practical reasons, we stop the digging at a metaconstitutional level that is relevant when individuals are in the process of constituting or reconstituting ongoing relationships. A metaconstitutional level occurs when participants examine the consequences of diverse rules for who is to represent them in a constitutional process.

In this chapter, we will focus first on linked action situations where the outcomes from one situation are eventually fed into a series of other situations, but where rules themselves remain relatively constant. Then we will address the deeper question of how to examine the linkage between one situation and its immediate deeper-level situation where the rules of the first situation may be changed.

Organizational Linkages

Behavior within any particular situation may depend upon expected outcomes in another situation. As mentioned above, a potential outcome of one situation may be to enter a second situation. Some social processes may need to be thought of as composed of a series of linked situations. The outcomes of any one situation become inputs into the next situation. The intermediate outcomes of an early situation may not have much value unless the full series of linked situations is completed. Thus, getting a bill passed by the House of Representatives can be viewed as an intermediate step in finally getting a bill passed into law. The full set of situations within the Senate and the signature by the president are necessary before a bill becomes a law. The intermediate outcome is a necessary step for the final outcome, but may not have much assigned worth.

An organization is composed of one or more (usually more) action situations linked together by prescriptions specifying how outcomes from one situation become inputs into others. Organizations may be thought of as a tree or a lattice with situations at each node. A particular set of rules structures the situation at each node. A general set of rules partially structures all internal situations and specifies the paths that may be chosen from one situation to the next. Thus, a tournament is one form of organization that prescribes how players will proceed through the tournament tree. Many bureaucratic organizations have a similar general structure to that of tournaments.

Where one draws the boundaries on the analysis of linked situations depends on the questions of interest to the analyst. In regard to collective-choice action situations, one may want to understand why some kinds of candidates are selected in elections and not others. If this is the only question, one can focus on primary elections and the relationships among diverse supporters and the policy position of candidates in a "candidate selection game" (see Downs 1957 for the classic analysis of this situation).

Other situations are only potentially linked together. Thus, many commercial transactions occur within organizations or across market situations. Most of these occur without any reference to a court. However, invoking court proceedings is a very important method available to participants in these transactions to constrain the action set of other participants to those that have been agreed to. If it is extremely costly to use court proceedings, then one would predict that the action sets of participants would be more likely to include some actions that are illegal or are outside the bounds of a contract. Thus, the relative ease and availability of such action situations as courts to serve as monitors, sanctioners, and to provide remedies is extremely important in understanding the behavior of actors within any particular situation.

Actions and outcomes that occur in one location may also stimulate reactions by others located in another situation located elsewhere. Firms that are highly profitable are frequently used as models by others as to how to organize themselves for success. Farm households who innovate and are successful or common-property arrangements that increase their joint yield are frequently copied by others. These connections are like a ripple across the landscape rather than strongly linked situations.

Multiple Levels of Analysis

Besides multiple and nested action arenas at any one level of analysis, nesting of arenas also occurs across several levels of analysis. All rules are nested in another set of rules that define how the first set of rules can be changed. The nesting of rules within rules at several levels is similar to the nesting of computer languages at several levels. What can be done at a higher level will depend on the capabilities and limits of the rules at that level and at a deeper level. Whenever one addresses questions about *institutional change*, as contrasted to ongoing actions within institutional constraints, it is necessary to recognize that:

> 1. Changes in the rules used to order action at one level occur within a currently "fixed" set of rules at a deeper level.
> 2. Changes in deeper-level rules usually are more difficult and more costly to accomplish, thus increasing the stability of mutual expectations among individuals interacting according to the deeper set of rules.

As mentioned earlier in the chapter, it is useful to distinguish three levels of rules that cumulatively affect the actions taken and outcomes obtained in any setting (Kiser and Ostrom 1982).[6] *Operational rules* directly affect day-to-day decisions made by the participants in any setting. These can change relatively rapidly—from day to day. *Collective-choice rules* affect operational activities and results through their effects in determining who is eligible to be a participant and the specific rules to be used in changing operational rules. These change at a much slower pace. *Constitutional-choice rules* first affect collective-choice activities by determining who is eligible to be a participant and the rules to be used in crafting the set of collective-choice rules that, in turn, affect the set of operational rules (Brennan and Buchanan 1985; Buchanan and Tullock 1962). Constitutional-choice rules change at the slowest pace. One can even think about a "metaconstitutional" level underlying all the others that is not frequently analyzed. One can think of the linkages among these rules and related level of analysis as shown in figure 2.3.[7]

For most practical applications, three levels are enough.[8] No theoretical justification exists for three and only three levels (Diermeier and Krehbiel 2003). For the purposes of formal theory, we may need to assume as long a series of layers as is needed until we hit rock bottom—the biophysical world. Very deep layering—even infinite layering—turns out to be needed in many aspects of formal theory. Game theorists, for example, have had to assume that the common understanding needed for one to assume that there is a game is nested infinitely. "Information is *common knowledge* if it is known to all players, each player knows that all of them know it, and each of them knows that all of them know that all of them know it,

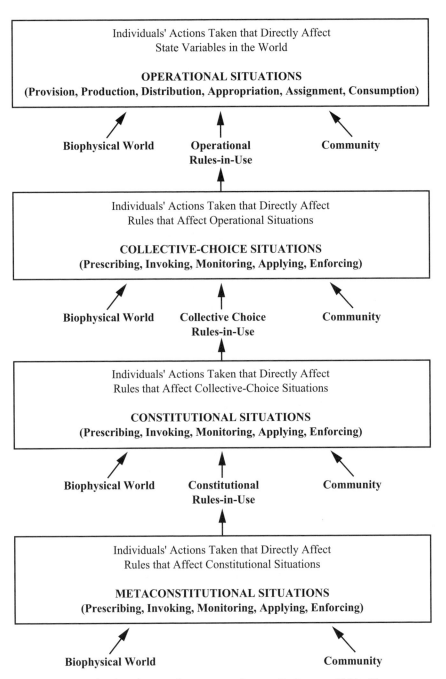

Figure 2.3 Levels of analysis and outcomes. *Source*: E. Ostrom 1999, 60.

and so forth ad infinitum" (Rasmusen 1989, 50). Thus, one can always assume that there are even more primitive rules underlying those that one is analyzing at any one level—thus our positing of a very general metaconstitutional level—until one gets to the constraints of a biophysical world. At that point, the only distinction that can be made among actors is their strictly physical strength, as Hobbes long ago recognized. For most institutional analyses, three nested levels are sufficient.

At an operational tier, participants interact in light of the internal and external incentives they face to generate outcomes directly in the world. Examples of operational-level situations include:

- Families deciding to move or not move into an urban neighborhood depending on the proportion of neighbors who share attributes (such as wealth, race, ethnicity) with them in the potential future neighborhood as compared to their present neighborhood (see H. Young 1998, 62–65; Schelling 1978).
- Workers hired by a boss to undertake a complex task who have private information about their level of effort and face incentives to keep effort at a minimum (for examples from a developed economy perspective, see Miller 2001; and from a developing economy perspective, see Ensminger 2001).
- Harvesters from a common-pool resource deciding how much, when, and with what technology to appropriate resource units (Gibson, McKean, and Ostrom 2000).

The participants in collective-choice games may be the same participants as in linked operational-choice games (as when all firms in an industry agree upon a particular industry standard that they will all use in manufacturing goods). Or, participants in collective-choice games may differ from those in operational games. They may, for example, be legislative representatives selected in electoral games (themselves part of the collective-choice level of action) to be the agents of a set of principals—the citizens engaged in a wide diversity of operational games that will be affected over time by legislative policies. Examples of collective-choice (policy choice) situations include:

- devising allocation schemes that can be used by NASA in allocating uses of space stations (Plott and Porter 1996);
- elected representatives in diversely structured legislatures devising policies based on popular preference distributions (Hammond and Butler 2003);
- citizens in diversely structured European countries making electoral decisions in light of the information generated by their political systems (Benz and Stutzer 2004).

Policy decisions affect the structure of arenas where individuals are making operational decisions and thus impacting directly on a biophysical world. The situation could as well be at a constitutional tier, where decisions are made about who is eligible to participate in policymaking and the rules that will be used to undertake policymaking.

Participants in the third level can again either be participants in the other two levels or not. And, participants in constitutional choices may not recognize that they are making a constitutional rule—they may be simply trying to fix a problem with the way that they have been making policy choices over the last several years. Examples of constitutional-choice arenas are:

- a group of groundwater producers meeting to discuss the formation of a public district in order to develop regulations on the amount of water withdrawn from the basin (Blomquist 1992);
- representatives from regions within a country debating the design or modification of a national constitution (V. Ostrom 1987; Reynolds 2002; Dougherty 2001);
- representatives from countries in regions that are developing strategies to create new multicountry unions for some purposes and possibly even to change their borders (O'Leary, Lustick, and Callaghy 2001).

At each level of analysis there may be one or more arenas in which the types of decisions made at that level will occur. In the collective-choice, constitutional, and metaconstitutional situations, activities involve prescribing, invoking, monitoring, applying, and enforcing rules (Lasswell and Kaplan 1950; Oakerson 1994).

The concept of an "arena" as described earlier does not necessarily imply a formal setting, but can include such formal settings as legislatures and courts. Policy making (or governance) regarding the rules that will be used to regulate operational-level choices is usually carried out in one or more collective-choice arenas, as shown in figure 2.4. Constitutional arenas are frequently formal arenas, but these may occur within specially called conventions, within formal courts, or within a legislature that changes a basic rule about making collective-choice rules.[9]

When a theorist chooses to analyze a situation at any particular level, the theorist must assume that the institutional rules at that level are temporarily fixed for the purpose of analysis. These rules form a part of the *structure* of the situation rather than the *solution* to the game created by that structure. When the purpose of analysis is to understand the origin of the rules at one level, knowing the structure of the situation at the next level is essential for that enterprise. The equilibria achieved at one level are thus supported by equilibria that have been achieved at deeper levels.[10] Understanding the role of these nested levels does not, however, require that the analyst specify the full supporting infrastructure in elucidating how individuals are expected to behave at one level.[11] Thus, assuming that there are multiple levels where decisions are made that affect actions at other levels actually greatly simplifies analysis rather than complicating it.

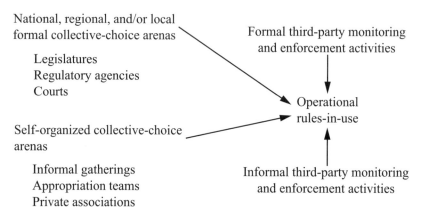

National, regional, and/or local
formal collective-choice arenas

    Legislatures
    Regulatory agencies
    Courts

Formal third-party monitoring
and enforcement activities

Operational
rules-in-use

Self-organized collective-choice
arenas

    Informal gatherings
    Appropriation teams
    Private associations

Informal third-party monitoring
and enforcement activities

Figure 2.4 Relationships of formal and informal collective-choice arenas. *Source*:
Adapted from E. Ostrom 1990, 53.

Level-Shifting Strategies

An individual engages in "level shifting" whenever he or she begins to
contemplate how to change any of the constraints on an operational situation (or, on a collective-choice situation) that are potentially under the
control of the participants in that situation. A groundwater pumper, for
example, attempts to shift levels when he or she states to another pumper,
"Hey, this race of ours to withdraw water is going to destroy the basin
and leave us all worse off than we could be. Why don't we change our
rules so as to avoid such a disaster?"

Any participant can shift *levels of analysis* in his or her own thinking
at any point in time while engaged in action at a different level. Before a
resource user suggests a rule to another user, the first has already analyzed
some of the consequences of adopting a revised set of rules. Shifting levels
of analysis can be accomplished by any actor operating independently of
others. That actor simply contemplates the opportunities and constraints
that might be available at a different level for solving some of the problems occurring at a current level.

When the individual estimates that substantial benefits are likely to
occur if others agree to an actual shift of levels of action and to change
rules, the individual may then be willing to invest resources to try to convince others that they should agree on a shift and consider the constraints
that are currently in effect. Shifting levels of action does not mean deciding to change the rules by making the shift. Shifting enables only those
who shift to contemplate overtly a different set of rules (or other constraints that may potentially be under their control, such as making a
capital investment in their joint enterprise.) One possible result of a shift
of levels may be to keep the status quo rules.

In field settings, it is hard to tell where one situation starts and another stops. Life continues in what appears to be a seamless web as individuals move from home to market to work (action situations typically characterized by reciprocity, by exchange, or by team problem solving or command). Further, within arenas, choices of actions *within* a set of rules as contrasted to choices *among* future rules are frequently made without recognizing that the level of action has shifted. So, when a "boss" says to an "employee," "How about changing the way we do X?" and the two discuss options and jointly agree upon a better way, they have shifted from taking actions *within* previously established rules to making decisions *about* the rules structuring future actions. In other words, using IAD language, they have shifted to a collective-choice arena.

The costs of shifting levels of decision making vary dramatically from one setting to another. In some settings the same individuals are involved in constitutional, collective-choice, and operational situations. Shifting levels may be accomplished at low costs. A group of resource users discussing common problems at an operational level may somewhat naturally turn to a discussion of what could be done to solve any of their current problems potentially including overuse, underinvestment, lack of information, and the like. Part of this discourse may be focused on enforcing their current rules more effectively. Another part of their discussion may include reference to alternative rules that might reassign their own rights and duties. After such a discussion, they may agree to stay with their current rules or seriously evaluate the likely effect of changing rules and agreeing on a change.

Formal procedures—including petitions, court hearings, legislation, and/ or referenda—may be required to shift levels of action in many situations. Bureaucratic officials may control access to an arena in which rules and other constraints could be changed. Judicial procedures may be used for this purpose. The transaction costs of shifting levels and transforming an ongoing situation may be very high. In such cases, participants at one level may continue to rely for long periods on rules that produce suboptimal outcomes at that level because the expected costs of changing rules are higher than the benefits they could derive from a better set of rules. Alternatively, they may devise their own de facto rules that they enforce themselves since they cannot turn to authorities to enforce them. Developing de facto rules outside formal channels may be less costly than trying to use the formal channels available to participants in some political systems.

It is through shifting levels of action that participants may be able to self-consciously design rules in their efforts to change patterns of undesirable interactions and outcomes at operational or collective-choice levels. The lack of a self-conscious examination of this strategy leads some scholars to presume that individuals facing social dilemma situations have no way out but continuing suboptimal outcomes or relying on "external actors" to change the constraints they are facing. Garrett Hardin (1968), for example, asks readers to picture a set of herders trapped in a "tragedy of the commons" that they could not themselves overcome. In an open, self-organizing society with considerable opportunities for individuals to devise their own rules for the public and private enterprises they establish, shifting levels of analysis is, however, something that participants do frequently.

Once this possibility is seriously considered, however, it raises the problem of how to analyze rules themselves rather than simply taking them as unchangeable constraints. This is the major challenge that will be addressed in chapters 5 to 9 of this volume. If rules are to be used as the tools of a self-governing society, the diversity of tools themselves must be examined. This is a nontrivial problem, especially given the importance of the biophysical world and the broader communities in which rules are only one factor affecting structure.

Predicting Outcomes

Depending upon the analytical structure of a situation and the particular assumptions about the actor used, the analyst makes strong or weak inferences about results. In tightly constrained, one-shot action situations under conditions of complete information, where participants are motivated to select particular strategies or chains of actions that jointly lead to stable equilibria, an analyst can frequently make strong inferences and specific predictions about likely patterns of behavior and outcomes. Game theorists draw on solution concepts, such as the Nash equilibrium, to predict outcomes.

Many field situations, however, do not facilitate making clear predictions. Instead of completely independent decision making, individuals may be embedded in communities where unobserved norms of fairness and conservation may change the structure of a situation dramatically. Within these situations, participants may adopt a broader range of strategies than expected using an assumption of a narrow self-interest. Further, individuals may change their strategies over time as they learn about the results of past actions. The institutional analyst examining these more open, less-constrained situations must make weaker inferences and predict the patterns of outcomes that are relatively more or less likely to result from a particular type of situation. In an experimental laboratory, for example, giving subjects in many types of social dilemmas an opportunity to communicate on a face-to-face basis is likely to substantially change the strategies chosen by subjects to ones that are not predicted by noncooperative theory (see E. Ostrom, Gardner, and Walker 1994 and cites contained therein). This is not, however, a determinate process. The variation in outcomes achieved is relatively large in groups that engage in face-to-face communication, as discussed in chapter 3.

In field settings, one can assume that providing arenas where at least some individuals engage in face-to-face discussions will usually change the outcomes achieved. The important role of communication is achieving a common understanding of the problems jointly faced. Discourse frequently generates ideas concerning various ways of coping more effectively with these problems. Further, communication helps participants to learn what norms individuals share or do not share and whether sufficient trust exists that individuals can adopt plans of actions that depend on trustworthy behavior (see E. Ostrom 1998, 2001). Even large communities whose forests are degraded can potentially turn a bad situation around through their own efforts. Varughese (2000) documents how a community of over twenty-five hundred people organized its own forest association and created subcommittees so as to involve more members in face-to-face discussion and decisions. This community has devised many innovative strategies for improving forest conditions while trying to keep the costs on community members relatively low. Many historical factors, as well as the current structure of the situation, affect the likelihood of organization and communication. Thus, no determinate predictions can be made.

Some situations within any one of these levels may be simple enough that one can generate a clear and empirically supported prediction about likely behavior and outcomes—as one can, for example, in a highly competitive market producing goods characterized by low costs of exclusion and subtractability. Here, one can rely on well-tested results from prior theoretical and empirical work. It is usually much more difficult to predict results when one is analyzing a collective-choice or constitutional-choice level situation as it impacts on operational-level settings. The process of changing the property rights of inshore fisheries in New Zealand by the national government involved substantial conflict and reorganization throughout its early history (Yandle and Dewees 2003). From an effort to create strictly private transferable rights, the system has evolved into a complex but workable system. Comanagement institutions have been crafted to complement individual property rights—something not predicted by anyone when the initial institutional change was initiated (ibid.).

The problem of predicting outcomes is especially challenging when new and unfamiliar collective- or constitutional-choice rules are selected.[12] When new and unanalyzed situations are created by the process of changing parts of a rule configuration, institutional analysis needs to proceed to undertake a deeper analysis of how participants view the new rules, how they come to understand them, how they will be monitored and enforced, and what types of individual actions and collective outcomes are produced. This is frequently a difficult and complex theoretical and empirical task. As Mantzavinos, North, and Shariq (2004, 75) stress, the "greatest challenge for the social sciences is to explain change—or more specifically, social, political, economic, and organizational change."

Evaluating Outcomes

In addition to predicting outcomes, the institutional analyst may also evaluate the outcomes that are being achieved as well as the likely set of outcomes that could be achieved under alternative institutional arrangements. Participants in action situations and those observing these situations use evaluative criteria that are applied to the outcomes as well as the processes of achieving outcomes. The number of potential evaluative criteria is large. In this chapter, we can only briefly focus on (1) economic efficiency; (2) equity; (3) adaptability, resilience, and robustness; (4) accountability; and (5) conformance to general morality.

Economic Efficiency

Economic efficiency is measured by the magnitude of the change in the flow of net benefits associated with an allocation or reallocation of resources. The concept of efficiency plays a central role in studies estimating the benefits and costs or rates of return to investments that are often used to determine the economic feasibility or desirability of public policies. When considering alternative institutional arrangements, therefore, it is important to consider how revisions in the rules affecting participants will alter behavior and, hence, the allocation of resources.

Equity

Assessing equity is undertaken in two ways: (1) on the basis of the equality between individuals' contributions to an effort and the benefits they derive and (2) on the basis of differential abilities to pay. The concept of equity that underlies an exchange economy holds that those who benefit from a service should bear the burden of financing that service. This is called *fiscal equivalence*. Perceptions of fiscal equivalence or a lack thereof can affect the willingness of individuals to contribute toward the development and maintenance of public facilities.

Outcomes that tend to redistribute resources to poorer individuals are considered to improve equity from a *redistributional equity* perspective. Thus, in some cases, efficiency criteria would urge that scarce resources be used where they produce the greatest net benefit, while equity goals would urge an effort to benefit particularly needy groups. Likewise, redistributional criteria may differ in rankings from those of achieving fiscal equivalence.

Adaptability, Resilience, and Robustness

Another criterion that can be applied to repeated situations is how behavior changes over time. Do individuals learn from experience within an action situation? Do they adapt to new circumstances as they arise or become rigid in their responses over time? The concept of resilience that originally was developed in ecology has now been applied to social systems. Resilience is defined as the amount of disruption needed to transform a system from stability domain (characterized by a configuration of mutually reinforcing processes and structures) to another (Holling 1973; Gunderson and Holling 2001). The concept of robustness tends to be used more in engineering, while resilience was initially defined related to ecological systems. Robustness refers to the maintenance of a system's performance even when it is subject to external, unpredictable disturbances (Carlson and Doyle 2002; Anderies, Janssen, and Ostrom 2004).

Accountability

When evaluating collective-choice or constitutional-choice levels, one can ask whether officials are accountable to citizens concerning the policies and rules chosen. Without accountability, actors can engage in the various opportunistic, strategic behaviors. Concern for accountability may not conflict with efficiency and equity goals. Indeed, achieving efficiency requires that information about the preferences of citizens be available to decision makers, as does achieving accountability. Institutional arrangements that effectively aggregate this information assist in realizing efficiency at the same time that they serve to increase accountability and to promote the achievement of redistributional objectives.

Conformance to General Morality

In addition to accountability, one may wish to evaluate the level of general morality fostered by a particular set of institutional arrangements. Are those who are able to cheat and go undetected able to obtain very high payoffs? Are those who keep promises more likely to be rewarded and advanced in their careers? How do those who repeatedly interact within a set of institutional arrangements learn to relate to one another over the long term? Are the procedures fair? (Frey, Benz, and Stutzer 2004)

The Need for Trade-offs

Trade-offs are often necessary in using performance criteria as a basis for selecting from alternative institutional arrangements. Some criteria are more important when evaluating patterns of actions and outcomes at a collective-choice or constitutional-choice level than at an operational level. The trade-off issue arises most explicitly in considering alternative methods of funding public projects at a collective-choice level. Evaluating how institutional arrangements compare across overall criteria is quite a challenge. Analytical examination of the likely trade-offs between intermediate costs is valuable in attempting to understand comparative institutional performance (see E. Ostrom, Schroeder, and Wynne 1993, chap. 5).

In this chapter, we have focused first on a core analytical unit of the IAD framework—the action situation. This is where the institutional analyst focuses on explaining results that affect the daily lives of participants as well as the resources affected by participants. Fortunately, the same components—participants, positions, actions linked to outcomes, control, information, and costs and benefits—characterize collective-choice as well as constitutional-choice arenas.

Given the importance of this theoretical concept, we will devote one more chapter to illustrate the working parts and outcomes of differently structured action situations. Chapter 3 moves into the experimental lab, where the researcher must self-consciously create an action situation designed to enable the testing of theoretical predictions. Chapter 3 will help the reader really understand the working components of this core unit of analysis.

Chapter 4 will then be devoted to the other component of an action arena—the participants. The reader will be well aware by the end of chapter 3 that the primary model of individual behavior used extensively in game theory, economics, and institutional analysis yields predictions that are not supported in many experiments discussed in chapter 3 and the literature cited therein. Thus, we face a substantial challenge in animating institutional analyses.

Chapters 5 through 9 then turn to the question of how we can analyze the rules used as tools to change the structure of action situations. Unfortunately, the language used by social scientists to discuss the rules, norms, and strategies used by participants in situations is extremely confusing. Thus, considerable effort has to be expended in chapters 5, 6, and 7 to develop a consistent, theoretical language to define and then use these terms in a coherent and cumulative manner. Once this is accomplished, we will illustrate the usefulness of the concepts that we have carefully defined with extensive examples from empirical research.

Three

Studying Action Situations in the Lab

READERS OF PAST descriptions of the working components of the Institutional Analysis and Development (IAD) framework have frequently urged me to provide some examples of an action situation to help them make this abstract concept more meaningful. Studying action situations in an experimental laboratory turns out to be an excellent way to understand how the components of an action situation and changes in these components, even small changes, can make a difference in behavior and outcomes. Experiments provide very good examples of how action situations work. In the laboratory, the researcher carefully establishes the specific components of an action situation to be studied.

While it is never possible to establish a perfect experiment, extensive methodological work has been undertaken since the pathbreaking work of Vernon Smith (1982). Smith challenged social scientists to exhibit great care in the design of experiments by having the payoffs closely tied to the incentives of the decision environment. He further urged researchers to ensure that the assumed structure was clear to the subjects by pretesting instructions extensively. Smith helped to establish a tradition of paying subjects well and closely related to the theoretical payoff structure being investigated, instead of having the subjects participate in experiments as part of required entry-level courses. Further, researchers have now developed a real commitment to share experimental instructions and their data with one another and to encourage replications in order to ensure that there was nothing "unique" about one implementation of an experiment. Still further, experimental studies are now being used to "test bed" competing strategies for implementing new public policies (see Plott and Porter 1996).

In this chapter, I will provide a brief overview of two action situations that have been studied extensively in experimental laboratories in many countries. The first is the Trust Game, similar to the Snatch Game discussed in chapter 2. The second is a Commons Dilemma, which we will discuss again in later chapters. I do so for three reasons: (1) to allow the reader who is not familiar with the concept of an action situation or a game to see how this concept has been operationalized; (2) to illustrate how small changes in the structure of an action situation can lead to big differences in outcomes; and (3) to illustrate how the findings from experiments challenge the presumption that all participants use the same internal form of rationality to make decisions in all settings. In light of these findings, in chapter 4 we will examine the puzzle facing institutional analysts of how to model individual behavior.

Both of the experiments discussed in this chapter are social dilemmas. In all social dilemmas, individuals face short-term incentives that, if followed, would lead them all to be worse off than feasibly attainable outcomes. The first action situation to be discussed is the Trust Game. Subjects in a laboratory experiment are assigned cash or tokens that have varying values to be converted into cash immediately after an experiment is concluded. The Trust Game has been studied extensively (E. Ostrom and Walker 2003). Behavior in the laboratory is not fully consistent with what is predicted by noncooperative game theory when monetary payoffs are assumed to be monotonically related to the internal utility values that a subject assigns to outcomes.

The second type of experiment is of appropriation (harvesting) from a common-pool resource—a Commons Dilemma. Many of the experiments described in the second section of this chapter have been conducted by colleagues at Indiana University as well as being replicated by scholars at other universities. Common-pool resource situations will help the reader think about more complex N-person situations that are closely related to specific field settings including inshore fisheries, irrigation systems, forest resources, and groundwater basins. While behavior in the laboratory is broadly consistent with noncooperative, game-theoretic predictions in a baseline common-pool resource experiment, interactions and outcomes are not consistent with this prediction when face-to-face communication is allowed or when subjects can use costly punishment against one another. There is, thus, a lot to learn about operationalizing action situations from experimental work. Given the multiplicity of findings that are not consistent with conventional game-theoretical analysis, we will be setting the stage for an extended discussion of "animating institutional analysis" in chapter 4.

The Trust Game in the Experimental Laboratory

In an elegantly simple, two-person game, Berg, Dickhaut, and McCabe (1995) designed a game that enables researchers to focus in clearly on factors that affect the likelihood that an individual will take a costly action because she places trust in a second individual. As we discussed in chapter 2, unless the first household in the Snatch Game trusted that the second household would exchange goods rather than snatch Household 1's goods, no positive transaction would occur. There are many such situ-

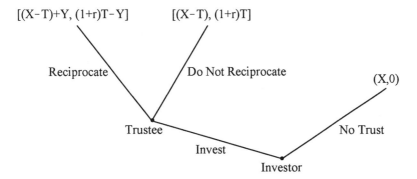

Figure 3.1 The Trust Game.

ations that individuals face in all aspects of life. The most simple baseline game is composed of the following elements (see figure 3.1):

 1. *Participants.* Two subjects play the game.

 2. *Positions.* The two positions are the Investor and the Trustee.

 3. *Actions.* The Investor is given X at the beginning of the game. The Investor then decides to keep all of X, to give T to the Trustee and to keep $X - T$, or to give all of it $(T = X)$ to the Trustee. The Trustee then decides how much of the funds—Y—to return to the Investor.

 4. *Outcomes.* The outcomes are the size of the funds allocated to the two players in light of the decisions they have made.

 5. *Action-outcome linkages.* The amount invested in the Trustee earns a rate of return (supplied by the experimenter) of $1 + r$.

 6. *Information.* Both players are told the full tree of possibilities and that their own identity will remain anonymous to the other player and to the experimenter (double-blind).

 7. *Potential payoffs.* The payoffs are affected by the rate of return $(1 + r)$. r has frequently been operationalized as 2, so that the amount that the Investor sends to the Trustee is tripled. The payoff to the Investor is $(X - T) + Y$. The payoff for the Trustee is $(1 + r) T - Y$, assuming the Investor sent something in the first place or zero otherwise.[1] T can then be used as a measure of trust and $(1 + r) T - Y$ for $T > 0$ as a measure of trustworthiness. The original payoff rates of Berg and colleagues were $X = \$10.00$, $r = 2$. Thus, if the Investor allocated all of the funds to the Trustee, the Trustee had $30.00 to keep or share. Beyond the objective pecuniary payoffs, it is also possible that the individual assigns a utility to the objective, external payoffs that increases or decreases the value of the objective payoff to the individual or assigns utility to the objective values that the other player receives.

A self-interested Trustee wanting to maximize pecuniary returns would return zero to the Investor. If the Investor expects this, no funds will be invested in the first place. Similar to the predicted outcome for the Snatch Game, the predicted outcome using noncooperative game theory and assuming that individuals attempt to maximize monetary returns is zero invested. The baseline game is barren of many of the social factors that are thought to affect trust. The players are strangers and do not even see one another. There is no way that they can establish a link to one another through promise-giving or the like. The Trust Game is similar in structure to a sequential Prisoner's Dilemma. The baseline game represents a situation requiring trust in about as pristine a form as one can imagine.

Using a one-shot decision setting with double-blind experimental procedures to ensure complete anonymity, Berg, Dickhaut, and McCabe found that 30 of 32 subjects in the position of Investor sent money to the Trustee ($5.16 on average). Of the 30 subjects in the position of Trustee, 18 returned more than $1.00 ($4.66 on average) and one-third of them sent more funds to the Investor than they received. On average, those Investors who sent $5.00 or more received an average return in excess of the amount they sent. It was those Investors sending less than $5.00 who received a negative net-average return. In other words, on average, those Investors who trusted their counterpart the most were the ones who left the game with more wealth than those who were less trusting.

This experimental design of the Trust Game is simple, but captures the essence of trusting and reciprocal behavior so effectively that it has been replicated and extended in many diverse settings and countries (see Cook and Cooper 2003). The initial Berg, Dickhaut, and McCabe experiment can be thought of as examining the level of trust and reciprocity among relatively equal players. All of the subjects were students at the University of Minnesota. Which subjects were chosen as the Investor or the Trustee was determined randomly.

Ernst Fehr and colleagues at the University of Zurich have undertaken a related set of experiments that shifted the framing and structure of the situation from one involving participants who related to one another in a horizontal manner to one that self-consciously involved hierarchy involving either "employers or buyers" and "workers or sellers" in a vertical relationship (see Fehr, Kirchsteiger, and Riedl 1993; Fehr and Falk 1999; Fehr and Gächter 1998). In one of the Swiss experiments (Fehr, Kirchsteiger, and Riedl 1993), the experimenters randomly assigned subjects to two groups placed in separate rooms without capacity to see or talk directly with one another (as did Berg and colleagues). For all rounds of the experiment, one set of subjects was told they were "Workers" and would be paid a wage if employed, and another set of subjects was told they were "Employers." There were always more Workers than Employers so that not all of them would be "hired." All were informed about the specific wages that could be offered and the range of effort that a Worker could expend at a monetary cost. The Employer's income depended on the effort expended by their Workers.

Employers made the first move in each of the twelve periods of an experimental session by making contract offers of wage rates. The size of the payoff to the Employer depended on the effort that a Worker expended once he was hired with a specific wage. Since there were more Workers than Employers, however, several Workers would remain unemployed and receive only a set fee for showing up at the experiment. Thus the Workers were at an initial disadvantage and might expect to receive a minimal wage offer.

In the second stage, the experimental Workers who had accepted a wage offer in a period made a decision regarding the level of effort they would return to their Employers, ranging from a minimum of 0.1 to a maximum of 1.0 with a reduction in their payoffs dependent on the level of effort chosen. Any level of effort above 0.1 would be a "return gift" back to the Employer, at a cost to the Employer that was much less than the benefit that the Employer would receive. For a wage of 60, for example, increasing effort by 0.1 would increase the cost to the Worker by 2 units at most, but would increase the return to the Employer by 6 units. The anonymity of all subjects was assured by the experimenters.

The game-theoretical prediction for this experiment is similar to that for the Berg, Dickhaut, and McCabe setting. The Employer should offer a minimum wage since the person in this position can expect that the Worker will return minimal effort (Fehr, Kirchsteiger, and Riedl 1993, 443). On the other hand, subjects in both positions lose potential income if they follow the theoretically "rational" thing to do (as is the case for Investors and Trustees in the Berg, Dickhaut, and McCabe experiment). Fehr and colleagues repeatedly found, however, that subjects in the position of Employer offered substantially more than the theoretical minimum expected and that Workers reciprocated by allocating higher than minimal costly effort. In this and a replication in a more challenging experiment, where a double auction determined wages (Fehr and Falk 1999), average effort was a positive function of the level of wage offered and far above the predicted level.

Kenneth Koford (2003) has replicated both the original Berg, Dickhaut, and McCabe horizontal experiments as well as some of the vertical (Employer-Worker) experiments run by Fehr and colleagues, with students recruited from Sofia University and Varna Economics University, both in Bulgaria. This enabled Koford to directly examine the impact of the relative horizontal or vertical standing of the two positions in the experiment. In the horizontal experiment, 44 out of 47 of the subjects in the position of Investor sent some money, which was quite similar to the 30 out of 32

Investors in Berg, Dickhaut, and McCabe's experiment. The distribution of amounts sent was also quite similar.

In the vertical experiment, Koford found a different pattern to that of Fehr and Falk (1999). The effort levels of the subjects in the position of Worker were much lower: "16 of the 41 effort levels were the minimum, .1. The mean effort is just .368" (Koford 2003, 17). Further, the wage level was not associated with the level of effort. Thus, in the horizontal design, Koford found the same level of trust and reciprocity as the U.S. and Swiss experiments, but not in the vertical designs.

Koford explains the intriguing difference in findings by drawing on the business and cultural traditions and history in Bulgaria and the Balkan countries more generally. Given the long history of exploitative Ottoman and then communist rulers, government provided no basic security or trust for a people. Folks had to trust others in similar circumstances. Those in business in Bulgaria report extensive fraud and difficulties with trusting others, however (see Koford and Miller 1995). Students are more likely to engage in a general trust relationship with one another.

> It seems that under specific conditions Bulgarian students trust as much as American students, and very likely more. This may be due to the focus upon "students," who feel that they should share a principle of solidarity in Bulgaria. Then, when they are divided into Workers and Employers, this solidarity disappears. Discussion with students suggested that if the horizontal experiment were run with the other group being significantly different—say, ordinary Workers, or a different ethnic group . . . the level of trust would be considerably lower. (Koford 2003, 21)

The horizontal Trust Game has also been replicated by Buchan, Croson, and Johnson (1999) in another cross-country design intended to assess the impact of the socioeconomic setting of participants on behavior. They conducted the Trust Game with 188 subjects from China, Japan, Korea, and the United States. They find no pure country effects in terms of the amount sent by subjects in the role of the Investor (on average, 67 percent of the endowment) or in the amount returned (on average, 31 percent of the amount received).

In addition to examining country effects, the researchers examined several other contextual variables including: the cultural beliefs of the participant (based on questionnaire data where questions relate to an individual's attitude toward group versus individual outcomes), social distance (manipulated experimentally), and communication (manipulated experimentally). Subjects who showed a greater orientation toward group outcomes sent more funds as both an Investor and as Trustee. The opportunity to communicate information about one's self and learn something about the other person with whom a subject was paired also had a positive effect on amounts sent and returned. Buchan and colleagues found that "trusters prosper." In other words, "subjects who sent above average amounts to their partners, took home greater wealth than did subjects who sent only average amounts or less" (Buchan, Croson, and Johnson 1999, 22).[2]

In a follow-up study to examine the impact of enabling the Trustee to build a reputation, Dickhaut et al. (1997) added a publicly announced second round to the basic structure of the base experiment. Both participants played in both rounds. According to standard, noncooperative game theory using backward induction, this second round should make no difference to the behavior of individuals in the first round. Dickaut and colleagues wanted to ascertain if Trustees would act even more trustworthy than those who had participated in the first study in order to assure Investors that they could be trusted.

In the first round, they found that 10 of the 23 Investors sent the maximum sum ($10.00) to the Trustee and that none of them sent zero. Trustees exhibited higher levels of reciprocity in the first round than had been exhibited in the baseline study. Twenty of them returned more than their counterpart had sent to them, leading to a positive-sum outcome for all involved. The findings for the second and final round, however, followed a different pattern. Nineteen out of 20 of the Investors who had received positive returns in round one made a positive investment again in round two, and all three of the Investors who had received a negative return in the first round sent zero to the Trustee in the second round. The big difference was that only 7 of the 19 Investors received a positive net return in round two. The reciprocity that had been exhibited in round one was substantially reduced in the second, and known-to-be final, round.

Güth, Ockenfels, and Wendel (1997) simplified the experimental conditions so that Investors had similar dichotomous options as Household 1 in the Snatch Game—to trust or not trust the Trustee. The Trustee could then either "exploit" the Investor by choosing an option that paid the Trustee a high payoff and gave the Investor very little, or the Trustee could reciprocate the trust by choosing an option that led to lower but equal payoffs for both. Güth and colleagues found that the majority of the subjects in the first position (21 out of 28) extended trust, but that their trusting action was not reciprocated by a majority of those in the second position. On the other hand, in a replication of this experimental structure, Kirchler, Fehr, and Evans (1996) had results very close to those of Berg, Dickhaut, and McCabe with high levels of trust and reciprocity exhibited (see also Dickhaut et al. 1997).[3] Güth, Ockenfels, and Wendel (1997) also experimented with a further modification of the Trust Game. In this experiment, they had subjects experience the game once and receive the payoffs from that round. Then they asked the subjects to bid for the role of Investor and Trustee. Very low levels of trust were extended when played by those who bid for the Investor position (and low levels of reciprocity were extended by those who were trusted).

In an experiment that explores the impact of changes in the information exchanged as well as threatened sanctions on outcomes of a Trust Game, Fehr and Rockenbach (2003) obtained some fascinating results (see also Fehr, Gächter, and Kirchsteiger 1996 and Fehr and Gächter forthcoming for related experiments). In one series of experiments—which they call the "trust condition"—both the Investor and the Trustee receive ten money units (MUs). As in the above games, the Investor may either send zero or some number between 1 and 10 MUs to the Trustee. Whatever amount is sent is tripled. At the time of sending funds, the Investor has to indicate a "desired back-transfer" that can range from zero to the full amount of the tripled transfer. The information about the amount sent and the desired back-transfer is given to the Trustee, who then decides how much, if any, to send back. The only difference between this experiment and the Berg, Dickhaut, and McCabe experiment is the information given to the Trustee about the amount the investor expects back.

In a second condition—which they call an "incentive condition"—the Investor is given a choice between indicating whether he or she has chosen a fining option that will deduct four MUs from the Trustee if the Investor does not receive at least as much as the specified desired level. The Investor can overtly waive this opportunity to have these funds deducted if the returned level is not as desired. If chosen by the Investor, the deduction is subtracted from the Trustee's payoff, and the Investor receives whatever funds the Trustee decides to send back without contributing to the deduction. Fehr and Rockenbach explored this incentive option in order to examine the proposition that a threatened sanction would increase the level of funds returned by the Trustee.

They found that Trustees sent substantial returns in all conditions. Like Berg and colleagues, they found that the amount of funds returned were positively associated with the amount of money invested in the first place. Nineteen of the 24 Trustees in the trust condition (79 percent) paid back more than zero, and 19 of the 45 subjects in the Trustee position in the incentive condition (42 percent) paid back more than zero (Fehr and Rockenbach 2003, 138). As shown in figure 3.2, the highest return occurred when the Investor refrained from imposing a fine in the incentive condition. The lowest level of return occurred when the Investor indicated a high desired back-transfer and a fine for not meeting this level. Fehr and Rockenbach explained both findings as the result of what they refer to as "strong reciprocity." "First, refraining from the threat of fining, although the threat is available, could itself be perceived as a fair act, which induces

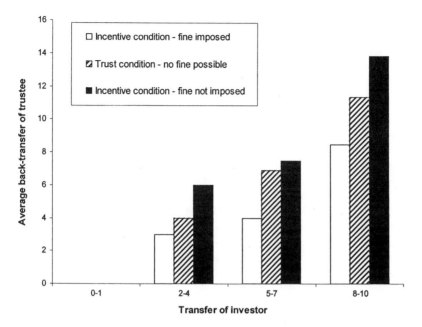

Figure 3.2 Trust and reciprocity under three experimental conditions. *Source*: Fehr and Rockenbach 2003, 138, and data provided by Ernst Fehr.

the trustees to increase their cooperation. Second, attempts to use the sanction to enforce an unfair distribution of income may be perceived as hostile acts, inducing the trustees to reduce cooperation" (2003, 139–40). Thus, the threat of a fine, which is frequently thought to be a major technique for solving problems related to trust, backfired. Instead of enhancing the level of reciprocity shown by Trustees, an externally established fine that is endogenously used as a threat by the Investor reduces reciprocity rather than increasing it. This is consistent with the theoretical and experimental work of Bruno Frey (1994, 1997a) on external sanctions crowding out reciprocity. We will return to the question of how sanctions are arrived at, and their impact, when we discuss sanctions again in the context of the common-pool resource experiments as well as in later sections of this book.

The findings from these rich experimental studies of the Trust Game are consistent with empirical studies of trust in other settings (Gambetta 1988; Rothstein 2005; Delhey and Newton 2003). They also provide important insights for an institutional analyst. First of all, it is relatively easy to see how Berg, Dickhaut, and McCabe initially created an action situation in an experimental lab. We can also observe how small changes in these working parts—including: (1) the relative standing of the partici-pants, (2) the number of rounds, (3) the range of actions authorized, (4) the benefits and costs of actions and outcomes, (5) the diverse ways of choosing subjects to hold a position (e.g., random assignment or an auc-tion), or (6) the diverse sanctioning mechanisms—affected interactions and outcomes. Hopefully, the concept of an action situation is now a little clearer for the reader.

Many readers, however, will be surprised at the high levels of trust exhibited in the first experiment and its replications in multiple cultures. The game-theoretic prediction for this game is very stark and clear. Be-cause the Trustee is expected by a rational player not to return anything to an Investor, the Investor is not expected to trust an unknown stranger by sending *any* funds. Like all social dilemmas, this prediction leaves all participants worse off than they could have achieved. The multiple replications in which a substantial level of trust is exhibited raises serious questions about the universal validity of relying entirely on the rational choice model of the individual (a topic to be explored in some depth in chapter 4).[4]

Still further questions are raised about the capability of the classic model of self-interested rationality to explain the adverse impact of exter-nally imposed threats of sanctions on the willingness of Trustees to recip-rocate Trust. When faced with a threat of sanction, if the Trustee did not return the level of funds specified by the Investor, many Trustees did not return the funds specified—thus, levels of reciprocity were reduced by the externally imposed threat of a sanction. This empirical result challenges not only the model of the individual that is widely used but also the stan-dard recommendation that external sanctions are the best way to solve social dilemmas that lie at the heart of many types of basic economic, social, and political problems. We will discuss the core difference in out-comes achieved between externally imposed sanctions and sanctions agreed upon by those involved in the next section of this chapter.

A Commons Dilemma in the Experimental Laboratory

The Trust Game characterizes a wide diversity of settings where one per-son has to trust someone else and that person has to reciprocate in order for both to be better off. This game seems too simple for some scholars. "All one needs to do is create a form of contract law," they say, "in order for the Investor to bind the Trustee to a contract so as to return the invest-ment." Then they argue, you would not have to depend on reciprocity but rather on the legal system. One of the expected benefits of creating a relevant legal structure is to use sanctions against those who are not trustworthy. As we have seen, however, from the experiments using sanctions, the way that legal structures are implemented can make a big difference. Externally imposed sanctions can lead to resentment rather than guilt and adversely affect the willingness to reciprocate trust.

Creating contract law or property rights is more difficult than it appears on the surface (as we will discuss in chapter 8, and as many advisers have learned in Eastern Europe and the former Soviet Union—see, for example, de Soto 2000). Many contracts in Western economies are undertaken based on trust and reciprocity (Arrow 1974) rather than drawing on the legal system. Further, the Fehr and Rockenbach experiments demonstrate that a sanctioning system imposed without agreement of the participants may reduce reciprocity rather than increase it. Hopefully, the reader can by now appreciate both how to operationalize an action situation as well as learning about the substantial findings of experimental research on trust. Further theoretical developments on trust have now been achieved as a result of this extensive research (see Bacharach and Gambetta 2001; Ahn et al. 2003; McCabe and Smith 2003; E. Ostrom and Walker 2003).

We will now look at a second illustration of an action situation in the laboratory that is inherently far more complex than the Trust Game— a common-pool resource situation. When the users of a common-pool resource are tempted to overuse the resource, the structure of the situation is a social dilemma. Social dilemmas are pervasive in social life, and proposed solutions to these dilemmas have occupied all great political philosophers including Aristotle, Hobbes, and Hume. There are many differently structured social dilemmas, but they all are characterized by a situation where everyone is tempted to take one action but all will be better off if all (or most of them) take another action. Studying how subjects behave in this type of social dilemma helps us understand more general questions of relevance across the social sciences than simply the study of natural resources. We will also return to discuss the common-pool resource setting in chapters 8 and 9 to examine how actual users of these kinds of resources create their own rules to deal with the problems of overuse.

The Definition of a Common-Pool Resource

A common-pool resource, such as a lake, an ocean, an irrigation system, a fishing ground, a forest, the Internet, or the stratosphere, is a natural or man-made resource from which it is difficult to exclude or limit users once the resource is provided by nature or produced by humans (E. Ostrom, Gardner, and Walker 1994). One person's consumption of resource units, such as water, fish, or trees, removes those units from what is available to others. Thus, the trees or fish harvested by one user are no longer available for others. As discussed in chapter 1, the difficulty of excluding beneficiaries is a characteristic that common-pool resources share with public goods. Further, the subtractability of resource units from a common-pool resource is an attribute shared with private goods. In the rest of this chapter, I will focus primarily on renewable natural resources as exemplars of common-pool resources, but the theoretical arguments are relevant to man-made common-pool resources, such as the Internet, as well.

When the resource units produced by a common-pool resource have a high value and institutional rules do not restrict the way resource units are appropriated (an open-access situation), individuals face strong incentives to appropriate more and more resource units leading eventually to congestion, overuse, and even the destruction of the resource itself. Because of the difficulty of excluding beneficiaries, the free-rider problem is a potential threat to efforts to reduce appropriation and improve the long-term outcomes achieved from the use of a common-pool resource. If some individuals reduce their appropriation levels, the benefits they generate are shared with others whether the others also cut back on their appropriation or not. Some individuals may free-ride on the costly actions of others unless ways are found to reduce free-riding as an attractive strategy. When free-riding is a major problem, those who would willingly reduce their own appropriations if others did are unwilling to make a sacrifice for the benefit of a large number of free riders.

Consequently, one of the important problems facing the joint users of a common-pool resource is known as the "Commons Dilemma," given the potential incentives in all jointly used common-pool resources for individuals to appropriate more resource units when acting independently than they would if they could find some way of coordinating their appropriation activities. Joint users of a common-pool resource often face many other problems including assignment problems, technological externality problems, provision problems, and maintenance problems (E. Ostrom, Gardner, and Walker 1994). And, the specific character of each of these problems differs substantially from one resource to the next. In this chapter, I focus on the problem of controlling appropriation since this is what most policy analysts associate with "the tragedy of the commons" (G. Hardin 1968; Dietz, Ostrom, and Stern 2003).

A Baseline Appropriation Situation

We need to start with a static, baseline situation that is as simple as we can specify it without losing crucial aspects of the problems that real appropriators face in the field. This static, baseline situation is composed of:

1. *Participants.* A set of n symmetric subjects who do not have any outside relationships with one another.

2. *Positions.* No differentiation exists in the positions these subjects hold relevant to the common-pool resource. In other words, there is only one position of appropriator.

3. *Actions.* Appropriators must decide how to allocate tokens assigned to them in each time period. Basically, one can think of these appropriators as being "endowed" with a total set of assets, e, which they are free to allocate in any proportion during each time period to two activities. In a field setting one can think that every day, each appropriator must decide between spending time trying to harvest resource units from the common-pool resource or using their time to earn money in an outside option, such as working in a local factory. To simplify the problem, we posit that all appropriators have the same endowment (just as we all have only twenty-four hours per day), and face the same outside opportunity. Thus, they have to decide how much of their endowment to devote each round to appropriation from the common-pool resource or in gaining returns from an outside option.

4. *Outcomes.* The actions they take affect the amount of resource units that can be appropriated from the common-pool resource or returns earned from the outside option.

5. *Action-outcome linkages.* The function maps the actions of all of the appropriators given the biophysical structure of the resource itself onto outcomes. While these functions are frequently stochastic in field settings and affected by many variables in addition to the actions of individuals, we will consider only determinant functions of appropriation actions in the baseline setting. The wage function simply multiplies the amount of time allocated to it by whatever is the standard wage. The resource function is a concave function, F, which depends on the number of assets, x_i, which is a fraction of e allocated to appropriation. Initially, the sum of all of the individuals' actions, Σx_i, generates better outcomes than the safe investment in wage labor. If the appropriators decide to allocate a sufficiently large number of their available assets, the outcome they receive is less than their best alternative. In other words, allocating too many assets to the common-pool resource is counterproductive (see Gordon 1954; Scott 1955).

6. *Information.* As an initial information condition (because of the instructions carefully given to all subjects), we assume that appropriators know the shape of the function linking actions to outcomes and know that they are symmetric in assets and opportunities. Information about outcomes is generated after each decision round is completed. Appropriators may not communicate with one another. It is assumed that each appropriator will assume that all other appropriators are rational actors and will adopt the "best response" to their own actions. The best response function should lead all appropriators to over-harvest from the resource.

7. *Potential payoffs*. Payoff functions specify the value of the wage rate and the value of the resource units obtained from the common-pool resource. Specifically, the payoff to an appropriator is given by:

$$we \qquad\qquad\qquad\qquad \text{if } x_i = 0$$
$$w(e - x_i) + (x_i / \Sigma x_i)\, F(\Sigma x_i) \quad \text{if } x_i > 0. \qquad (1)$$

Basically, if appropriators put all of the assets into their outside option, they receive a certain monetary return equal to the amount of their endowment times an unchanging rate of return (w).[5] If appropriators put some of their endowed assets into the outside option and some into the common-pool resource, they get part of their return from the outside option and the rest from their proportional investment in the common-pool resource times the total output of the common-pool resource as determined by function F.

Predicted Outcomes for a Commons Dilemma in the Laboratory

In a series of laboratory experiments conducted at Indiana University, we thought it crucial to examine behavior in an appropriation situation with a nonlinear transformation (action-outcome) function and a sufficient number of players that knowledge of outcomes did not automatically provide information about each player's actions. In this chapter, I can only briefly discuss the results of these experiments. All procedures and specifications are thoroughly documented in E. Ostrom, Gardner, and Walker 1994 and in journal articles cited therein.

In the baseline experiments, we utilized the following equation for the transformation function, F, measured in units of output (outcome units):

$$23(\Sigma x_i) - 25(\Sigma x_i)^2. \qquad (2)$$

Instead of asking subjects to pretend they were fishing or harvesting timber, the situation was described as involving a choice between investing in either of two markets having the structure as specified above. All eight subjects were assigned either 10 or 25 tokens as their endowment in each round of play. Their outside opportunity was valued at $.05 per token. They earned $.01 on each outcome unit they received from investing tokens in the common-pool resource. Subjects were informed that they would participate in an experiment that would last no more than two hours. The number of rounds in each experiment varied between twenty and thirty rounds. In addition to being told the payoff function specifically, subjects were provided with look-up tables that eased their task of determining outcomes depending on their own and others' decisions.

With these specifications, the predicted outcome for a finitely repeated game where subjects are not discounting the future and each subject is assumed to be maximizing monetary returns is for each subject to invest 8 tokens in the common-pool resource for a total of 64 tokens. By design, the prediction is the same for both endowment levels. At this level of investment, they would each earn $.66 per round in the 10-token experiments and $.70 per round in the 25-token experiments (players were paid one-half of their computer returns in the 25-token experiments to keep the payoffs roughly similar). The players could, however, earn considerably more if the total number of tokens invested was 36 tokens (rather than 64 tokens) in the common-pool resource. This optimal level of investment would earn each subject $.91 per round in the 10-token experiment and $.83 per round in the 25-token experiment. The baseline experiment is an example of a commons dilemma in which the game-theoretic, predicted outcome involves substantial overuse of a common-pool resource, while a much better outcome could be reached if subjects were to lower their joint use.

Behavior in a Sparse Experimental N-Person, Repeated Commons Dilemma

Subjects interacting in baseline experiments substantially overinvested as predicted. Subjects in the 10-token experiments achieved, on average, 37 percent of the maximum earnings from the common-pool experiment available to them, while subjects in the 25-token experiments received −3 percent (E. Ostrom, Gardner, and Walker 1994, 116). At the individual level, however, subjects rarely invested 8 tokens, which is the predicted level of investment at equilibrium. Instead, all experiments generated an unpredicted and strong pulsing pattern in which individuals appear to increase their investments in the common-pool resource until there is a strong reduction in yield, at which time they tend to reduce their investments leading to an increase in yields. The pattern is repeated over time. At an aggregate level, behavior approximates the predicted Nash equilibrium in the 10-token experiments. Outcomes are far lower than predicted in the early rounds of the 25-token experiment and only begin to approach the predicted level in later rounds. No game-theoretical explanation yet exists for the pulsing pattern or the substantial difference between the 10-token and the 25-token experiments.

In response to postexperiment questions, subjects explained that they were using several heuristics. One of the heuristics they used was to invest more in the common-pool resource whenever the rate of return on the previous round was above $.05 (what they could earn in their next best alternative) and less if the return was below $.05. In the 10-token experiment, some players invested all 10 of their tokens whenever the rate of return in the prior round was above $.05. With such heuristic strategies, equilibrium is never reached at the individual level. Each player is revising his or her response to the results obtained in the most recent round, creating considerable turbulence in the outcomes jointly reached.

Replication in Agent-based Models

An extremely interesting follow-up study was undertaken by Peter Deadman (1997) in which artificial agents were programmed to use a variety of heuristics similar to those used by the human subjects in these common-pool resource (CPR) experiments and to interact in a simulated environment that exactly replicated the baseline experiments. Deadman found that the specific results obtained in any series of runs depended on the particular heuristic (or mix of heuristics) programmed, but the artificial agents did consistently produce the same kind of pulsing returns and the consistent difference between 10-token and 25-token environments was also observed. Deadman describes his results:

> As in CPR experiments, the group performance for the simulation follows an oscillating pattern in which high performance leads to over investment in the CPR and the resultant drop in performance causes a reduction in group-wide investment in the CPR. . . . Still more interesting is the observation that the simulations perform similarly to subjects in laboratory experiments in terms of average performance over time. At the ten token endowment, the simulations perform near the Nash equilibria over time. At the 25 token endowment, the simulations perform near zero percent of optimum over time. (Deadman 1997, 175–76)

Jager and Janssen (2003) also developed a multiagent model using the consumat framework derived from social psychology (Jager, Janssen, and Viek 2001). They thought that they could replicate the data from the baseline commons dilemma experiments described above with an assumption that individual subjects differed in regard to their Social Value Orientations (SVOs). In their first series of simulations, they were indeed able, as Deadman had done independently, to explain the aggregated pattern of appropriation behavior. Jager and Janssen were not as successful in replicating individual appropriation decisions (from the experimental data) as they had been in simulating aggregate outcomes. Jager and Janssen (2003) suggested that the cognitive processes that subjects use appear to be important in behavior. Those with low aspiration levels may lock into a habitual response too soon. Further, those agents "conforming to the Homo psychologius have a better performance than the Homo economicus in approximating the empirical data" (98).

Structural Changes in the Laboratory

In addition to the baseline experiments, we and many other researchers have explored how changes in the structure of the action situation affect outcomes. These changes are operationalized in the set of instructions given to subjects and in the procedures adopted within the experiment.

The first structural change is related to the information component of an action situation. Instead of forbidding communication among subjects, as in the baseline experiments, subjects are now authorized to communicate with one another on a face-to-face basis in a group setting before returning to their own enclosed terminals to make their private decisions. This introduction of an opportunity for "cheap talk" in a social dilemma, where agreements are not enforced by an external authority, is viewed within the context of noncooperative game theory as irrelevant. The same outcome is predicted as in the baseline experiment.

In a second set of experiments, colleagues also explored whether cheap talk would enable individuals who acquired heterogeneous assets to achieve better outcomes than predicted by theory. In a third series of experiments, the payoff component was changed to allow subjects to sanction one another at a cost to themselves. Since using this option produces a benefit for all at a cost to the individual, the game-theoretic prediction is that no one will choose the costly sanctioning option. Fourth, the authority rule was changed to allow subjects to covenant with one another to determine their investment levels and to adopt a sanctioning system if they wished. Again, the predicted outcome is the same. In all four of these appropriation experiments, however, subjects demonstrate their willingness and ability to search out and adopt better outcomes than those predicted.

Face-to-Face Communication

In the repeated communication experiments, subjects first made ten rounds of decisions in the context of the baseline appropriation situation described above. After the tenth round, subjects listened to an announcement that told them they would have an open group discussion before each of the next rounds of the experiment. The subjects left their terminals and sat in a circle facing one another. After each discussion period, they returned to their terminals to enter their anonymous decisions. Subjects used face-to-face communication to discuss together what strategy would gain them the best outcomes and to agree on what everyone should invest in the subsequent rounds. After each decision round, they learned what their aggregate investments had been, but not the decisions of individual players. Thus, they learned whether total investments were greater than the total investments they had earlier agreed upon. While in many rounds, subjects did exactly as they had promised one another they would do, some defections did occur. If promises were not kept, subjects used this information about the aggregate investment levels to castigate the unknown participant who had not kept to the agreement.

This opportunity for repeated face-to-face communication was extremely successful in increasing joint returns. In the 10-token experiments, subjects obtained close to 100 percent of the maximum available returns. There were only 19 instances out of 368 total opportunities (5 percent) where a subject invested more in the common-pool resource than agreed upon (E. Ostrom, Gardner, and Walker 1994, 154). In the 25-token experiments, subjects also improved their overall performance. The temptation to defect, however, was greater in the 25-token experiments. Subjects in the 25-token baseline experiments had received total returns that were slightly below zero, while in the communication experiments, they obtained on average 62 percent of the maximum available returns (with considerable variation across experiments). The defection rate was 13 percent. Our conclusion in completing an analysis of these experiments was:

> Communication discussions went well beyond discovering what investments would generate maximum yields. A striking aspect of the discussion rounds was how rapidly subjects, who had not had an opportunity to establish a well-defined community with strong internal norms, were able to devise their own agreements and verbal punishments for those who broke those agreements. . . . In many cases, statements like "some scumbucket is investing more than we agreed upon" were a sufficient reproach to change defectors' behavior. (E. Ostrom, Gardner, and Walker 1994, 160)

That subjects had internalized norms regarding the importance of keeping promises is evidenced by several of their behaviors. Simply promising to cut back on their investments in the common-pool resource led most subjects to change their investment pattern. Secondly, subjects were indignant about evidence of investment levels higher than that promised and expressed their anger openly. Third, those who broke their promise tended to revert to the promised level after hearing the verbal tongue-lashing of their colleagues (see A. Simon and Gorgura 2003 for an intensive analysis of the recorded transcripts). The findings from these initial communication experiments are consistent with a large number of studies of the impact of face-to-face communication on the capacity of subjects to solve a variety of social dilemma problems (see Bohnet and Frey 1998; E. Ostrom and Walker 1991; Sally 1995 and literature cited therein).

Communication among Heterogeneous Players

Steven Hackett, Edella Schlager, and James Walker (1994) conducted a series of commons dilemma experiments where they explored whether communication could ameliorate the problems identified in field and experimental settings related to heterogeneity among appropriators (R. Hardin 1982; R. Johnson and Libecap 1982; Libecap and Wiggins 1984; Isaac and Walker 1988a, 1988b; Wiggins and Libecap 1987; Hackett 1992).

The task of agreeing to and sustaining agreements for efficient appropriation from a common-pool resource is more difficult for heterogeneous appropriators because of the distributional conflict associated with alternative sharing rules. In heterogeneous settings, all appropriators may be made better off by adopting a new rule; some will benefit more than others, depending upon the sharing rule chosen. Consequently, appropriators may fail to cooperate on the adoption of a sharing rule because they cannot agree upon what would constitute a fair distribution of benefits produced by cooperating.

In order to address appropriator heterogeneity, the Hackett, Schlager, and Walker experimental design allows for two levels of input endowments. One subset of appropriators has large endowments of tokens (24); the other appropriators have small token endowments (8). Group allocations to invest in the commons at the asymmetric Nash equilibrium are greater than optimal, but not all potential returns dissipated.

In order for communication to enhance joint payoffs to a heterogeneous set of subjects, they must agree on (1) the target level of group allocations to the common-pool resource, and (2) a rule for allocating the target input allocation across appropriators, and they must create (3) the necessary "social capital" to attenuate cheating, since agreements are nonbinding. The existence of heterogeneity in endowments and in historic allocation levels has no effect on the first problem, but is likely to elicit disagreement over the second problem. Disagreements then impair the building of social capital—the third problem.

Subjects knew with certainty the total number of decision makers in the group, their own token endowment and that of the others, the total number of tokens in the group, the transformation function, and the number of decision rounds in the current treatment condition. After each round, subjects were shown a display that recorded their payoffs in each market for that round, total group token investments, and a total of their cumulative profits for the experiment, but not the allocations made by specific other players.

Subjects participated in two (consecutive) ten-round sequences of the asymmetric game. In the first ten rounds, subjects were not allowed to communicate, but face-to-face communication was allowed during the second set of ten interactions. Prior to each ten-round treatment sequence, four subjects were assigned the "large" token endowment, while the other four subjects were assigned the "small" endowment. Two different mechanisms were used for assigning these endowments: random and auction (based on Güth 1988). In the first method, large endowments were assigned randomly prior to the ten decision rounds without communication, and again prior to the ten decision rounds with communication. A multiple-unit ascending price auction was used as the alternative mechanism for assigning endowment positions because of its demand-revealing characteristics. In particular, the price paid for the large endowment position should theoretically correspond with the maximum value placed on this position by the subject with the fourth highest valuation.

The opportunity to communicate led to a noticeable change in the pattern of allocations. With the allocation rules agreed upon in communication rounds, subjects concentrated near the optimal allocation of 56 tokens in total. In the random-assignment and communication condition, individual allocations of 8 tokens represented the modal response (67 percent). In the auction and communication condition, however, Hackett, Schlager, and Walker (1994) observed a spread of allocations clustered between 6 to 10 tokens. For both treatment conditions with no communication, they observe a level of rent accrual relatively close to that predicted by the Nash equilibrium (49 percent). Thus, even in an environment of extreme heterogeneity in subject endowments, communication remains a powerful mechanism for promoting coordination, resulting in rents very close to those observed in the homogeneous decision setting discussed above.

Three follow-up experimental designs were conducted by Pamela Schmitt, Kurtis Swope, and James Walker (2000). They used the same baseline design as first described above with three variations in regard to the information component of the situation. In all of their protocols for the communication aspects of the experiment (rounds eleven through twenty-five), six out of the eight players were invited to communicate with one another in one location. In their first protocol, two of the remaining "players" were computerized decision makers whose decisions were each the result of a random draw of a number between four and twelve. The other six, who could communicate with one another, were informed about the constraints on the random draw for "Players 7 and 8." In their second protocol, two of the players were real subjects who had been separated from the other six players. These real players did not face a constraint on their decisions. In the third protocol, the two separated players were constrained to invest between 4 and 12 tokens in the common-pool resource. As in the baseline experiments, subjects were informed about the aggregate investment of all eight players after each round.

In all three protocols, subjects substantially improved their overall efficiency in the communication rounds as contrasted to the noncommunication rounds. Limiting who could communicate to six out of the eight players did, however, make a difference. The six communicating subjects were never certain if the announced aggregated investment level reflected higher investments by the two "noncommunicating" players or whether some of the communicating groups did not follow their agreement. This uncertainty affected the capacity of the communicating group to keep to their own agreements. They could always blame the outsiders for any major overinvestment.

Major differences in interactions and outcomes occurred across the three protocols. The outsiders in Protocol 2 were the least constrained in their decisions. The members of the communicating group had the most difficulty in reaching agreements and following them in Protocol 2. The six communicating subjects in Protocol 2 had a "scapegoat" they could blame for high investment levels in rounds eleven through twenty-five. As shown in table 3.1, the subjects in Protocol 2 were less likely to come to an agreement in the first place, had a much higher deviation rate and size of deviation when they did agree, and obtained lower payoffs than in the earlier Ostrom, Gardner, and Walker experiments (discussed above and labeled as OGW in table 3.1) or in Protocols 1 or 3. The problem of imperfect monitoring was less severe in Protocols 1 and 3. Some subjects among the communicating group were able to deviate without raising suspicion of cheating in these protocols, but they made only small increases over what the group had promised each other.

What this series of experiments found does have considerable implications for those trying to achieve an agreement in the field not to overharvest from a common-pool resource. The results provide evidence that communication is less likely to be effective in preventing overharvesting in Commons Dilemmas "in which a subset of appropriators either cannot or will not participate in collective action" (Schmitt, Swope, and Walker 2000, 852). The lack of commitment by an outside group is not only a source of additional investment but also gives "insiders" a scapegoat to

TABLE 3.1
Summary results across environments

Decision environment 25 tokens Repeated communication	OGW	Protocol 1 (5 experiments)		Protocol 2 (3 experiments)		Protocol 3 (3 experiments)	
		Group	Random	Group	Outside	Group	Outside
Number of subjects	8	6	2	6	2	6	2
Average rents	−2%	−9.4%		−12.3%		28.5%	
Rounds 1–10							
Average investment in market 2	8.71	9.08	8.84	8.76	9.50	8.40	7.23
Average payoffs	1.24	1.11	1.21	1.20	1.17	1.37	1.36
Average rents	73%	68.5%		6.1%		80.4%	
Average investment in market 2	5.65	5.95	8.13	9.00	9.90	5.61	8.28
Average payoffs	1.54	1.57	1.71	1.27	1.30	1.54	1.70
Rounds 11–25							
Agreement rate	95%	64%		31.1%		97.8%	
Deviation rate	13%	15.3%		50%		15.9%	
Average deviation size	3.3	2.75		7.83		2.52	

Source: Schmitt, Swope, and Walker 2000, 849.

blame if their own harvests are higher than agreed upon. "The problem becomes more severe when outsiders have less constraints on their overall appropriation behavior and their ability to behave strategically" (852).

Sanctioning Experiments

Participants in field settings are frequently able to communicate with one another on a face-to-face basis, at least from time to time, either in formally constituted meetings or at social gatherings. In many field settings, where the resource has been sustained over a long time, participants have also devised a variety of formal or informal ways of monitoring and sanctioning one another if rules are broken (discussed in chapters 8 and 9). Engaging in costly monitoring and sanctioning behavior is, however, not consistent with the theory of norm-free, complete rationality (Elster 1989a, 40–41). Thus, it was important to ascertain whether subjects in a controlled setting would actually pay funds from their own earnings in order to sanction the less cooperative behavior of other participants. The short answer to this question is yes, they will.

All sanctioning experiments used the 25-token design since appropriation levels had been much higher in this design. Subjects played ten rounds of the baseline game modified so that the individual contributions in each round were reported as well as the total outcomes. Subjects were then told that in the subsequent rounds they would have an opportunity to pay a fee in order to impose a fine on the payoffs received by another player. The fees ranged in diverse experiments from $.05 to $.20 and the fines from $.10 to $.80. In brief, the finding from this series of experiments was that much more voluntary sanctioning occurs than the zero level predicted.

Subjects react both to the initial cost of sanctioning and to the fee-to-fine relationships. They sanction more when the cost of sanctioning is less and when the ratio of the fine to the fee is higher. Sanctioning is primarily directed at those who invested more in the common-pool resource. A few sanctions, however, appear to be a form of "blind revenge." These were fines made by subjects who had themselves been fined by unknown others for their high levels of investment. In these few cases, the sanctioners picked on those whose investments were lower than others, and thus were suspected of being the ones who had previously sanctioned them (E. Ostrom, Walker, and Gardner 1992).

In this set of experiments, subjects were able to increase their returns from the common-pool resource modestly to 39 percent of maximum, but when the costs of fees and fines were subtracted from the total, these gains were wiped out. When subjects were given a single opportunity to communicate prior to the implementation of sanctioning capabilities, they were able to gain an average of 85 percent of the maximum payoffs (69 percent when the costs of the fees and fines were subtracted).

Covenanting Experiments

In self-organized field settings, participants rarely impose sanctions on one another that have been devised exogenously as was done in the above sanctioning experiments and in the trust experiments, where the experimenters assigned one position the authority to sanction the holder of the other position. In the field, sanctions are much more likely to emerge from an endogenous process of crafting their own rules, including the punishments that should be imposed if these rules are broken. Spending time and effort in a linked collective-choice situation designing rules creates a public good for all of those involved. Crafting rules for an operational situation is thus a second-level dilemma that theorists have argued is no more likely to be solved than the original commons dilemma.

Noncooperative game theory predicts that participants will not undertake such efforts. This is the foundation for the repeated recommendation that rules must be imposed on participants by external authorities who then assume official responsibility for monitoring and enforcing these rules and are paid a salary for their work. Since self-organized rules are found in many local common-pool resource situations, it appears that participants frequently do design their own rules contrary to the theoretical prediction. Few scholars are able to witness these processes, however, in the field.

In order to observe what happens in these settings, subjects experienced with baseline and sanctioning experiments were recalled and given an opportunity to have a "convention" in the laboratory. In a face-to-face discussion, subjects could decide whether or not they would like to have access to a sanctioning mechanism like the one described above, how much the fines and fees should be, and on the joint investment strategy that they would like to adopt. All of the subjects in these groups were endowed with 25 tokens in every round. Four out of six experimental groups adopted a covenant in which they specified the number of tokens they would invest and the level of fines to be imposed. The fines determined by the participants ranged in size from $.10 to $1.00 (E. Ostrom, Walker, and Gardner 1992).

The groups that crafted their own agreements were able to achieve an average of 93 percent of the maximum in the periods after their agreement. And, the defection rate for these experiments was only 4 percent. The two groups that did not agree to their own covenant did not fare as well. They averaged 56 percent of the maximum available returns and faced a defection rate of 42 percent (E. Ostrom, Walker, and Gardner 1992). Consequently, those subjects who used an opportunity to covenant with one another to agree on a joint strategy and choose their own level of fines received very close to optimal results based entirely on their own promises and their own willingness to monitor and sanction one another when it was occasionally necessary (see Frohlich, Oppenheimer, and Eavey 1987 for similar findings).

Replications and Extensions of Commons Dilemma Experiments

One of the great advantages of laboratory experiments, as we saw with the Trust experiments in the first part of this chapter, is that they can be replicated as well as modified by other researchers so that one can gain ever greater confidence in the findings. One of the first replications was conducted by Rocco and Warglien (1995), who found very similar outcomes in the baseline, no-communication situation as well as in the face-to-face communication settings. They were interested, in addition, in the question of whether similar results would be obtained in an experimental design where communication was *not* organized on a direct face-to-face basis. They used identical structural variables of our earlier Commons Dilemma design with and without face-to-face communication. Then, they added a design with limited communication in a form of computerized exchange. They replicated the substantial improvement in efficiency that was earlier obtained in face-to-face communication. When the communication was conducted electronically without a face-to-face discussion, subjects did not increase their cooperation levels to the same extent.

Another very interesting series of replications and extensions was conducted by Juan-Camilo Cardenas (2000, 2003) using field laboratories set up in school buildings in rural Colombia rather than a computer-based laboratory on a university campus. Cardenas initially invited over two hundred villagers to participate in a series of common-pool resource experiments. Several closely paralleled the ones conducted at Indiana University and discussed above. Others extended the questions that could be addressed. The villagers who Cardenas invited were actual users of local forests for the extraction of firewood, natural fibers, and log timber as well as local water resources. One of the basic questions he wanted to pursue was whether experienced villagers who were heavily dependent on local forests for wood products would behave in a manner broadly consistent with that of undergraduate students at an American university.

The answer to this first question turned out to be positive. He wrote his instructions in Spanish and in a manner that would be easily understood by villagers. Instead of tokens—which are an easy medium for undergraduates to understand—he asked villagers to decide on how many months a year they would spend in the forest gathering wood products as contrasted to using their time otherwise. Each villager had a copy of a payoff table, which was the same as that of the other seven participants, showing that as the number of months that each individual would spend in the forest increased, she would gain more returns, but that the return to all of them depended on their own keeping the harvesting time to a very low level.

In the baseline, no-communication experiments, Cardenas found a similar pattern as we had found with subjects from Indiana University. Villagers substantially overinvested in the resource. While there was considerable variation among groups, villagers on average achieved 57.7 percent of their optimal return in the last three rounds of the baseline experiments (Cardenas 2000, 316). The daily wage that most of the villagers could earn at the time of the experiment was around 7,000 pesos (or around U.S. $5.40 at the time). If they all invested at an optimal level, they would earn around 12,900 pesos. They did earn around 7,884 pesos in these experiments for the two or three hours they were involved in initial practice sessions and the actual experiments themselves.

Face-to-face communication enabled them to increase efficiency on average to 76.1 percent of optimal. Considerable variation among groups existed, which Cardenas was able to explain using information about the participants filled in after that experiment was completed. He found, for example, that when most members of the group were already familiar with common-pool resources such as the collective use of a mangrove, they used the communication rounds more effectively than when most members of the group were dependent primarily on their own assets. Cardenas also found that "social distance and group inequality based on the economic wealth of the people in the group seemed to constrain the effectiveness of communication for this same sample of groups" (2000, 317; see also Cardenas 2003).

Cardenas, Stranlund, and Willis (2000) report another fascinating extension. In five experiments, the villagers were given a chance to communicate after the initial ten rounds of the baseline condition. In five other experiments, they were also told that a new regulation would go into force that mandated that they should spend no more than the optimal level of time in the forest each round (which in this case was one month per villager). They were also told that there would be a 50 percent chance that conformance to the rule would be monitored each round. The experimenter rolled a die in front of the subjects each round to determine whether an inspection would take place. If an even number showed up, there would be an inspection. The experimenter then drew a number from chits numbered between one and eight placed in a hat to determine who would be inspected. Thus, the probability that anyone would be inspected was 1/16 per round—a low but very realistic probability for monitoring forest harvesting in rural areas. The monitor checked the investment of the person whose time had come without revealing the result to others. If the person was over the limit imposed, a penalty was subtracted from the payoff to that person. No statement was made to others whether the appropriator was complying with regulations or not.

The subjects in this experimental condition actually increased their harvesting levels in this externally imposed sanctioning experiment in contrast to behavior when no rule at all was imposed, and the subjects could communicate on a face-to-face basis. What was remarkable about these outcomes was that subjects, who were simply allowed to communicate with one another on a face-to-face basis, were able to achieve a higher joint return than the subjects who had an optimal but imperfectly enforced external rule imposed on them. These experiments provide further support for Bruno Frey's (1997a, 1997b) hypothesis that external rules imposed on citizens can crowd out intrinsic motivation and lead to worse outcomes than reached through voluntary agreements.[6] As the authors conclude:

> We have presented evidence that indicates that local environmental policies that are modestly enforced, but nevertheless are predicted by standard theory to be welfare-improving, may be ineffective. In fact, such a policy can do more harm than good, especially in comparison to allowing individuals collectively to confront local environmental dilemmas without intervention. We have also . . . presented evidence that the fundamental reason for the poor performance of external control is that it crowded out group-regarding behavior in favor of greater self-interest. (Cardenas, Stranlund, and Willis 2000, 1731)

Common-pool resource experiments have also been replicated and extended upon by Marco Casari and Charles Plott (2003). Casari and Plott wanted to explore whether an institution that had been used in the Italian Alps for centuries and was thought to be highly effective would generate positive results in a laboratory setting. The Alpine system had a relatively simple structure.

> The population of a village developed a contract among themselves, subject to the approval of the regional government, called "Carte di Regola," where they described a system for monitoring and sanctioning those who are discovered violating or exceeding patterns of use that the villagers agreed upon in the contract. The "Carte di Regola" specified in advance the conditions under which a sanction could be inflicted on a person found in violation of the contract and the amount of the fine. . . . Any villager could report a violation but he usually incurred a cost in the form of a monitoring effort to discover the violator and additional costs to bring him to court. A share of such a fine usually went to the person who discovered the violator in order to give an incentive to monitor. (Casari and Plott 2003, 218)

Casari and Plott used the same functional form for a payoff function as we had earlier used with Indiana University subjects (see equation 1 above), but they increased the monetary incentives by more than three-fold.[7] Using Cal-Tech subjects, they first ran a baseline experiment that closely paralleled our earlier baseline experiments. Without communication or sanctioning, they found—as we had earlier found—that the resource was substantially overused, even more than the Nash equilibrium. Subjects earned only 28.4 percent of the optimal return, while the Nash equilibrium would have earned them 39.5 percent. They also found substantial variations among individual subjects in the amount they overused the resource, as we had earlier.

Casari and Plott then changed the transformation function and the payoffs of the game. They used two sanctioning conditions—weak and strong. In both conditions, after the decision regarding harvesting had been made and the total investment levels had been announced, a subject could select an option to inspect the decision made by any of the other subjects at a set cost. After this decision had been made, the harvesting decision of the inspected subject was made public information, but not the identity or number of subjects requesting an inspection. A fine was imposed for each unit appropriated above the announced level and transferred to the inspector. The "inspector" made a profit when the fee that had been paid to carry out the inspection was less than the amount transferred, which was in turn dependent upon the amount in which the inspected appropriator had exceeded the announced level. The weak sanctioning option did not change the predicted Nash equilibrium for the game, but the strong sanctioning option made the predicted Nash equilibrium approach the socially optimal level of appropriation.

In the experiments conducted with weak sanctions, slightly over half of the actions were inspected—a much higher level than predicted by classical game theory. And subjects obtained closer to optimal levels of returns than they had without sanctions. In the strong sanction condition, the efficiency of the joint return was 94 percent, but when inspection fees are subtracted, the net return was 77 percent of optimal (238). Almost all actions were inspected. It turned out that the subjects making the lowest uses were more aggressive inspectors than those making the highest uses.

Casari and Plott found that the subjects behaved in a manner consistent with having heterogeneous preferences rather than all subjects having preferences that were monotonically aligned with the available payoffs. Some individuals appeared to be more spiteful than others. This helps to explain the success of the "Carte di Regola" system, as it would appear that it was able to use the "heterogeneity of preferences to socially advantageous ends" (241). By sharing the fine with the person who reported the violation, the system channeled the behavior of the more spiteful individuals into socially useful purposes. Overall, they found that the experiment mimicking the set of rules used in the Italian Alps greatly improved the efficiency of resource use as contrasted to the baseline experiment without the sanctioning options.

Casari and Plott provide a cogent and important theoretical explanation for their findings based on a model of individual choice called a "heterogeneous, linear other-regarding model." Their model predicts the outcomes of their experimental designs well, while the model of individual behavior focused only on monetary returns does not explain the behavior in their common-pool resource experiments (or that of our own earlier experiments) well at all. Given that the results from both types of experiments—as well as many other extensively replicated experiments—are not consistent with what is predicted from classical game theory, it is time to discuss the deep problem of animating institutional analysis. We will do so in chapter 4.

Conclusions

My intention in writing this chapter was to provide several concrete illustrations for the reader of the working components of an action situation and how they combine to generate a clear-cut structure of extrinsic incentives. The experimental researcher must create all of the working parts of an action situation in the protocols for an experiment and attempt to isolate the experiment from external, confounding variables. The experimental lab is thus an excellent environment to learn about action situations and how changes in one component of a situation affect interactions and outcomes.

We have also learned a great deal about interactions and outcomes in two particular games: the Trust Game and the Commons Dilemma. Basically, we have learned that:

1. In a two-person Trust Game, both Investors and Trustees engage in more cooperative behavior than predicted when using a model of behavior based on purely monetary returns.

2. The level of trust and reciprocity achieved in a Trust Game depends on many factors associated with the relative position of the subjects, the information they have, and the type of sanctions made available to participants.

3. When participants in an N-person Commons Dilemma are held apart and unable to communicate on a face-to-face basis (or via the type of signaling that is feasible in two-person situations), they overuse a common-pool resource.

4. Participants initially use an opportunity for face-to-face discussions to share their understanding of how their actions affect the joint outcomes and arrive at a common understanding of the best joint strategy available to them.

5. Participants are willing to promise others whom they assess as being trustworthy that they will adopt a joint plan of action. Most individuals keep their promises (in situations where substantial advantage can accrue for breaking the promise).

6. If agreements are broken, individuals become indignant and use verbal chastisements when available. They are also willing to use costly sanctions when they have the opportunity to select this option, and even tend to overuse them.

7. Participants use heuristics in dealing with complex problems.

8. Heuristics vary in their capabilities to cope with a changing configuration of actions by other participants.

9. When given an opportunity to communicate, craft their own rules, and sanction nonconformance to these rules, some groups were willing to do so. Through their own efforts, these groups achieve close to optimal results. Those who forego such an opportunity are not able to sustain a high level of performance.

In other words, a substantial number, but not all, of the individuals in these carefully controlled experiments are trustworthy and reciprocate trust if it has been extended. When behavior is discovered that is not consistent with reciprocity, individuals are willing to use retribution in a variety of forms.[8] Individuals also initially rely on a battery of heuristics in response to complexity. Without communication and agreements on joint strategies, these heuristics lead to overuse. On the other hand, individuals are willing to discuss ways to increase their own and others' payoffs over a sequence of rounds. Many are willing to make contingent promises when others are assessed as trustworthy (Bendor and Mookherjee 1990).

These conclusions are *not* consistent with predictions derived from classical game-theoretic models of participants focusing entirely on monetary returns in these situations. They are, however, consistent with evidence gathered from empirical research in the field (Van Vugt et al. 2000). Thus, it is time that we address the question of how institutional analysis should be animated. In chapter 4, I dissect the other holon—the participant—which, together with an action situation, creates an action arena. To make a prediction about the likely outcomes to be achieved in a particular arena, one must animate the analysis by specifying key assumptions about the individual actors holding positions in the situation.

Four _____

Animating Institutional Analysis

IN THE FIRST three chapters of this book, I focused on the exogenous variables that underpin all action situations and the components of action situations at operational, collective-choice, or constitutional-choice levels of analysis. So far, I have provided only a minimal sketch (in chapter 3) of the contemporary theory used to explain and predict how participants in action situations are expected to choose among actions. It is this theory (and models of this theory) that analysts use to predict likely actions of diverse participants and their cumulative outcomes. Participants are the second holon of an action arena and the animators of institutional worlds. Without humans who make decisions in a situation, there is nothing but the biophysical world to explain.

In this chapter, I discuss the approaches taken by scholars to the puzzle of animating diverse types of situations ranging from highly competitive markets to various types of social dilemmas. We will start with situations that are relatively well understood—open, competitive, posted price markets. In these settings, a theory of full-information, rational behavior focusing on material outcomes has been shown to be a powerful engine of prediction and is consequently very valuable for institutional analysis. Then, I add complicating assumptions that redefine the information processes, the valuation mechanisms used by individuals, and/or the selection processes that individuals adopt.

An institutional theorist must self-consciously posit the kind of information participants possess, the relevant preference structure of the participants, and the process they use for choosing among actions. Assumptions about information, preferences, and choice mechanisms are thus the essential components of this holon. All three need to be specified in order to generate hypotheses about interactions and outcomes that can be tested in a particular type of action situation or linked set of action situations.[1] As a scholar trained extensively in both political science and economics, I have used (and plan to continue to use for many purposes) the basic assumptions about human behavior in models developed to represent what is called "rational choice theory" as it has currently evolved in contemporary microeconomics and game theory (for basic textbooks see Gardner 2003; Dixit and Skeath 1999; Gintis 2000a).

Animating Open, Competitive Processes

First-generation rational choice theory and related models have proved valuable for predicting human behavior in stable, competitive market settings and in competitive electoral and legislative settings where the issue space is constrained (Aldrich 1995; Nardulli 1995; V. Smith 1991, 2000). In these stable and repetitive settings, individuals are able to learn about the full, relevant structure of the situation and attach positive or negative preferences to actions and outcomes. When one is explaining behavior in familiar and often-used situations with complete information, one is not faced with the problem of explaining how individuals learn about the situation and its likely outcomes and payoffs. One can assume that learning has taken place and proceed with an explanation of behavior by informed participants using a mental model of the situation that is at least roughly approximate to the external situation itself. Explaining how individuals learn turns out to be extremely challenging.[2]

Predictions from these models are empirically supported at an aggregate level in open, competitive, posted-price market settings and at an individual level in carefully designed experimental settings of competitive market situations (see V. Smith 1982; Kagel and Roth 1995; Lian and Plott 1998; Noussair, Plott, and Reizman 1995). If open, posted-price, competitive markets for the exchange of goods (or similar situations) were the only type of action situations that individuals faced, then rational choice theory and its currently accepted models would clearly be the only theory (and related models) of human behavior that one would need for prediction of outcomes. Frohlich and Oppenheimer (2001, 22) assess "the traditional spare economic model of decision making" as being "useful and robust in predicting behavior in contexts of choice which are relatively stable, hence in which subjects have learned to call up particular representations on a repeated basis" (22).

Thus, it is important to learn about relatively simple situations that have been successfully analyzed and shown to have empirical support before venturing off into the interesting but difficult work of understanding and explaining behavior in more complex settings.[3] To some extent, we can think of learning how to analyze behavior in these games as somewhat similar to a young chemist learning how to make simple compounds or a biologist learning how to dissect a frog. These tools are not all that are needed to explain complex chemical and biological phenomena, but they are a useful starting place. Further, the ways of analyzing relatively simple situations as formal games have already been developed. It makes little sense to try to utilize a complex form of analysis, or develop entirely new forms of analysis, when tools are already available for the analysis and explanation of behavior in many situations.

Thus, I strongly advise institutional analysts to learn how to use the working assumptions of models developed to apply contemporary rational choice theory. These are:

1. Individuals possess as much *information* about the structure of a situation as is contained in the situation itself.

2. Individuals assign a complete and consistent, internal *valuation* to outcomes that is a monotonic function of an individual's own net external payoff.[4]

3. After making a complete analysis of the situation, individuals choose an action in light of their resources to *maximize* expected material net benefits to themselves given what others are expected to do.

We will use the term *rational egoist* to describe a participant in a situation whose behavior can be predicted using these three assumptions. Knowing the assumptions of a rational egoist and how to use them enables an analyst to begin using theoretical tools to predict how individuals make choices and generate outcomes in competitive situations. Further, some individuals are present in most situations whose choices of strategies can be predicted using a model of a rational egoist who focuses on the immediate material payoffs to self and not on other values.

Armen Alchian (1950) demonstrated long ago that those who do not behave as rational egoists in an open, competitive market will not be present in any significant number once demand and supply have led to an equilibrium. More recently, Gode and Sunder (1997) demonstrated that it is not even necessary to assume that all individuals are rational egoists— even at equilibrium—to establish efficient markets. Rather, they show that the efficiency of market exchanges derives from the set of rules constituting a market, rather than the sophisticated calculation of the participants. In their model, they show that "zero intelligence traders" reach efficient outcomes when seven essential rules constrain the actions of buyers and sellers and not otherwise (see chapter 7, note 13). Thus Alchian, as well as Gode and Sunder, show that it is the structure of markets that leads participants to make efficient choices rather than the assumptions made in economic theory about the internal structure of individual valuation and choice.

The Challenge of Imperfect Information

Competitive markets or other full-information, competitive situations are not the only situations facing individuals that are of interest to institutional analysts. Further empirical research has uncovered a rich array of anomalies that systematically occur in situations that were once thought to have properties leading to clear predictions.[5] Situations that are relatively simple social dilemmas that make clear predictions about expected behavior, for example, frequently evoke positive or negative internal values for participants who are not monotonically related to the objective payoffs involved (as discussed in chapter 3).

When other-regarding preferences and/or intrinsic values are assigned to outcomes and actions, the situation is one of incomplete, rather than complete, information because other players cannot know exactly how an individual is valuing these actions and outcomes. In order to analyze these situations, one needs to make different assumptions about the values taken into account by individuals. Further, as Kenneth Koford (2003) illustrated with his research conducted in Bulgaria, the way a situation is framed may strongly affect how individuals embedded in a particular culture and history view it and value actions and outcomes (McDermott 2001). Frohlich, Oppenheimer, and Kurki (2004) have analyzed simple situations where small changes in the structure of the situation itself— what they call the context of the situation—evoke norms in some participants that were not expressed in a baseline situation.

Instead of complete information, some situations generate only partial information. Further, the distribution of the information may be asymmetric. One may also be confronted with the need to examine how individuals view risk, uncertainty, and information asymmetries and how they react to the actions and perceived attributes of other participants. Situations also differ in regard to the extent of repetition and whether the same individuals continue to interact with one another over time or whether interactions are largely with a continuous stream of strangers. How do all of these affect choice? When rational choice models—as usually operationalized—fail to predict outcomes, other theoretical tools are needed (Vanberg 2002).

Political economists thus find themselves at a very interesting juncture. Experimental researchers have shown that behavior after several rounds in experimental markets and other tightly constrained, competitive processes tends to be consistent with the predictions stemming from a rational egoist model of human behavior. On the other hand, experimental researchers have also shown that behavior in many forms of social dilemmas and other games is *not* consistent with what would be predicted if all individuals behaved in a manner consistent with the rational egoist model (see Gintis 2000a for a review). Further, the level of trust and cooperation exhibited varies substantially from one experimental design to another. The combination of the extensive experimental research and the strong theoretical arguments made first by Alchian (1950) and then by Gode and Sunder (1997) that the institutional structure of a market, rather than the model of the individual, leads to the outcomes predicted by market theory challenges all political economists. We need to know when to use the assumption of a rational egoist for *all* participants or to assume some individuals may have other-regarding preferences or value norms such as trust or reciprocity.

Assumptions Used in Animating Participants

Consequently, I strongly advise institutional analysts not to rely on one and only one theoretical tool to explain human behavior unless they wish to confine their analyses entirely to situations that can be successfully modeled as simple, competitive, complete-information situations. The three basic assumptions of rational choice theory are, however, a useful starting point for doing institutional analysis. They illustrate the components of any theory of human behavior that an institutional analyst would use in analyzing situations other than highly competitive situations. Thus, whether a participant is an individual or a corporate actor, the analyst must make assumptions about three components of human behavior in order to animate an institutional analysis. These assumptions are the components of the holon called "participants" in the Institutional Analysis and Development (IAD) framework. Each of these assumptions can also be unpacked into multiple layers. These are:

1. the way that participants acquire, process, represent, retain, and use *information*;

2. the *valuation* that participants assign to actions and outcomes; and

3. the processes (maximizing, satisficing, or using diverse heuristics) that participants use for *selecting* particular actions or strategic chains of actions in light of their resources.

Once one decides to explore alternative assumptions about human behavior, the number of choices that the researcher has to make are substantial. Alternative assumptions are not likely to be as clean and elegantly simple as those of rational choice models. Frohlich and Oppenheimer (2001, 22) reflect that the "standard rational choice model, simple, elegant and decisive, is not liable to be replaced with as simple and manipulable a model. The anomalies which have been identified are broad and diffuse and they are likely to require more theoretical superstructure for their explanation" (see also Levi 1997b). The grave hesitation of some theorists to adopt "more realistic" assumptions stems, to a large extent, from the messiness of the alternative superstructures.

One strategy adopted by many (including the author) is not to change all of the assumptions at the same time when trying to model a particular type of situation. In stable and repetitive situations where intrinsic values are important, one may retain assumption one—regarding full information about the structure of the situation—while focusing primarily on the types of values of importance to individuals and the resulting strategies they select (see Ahn et al. 2003; Cox 2004). Alternatively, one may focus primarily on the information processing and assume individuals are boundedly rational (Selten 1998; B. Jones 2001). If the situation is uncertain and complex, one may focus on the third assumption related to how individuals make decisions about their choices. In many field settings, participants use heuristics or rules of thumb that they have learned over time—or were taught to them by their seniors—that give them good enough solutions that there is little need to pay the costs of a full search (see Gigerenzer and Selten 2001). Thus, which assumption (or assumptions) one changes and the particular assumptions made depend on the situation to be explained.

A thick book could be devoted to elucidating the different theories and models that posit diverse assumptions about these three broad components of human choice. In order to keep the present book focused, I will briefly discuss here only some of the most relevant alternative assumptions that are used by institutional theorists and will refer the reader to contemporary literature related to these assumptions. I will conclude with a discussion of the importance of the institutions within which individuals interact to the likelihood that individuals with normative orientations and other-regarding preferences may be able to achieve higher outcomes over time in social dilemmas and may even change the distribution of strategies used by individuals over time.

Assumptions about Information Processing and Mental Models

Many of the situations of interest to institutional analysts are uncertain and lack the kind of rules leading to the selective pressures and information-generating capabilities of highly competitive processes. In analyzing these situations, theorists frequently substitute the assumption of bounded rationality—that participants are goal oriented and try to be rational but face cognitive limits—rather than the assumptions of complete information (see Simon 1957, 1972, 1995; Williamson 1985, 2000; V. Ostrom 1997; B. Jones 2001). In some complex situations, the available information may greatly exceed the competence of an individual to compute a solution based on fuller analysis (Heiner 1983). As discussed in chapter 2, the game of chess exceeds the capacity of any human to compute an analytical solution. In analyzing the behavior of chess players, one can assume that they know the current pattern of chess pieces on the board, but not that they know all of the action-outcome linkages.

Most cognitive scientists stress that humans expend substantial effort to make sense out of the variety of signals (and symbols) they receive as

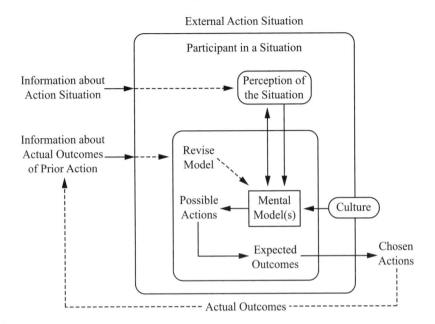

Figure 4.1 The relationship between information, action-outcome linkages, and internal mental models. *Source*: Adapted from Denzau and North 2000, 36.

they interact within a variety of situations in life (Busemeyer and Myung 1992). Individuals attempt to create a mental model or a representation of diverse situations so as to be able to make reasonable decisions in these multiple settings (Holland et al. 1986). Mental models are affected by at least two basic sources—feedback from the world and the shared culture or belief system in which an individual is embedded.

As individuals interact in a diversity of situations, they receive information about the structure of the situations they are in prior to making a decision and usually receive some kind of feedback after they take an action. Participants need to discover an appropriate model of the situation they are in through repeated interactions in it or similar structures (Plott 1996). Drawing on Denzau and North (2000), one can envision a participant in a situation receiving information about its structure (how many participants, who they are, the benefits and costs of action-outcome linkages, etc.) (see figure 4.1). The participant initially relies on earlier mental models formed of this situation to calculate expected outcomes of diverse actions. If satisfied with the outcomes, they may not search for further information. What they learn about the outcome of their own and others' actions, however, will potentially stimulate an effort to revise their mental model if there is an incongruity or a lack of satisfaction.

Cultural belief systems also affect the mental models that individuals utilize. Most of childhood is spent in a combination of observing others interacting, being told the prudent or proper way to perceive situations and to act within them, and taking actions based on both observation and instruction (Tomasello 2004). Parents actively encourage their children to learn a culturally appropriate set of strategies, including industriousness, responsibility, and self-reliance, for doing well in a variety of situations (Low 1989). The distribution of imparted traits varies by whether a culture is highly stratified or not, and by the gender of the child (ibid.). When we indicate that people share a culture, it is a shorthand way of indicating that the wide diversity of mental models that individuals have invented has been reduced to a smaller set within those sharing the culture (Benedict 1934). Culture may also be viewed as an intergenerational transfer of past experience. The mental models that scientists hold come about initially from what they learn in school as these are modified by their own research and that of others (Gopnik 2004).

Individuals learn from experience and from shared mental models. Learning is enhanced in situations that are often repeated. Interactions with the same set of individuals enable an individual to obtain a better estimate of the strategies that specific others adopt. Theoretical and experimental work has shown that individuals tend to experiment with diverse actions and then adopt those that have returned the highest payoffs in the past (Selten, Abbink, and Cox 2001; Busemeyer and Myung 1992). If the situation in which individuals interact is relatively stable and repetition occurs frequently, and if there is pressure to improve performance, individuals will tend to discover those strategies that an omniscient individual would have selected.[6] Of course, the larger the number of individuals involved in a repeated situation, and the more diverse their strategies, the more difficult it is for anyone to gain an accurate perception of others' strategic behavior.

The convergence through learning to the same strategy as is predicted under full rationality is unlikely to happen when the number of participants in a situation is large and the situation itself is complex, changes frequently, and/or the individuals do not participate in that situation with regularity or any induced need to increase performance. Information search is costly. The information-processing capabilities of human beings are limited. Individuals must often make choices based on incomplete knowledge of all possible alternatives and their likely outcomes. With incomplete information and imperfect information-processing capabilities, individuals may make errors in perception, in their comprehension of how a complex structure works, or simply in computations (V. Ostrom 1986, 1997).

The experiences that different individuals have had and their interpretation of them may differ substantially. It is thus possible that a single individual might be able to call up more than one mental model or that the mental model of participants in the same situation will differ. This presents a theoretical problem for the analyst trying to understand behavior. "How can we understand a person's choices if, when confronting a given environment, she can have multiple representations, each of which is associated with different values?" (Frohlich and Oppenheimer 2001, 6).

Denzau and North (2000) stress the importance of communication as one way to enable individuals to develop a shared mental model. If the same individuals repeatedly interact in free and open communication, and if they already share some broad cultural views of the world, mental models are more likely to converge. The positive impact of communication—particularly face-to-face communication on joint outcomes in a wide diversity of social dilemma experiments—has been replicated frequently, as discussed in chapter 3.

Individuals may not always be able to engage in open, repeated communication, however. John Schiemann (2002) examines this problem in his analysis of the mental models used by different age groups coming from the same culture but who have had vividly different experiences in life. Older Hungarians, who had directly experienced the bloodshed of World War II, interpreted the situations following the ending of the Soviet Union differently than did younger Hungarians who only read about the earlier, dramatic events. A generational difference also exists on how individuals view the Chinese leadership's decision to use force in the Tiananmen incident in 1989.[7] Unless there is open and active communication among participants over some time, they may simply use different mental models when interacting in the same external situation. This can lead to gross misunderstandings and disappointments or even to major violence.

Frohlich and Oppenheimer (2001) address the puzzle of multiple internal models by asking what factors in an environment are likely to affect the way a participant perceives a situation and the way the individual optimizes in that situation given that "paying attention" is costly. Few humans gain full mastery of all of the potentially relevant details in a complex, ongoing situation. Frohlich and Oppenheimer single out two properties of a situation as most important in affecting the way a situation is perceived. "The first property is the *salience* of the elements in a choice situation," by which they mean "the degree to which an element is linked to possible changes in the welfare of the decision maker" (8). The second property is the *vividness* of the situation or the "amount and quality of the sensory details of the objects encountered" (8). These attributes are important in gaining attention given the variety of signals an individual receives. "In order for something to grab one's attention it must displace

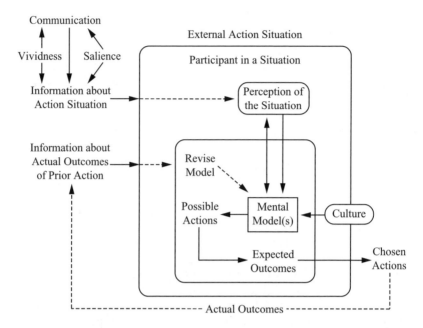

Figure 4.2 The impact of communication, vividness, and salience on the relationship between information, action-outcome linkages, and internal mental models.

something else to which one is attending. To accomplish this, a new focus of attention must have a higher claim. Attention shifts from one object of attention to another as if there were a threshold of value attached to the former which has to be surpassed for the competitor to displace it" (8). The repeated finding that face-to-face communication in social dilemmas is more effective than written communication may be related to its being a more vivid form of communication.

The role of vividness of symbols or rituals in solidifying the shared mental models of large groups of individuals is an important theme in the work of anthropologists (Rappaport 1979, for example). The philosopher Allan Gibbard (1990) stresses the importance of rituals in achieving shared norms of what participants should do in particular situations and helping to increase the probability that they will do so in the future partly because they share a vivid memory of what should be done.[8] Thus, the vivid ritual or symbol helps to select one mental model over others. The resulting congruence in behavior and outcomes helps to reinforce that model among those sharing the same culture. The role of communication, salience, and vividness in affecting mental models can be represented as in figure 4.2.

The architecture of information processing broadly reflected in figure 4.2 illustrates that individuals do not respond immediately to all information but rather to that which is communicated in a salient and vivid manner.[9] On the basis of his own and others' research, Bryan Jones argues that individuals and the organizations with which they work are disproportionate information processors. "Disproportionate information processing means that inputs into a decision-making process do not link directly to outputs. As a consequence, there is an imperfect match between the adaptive strategies people devise and the information they receive. This mismatch is the inner cognitive and emotional architecture of the human brain 'showing through' in responding to information" (Jones 2001, 9). Jones illustrates this mismatch with a variety of imaginative quantitative studies of disproportionate information processing in shifting electoral responses over time, in public budgetary changes, and in the level of coverage of national policy issues by Washington-based news publications. The substantive interpretation of his results for an institutional analyst is that: "change in human institutions tends to be quite conservative—most cases cluster around a central peak—but is subject to occasional quite large punctuations (the tails). . . . It would seem that a hypothetical decision maker would have to be prepared either for virtually no change or a very large change—he or she could not hope for moderate adjustments to changing circumstances" (184; see also Jones, Baumgartner, and True 1996).

Denzau and North (2000) reflect a similar view of the way change happens. They use the term "punctuated equilibrium" to reflect their sense that the internal models used by individuals remain relatively similar until some event triggers a large change in the mental model and resulting changes in the actions that individuals (or organizations) take. Denzau and North, as well as Jones, also illustrate how individuals are able to overcome some of their own information-processing limits by establishing rules and routines that structure situations in such a way as to enhance the likelihood that individuals will share a mental model of the situation and take actions that lead to better rather than worse outcomes (North 2005). Humans are thereby able to compensate for—as well as replicate—cognitive processing limits by the way they organize themselves and the procedures they follow (see also Dawes 1988).

Assumptions about Valuation Processes

How individuals value actions and outcomes has become a very active discourse among scholars interested in institutional questions (Fehr and Falk 1999; Fehr and Gächter 2000a, 2000b; Bolton and Ockenfels 2000; Casari and Plott 2003; Frohlich, Oppenheimer, and Kurki 2004; Janssen and Ahn 2003). Assuming that all individuals are self-interested utility maximizers without exploring how individuals reach utility judgments was a satisfactory scholarly strategy for many years when explaining behavior in highly competitive market settings where one could implicitly equate utility with profits. As mentioned above, substantial field and experimental research supports the second assumption of rational choice when individuals are interacting in a stable, competitive environment with full information about the short-term options available to them.

When one turns to the large realm of social dilemmas, however, little empirical support exists for an assumption that *all* individuals value *only* the material outcomes that flow only to them.[10] If this were the case, we would not have seen the extensive evidence presented in chapter 3 that Investors frequently send funds to Trustees and Trustees often send funds back to the Investor at a personal cost to themselves to fulfill the trust that the Investor placed in them. Nor would we have seen subjects keeping promises that they have made in face-to-face communication rounds to other subjects in a Commons Dilemma experiment to keep their appropriation levels low. Many subjects appear to have other-regarding preferences and to accept norms of behavior backed up by emotions including pride, guilt, shame, and anger. Whether norms are invoked and lead to cooperative behavior varies across experiments that differ only in regards to relatively small structural features.

The results discussed in chapter 3 are hard to explain using the standard rational choice model that all individuals who face the same objective game structure evaluate decisions the same way![11] And, we cannot simply resort to the easy criticism that undergraduate student subjects are being paid a modest sum (or nothing at all) and thus the game is not a valid test of the theory. Many subjects were not students in these and other experiments conducted in multiple countries (Henrich et al. 2004).[12] Increasing the size of the payoffs offered in experiments does not appear to change the broad patterns of empirical results obtained.[13] Nor, on the basis of experimental evidence, can we simply change from an assumption of universal selfish behavior to an assumption of universal altruism. As Fehr and Gächter (1998, 847) stress, "*Homo Oeconomicus* Also Exists." In all social dilemma experiments, a "non-trivial minority of subjects exhibits selfish behavior" (847).

Thus, the results of the experiments summarized in chapter 3—and many others documented by Camerer (2003)—substantially challenge the second assumption of contemporary rational choice models that valuation of all players is always focused entirely on extrinsic, immediate, net benefits to the individual. These well-substantiated facts provide an essential foundation of a more eclectic (and classical) view of human behavior. Further, as Ben-Ner and Putterman (2000a) stress, humans invest substantial time in their attempt to "mold the character" of their offspring. If this were truly impossible, it would be irrational for adult humans to spend so much time trying to transform the preference structure of their offspring. On the other hand, adopting the closely related, internal norms of trustworthiness and trust are not the unchanging, universal attributes of all individuals. It is important that we develop tools of analysis that reconnect the normative side of individual orientations with the calculation of individual benefits.[14]

Recent research by Rilling and his colleagues (2002) provides an even further challenge. Freely recruited and paid subjects participated in a series of repeated Prisoner's Dilemma games while connected to a magnetic resonance imaging (fMRI) scanner. In each round, subjects pressed a button to indicate their choice of cooperation or defection leading to a payoff per round of $2 each if both cooperated, or of $3 if a subject defected and if the other cooperated, or $1 if both defected. The researchers compared levels of cooperation and brain activities in several designs including one in which the second player was a programmed computer strategy. The results of each round were projected onto a screen that the player in the scanner could see and onto the computer screen of the other player (where applicable). The observed behavior was similar to that of other repeated dilemma experiments.

While the observed interactions and outcomes were not novel, linking the portrait of brain activity to behavior in social dilemmas adds a new dimension to the body of findings. And what they found was surprising to the research team (as reported to Angier, July 26, 2002) as well as to many readers. Pressing the cooperate key in a reciprocating relationship generated the brightest reactions in the pleasure zones of the brain (the anterovential striatum and the orbitofrontal cortex). The researchers also tested whether the same level of brain activity was associated with receiving a payoff of $2 in a nonsocial context. They found different patterns of neural activation depending on whether the scanned player thought she was playing a real human or a computer (see also McCabe 2003). They concluded that they had "identified a pattern of neural activation that may be involved in sustained cooperative social relationships, perhaps by labeling cooperative social interactions as rewarding, and/or by inhibiting the selfish-impulse to accept but not reciprocate an act of altruism" (Rilling et al. 2002, 403). These findings are consistent with the earlier theoretical work of Robert Frank (1988), who posited that human emotions underpin a commitment to reciprocity so that humans feel good when achieving mutual cooperation and feel bad when defections (their own or others) occur.

Given the extensive evidence from many empirical studies, at least some social scientists now tend to follow Amartya Sen's (1977) advice to stop assuming that all individuals are "rational fools." Instead, they assume that at least some individuals in some situations do have other-regarding preferences and do follow norms of behavior (see, for example, Frohlich and Oppenheimer 1996; McCabe and Smith 2003). As discussed in some detail in chapter 5, norms can be thought of as shared concepts of what must, must not, or may be appropriate actions or outcomes in particular types of situations. Individuals add positive or negative values to objective payoffs invoked by emotions such as pride (when positive) or shame (when negative). Norms such as those of trustworthiness, trust, and fairness will lead individuals to take actions in some situations—like those reported earlier—that are directly contrary to those predicted using a rational egoist assumption. While "foolish" according to these models, if those following norms can identify others with similar norms, they will actually earn more than those seeking their own short-run selfish objectives.[15]

The behavior of many participants can be thought of as partially based on intrinsic preferences related to how they prefer to behave (and, obviously would like others to behave) and the kind of outcomes they wish to see themselves and others obtain. Norm-following individuals take into account other individuals' interests as well as their own in the decisions they make (Frey 1994, 1997a). These "nonselfish" individuals, however, differ among themselves in terms of the extent to which they depart from purely selfish motivations and do not adopt an unchanging strategy when interacting with others in repeated situations. Further, individuals differ in regard to how they interpret actions by others that *reduce* their own payoffs. Some individuals can easily find themselves enmeshed in ever-expanding threat systems (Boulding 1963) whereby one bad deed cannot rest unpunished. Reciprocity can have a very dark side when bads have to repay bads over time. Unfortunately, "envy, vengeance and the desire to dominate are not less intrinsically motivated than altruism, conscientiousness, and love. All of these motives contribute to immediate satisfaction rather than to achieving externally set goals" (Osterloh and Frey 2000, 540).

Turning to the bright side, psychological research provides evidence that positive intrinsic motivation is increased when individuals feel that their own self-determination or self-esteem is enhanced (Deci and Ryan 1985; Deci, Koestner, and Ryan 1999). This leads to the possibility that intrinsic motivation can be "crowded out" in situations where individuals do not perceive themselves to have sufficient self-control over the actions they take. The recent experiments by Fehr and Rockenbach (2003) and Cardenas, Stranlund, and Willis (2000), discussed in chapter 3, provide strong evidence for the crowding out of reciprocity by the imposition of external sanctions. In a review of crowding-out theory, Frey and Jegen

(2001, 591) identify the conditions that affect the level of intrinsic motivation that individuals may feel:

1. External interventions *crowd* out intrinsic motivation if the individuals affected perceive them to be *controlling*. In that case, both self-determination and self-esteem suffer, and the individuals react by reducing their intrinsic motivation in the activity controlled.

2. External interventions *crowd in* intrinsic motivation if the individuals concerned perceive it as *supportive*. In that case, self-esteem is fostered, and the individuals feel that they are given more freedom to act, which enlarges self-determination.

Just as individuals may have different mental models of the situations they are in, they may differ in regard to their internal valuation patterns— the extent they take others into account in the decisions they make and the intrinsic valuation they may place on taking particular types of actions (e.g., being trustworthy) or reaching particular types of outcomes (e.g., more equitable). Further, the form that normative and other-regarding behavior takes "may be substantially context dependent. No 'single' model which explicates a particular set of values is likely to be adequate to capture behavior in all contexts" (Frohlich, Oppenheimer, and Kurki 2004, 116).

Assumptions about Selection Processes

Reviewing the assumptions about information and valuation processes has already opened a Pandora's box of complexity. Examining alternative assumptions about the selection processes that individuals use does not help reduce the complexity. One can make statements like: "Individuals will try to do as well as they can given the information they obtain." Or, "Individuals will use heuristics that have been proved to work in the past."

In *Rules, Games, and Common-Pool Resources*, for example, we examined the possibility that individuals in an experimental common-pool resource situation were using a heuristic that we called "measured reaction" (E. Ostrom, Gardner, and Walker 1994, 199). After engaging in face-to-face discussions where subjects had reached a simple agreement regarding what they all should do in future rounds, each subject had to make a personal decision as to whether to keep to the agreement and what to do if someone deviated from their agreement. Most subjects kept to their agreement. When deviations did occur, most subjects first reacted with a moderate increase in their own harvest rates.

A different strategy that scholars have posited that participants will use in coping with this type of situation is called the "grim trigger." A person using a grim-trigger strategy would react to any deviation from a verbal agreement by withholding cooperation on *every* play for the rest of the game. While subjects discussed such an option, they always rejected it. In trying to understand how they were behaving, we posited that players were reacting mildly (if at all) to a small deviation from an agreement. If defections continued over time, subjects using a measured response slowly changed from keeping the agreement toward actions consistent with the Nash equilibrium (E. Ostrom, Gardner, and Walker 1994, 200). An analysis of the round-by-round decisions by subjects to the deviations that did occur generated strong statistical support for the use of the measured reaction heuristic (200–215). By following this heuristic, individuals achieved a much higher payoff than predicted if they had used a maximization of expected net benefits assumption.

That experience certainly increased the warrantability of the claim that individuals use heuristics, in my view. And, the extensive research by Gigerenzer and his research team on "fast and frugal heuristics" provides substantial evidence across a diversity of situations (Gigerenzer, Todd, and the ABC Research Group 1999; Gigerenzer and Selten 2001). There is, however, a "serious and perhaps intractable induction problem in inferring the structure of a black box from the structure of the behavior it produces" (J. Anderson 1991, 471). In other words, it is hard to tell from behavior which of a variety of potential heuristics individuals are really using.

In an effort to answer this question, scholars are using a variety of ingenious methods. Rieskamp and Hoffrage (2003), for example, devised a series of experiments where they asked subjects to make decisions about a business firm's profitability based on their best estimate obtained from a cursory examination of an array of cues. By observing the cues subjects used—by opening a box on a computer screen—and how much time they spent, Rieskamp and Hoffrage could assess the heuristics that the subject used. As part of the experimental conditions, they also changed the amount of time allowed to subjects in order to observe how time constraints affect the selection process.

Rieskamp and Hoffrage identified the eight heuristics shown in table 4.1 as among those that subjects might use in this kind of a choice situation. As one can see from table 4.1, there is a rich array of potential heuristics that subjects could potentially use. Under low time pressure, Rieskamp and Hoffrage found that subjects tended to use noncompensatory heuristics—the PROS heuristic shown on table 4.1. The simple heuristic LEX was the best behavioral model to describe their behavior under high time pressure. They then conducted a Monte Carlo simulation to evaluate the performance of the eight heuristics listed on the table against using a multiple regression method to make the same decision. They

TABLE 4.1
Description of various decision strategies

Strategy*	Description of strategies
LEX	The lexicographic strategy (Fishburn 1974) selects the alternative with the highest value on the cue of the highest validity. If two or more alternatives have the same highest cue value, then for these alternatives the cue with the second highest validity is considered, and so on. LEX is the general form of the "Take the Best" heuristic investigated in Gigerenzer and Goldstein (1996).
LEX-Semi	Lexicographic semiorder (Luce 1956) works like LEX, with the additional assumption of a negligible difference (in the present paper, this difference was set at 1). Pairs of alternatives with a negligible difference between the cue values are treated as not discriminative.
EBA	Elimination by aspects (Tversky 1972) eliminates all alternatives that do not exceed a specified value on the first cue examined (in the present paper, this value was set at 2). If more than one alternative remains, another cue is selected. This procedure is repeated until only one alternative is left. Cues are selected in order of their validity.**
Features	The features strategy (Alba and Marmorstein 1987) selects the alternative with the highest number of good features. A good feature is a cue value that exceeds a specified cutoff (in the present paper, this cutoff value was set at 3).
ADD	The additive strategy calculates for each alternative the sum of the cue values (multiplied by a unit weight of 1) and selects the alternative with the highest score.
LEX-ADD	The LEX-ADD strategy is a combination of two strategies. It first uses LEX-Semi to choose two alternatives as favorites, then evaluates them by the ADD strategy and selects the one with the highest sum.
PROS	The weighted pros strategy (Huber 1980) selects the alternative with the highest sum of weighted "pros." A cue that has a higher value for one alternative than for the others is considered a pro for this alternative. The weight of each pro is defined by the validity of the particular cue.
WADD	The weighted additive strategy calculates for each alternative the sum of the cue values multiplied by the corresponding cue validates and selects the alternative with the highest score.

Source: Rieskamp and Hoffrage 2003, 50.

* Strategies occasionally do not end up with one single prediction; in this case, it was assumed that the strategy would randomly choose between the remaining alternatives.

** In contrast to this deterministic selection, in the original formulation of the EBA heuristic the cues are selected with a probability proportional to their weights (Tversky 1972).

found that the simple heuristics—particularly the LEX heuristic, which actually requires the least information—did very well in comparison to the "optimal" method for making this decision.[16] In their effort to understand the use of heuristics, Jager, Janssen, and Viek (2001) used the dimensions of uncertainty and satisfaction to determine which heuristic would be used. The more an individual is both satisfied and certain about the environment, the less likely they will put much effort into making a calculated choice.

Another puzzle in regard to the use of heuristics is: What is the effect of diverse heuristics on outcomes achieved? Gigerenzer and his colleagues (1999) have identified a number of heuristics that they have found to enable individuals and firms to make quick decisions and do very well over time. Other researchers are somewhat more skeptical of the efficiency of heuristics—especially in highly volatile environments. Güth and Neuefeind (2001), for example, explore the over-time efficiency of a heuristic that appears to be used in many consumer choices—a form of directional learning. This involves continuing or increasing an action if past actions have generated good outcomes and decreasing if bad outcomes occurred. In relatively stable environments, they found that the heuristic helped individuals move toward an efficient set of decisions. In a highly volatile environment, however, learning from the use of this heuristic only slowly improves achieved outcomes.

Variety and Complexity: An Asset or a Liability?

What I hope the reader gains from this brief overview of the broad set of assumptions used by theorists to animate analyses of multiple situations is a good sense that research in the behavioral social sciences is gradually increasing our capabilities to understand and predict interactions and outcomes in a diversity of action situations. The large number of replicated experiments provide substantial evidence for theorists to use in testing out a diversity of assumptions about basic human behavior (see Bolton and Ockenfels 2000; Fehr and Schmidt 1999; Frohlich and Oppenheimer 2001; Charness and Rabin 2003; Bowles 1998; Cox, Friedman, and Gjerstad 2004; Cox and Sadiraj 2004; Gintis 2000a; Rabin 1993; E. Ostrom 1998; Camerer 2003). What is also encouraging is that research in biological evolution (Maynard Smith and Szathmáry 1997; Kurzban 2003), cultural evolution (Boyd and Richerson 1985), and their interrelationships (Henrich 2004; Richerson and Boyd 2002; Sethi 1996) is helping to provide a better foundation for understanding how humans could have evolved such a rich set of preferences in addition to the universal goal of seeking to do well in regard to material payoffs.

The reaction of some scholars, however, to the growing richness of behavioral theories of human decision making is to view the variety as leading to messy complexity. Given that humans may be viewed as pursuing multiple values in diverse situations depending to some extent on their prior life's experiences, does it matter anymore which assumptions one uses? Does theory underlie all of these models? Is it just a hodgepodge of assumptions? Or, are there some major lessons to be learned?

My answers to these questions are: Yes, there is a broad underlying theory of human behavior that is itself developing over time as a result of the extensive empirical research and theoretical effort. Yes, it matters a lot that we can make multiple assumptions about how participants in a situation make decisions. The variety of assumptions is an asset and not a liability when used to design research so as to test out the implications of one set of assumptions versus others (see McCabe and Smith 2003; Cox 2004). We are beginning to make some real headway in understanding the behavior of the extremely complex animal called *Homo sapiens*. In this effort, we can learn a lot from engineers and how they draw on the general laws of physics.

Engineers work with multiple types of motors that are used to propel vehicles. To predict energy use, length of service, fragility to impact, and other important outcomes, an engineer needs to know specific facts about the situation (the kinds of roads or rail systems, their roughness and steepness, the amount of traffic, etc.) and about the motor involved (its internal composition, fuel needs, horsepower, etc). A skilled engineer is trained to work with multiple types of animation devices—motors—that are all consistent with underlying laws of physics. The underlying laws are too broad and general to provide specific guidance as to what to expect in particular settings. Engineers must design motors to perform well in specified contexts rather than in any and all contexts. Engineers use very detailed specifications. This does not mean, however, that the design of motors lacks a foundation in general physical laws.

Like engineers, social scientists need to recognize that to predict outcomes we must *match* the animating assumptions about the participants to the structure of the situation or linked set of relevant situations we are analyzing. While social scientists do not *design* the animators of action situations, we must understand how humans tend to behave in diverse situations. Our explanatory models of human behavior will differ when we explain behavior in a repeated social dilemma among individuals who have built reputations for trustworthiness and conditional cooperation as contrasted to total strangers who cannot even communicate with one another. When the situation relates to private goods and is competitive and stable; when it generates considerable information about its structure and the actions of participants; and when participants voluntarily enter primarily to achieve material outcomes, animating the situation with rational egoists generates empirically supported propositions. Or, if the situation is extremely simple and lacks any context that provides a clue as to who else is involved and the appropriate norms to use, individuals tend to rely primarily on what is best for themselves (Frohlich, Oppenheimer, and Kurki 2004).

Unlike motors, however, the animators of social life adapt and change over time. Humans do not have fixed characteristics. What makes understanding human behavior so difficult is exactly our capacity to try out multiple norms, heuristics, or strategies, and to learn to use one set in one situation while using different mixes in other situations. The reason we can characterize participants as rational egoists in an open, competitive market is because of the institution, *not* that all of the participants are narrowly selfish! The same individuals who energetically pursue profit-maximizing strategies from 8 A.M. to 5 P.M. every workday may also volunteer several evenings a month on neighborhood projects, contribute substantial funds to diverse charities, regularly vote, and be known to friends and coworkers as kind, considerate individuals who always do more than their share of any team project. These individuals are also likely to have biases in the way the world is interpreted and a variety of other human failings.

All of these aspects of humans are consistent with a theory of boundedly rational, fallible individuals who pursue multiple goals for themselves and others, adopt contextually relevant norms of behavior, and can learn better strategies in a particular situation over time—particularly if it generates accurate information about key variables. We need to draw on and expand the basic work of Herbert Simon, Vincent Ostrom, Douglass North, Reinhard Selten, Bryan Jones, Oliver Williamson, and others who have posited and continue to develop a general theory of bounded rationality.

Like all creatures honed by millennia of evolutionary processes, humans do seek beneficial outcomes for themselves. Information search is costly, and the information-processing capabilities of human beings are limited. Individuals, therefore, often must make choices based on incomplete knowledge of all possible alternatives and their likely outcomes. With incomplete information and imperfect information-processing capabilities, all individuals may make mistakes in choosing strategies designed to realize a set of goals (V. Ostrom 1986). Over time, however, individuals can acquire a greater understanding of their situation and adopt strategies or heuristics that result in higher returns. Bounded rationality, however, has focused mostly on the information condition related to how participants choose.

The theoretical challenge facing scholars today is developing an appropriate family of assumptions to make about the intrinsic values individuals place on actions and outcomes—particularly outcomes obtained by others. Individuals adopt norms of behavior taught them by parents and others in the situations in which they find themselves. Which norms are supported and become a strong influence affecting decisions is affected by the history of experiences that individuals have (or have not) shared and by the specific experiences they face in a particular decision situation. Humans tend to partition action situations into those where norms are not taken seriously into account and those where norms matter (Harsanyi 1955).

Social scientists have to match their initial assumptions about the orientations of participants to the situation they are trying to understand and explain. What kind of goods and services are involved, what rules, and what kind of community surrounds a particular situation? We have to ask whether the situation is stable or changing, conveys substantial information about its structure and the behavior of participants, tends to invoke norms such as trust and reciprocity (or those of an eye for an eye), and allows participants to adapt more effective strategies over time? The effort to develop better theory, specify testable propositions, and undertake carefully designed field and experimental work is crucial to our enterprise.

The two fundamental lessons from the vast empirical and theoretical research of the last several decades are: first, humans have complex motivations including narrow self-interest as well as norms of proper behavior and other-regarding preferences; and second, institutions matter! To move beyond these important lessons to better understand institutional diversity, we need to address three major issues: (1) How can we cut through the complexity to focus on problems that are ripe for further growth? (2) How can we include norms in our analysis without falling into the trap that all that is needed is to assume that individuals learn and use norms? and (3) How can we gain a better grasp of what we mean when we say that institutions matter?

A Focus on Collective Action to Overcome Social Dilemmas

First, to cut through the complexity we need to concentrate on broad areas of nonmarket situations. Market institutions work well when the goods involved are private goods. Individuals trying to provide public goods or sustain common-pool resources (as defined in chapter 1) find themselves facing a variety of social dilemmas that are not easy to solve. We are likely to make more progress if we do not try to develop a single *model* of human behavior that can be used to predict behavior in *all* market and nonmarket action situations. A more focused effort to explain collective action in overcoming social dilemmas appears to have a higher probability of success in the near future.

After all, traditional rational choice theory emerged from a consistent effort of many scholars to develop a rigorous theory and models of human choice within one broad type of institutional arrangement—that of a competitive market. The expansion of this theory to other types of action situations did not occur until long after it had proved itself to be successful in predicting outcomes in one type of institutional arrangement. It was not until the influential work of Kenneth Arrow (1951), Anthony Downs (1957), Mancur Olson (1965), William Riker (1962), and James Buchanan and Gordon Tullock (1962) that scholars began to take seriously the possibility of using rational choice theory to explain voting, legislative decisions, decisions within a hierarchy, and engagement in collective action to overcome social dilemmas. And we have learned a lot from this effort to apply a systematic theory to explain behavior in nonmarket situations.

Part of what we have learned is that highly competitive situations exist outside of the market where the narrow theory of rational behavior generates useful explanations for important empirical phenomena (Shepsle and Weingast 1984, 1987; Tsebelis 2002). We have also learned that the predictions of zero contributions derived from this theory are not supported in many social dilemmas. Explaining successful and unsuccessful efforts to engage in collective action to overcome social dilemmas should be a high priority for institutional theorists.

Explaining the diversity of outcomes in social dilemma situations is a puzzle that is ripe for further development given the quality and quantity of relevant research. It is also an important question to pursue if one presumes that humans are capable of developing, transmitting, and learning norms of trust, trustworthiness, reciprocity, and equity as well as learning how to govern themselves. Without further progress in developing our theories and models of human valuation in social dilemma situations, those convinced that all human behavior can be explained using rational egoist models will continue to recommend Leviathan-like remedies for overcoming all social dilemmas. Hopefully, much of what we learn from focusing on behavior in social dilemmas will be useful in other puzzling nonmarket situations.

In focusing on social dilemmas, we need to address how to focus on the role of norms and other-regarding preferences. Simply explaining puzzling findings post hoc, as "they must somehow share some norms," is not a satisfactory strategy in the long run. Focusing on norms and other-regarding preferences is not enough, however, to explain fully how individuals do overcome social dilemmas. Rules are needed to back up these norms (or counteract dangerously escalating negative reciprocity). We then need to dig into the analysis of institutions so that we can understand how individuals adopt norms as well as rules to overcome social dilemmas.

In the remainder of this chapter, we will focus on the role of norms in overcoming social dilemmas—how to represent norms, why they are important, why norms alone are not sufficient to cope with many collective-action problems, and how norms may evolve. Then, the rest of this book digs into the concept of institutions and tries to clarify the meaning of key concepts, the reason we need to develop a theoretically relevant way of classifying rules, the way we identify classes of rules used in the field, and the manner in which rules may be used as tools to affect the orientations of participants over time.

Norms Fostering Collective Action

Some scholars are hesitant to use the concept of norms because a generally accepted method for representing norms in formal models does not yet exist. Sometimes norms are simply used as a casual explanation after observing behavior that is not consistent with that predicted by noncooperative game theory. Arguing that "Oh, they must have been using a norm of reciprocity" as a post hoc explanation of puzzling behavior is not sufficient in the long run for arriving at empirically warrantable theory.

Representing norms in formal theory and then positing testable propositions from these theories is not immensely difficult. Many contemporary theorists add one or more symbols to the payoff function they examine in a formal game to represent the internal valuation that participants may place on outcomes that others may receive—other-regarding preferences—or on actions or outcomes to which an individual assigns an intrinsic value that differs from its extrinsic value (see Fehr and Gächter 1998; Frey 1997a, 1997b; Bolton and Ockenfels 2000).

Sue Crawford and I tackled this problem in 1995 in our *American Political Science Review* article "A Grammar of Institutions," which has been revised and updated as chapter 5 of this book. As we define them, norms are prescriptions held by an individual that an action or outcome in a situation must, must not, or may be permitted. Norms can be represented in formal analyses as a delta parameter that represents the intrinsic benefits or costs of obeying a normative prescription in a particular situation. The changes may occur as a result of intrinsic motivation such as pride

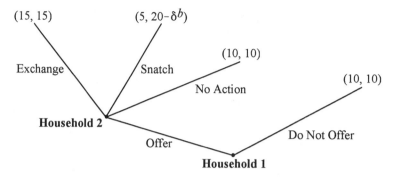

Figure 4.3 The Snatch Game with norms.

when keeping a norm or guilt when breaking a norm.[17] The delta parameter may also occur as a result of the action being observed by others leading to esteem for following a norm or shame for breaking it.

The Snatch Game—with Norms

As an example for the reader, it would be useful to illustrate how one could explicitly introduce the concept of norms into a formal game—the Snatch Game—presented in chapter 2. Norms change the internal value that participants place on an action or outcome in a situation (see figure 4.3). In the initial Snatch Game, participants did not possess norms against snatching goods. Thus, their internal preference functions could simply be represented as the value placed on the goods they received (or as a monotonic function thereof). Given this preference, Household 1 would predict that Household 2 would snatch any goods put out for exchange. Thus, Household 1 would not offer any goods in the first place.

Let us now assume that Household 2 has a norm against snatching goods. The preference function for Household 2 could now be represented as:

$$u_2 = \pi_2 - \delta^b, \text{ where}$$
$$\pi_2 = \text{payoff obtained by Household 2,}$$
$$-\delta^b = \text{decrease in the value of } \pi_2 \text{ for breaking the norm.}$$

Now, if Household 1 has good reason to believe that Household 2 has a norm against snatching, and that the size of the norm is greater than the value of the goods that could be snatched, then Household 1 is likely to put the goods out for exchange. Both Households are better off than they would be simply keeping their own commodities.

Whether the strength of the norm is sufficient to motivate Household 2 to refrain from snatching the commodities depends on the size of the delta parameter and not simply its presence. In this example, Household 2 would need to suffer a loss of more than five payoff units to offset what could be obtained by snatching. If the two households were embedded in a community with an effective observation and gossip network, so that anyone who snatched goods offered for sale would be likely to be observed and shamed, the shame of snatching might be enough to lead Household 2 to prefer an exchange rather than to snatch the goods.[18] If the intrinsic value of the norm is not high enough to compensate for the potential gain of material payoffs in a Snatch Game, then the behavior will be the same as in the earlier game. Thus, in addition to specifying that norms exist, the theorist needs to posit the relative size of the costs or benefits of following a norm. Norms can definitely change behavior but may not do so. Whether norms have an impact on behavior depends both on the strength of the norm and the context of the situation.

For norms against snatching goods offered for exchange to be effective without any rule enforcement present, a community in which the households are located needs to be relatively stable. All households must teach children the prescription against snatching other people's goods. All households must share the knowledge that all the other households are doing this. In other words, the presence, size, and sign of delta parameters must become common knowledge over time. A small clique of households who obtain a positive internal reward from the daring act of snatching goods could unravel years of stability in the exchange of agreements among the households.[19] In most market economies, where rules are relatively well enforced, shared norms play an important complementary role in enabling participants to engage in a wide diversity of economic transactions without relying entirely on external rule enforcers (Cooter and Ulen 1996).

The Problem of Heterogeneity

More puzzling than finding ways of representing norms in formal analyses is coping with the wide heterogeneity of norms that individuals learn and the internal strength that they attach to these norms. As illustrated by the experiments discussed in chapter 3, a substantial proportion of participants in social dilemmas is observed to take actions that are more cooperative than predicted for rational egoists. One must stress, however, that not all of the participants appear to have intrinsic delta parameters attached to the actions of trusting others, reciprocating trust, cooperating to solve collective-action problems, or sanctioning others who are not cooperative. Nor can we assume a uniform "delta" that everyone who is not a rational egoist would share.

Different participants have their own orientations and adopt diverse strategies in the same situation. In other words, we need to assume heterogeneity of preferences. The classic model of noncooperative game theory now becomes a *special* case for modeling situations where one assumes that individuals do not attach any internal value to following norms or to the payoffs received by others. Further, one can expect some individuals to behave in most situations in a manner consistent with this model.

Many new models have been posed in an effort to devise another *general* model of human behavior (see Rabin 1993; Ito, Saijo, and Une 1995; Chan et al. 1997; Levin 1998; Fehr and Gächter 2000a; Bolton and Ockenfels 2000; Gintis 2000a; Casari and Plott 2003). None of these general models are yet sufficiently well supported by experimental and field data that we can just substitute a new general model for the old classical general model. What is exciting, however, is that scholars are developing careful experimental designs precisely to examine how these competing models fare in critical experiments (see Cox 2004; Cox and Sadiraj 2004; Cox, Friedman, and Gjerstad 2004).

Many reasons exist for a concern that all of the explanations for cooperative behavior can be placed on a new model of individual behavior. Fundamentally, one has to know key information about the situation before one can specify the kind of values participants are likely to adopt. As discussed above in relation to the Snatch Game with norms, the norms that individuals may adopt in general may or may not be strong enough to overcome a temptation to break a norm in a particular situation. Further, for norms such as those leading an individual to be a conditional cooperator to generate positive returns, some arrangement for clustering conditional cooperators together is needed. Studies that look at niches, or spatial relationships among participants, often show that conditional reciprocity can lead to cooperation to overcome social dilemmas (Laland, Odling-Smee, and Feldman 2000).

A key requisite for successful cooperation is that conditional cooperators must be able to find one another—due to either institutional or spatial connections. If too many rational egoists surround conditional cooperators, cooperation can just collapse. It is also the case that some norms are potentially destructive rather than constructive (Boulding 1963). McGinnis (forthcoming) demonstrates for us how individuals engaged in threat systems can find themselves in ever deepening conflict situations.

What is important about recognizing that not all individuals in all situations act like rational egoists is that we can begin to take institutions very seriously. As Colin Camerer (2003, 117) captured the current situation:

"Institutional arrangements can be understood as responding to a world in which there are some sociopaths and some saints, but mostly regular folks who are capable of both kinds of behavior." Thus, institutions are among the tools that fallible humans use to change incentives to enable fallible humans to overcome social dilemmas. Sadly, however, institutions can also exacerbate bad outcomes as well as ameliorate them. We need to recognize that not only are humans complex systems; so are the structures they build. Thus, we need to really dig in and examine what we mean by institutions and how they can be used to overcome social dilemmas—a task that we will begin in chapter 5 and continue through the rest of the volume. Before we turn to this task, however, we need to examine the question of how human norms could survive in settings where rational egoists are initially a large part of a population.

Emergence and Survival of Norms in Evolutionary Processes

While evolutionary theory has been used for years to explain why only rational egoists can survive in a competitive process, recent developments in evolutionary theory are coming to a different set of conclusions (Maynard Smith and Harper 2003; Marcus 2004; Richerson, Boyd, and Paciotti 2002). Contemporary evolutionary theories provide useful ways of modeling the emergence and survival of multiple strategies in a population of participants. In a strict evolutionary model, individuals inherit strategies and do not change strategies in their lifetime. Those carrying the more successful strategies for a particular environment reproduce at a higher rate (Axelrod 1986). After many interactions, the more successful strategies come to prominence in the population.[20]

Human evolution occurred mostly during the long Pleistocene era that lasted for about 3 million years to about 10,000 years ago. During this era, humans roamed the earth in small bands of hunter-gatherers who were dependent on each other for mutual protection, sharing food, and providing for the young. Survival was dependent not only on aggressively seeking individual returns but also on solving many day-to-day collective-action problems. Those of our ancestors who solved these problems most effectively and learned how to recognize who was deceitful and who was a trustworthy reciprocator had a selective advantage over those who did not (see Barkow, Cosmides, and Tooby 1992; Ben-Ner and Putterman 2000a; Brown and Moore 2002). Humans have acquired well-honed skills at face recognition and strong abilities to detect cheating. Research provides evidence that humans keep rough internal accounts—both in regard to goodwill (McCabe and Smith 2003) and threats (Boulding 1963).[21]

Evolutionary psychologists who study the cognitive structure of the human brain speculate that humans do not develop general analytical skills that are then applied to a variety of specific problems. Humans are not terribly skilled at general logical problem solving (as any scholar who has taught probability theory to undergraduates can attest). Rather, the human brain appears to have evolved a domain-specific, human-reasoning architecture (Clark and Karmiloff-Smith 1991). For example, humans appear to use a different approach to reasoning about deontic relationships—what is forbidden, obligated, or permitted—as contrasted to reasoning about what is true and false. When reasoning about deontic relationships, humans tend to check for violations or cheaters (Manktelow and Over 1991). When reasoning about whether empirical relationships are true, they tend to use a confirmation strategy (Oaksford and Chater 1994). This deontic effect in human reasoning has repeatedly been detected even in children as young as three years old, and is not associated with overall intelligence or the educational level of the subject (Cummins 1996).

Recent studies have also examined how strategies are transmitted via diverse cultural processes and thus can evolve rapidly (Richerson and Boyd 2002; Henrich 2004; Sussman and Chapman 2004). Cultural transmission is largely enhanced by language. While evidence is mounting that some animals have gained simple languages (Kaminski, Call, and Fisher 2004), humans have acquired language skills involving thousands of words that can be combined, given the rules of a grammar, into an infinite number of sentences conveying both specific information about a situation as well as general conceptual and normative information (Bloom 2000). The acquisition of human language provides "a second system of 'heredity'" (Maynard Smith and Harper 2003, 140). This second system of heredity links the generations and is able to support rapid cultural change. "With language, genetic change ceases to be the main basis of change: history begins" (140).

Developments in evolutionary theory and supporting empirical research provide strong support for the assumption that modern humans have inherited a propensity to learn rules and norms similar to our inherited propensity to learn grammatical rules (Pinker 1994). In their chapter on the acquisition of language, Maynard Smith and Szathmáry (1997) stress the formal similarity between an "action grammar" and a "language grammar." Children begin to learn strategies of constructing sentences and undertaking rule-ordered actions in the world at about the same time in their development. Which prescriptions are learned, however, varies from one culture to another, across families, over time, and with exposure to diverse social norms expressed within various types of situations. In most societies, however, the norm of reciprocity—that one should return cooperative actions of others that benefit self, with similar efforts to help others—appears to be present to some extent related to specific activities, locations, and relationships among individuals. The evidence that individuals do learn norms of reciprocity—including a norm of punishing others who do not reciprocate cooperation as well as punishing those who do not punish others—is steadily mounting (Bowles and Gintis 2004).

The Indirect Evolutionary Approach to Adaptation through Experience

Recent work on an *indirect* evolutionary approach to the study of human behavior offers a rigorous theoretical approach for understanding how preferences—including those associated with social norms—may evolve or adapt in shorter time horizons than posited in biological evolutionary theory (Güth and Yaari 1992; Güth 1995). In an indirect evolutionary model, players receive objective payoffs (measuring economic or reproductive success), but make decisions based on the transformation of these material rewards into their own intrinsic values. Those who place a value on reciprocity, fairness, and being trustworthy can be thought of as adding a subjective delta parameter to actions (of themselves or others) that are consistent or not consistent with their norms. This approach allows individuals to start with a predisposition to act in a certain way, but it allows preferences to adapt within a generation (rather than over many generations) given the objective payoffs received depending on the interpretation of the evolutionary dynamics.[22]

Social dilemmas are particularly useful for exploring the indirect evolutionary approach. An indirect evolutionary approach explains how a mixture of norm-users and rational egoists would emerge in settings where standard rational choice theory assumes the presence of rational egoists alone. In this approach, social norms may lead individuals to behave differently in the same objective situation depending on how strongly they value conformance with (or deviance from) a norm. Rational egoists can be thought of as having intrinsic payoffs that are the same as objective payoffs since they do not value the social norm of reciprocity.

Conditional cooperators (to add one additional type of player) would be modeled as placing a positive delta parameter on (1) contributing to a group outcome in a Commons Dilemma or (2) trusting others when in the position of an Investor or on being trustworthy when in the position of a Trustee in the Trust Game. By their behavior and resulting interaction, however, different types of players are likely to gain differential objective returns. In a Trust game where players are chosen from a population that initially contains some proportion of rational egoists and conditional co-operators, the level of information about player types affects the relative proportion of rational egoists and conditional cooperators over time. With complete information regarding the presence and size of a delta parameter, conditional cooperators playing a trustworthy strategy will more frequently receive the higher extrinsic payoff, while rational egoists will consistently receive a lower payoff since others will not trust them.

In indirect evolutionary theory, only trustworthy participants survive in an indefinitely repeated social dilemma characterized by complete information about the past actions of all subjects (Güth and Kliemt 1998, 386). If one thinks of this theory as a learning process, those who were less successful would tend to learn the intrinsic values or delta parameters of those who had achieved higher material rewards (Börgers and Sarin 1997).[23] Where a player's type is common knowledge, rational egoists would not survive. Conditional cooperators interacting with other known conditional cooperators will obtain higher payoffs and come to dominance.

Full and accurate information about all players' intrinsic preference, however, is a strong assumption and difficult to achieve. When participants try to limit who else is involved in overcoming dilemmas to others who live in a community and who can establish a reputation for being trustworthy, they may be able to create the conditions needed for the evolution of conditional cooperators to become the dominant type of player.

If there is no information about player preferences for a relatively large population, preferences are predicted to evolve so that only rational egoists survive.[24] If information about the proportion of a population that are trustworthy is known, and the first player has no information about the trustworthiness of a specific second player, Güth and Kliemt (1998) derive a prediction that first players will trust second players as long as the expected return of meeting trustworthy players and receiving the higher payoff exceeds the expected payoff obtained when neither player trusts the other. In such a setting, however, the share of the population held by the norm-using types is bound to decline. On the other hand, if there is a noisy signal about a player's type that is at least more accurate than a random signal, trustworthy types can survive as a substantial proportion of the population. Noisy signals may result from seeing one another, face-to-face communication, and various internal accounting mechanisms that humans have evolved to monitor each other's behavior. As we discuss later in this volume, the institutions that humans craft to cope with diverse problems can affect the kind of information that individuals obtain about each other's past actions.

Evidence Testing the Indirect Evolutionary Theory

Indirect evolutionary theory is able to explain how a mixture of contingent cooperators and rational egoists would emerge in settings where traditional game theory predicts that only rational egoists should prevail. Given the recent development of this approach, *direct* tests of this theory are not yet extensive. From the viewpoint of an indirect evolutionary process, participants in a collective-action problem would begin an interaction with differential, intrinsic preferences over outcomes due to their initial predispositions toward norms such as reciprocity and trust. Participants would learn about the likely behavior of others and shift their behavior in light of the experience and the objective payoffs they have received. Several recent experiments provide evidence of these kinds of contingent behaviors and behavioral shifts.[25]

In a one-shot, sequential, double-blind, Prisoner's Dilemma experiment, for example, the players were asked to rank their preferences over the final outcomes after they had made their own choice, but before they knew their partner's decision. Forty percent of a pool of 136 subjects ranked the cooperative outcome (C,C) higher than the outcome if they defect while the other cooperates (D,C), and 27 percent were indifferent between these outcomes, even though their individual monetary payoff was higher in the latter outcome (Ahn, Ostrom, and Walker 2003). This finding confirms that not all players enter a collective-action situation as pure forward-looking rational egoists who make decisions based solely on individual outcomes.[26] Some bring with them a set of norms and values that can support cooperation.

On the other hand, preferences based on these norms can be altered by bad experiences. One set of 72 subjects played 12 rounds of a finitely repeated Prisoner's Dilemma game where we randomly matched partners before each round. Rates of cooperation were very low. Many players experienced multiple instances where partners declined to cooperate (Ahn, Ostrom, and Walker 2003). In light of these unfortunate experiences, only 19 percent of the respondents now ranked (C,C) above (D,C) while 17 percent were indifferent (ibid.). In this uncooperative setting, the norms supporting cooperation and reciprocity were diminished by experience, but not eliminated.[27]

In another version of the Prisoner's Dilemma game, Cain (1998) first had players participate in a "Dictator Game"—in which one player divides a sum of money, and the other player must accept the division, whatever it is—and then a Prisoner's Dilemma game. "Stingy players," defined as those who retained at least 70 percent of their endowment in the earlier Dictator Game, tended to predict that all players would defect in the Prisoner's Dilemma game. "Nice players," defined as those who gave away at least 30 percent of their endowment, tended to predict that other nice players would cooperate and stingy players would defect. Before playing the Prisoner's Dilemma game, players were told whether their opponent had been "stingy" or "nice" in the dictator game. Nice players chose cooperation in the Prisoner's Dilemma game 69 percent of the time when they were paired with other nice players and 39 percent of the time when they were paired with stingy players.

Finally, interesting experimental (as well as field) evidence has accumulated that external imposed rules tend to "crowd out" endogenous cooperative behavior (see Frey 1994). For example, consider some paradoxical findings of Frohlich and Oppenheimer (1996) from a Prisoner's Dilemma game. One set of players—the control group—played a regular Prisoner's Dilemma game (some with communication and some without). A second set of players used an externally imposed, incentive-compatible mechanism designed to enhance cooperative choices. In the first phase of the experiment, the second set of participants gained higher monetary returns than those in the control group, as expected. In the second phase of the experiment, both groups played a regular Prisoner's Dilemma game. To the surprise of the experimenters, a higher level of cooperation occurred in the control groups that played the regular Prisoner's Dilemma in both phases, especially for those who communicated on a face-to-face basis. The greater cooperation that had occurred due to the exogenously created incentive-compatible mechanism appeared to be transient. The authors speculated that removing the external mechanism undermined subsequent cooperation. Having an effective rule imposed on them, even though it induced them to improve their outcomes, appeared to leave the players worse off once it was removed, in comparison with the players in the control group who relied entirely on face-to-face communication.

The studies by Fehr and Rockenbach (2003) and Cardenas, Stranlund, and Willis (2000), discussed in chapter 3, have confirmed the notion that external rules and monitoring can crowd out cooperative behavior. These studies typically find that a social norm, especially in a setting where there is communication between the parties, can work as well or nearly as well at generating cooperative behavior as an externally imposed set of rules and system of monitoring and sanctioning. Moreover, norms seem to have a certain staying power in encouraging a growth of the desire for cooperative behavior over time, while cooperation that is primarily there due to externally imposed and enforced rules can disappear very quickly. Finally, the worst of all worlds may be one where external authorities impose rules but are able to achieve only weak monitoring and sanctioning. In a world of strong external monitoring and sanctioning, cooperation is enforced without any need for internal norms to develop. In a world of no external rules or monitoring, norms can evolve to support cooperation. In an in-between case, a low level of external monitoring discourages the formation of social norms, while also making it attractive for some players to deceive and defect, given the low risk of being caught.

Conclusion

The institutional analyst at the beginning of the twenty-first century faces a challenging task in animating analyses of expected behavior in a wide diversity of situations. To do a detailed analysis of expected behavior, the analyst must first ask some crucial questions about the action situation. First, does the situation generate substantial information about the structure of the situation itself? Second, do individuals voluntarily enter the situation in order to compete for valued, objective outcomes such as income, commodities, winning an election, beating others in a sports tournament? Third, do those who engage in this type of situation place primary value on obtaining the immediate objective outcomes of the situation? If the answers to these three questions lead the analyst to conclude that the situation is an open competitive situation focused primarily on objective payoffs, then using the assumptions of a rational egoist to animate the model is the best strategy. When all of these factors are present, the theorist is likely to make predictions about behavior and outcomes that are supported by empirical data.

On the other hand, if the situation is a social dilemma rather than an open competitive process, I would urge the analyst to animate an initial analysis assuming that participants hold multiple value orientations and use strategies ranging from those used by rational egoists to those used by players who value trust, reciprocity, and equity very highly. The relative proportion of each type of player that would survive after repetition of the situation would depend heavily on multiple aspects of the structure of the situation and the initial distribution of types as affected by the biophysical world, the rules in use, and the community in which it is embedded.

If the dilemma involved many individuals located in diverse settings around the world who have little opportunity to communicate and share no common rules—like an open-access ocean fishery or the global atmosphere—then the best predictions and explanations of behavior would be derived from assuming that most participants are rational egoists. Conditional cooperators can do little without an appropriate institutional structure to support their norms. Those who would like to cooperate with others find themselves unable to do anything but follow the dominant strategy. Recent evidence related to the massive depletion of fisheries in the open oceans confirms this prediction (Myers and Worm 2003).

This points to the importance of larger institutions that enable participants in social dilemma situations to have sufficient autonomy that they can change the rules that affect their ongoing situations. If individuals face a social dilemma situation repeatedly and they have the autonomy to change the rules that structure it so as to enhance the probability that the proportion of conditional cooperators and willing punishers can grow over time, many individuals have crafted ingenious institutions that help them reach mutually productive rather than mutually unproductive outcomes.

Given the importance of institutions in affecting the structure of a situation and the population of types of individuals who are most likely to come to prominence in a particular type of situation, we now need to tackle a major focus of this book—the rules that humans can use as tools to fashion the action situations they engage in repeatedly. The biophysical world and the attributes of a community work together with rules to constitute action situations that enhance or reduce the likelihood of individuals reaching better outcomes. Rules are the tools, however, that fallible humans can use to try to change situations to achieve better outcomes.

In chapter 5, we will focus on how rules, norms, and strategies share some attributes and differ on others. A high level of confusion exists in the literature as to what these concepts mean. It is hard to develop better policies to overcome collective-action problems when scholars disagree on fundamental terms such as these. In chapter 6, we will then focus on the question of why we should classify rules themselves. In chapter 7, we will develop a systematic language for identifying and classifying rules. In chapter 8, we will illustrate many of the rules actually used in field settings and develop a theoretical calculus for how appropriators from a common-pool resource decide to change the rules affecting their interactions. Chapter 9 will then focus on what types of resource governance regimes tend to be robust in a changing world.

As scholars and as policy analysts, we need to learn the artisanship of working with rules so as to improve how situations operate over time. Human beings are neither all-knowing saints nor devilish knaves. The institutions they grow up in—families, schools, playgrounds, neighborhoods—differentially reward or punish them over time so that intrinsic and extrinsic motivations are learned and developed over time. The situations they find themselves facing as adults in the workplace and their community also affect which norms they use and the outcomes they reach.

When individuals learn the artisanship of crafting rules, they can experiment and learn to create more productive outcomes (as well as participants) over time. Learning to craft rules that attract and encourage individuals who share norms of reciprocity and trustworthiness, or who learn them over time, is a fundamental skill needed in all democratic societies.

Part II

FOCUSING ON RULES

Five

A Grammar of Institutions

SUE CRAWFORD AND ELINOR OSTROM

CHAPTER 4 focuses on the challenge that social scientists face in animating analyses of social situations so as to generate understandings and predictions that are then tested.[1] The need to study holons within holons makes this a difficult process. Until recently, political economists had at least one unchanging constant in their analyses—the model of the individual used. One paid primary attention to the focal action situation and then asked what participants modeled as rational egoists would do in this situation. The general strategy recommended in this book is similar but more difficult. First, one needs to examine the structure of the situation. Then one asks how boundedly rational, fallible but adaptive individuals would interact in that situation over time.

In this chapter, we return to the task of analyzing the structure of situations so as to better model the interaction of actors in those situations. Earlier chapters establish the basic components of diverse action situations. Here we turn to analysis of specific kinds of institutional statements that shape incentives in action situations. Specifically, we elucidate a syntax that illustrates the similarities and differences between shared strategies, norms, and rules. These concepts are not clearly distinguished in much contemporary social science literature. In this chapter, we show why there is so much confusion and provide tools to clarify the distinct influences of each kind of institutional statement on human interaction in diverse action situations. As in other chapters, we illustrate how the grammar works for institutional analysis that uses various research approaches.

Parsing Institutional Statements

We view the concept of an *institutional statement* as a broad term encompassing three types of statements—rules, norms, and shared strategies. These statements describe opportunities and constraints that create expectations about other actors' behavior. In other words, an "institutional statement" encompasses a broad set of *shared* linguistic constraints and opportunities that prescribe, permit, or advise actions or outcomes for participants in an action situation. We stress the shared nature of these concepts. Many written statements have the form of a rule (or a norm or strategy) but are not known to participants and do not affect behavior. Such statements are considered rules-in-form rather than rules-in-use (Sproule-Jones 1993). We concentrate our attention here on rules-in-use. As the Institutional Analysis and Development (IAD) framework stresses, these shared linguistic constraints interact with influences from the bio-physical world and those attributes of the community not easily under-stood as institutional statements (for example, ethnic heterogeneity) to shape the structure of the action situation.

The grammar tool allows analysts to distinguish more systematically between institutional statements that are best understood as attributes of the community (strategies and norms) and those that are best understood as rules. This distinction recognizes that rules operate in such a distinct way in action situations that analysts need to know when an institutional statement is a rule and when it is not.

We focus on rules for two basic reasons. First, institutional analysts conducting policy analysis are frequently asked to analyze the impact of some change in rules—either a change that has already occurred or the possible impacts of a proposed change. Second, institutional analysts working to craft solutions to negative outcomes in an action situation recognize that changes in the rules may be easier or more stable than attempts to change the situation through changes in the biophysical world or attributes of the community. The grammar of institutions provides a tool to help those crafting institutions to ensure that the institutional state-ments that they craft are indeed rules, so that they can better predict the influence that the institutional statement will have on the action situation and better tap into the institutional strengths that rules provide.

We assume with von Wright (1968) that rules can be expressed using two basic linguistic forms. One is a generative form: "let there be an X." Rules that create positions (e.g., voter, judge, mayor) or organized bodies (e.g., the U.S. Senate) are generative rules. The other is a regulatory form, which has a more complex syntax elucidated in this chapter. We return to a brief discussion of generative rules in chapter 7 when we examine the challenge of classifying and using rules.

In this chapter, we posit that regulatory rules are one grammatical step away from norms and two steps away from strategies. Our explicit recog-nition of the differences between rules, norms, and strategies clarifies ana-lytical questions about the similarities among these concepts and about the existence and origin of institutional rules. Using this grammar, one can ask *clear* questions about when strategies or norms evolve into rules and why.

The grammar of institutions thus provides a syntax for analyzing and expressing institutional statements that can be used to distinguish systematically among rules, norms, and shared strategies. It draws on and speaks to discussions of rules, norms, and institutions from a wide range of the social sciences. But first, a disclaimer: we do not assume that institutional statements affecting behavior can always be articulated easily and fully by participants. Knowledge of institutional statements often becomes habituated and part of the tacit knowledge of a community (Epstein 2001). Moreover, we do not assume that all individuals recognize the existence of an institutional grammar and explicitly use it to formulate institutional statements. The grammar of institutions is a logical tool that complements other ways of representing institutional phenomena. It is a useful tool for summarizing and analyzing the content of institutional statements, distinguishing between types of institutional statements, and studying the formation and evolution of institutional statements.

The Syntax of a Grammar of Institutions

In this section, we identify the syntax and components of a grammar of regulatory rules that can be used in the analysis of institutional statements. To ease the discussion of the syntax, we provide five examples of typical institutional statements. We refer to these examples throughout this chapter.

1. All male, U.S. citizens over eighteen years of age must register with the Selective Service by filling out a form at the U.S. Post Office or else face arrest for evading registration.

2. All senators may move to amend a bill after a bill has been introduced, or else the senator attempting to forbid another senator from taking this action by calling him or her out of order will be called out of order or ignored.

3. All villagers must not let their animals trample the irrigation channels, or else the villager who owns the livestock will have to pay a fine.

4. If you use the microwave, you must clean up your own mess!

5. The person who places a phone call, calls back when the call gets disconnected.

Let us now turn to the syntax that we will use to analyze these and other examples.

The general syntax of this grammar includes five components: [ATTRIBUTE], [DEONTIC], [AIM], [CONDITIONS], and [OR ELSE] where,

A ATTRIBUTES is a holder[2] for any value of a participant-level variable that distinguishes to whom the institutional statement applies. Examples include eighteen years of age, female, college educated, 1-year experience, or a specific position, such as employee or chairperson.

D *DEONTIC* is a holder for the three modal verbs analyzed by von Wright. These are "may" (permitted), "must" (obliged), and "must not" (forbidden).

I *AIM* is a holder that describes particular actions or outcomes in the action situation to which the deontic is assigned. An *AIM* may include a formula specifying an amount of action or outcome or a description of a process for an action.

C *CONDITIONS* is a holder for those variables that define when and where an action or outcome is permitted, obligatory, or forbidden.

O *OR ELSE* is a holder for the institutionally assigned consequence for not following a rule.

There are several advantages of using this ADICO syntax. First, elements from the syntax make up all three types of institutional statements. Second, elements from the syntax also distinguish among these three types of statements. Rules contain all five components (ADICO). Norms contain four components (ADIC) and shared strategies contain three components (AIC). Third, the syntax provides a format for writing institutional statements in a consistent manner. Regardless of how institutional statements are expressed in natural language, they can be rewritten or summarized in the ADICO format.

All regulative rules can be written as: [ATTRIBUTES] [DEONTIC] [AIM] [CONDITIONS] [OR ELSE]; all norms can be written as: [ATTRIBUTES] [DEONTIC] [AIM] [CONDITIONS]; and all shared strategies can be written as: [ATTRIBUTES] [AIM] [CONDITIONS]. By writing the statements in a consistent manner, we can then better compare the institutional statements in use in a variety of settings.[3] Finally, since the addition or subtraction of components switches institutional statements from one type to another, the syntax provides a tool for analyzing the evolution of institutional statements from one type to another.

The Syntax Components

We now turn to a discussion of the components of the ADICO syntax. Understanding the components helps analysts develop common methods of distinguishing between rules, norms, and strategies to cumulate knowledge for key questions such as: What difference does it make if the prescription is a rule or a norm? and What difference does it make if an institutional statement is a shared strategy or a norm? The syntax does not eliminate all gray areas. One gray area of particular concern to many scholars since the original publication of the syntax has been the precise point at which a norm can be said to have evolved into a rule. The discussion of the OR ELSE component here clarifies this distinction between norms and rules to address some of these concerns.

ATTRIBUTES

All institutional statements apply to a subset of participants in an action situation. The subset can range from one participant to all participants. A set of ATTRIBUTES establishes the subset of the participants affected by a particular statement. If individuals make up the participants in an action situation, the ATTRIBUTES will be individual-level values. Individual-level ATTRIBUTES include values assigned to variables such as age, residence, sex, citizenship, and position.[4] When the participants governed by a set of institutions are corporate actors, rather than individuals, the ATTRIBUTES refer to organizational variables such as size of membership, geographic location, or who owns the residuals.

In the first example, the relevant ATTRIBUTES are: male, citizen of the U.S., and over eighteen years old. Some version of the fourth example, the microwave cleanup statement, can often be found taped to the door of a community microwave. The beginning of that statement, "If you use the microwave," could be parsed as the ATTRIBUTE of "microwave users." In the last example, the ATTRIBUTE is the caller who placed the call. The other examples list no specific attribute. When no specific attribute is listed, the default value for the ATTRIBUTE component is: all members of the group.[5] This means that the ATTRIBUTE component always has something in it, even when a specific attribute is not contained in the statement. Thus, the second example applies to all senators in a legislature, and the third example applies to all villagers in a particular village.

Within a particular action situation, the ATTRIBUTE component of institutional statements maps the authority or prescription of an institutional statement to particular positions or to all positions. In order for this assignment to work, then, there must be other institutional statements that assign participants into positions (discussed as boundary rules in chapter 7). When analyzing an institutional statement with specific positions in the ATTRIBUTES component, it is important to extract the rules assigning participants into positions in order to understand how a specific institutional statement with that position actually works in the action situation.

DEONTIC

The DEONTIC component draws on the modal operations used in deontic logic to distinguish prescriptive from nonprescriptive statements (see von Wright 1951; Hilpinen 1971, 1981). The complete set of DEON-TIC operators, D, consists of permitted P, obliged O, and forbidden F. The logical relationships among the DEONTIC operators include the following:

$$D = P \cup O \cup F.$$
$$F \cap P = \varnothing; \; O \cap P = O; \text{ and } F \cap O = \varnothing.$$
$$\text{If } O \text{ then } P.$$

Institutional statements use the operative phrases *may, must/should*, and *must not/should not* to assign these operators to actions and outcomes. "Should" and "must" are both commonly used to oblige a person to act. Similarly, "must not" and "should not" both forbid. For the sake of simplicity, we use "must" and "must not" throughout this chapter in nearly all examples. However, the deontic terms can be used equally well for "should" statements. Generally, in everyday language, "must" obligates someone more strongly than "should," and "must not" forbids someone more strongly than "should not." Later in the chapter we describe how delta parameters allow more precision in the weight of the Oblige or Forbid and thus can be used to distinguish between "should" and "must" when needed in analysis.

The statement that all members *may* vote assigns the DEONTIC permitted, P, to the action of voting. The assignment of a DEONTIC operator to an action $[a_i]$ may be represented as $[D]\,[a_i]$, where D stands for P, O, or F. Similarly, $[D]\,[o_i]$ represents the assignment of a deontic to an outcome.

DEONTIC OPERATORS RELATE TO THE PHYSICALLY POSSIBLE

Regulation refers to statements about what is presumed to be physically possible. A person cannot logically be required to undertake an action that is physically impossible for anyone to do. As expressed by von Wright in regard to actions: "The notion of ability or can do . . . signifies ability so to say in its 'naked form,' subject only to the restrictions imposed by the laws of nature (including the limits of man's innate capabilities of growth and learning). Within this broad concept of ability (can do) one can distinguish a narrower concept. When, in this narrower sense, we say of an agent that he can do or that it is possible for him to do a certain thing, we mean that his doing of this thing will not violate a set of rules (norms) or conditions such as, for example, the rules of a certain legal order or moral code" (von Wright 1966, 33). The DEONTIC operators are related to each of the components of an action situation. In the above paragraph, the DEONTIC operators are related to actions. In scope rules, the operators refer to outcome variables. In information rules, the operators refer to communication channels.

The three DEONTIC operators are interdefinable (von Wright 1968, 143). In other words, if one of them is taken as a primitive, or the initial starting point, the other two can be defined in terms of this primitive. For example, let us use permission P as a primitive. If we are referring to a possible action $[a_i]$, then $[P] [a_i]$ would be read: One is permitted to do a_i, or one *may* do a_i. The statement that an act is forbidden $[F][a_i]$ can be restated using P as the primitive as $[~P][a_i]$. In other words, when an action is forbidden, one is not permitted to do $[a_i]$. On the other hand, if the negation of an action $[~a_i]$ is forbidden, one is obliged to take the action. The statement that an act must be done, $[O][a_i]$, can be defined as $[~P][~a_i]$. If an action is obligatory, one is not permitted to not do $[a_i]$. Alternatively, we could use F as the primitive. Then, P can be defined as $[~F][a_i]$ and O can be defined as $[F][~a_i]$. With O as the primitive, P can be defined as $[~O][a_i$ or $~a_i]$, while F can be defined as $[O][~a_i]$. This same interdefinability exists for prescriptions that refer to outcomes instead of actions. Any prescriptions with a DEONTIC assigned to some OUTCOME, o_i, can be restated using either of the other two DEONTIC operators.

The first four examples listed above can be restated using F as the primitive yielding the following:

1. U.S. citizens with [ATTRIBUTES] $[F] [~a_1]$ [CONDITIONS] [OR ELSE]
All male, U.S. citizens, over eighteen years of age are forbidden not to register with the Selective Service by filling out a form at the U.S. Post Office, or else face arrest for evading the draft.
2. Senators [All] $[~F] [a_2]$ [CONDITIONS] [OR ELSE]
All senators are not forbidden to move an amendment to a bill after a bill has been introduced, or else the senator attempting to forbid another senator from taking this action by calling him or her out of order will be called out of order or ignored.
3. Villagers [All] $[F] [o_3]$ [CONDITIONS] [OR ELSE]
All villagers are forbidden to let their animals trample the irrigation channels, or else the villager who owns the livestock will have to pay a fine.
4. [Microwave users] $[F] [~a_4]$ [CONDITIONS]
Microwave users are forbidden to not clean up their own mess.

Notice that the fifth example stated earlier has no DEONTIC. The fifth statement does not state a "must" and "must not" or a "may." This means that the strategy of the person, who initiated a telephone call being the one who "calls back" if the call is interrupted, does not contain a DEONTIC component. It is a strategy rather than a norm or a rule.

The meaning of the DEONTICS *Obliged* ("must") and *Forbidden* ("must not") fit well into most conceptions of normative statements. The meaning of *Permitted* ("may") is more perplexing for many scholars. For example, Susan Shimanoff (1980, 44) concludes that "it is incongruous to talk of rules prescribing behavior which is merely permitted." Her conclusion begs the question that we address here—namely, what does it mean for a rule or norm to *permit* an action?

Statements that assign permission (*P*) to an action influence the structure of action situations in at least three ways. Most often, rules and norms that assign permission define constraints on permission by establishing limited CONDITIONS in which permission exists. In the United States, consumers above the age of twenty-one may purchase alcohol in most states. In some states, Sunday liquor laws constrain this permission further and allow consumers above the age of twenty-one to purchase alcohol only Monday through Saturday. In effect, these rules establish the settings in which permission exists and thus forbid the action in circumstances that do not meet the stated CONDITIONS. A rule that grants permission to cut trees with a permit from a forestry agency implies that the absence of a permit renders tree cutting forbidden.

Less often, assigning a "may" to an action is the equivalent of "constituting" that action (Searle 1969). For example, a statement that an individual may vote in an election creates an action—voting—that did not exist before. The rule assigning the permitted action constitutes the action. These permission rules, then, add new action options to the action situation that did not exist before.

Finally, some permission rules change the action situation by granting participants with particular attributes a right to take an action. For example, voting in some political systems is a legal right. As Commons ([1924] 1968) warns, however, the permission to vote does not operate as an effective legal right unless at least one other rule assigns a duty to someone else. Others, who have a duty to recognize a person's right, are the ones who are forbidden or required to take actions or affect outcomes.[6] The Voting Rights Act of 1965 included rules that assigned the United States the duty of ensuring that African Americans were permitted to vote. That legislation converted a simple permission to vote into a right to vote.

John R. Commons ([1924] 1968), drawing upon the work of Wesley Hohfeld (1964), further develops the meaning of permission in the form

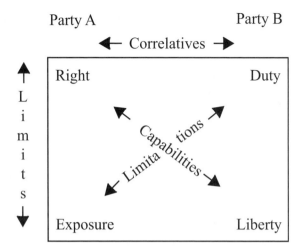

Figure 5.1 Authorized relationships: authority to act. *Source*: V. Ostrom and E. Ostrom 1999, 46.

of rights by clarifying the relationships between rights and duty. He argues that a *right* depends on a correlative obligation or *duty* on the part of others to act in accordance with the right being asserted. Rights are subject to limits. Limits bearing upon any right define the area of decision making where a claimant stands *exposed*. Thus, Commons has defined the limit of a *right* as an *exposure*. The correlative of an *exposure* is beyond the limit of a *duty*. A person who is no longer under duty is at *liberty* to act. Thus, the correlative of an *exposure* is a *liberty*. When these are represented in a boxed space, as in figure 5.1, the correlatives indicate the reciprocal interdependencies among two different legal parties or sets of legal parties. The limits are applied to each particular party. Taken together, the diagonal or reciprocal relationship represented by *right* and *liberty* establish the *capabilities* assigned to both parties. The *duty* and *exposure* establish the *limitations* assigned to their respective decision-making capabilities. The correlates in figure 5.1 result from rule configurations, not from a single permission rule. One would need to go beyond the parsing of single rules to define the full set of rights, liberties, duties, and exposures of actors within an action situation.[7]

   If a permission rule exists in an action situation, with no rule that assigns a duty to some position to ensure that those permitted to act are able to do so, then the permission rule simply establishes that one (or more) participants are allowed to take this action without having a right to take it. Others are exposed to this liberty. The U.S. Constitution permits people who meet certain attributes to run for the office of president. Labor laws permit individuals over a set age to be legal employees. These rules establish eligibility. They do not confer "rights" because another rule does not assign someone the duty to allow anyone meeting those attributes to be president. Nor do U.S. laws assign duties to anyone to ensure full employment of those of legal working age. Although these permission institutions do not confer rights, because they do not assign a duty to anyone to ensure that the actions can be carried out, these permission institutions *do* create liberties. They constrain efforts by others to *forbid* a participant to take the permitted A*I*M. Notice that the rule in the second example contains an OR ELSE that indicates what happens when senators attempt to treat the permitted action as forbidden (the offending senator is called out of order or ignored).[8] Even without an established right, the assignment of permission influences the opportunities and constraints in the action situation.

REPRESENTING DEONTICS IN FORMAL ANALYSIS

What does including a DEONTIC in an institutional statement imply for the way a formal game is analyzed? As initially discussed in chapter 4, it implies that the payoff structure for individuals in situations where they share common understandings related to prescriptions will differ from similar situations in which players merely accept a shared understanding of prudent, rational action. Our way to capture this change in the payoffs is to add parameters, called delta parameters, to the payoffs related to conforming or not conforming to a shared prescription. In simple terms, delta parameters are added to an individual's payoff to represent the perceived costs and rewards of obeying (o) or breaking (b) a prescription. The delta parameters can thus be defined as:

$\Delta = \delta^o + \delta^b$, where
Δ = the sum of all delta parameters
δ^o = the change in expected payoffs from *obeying* a prescription
δ^b = the change in expected payoffs from *breaking* a prescription.

One can further divide these rewards and costs into those that arise from external versus strictly internal sources of valuation. Thus:

$\delta^o = \delta^{oe} + \delta^{oi}$ and $\delta^b = \delta^{be} + \delta^{bi}$, where
e = changes in expected payoffs originating from external sources
i = changes in expected payoffs originating from internal sources.

The distinction between external and internal sources of delta parameters is similar to that of Coleman (1987) between "internalized norms" and "externally sanctioned norms." Delta parameters originating from external sources are a way to capture the benefits and costs of establishing a particular reputation (see Kreps 1990). The delta parameters originating from internal sources can be thought of as the guilt or shame felt when breaking a prescription and the pride or "warm glow" felt when following a prescription—particularly if it is costly to follow in a particular situation (Andreoni 1988; Ledyard 1995). "People who have developed an internal sanctioning system, for example, feel guilt and shame at behaving in a deviant way" (Bicchieri 1997, 19).

The analyst may not wish to focus on all four parameters in any particular analysis. Three of the four delta parameters could be assigned a zero value in a game-theoretic analysis involving a norm or a rule. In order to analyze the impact of a DEONTIC on expected outcomes of a game, however, at least one of the delta parameters must have a nonzero value. In situations where it is reasonable to assume that all players who break the prescription feel the same cost, the delta parameters can be modeled as if they were the same for all players and as if their magnitude is public information. As discussed in chapter 4, the theorist can also model players as having different orientations (Harsanyi 1967–68) for situations where actors react differentially to breaking prescriptions. One player can perceive the costs of breaking a prescription (δ^{bi} or δ^{be}) to be high while another perceives costs (δ^{bi} or δ^{be}) to be low. Coleman's (1988) zealot, for example, is a player with high external deltas for obeying norms (a high positive δ^{oe}).

If an action is forbidden by a norm and an individual engages in that action, we expect that player to experience some type of cost represented by at least one component of delta. If norms indicate that an A*I*M is *permitted*, then we expect that others, who treat that action as if it were forbidden, will experience some cost. In other words, norms or rules that forbid or require some A*I*M will be reflected in a cost parameter to the individuals to whom the prescription applies. Agreements that establish permission for an action place the cost parameter on others. Others may experience a cost if they try to obstruct an individual when a shared norm indicates that the individual is permitted to take that action.[9]

The existence of a DEONTIC implies the presence of additional information that individuals use in developing their expectations about others' behavior and thus their own best response. If players share a norm, the payoff structure looks different from the payoff structure for a similar situation in which the players do not share a norm. The payoffs may even change enough so that the predicted outcome of the game differs entirely from that predicted by a similar game that includes no delta parameters. Uncertainty about whether other actors, who have accepted certain norms, are present in a situation may be sufficient grounds for changing the behavior of players. Kreps and colleagues (1982) have analyzed repeated Prisoner's Dilemma games where information asymmetries exist among players concerning the probability that other players will play tit-for-tat.[10] In such games, players who are "perfectly rational" (i.e., the players' payoff functions have a zero value for delta components associated with playing tit-for-tat) will adopt behavior consistent with the norm for most of the game.

AIM

The AIM is the specific description of a working part in an action situation to which an institutional statement refers. The description can include information about a process (filling out a form at the U.S. Post Office) or a formula (pay $10 per hour worked). In order for an institutional statement to influence behavior, the AIM must be physically possible and its negation [$\sim a_i$] must also be physically possible. An individual cannot logically be required to undertake a physically impossible action, and prescribing an action can only influence behavior if it is physically possible to not do that action. The capability of voting implies the capability of not voting. Voting for candidate A implies the option of not voting for candidate A. The AIM sometimes specifies states of affairs in the world or an outcome instead of an action. Outcomes, like actions, must also be possible and avoidable to be parts of a well-formed institutional statement. Moreover, any particular outcome [o_i] implies the existence of its negation [$\sim o_i$].

In the first example given earlier, the AIM is the action (a_1) of registering for the Selective Service by filling out a form at the U.S. Post Office and the DEONTIC operator required, O, is assigned to the action for all individuals with the ATTRIBUTES listed in the rule. In the second example, the AIM is the action of offering a motion to amend a bill and the DEONTIC operator is P, or permitted for all senators. The AIM in the fourth example also includes an action—cleaning the microwave. The third example assigns the DEONTIC F, or forbidden, to the outcome of livestock damage. The AIM of the rule does not specify actions that an irrigator must or may take. The AIM specifies only the forbidden outcome. Villagers may select any actions that are not forbidden by another rule to keep their livestock from damaging the irrigation channel. Finally, in the fifth example of a strategy, the AIM, a_5, is the action of calling back.

The AIM often supplies the focus for formal and empirical studies. Once the set of actions or outcomes is selected, the next step is developing the analysis of institutional statements related to those AIMs. Scholars decide to study the impact of institutions on behavior for some subset of actions or outcomes. Studies of agenda setting and voting institutions, for example, focus on those actions related to setting agendas and voting within a particular forum. In studies of voting rules, it becomes particularly important to specify the formulas in the voting rules that indicate when the collective body has permission to change the status quo (Shepsle 1989). The A*I*M component for a majority rule will be different from the A*I*M component for a consensus voting rule. Analyses of the impact of different voting rules will often focus on the impact of different formulas here. In common-pool resource action situations, the A*I*M formulas are particularly important. Formulas in the A*I*M component of institutional statements indicate how much a participant may extract (e.g., three units per acre of land) and how much participants must contribute (e.g., two days per acre of irrigated land). Analysis of the effectiveness of rules, then, often turns to analysis of the effectiveness and costs of different formulas (Yandle and Dewees 2003).

CONDITIONS

CONDITIONS indicate the set of variables that define when and where an institutional statement applies. For example, the CONDITIONS for a statement might indicate when a statement applies, such as during certain weather conditions, at a set time, or at a particular step in some process. Likewise, the CONDITIONS might indicate where a statement applies, such as a particular jurisdictional area. If an institutional statement does not specify particular variables, the default value for the CONDITION is at all times and in all places covered by that rule, norm, or strategy. Thus, like the ATTRIBUTE, the CONDITION component always has some value in it even when the institutional statement fails to overtly specify it.

The CONDITIONS component in the second example indicates when the prescription applies. After a bill has been introduced, the prescription of the second rule applies. Thus, any senators may move to amend a bill after it has been introduced. The strategy in the fifth example applies when a telephone call is disconnected. The first, third, and fourth examples do not specify specific CONDITIONS; therefore, we assume that the rules apply for U.S. citizens, members of the village, and microwave users under all circumstances.

OR ELSE

The final component of our institutional syntax is the consequence that an institutional statement assigns to detected noncompliance with the other components of that statement. In some cases, the OR ELSE specifies a range of possible punishments if a rule is not followed. Individuals in the community know that if they violate a rule, they face the probability that a sanction in a specified range will be applied and that others in a similar situation face the same range. Only rules include an OR ELSE. This component, consequently, plays a crucial role in discerning what a rule is and how rules differ from other institutional statements.

Sanctions for breaking a rule are a common type of OR ELSE, but the OR ELSE may take other forms. The OR ELSE might also shift the DEONTIC assigned to some other action. For example, a violator might be forbidden to vote or engage in some other action that would otherwise be permitted. The OR ELSE might also shift the DEONTIC assigned to some activity for an individual from permitted to obligatory (P to O). The violator might be required to allocate resources to a public jurisdiction (i.e., pay a fine), or another actor might be required to check on the violator. Those actions might be permitted (P) under all other CONDITIONS, but obligatory (O) when the CONDITION of a violation of the rule is met.

Although the OR ELSE often refers to physical punishments, the OR ELSE may also involve institutional actions, such as taking away a position or refusing to accept an amendment as legal. For example, one of the rules governing the amendment process may state that legislators with [ATTRIBUTES] [must] [take a particular action] [when voting for an amendment] [OR ELSE—the amendment fails].

Three qualifications must be met for an OR ELSE to exist. First, the consequence stated in the OR ELSE must be the result of collective action. A collective decision must have been made in a relevant collective-choice arena to determine the consequence.[11] Second, the threat in the OR ELSE component of a rule must be backed by another rule or norm that changes the DEONTIC assigned to some AIM, for at least one actor, under the CONDITION that individuals fail to follow the rule. Often the actions threatened in the OR ELSE are forbidden under most CONDITIONS (e.g., imposing a fine, incarcerating a citizen, or taking someone's livestock and putting them in a village pen). The prescription backing the OR ELSE makes these actions permitted or required in the CONDITION that someone breaks a rule. The shift in the deontic is not always from F to P or O. The OR ELSE might involve forbidding some action that is usually permitted; a shift from P to F. For example, the OR ELSE might forbid a government agency from providing a tax incentive to a corporation on the condition that the corporation violated the specific provisions authorizing the incentives in the tax code (see Lederman 2003).

Third, in order for an OR ELSE to exist, a prescription must affect the constraints and opportunities facing an actor or actors with the responsibility of monitoring the conformance of others. Although the actors who monitor frequently sanction nonconforming actors, they may only report nonconformance to someone else responsible for sanctioning. We do not consider government sponsorship or government backing to be a necessary condition for a statement to include an OR ELSE. Many self-organized, communal, or private organizations develop rules that include (1) a sanction, (2) backed by another rule or norm that changes the DEONTIC assigned to some AIM for at least one actor if individuals fail to follow the rule, and (3) a norm or rule (a sanctioning prescription) that affects the constraints and opportunities facing an actor or actors to take the responsibility to monitor the conformance of others to the prescription (a monitoring prescription).

Turning again to the examples of institutional statements listed above, the first three examples appear to contain an OR ELSE. Of course, we would need to check to be sure that there are rules or norms regarding monitoring and sanctioning backing the stated OR ELSE before we would be sure that the stated sanction fully qualifies as an OR ELSE. For example, the potential punishment for villagers who let their livestock trample the irrigation channels qualifies as an OR ELSE only when rules or norms accepted in that village prescribe others to monitor and to employ the sanctions defined in the OR ELSE. Without the establishment of positions with the authority for monitoring and sanctioning, phrases that contain the words "or else" fail to constitute an OR ELSE that distinguishes an institutional statement as a rule as defined herein.

Institutional statements with content in the OR ELSE slot, then, are institutional statements that add information to the action situation about what will happen if a participant violates the prescription. The Senate example of a rule indicates that participants who violate the prescription will be called out of order. A participant in the Senate action situation, then, knows that if he or she chooses to violate the rule that he or she will have the consequence of being called out of order or at the very least having his or her attempts ignored. In effect, the institutional consequence of breaking this rule is the removal of legal standing. The senator has no legal standing to restrict another member from moving an amendment in this simple rule.

Compare the information about the consequences in the Senate action situation to that in the microwave example. The sign on the microwave does not provide any specific information about what will happen to a participant who chooses to ignore the norm and leave a puddle of soup at the bottom of the microwave. Office workers seeing the sign on the microwave have only information about their own internal costs or benefits of following the norm and their beliefs about how others in the office are likely to respond when they open the door and see the crusty soup spill there.

The OR ELSE component of a rule is frequently linked to a CONDITIONS component that specifies the number of times that a rule has been violated (Dana 2001). The range of sanctions is likely to be lowest when someone has committed their first offense against a specific rule. A different rule, specifying a more stringent range of sanctions, will then be applicable if that individual has committed a second, or a third, or more offenses. Many rules against drunk driving use this form of graduated sanctions and increase the sanction for this offense substantially for second or third offenders.

The content of the OR ELSE affects the very nature of a rule. Rowe (1989) discusses the difference between a speed limit law with minor sanctions and a speed limit law with the death penalty as the sanction. The prescription is the same. The severity of the sanction in the OR ELSE is the only difference. Yet a speeding law with a death penalty is quite a different rule than a speeding law with a minor fine. Given the same level of enforcement, the type of OR ELSE involved may make a substantial difference on the behavior of participants.[12] This example is not meant as an argument for severe sanctions. Rather, it points out that the OR ELSE is a fundamental part of rules and that the implications of the sanctions that are assigned to prescriptions are important for the analysis of institutional arrangements. This is particularly true for studies of rule compliance and stability.

Use of the grammar thus far suggests that the OR ELSE component of the grammar has been the most challenging for scholars to apply, but the discussions of determining whether this component exists have led to productive wrestling about the important theoretical differences between rules and norms in action situations.[13] The presence of an OR ELSE, then, is absolutely crucial to the effective use of the grammar for analysis of rules. Identifying when this component exists distinguishes when an institutional statement includes "rule information." These statements, then, influence the action situation so that one would describe the situation as "rule-governed" or "shaped by a rule." Thus, the OR ELSE clarifies the difference between institutional statements that influence the action situation as norms or strategies alone and those that can influence the action situation as rules.

Applying the Grammar

No one will want to spend time learning the intricacies of the grammar of institutions developed herein without a sense that it is useful for at least some purposes. In the remainder of this chapter, we illustrate initial applications of the grammar to three broad endeavors: (1) game-theoretical analyses, (2) the synthesis of diverse theoretical approaches to the study of rules and norms, and (3) learning about norms and rules in empirical research. The remaining chapters of the book will dig into these applications still further.

Using the Grammar in Game-Theoretical Analyses

Our first application demonstrates the grammar for a very simple game. By using a game familiar to most contemporary scholars, we illustrate the analytical usefulness of the working parts of the grammar. The concept of a strategy, as developed in the institutional grammar, is the same as the concept of strategy used in contemporary game theory. Thus, a game-theoretic analysis of a situation in which there are no norms or rules would not differ in any way from current usage. The Snatch Game, first presented in chapter 2, is such an analysis. To incorporate the syntax into formal analyses of behavior, the payoffs for actions governed by norms alone need to include delta parameters that capture the DEONTIC (as illustrated in chapter 4), and for rules they must also specify the institutionally assigned consequence defined in the OR ELSE (as we now illustrate).

If the enforcing players are brought into the analysis, the enforcing player would have a delta parameter assigned to the action of "not sanctioning," since there is a norm or rule that prescribes sanctioning. If the OR ELSE is backed by a rule, then we expect the payoffs for sanctioning or not sanctioning to include delta parameters and a variable representing the cost of the sanction defined in the OR ELSE of the sanctioning rule. A game that includes the enforcement players must also specify the monitoring institution influences on the monitor. Once a monitoring norm or rule comes into play, the delta parameters and possibly the OR ELSE parameters become part of the monitors' payoff formulas.

If it is costly to monitor the actions of others and/or to impose sanctions on them, those assigned these tasks may not be motivated to undertake these assignments unless (1) the monitor or sanctioner face some probability of themselves being sanctioned for not monitoring and/or sanctioning,[14] (2) social pressure to monitor or sanction is large and is salient to the monitor and sanctioner (large δ^{oe} and δ^{be}), (3) the monitor or sanctioner hold some strong moral commitment to their responsibilities (large δ^{oi} and δ^{bi}), or (4) the payment schemes for the monitor or sanctioners create prudent rewards high enough to offset the costs. When norms back an OR ELSE, monitoring and enforcement rests solely on the value of the normative delta parameters and on the payment schemes for the monitor and sanctioner (i.e., Are the monitors and sanctioners paid? If so, is payment a set fee regardless of the number of defectors they catch, based on the number of defectors caught and punished, or some mixture of a set fee and a commission?).

COLLECTIVE-ACTION PROBLEMS

To illustrate applications of the syntax to ongoing research, our discussion of applications uses shared strategies, norms, and rules related to an abstract social dilemma problem rather than the five examples discussed earlier in this chapter or the Commons Dilemma discussed in chapter 3. The scholarly discourse about social dilemmas and their solution through collective action has involved terms such as common understanding, shared beliefs, scripts, norms, rules, procedures, institutions, informal rules, informal institutions, conventions, internal solutions, external solutions, as well as a wide diversity of highly technical terms related to particular solution theories.

Collective-action problems can be represented by many different game structures (see discussion in Taylor 1987; E. Ostrom, Gardner, and Walker 1994; Gintis 2000b). Because almost all social scientists know the Prisoner's Dilemma (PD) game well, however, we can more easily jump into existing debates and rely on extensive earlier work. We start with a simple two-person Prisoner's Dilemma game and use the ADICO format to illustrate differences in the research issues, the game structures, and the predicted outcomes that arise from (1) changed expectations of other players' behavior only (AIC statements); (2) changed normative views of the appropriate actions to be taken or the adoption of norms (ADIC statements); and (3) changes in the rules (ADICO statements). Table 5.1 summarizes the institutional and payoff characteristics of four games based on a two-person Prisoner's Dilemma situation. The first game is the base two-person Prisoner's Dilemma game. The *shared strategies* game adds a set of shared strategies that equate to the *grim trigger* strategy. The *norms* game adds a cooperating norm to the base situation. The *rules* game adds a cooperating rule, a monitoring norm, and a sanctioning norm to the base Prisoner's Dilemma game. These four examples represent only one way to add the ADICO statements to a two-person Prisoner's Dilemma game. We do not develop a new solution theory. Rather, our effort is to illustrate how an application of the ADICO syntax distinguishes between three structural adjustments to social dilemma situations.

In figure 5.2, we present both the extensive and the normal forms of the base two-person PD game. We make only the assumption that the payoffs are related in the following way: $1 > c > d > 0$. Both players are better off choosing D, no matter what the other player chooses, so D is the dominant strategy for both players. The Commons Dilemma discussed in chapter 3 is frequently represented as an N-person Prisoner's Dilemma game under particular cost and benefit assumptions.

The game-theoretic solution to this game, if played only once, is for both players to choose D and receive d instead of the more desirable c

Table 5.1
Game summaries

Institutional statements	Payoffs
Base game	
NONE (physical world)	*Player 1 or 2*
	$C = c$ if other C
	$= 0$ if other D
	$D = 1$ if other C
	$= d$ if other D
Shared strategies game	
AIC statements	*Player 1 or 2*
[All players] [ ] [C] [first round] [ ]	$C = c + t\,(c)$ if other C
[All players] [ ] [C] [if all C in previous	$= 0 + t\,(d)$ if other D
round] [ ]	$D = 1 + t\,(d)$ if other C
[All players] [ ] [D] [all rounds after a D] [ ]	$= d + t\,(d)$ if other D
Norms game	
ADIC statement	*Player 1 or 2*
[P1* and P2] [must] [C] [always] [ ]	$C =$ base game payoffs $+ \delta^{oi} + \delta^{oe}$ if P3 $\Rightarrow M$**
	$=$ base game payoffs $+ \delta^{oi}$ if P3 $\Rightarrow \sim M$
	$D =$ base game payoffs $- \delta^{bi} - \delta^{be}$ if P3 $\Rightarrow M$
	$=$ base game payoffs $- \delta^{bi}$ if P3 $\Rightarrow \sim M$
	Player 3
	$M = E$ if (P1 and P2) $\Rightarrow C$
	$= R - E$ if (P1 or P2) $\Rightarrow D$
	$\sim M = 0$
Rules game	
ADICO statement	*Players 1 and 2*
[P1 and P2] [must] [C] [always] [f]	$C =$ norm game payoffs
ADIC statements	$D =$ norm game payoffs $+ f$ if (P3 $\Rightarrow M$) and
[P3] [must] [monitor] [always] [ ]	(P4 $\Rightarrow S$)
[P4] [must] [impose f on defector] [when	$=$ norm game payoffs if (P3 $\Rightarrow \sim M$) or
P3 reports a D] [ ]	(P4 $\Rightarrow \sim S$)
	Player 3
	$M =$ norm game payoffs $+ \delta^{o}_{m}$
	$\sim M =$ norm game payoffs $- \delta^{b}_{m}$
	Player 4
	Only plays if P3 $\Rightarrow M$
	$S = \delta^{o}_{s} - E_{s}$
	$\sim S = - \delta^{b}_{s}$

Source: Crawford and Ostrom 2000, 134.

* P1 refers to player 1, and so on.

** (P3 $\Rightarrow M$) indicates that player 3 chooses M.

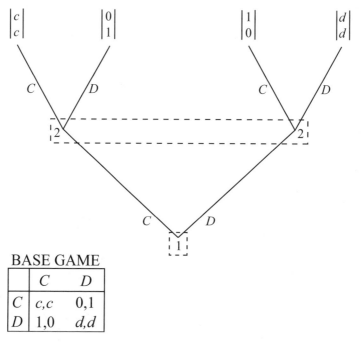

BASE GAME

	C	D
C	c,c	0,1
D	1,0	d,d

Figure 5.2 Base game. *Source*: Crawford and Ostrom 2000, 143.

that they could have received if they had both chosen C. In the Commons Dilemma game, this would mean that subjects would overinvest rather than investing at the optimal level. Even if repeated for a finite number of times, the solution is for both players always to choose *D*.

SHARED STRATEGIES

Predictions that individuals will select *C* rather than *D* in a PD game based on shared strategies rely upon changes in players' expectations about each other's future behavior. In order to incorporate those expectations into formal analysis, we use an indefinitely repeated version of the base game. By making the game repeated, we can include future expected payoffs as part of a player's calculation at any one round. It is now logically possible for individuals to adopt shared strategies involving plans of action to co-operate in the first round, and to defect for all periods thereafter, if the other player defects in a prior round.

Figure 5.3 illustrates the extensive form of an indefinitely repeated game with a set of shared strategies that create the famous grim trigger: "all players cooperate in each round of the game or else all other players will defect for the rest of the game." Both players cooperating in every

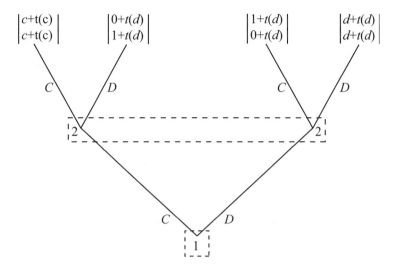

t = number of expected future rounds
$t( )$ = expectation of payoffs from future rounds of the game

Institutional Statements
Shared Strategies
[All Players] [C] [First Round]
[All Players] [C] [All Rounds in which All Players Play C in the Previous Round]
[All Players] [D] [All Rounds after a D]

Figure 5.3 Repeated game with shared strategies. *Source*: Crawford and Ostrom 2000, 144.

round is the predicted result if and only if $c + t(c) > 1 + t(d)$ where t is the expected number of future rounds, assuming that players do not discount future payoffs.[15] Whether all C is the predicted outcome to this game depends on the relative size of 0, d, and t, all features of the physical world.

Shared strategies, even the crude trigger strategy, are institutional statements. They require shared understanding. If all players do not consider it prudent to defect for all rounds after someone initially defects, the trigger strategy is not shared and will not work. Little empirical evidence exists that individuals share a belief in the prudence of a grim trigger (E. Ostrom, Gardner, and Walker 1994). Herein lies the frailty of the grim trigger as a resolution of PD situations.

The words "or else" in the grim trigger shared strategy might cause one to wonder whether it is a rule. The shared strategy with a grim trigger is not a norm or a rule, using the ADICO syntax because there is no DEON-

TIC and no OR ELSE here. If the advice to cooperate to avoid a trigger response is not discussed in terms of obligation nor backed by monitoring and sanctioning institutions, the massive defection that is threatened by the trigger can only be a prudent response of a player's defection.

The shared strategy with a grim trigger would be a rule, using the ADICO syntax, if we were to assume that there were a prescription to play the trigger strategy that is in turn backed by another rule or norm that changes the DEONTIC assigned to some AIM for at least one actor, and there is an additional institutional statement that affects the constraints and opportunities facing an actor to monitor the conformance of others. The institutional statements that could back a trigger rule might be a sanctioning rule, such as: "all other players must defect for the rest of the game when one player defects in any of the rounds OR ELSE the other players face the probability of a further sanction" and a monitoring norm that "all players must monitor all other players." Notice that the sanctioning rule changes the DEONTIC assigned to C from *obligatory* to *forbidden* in the CONDITION of a defection in the prior round.

NORMS

Predictions that individuals will select C rather than D in a PD base game based on norms rely upon changes in players' payoffs because of the addition of at least one delta parameter to the players' payoffs. Figure 5.4 illustrates a game in which the base PD structure has been modified by the addition of delta parameters in the payoffs for players 1 and 2. In order to make the discussion more applicable to situations with more than two players, we add a third player, a Monitor who chooses to monitor (M) or not to monitor ($< M$) and assume that external reinforcements for obeying or breaking a norm occur only when the Monitor reports the defection. In the simple two-person game, this assumption is usually not necessary; players 1 and 2 know whether the other player cooperated by simply looking at their own payoffs. As soon as the number of players in a PD is larger than two, however, identifying who defects is no longer trivial. To make the game more applicable to common's situations with multiple actors, we "blind" the actors here and assume that defection becomes common knowledge only when the Monitor does his or her job. Consequently, the negative external effects of breaking the norm only kick in when the Monitor chooses to monitor.

In this game, the Monitor is motivated solely by prudential rewards associated with discovering defection and not by any normative motives (delta parameters). In other words, we do not assume a monitoring norm. The absence of a monitoring norm is appropriate here because the game

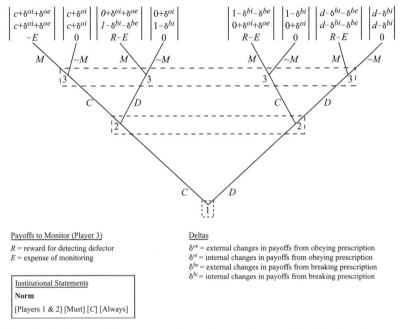

Payoffs to Monitor (Player 3)

R = reward for detecting defector
E = expense of monitoring

Deltas

δ^{oe} = external changes in payoffs from obeying prescription
δ^{oi} = internal changes in payoffs from obeying prescription
δ^{be} = external changes in payoffs from breaking prescription
δ^{bi} = internal changes in payoffs from breaking prescription

Institutional Statements

Norm

[Players 1 & 2] [Must] [C] [Always]

Figure 5.4 Game with a norm and monitoring. *Source*: Crawford and Ostrom 2000, 145.

represents the addition of a cooperating norm only, not a cooperating rule. Freelance reporters are an example of this type of monitor. They receive payment for detecting and reporting nonconformance with accepted norms. Rewards include fees for stories accepted and increased probabilities of receiving prizes for good reporting. It is, of course, possible to illustrate the addition of norms without a player who is assigned a specialized role as a Monitor by simply assuming that the existing institutional statements allow players to monitor each other (Weissing and Ostrom 1991a, 1993). To do this, however, one needs to model a sequential structure, which introduces more complexity than we desire in this initial application.

In the game represented by figure 5.4, predictions about players' strategies depend on the relationships among the original payoffs in the base game, the added delta parameters, and the benefits the Monitor receives for reporting nonconformance. This game has many equilibria. Assuming that all of the delta parameters are symmetric (players 1 and 2 have the same values for each delta parameter) and that the sum of the external parameters is greater than the sum of the internal parameters (i.e., the social pressure to follow the prescription is greater than the internal pres-

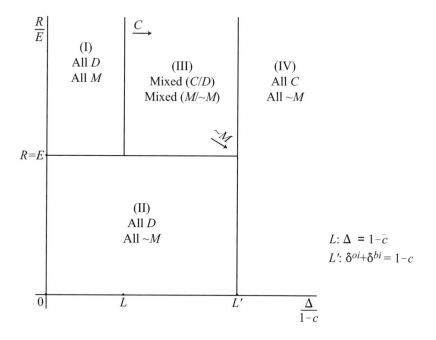

Figure 5.5 Equilibrium diagram: game with a norm and monitoring. *Source*: Crawford and Ostrom 2000, 136.

sure), four equilibrium regions exist as shown in figure 5.5. The vertical axis is the ratio of the Monitor's reward for detecting defection to the expense of monitoring (R/E). The vertical axis is divided into regions above and below the point at which the reward to the Monitor equals the expense ($R = E$).

The reward is higher than the cost above this point and lower than the cost below this point. The horizontal axis on figure 5.5 is the ratio of the sum of all delta parameters to the advantage of defecting ($1 - c$). As one moves to the right, the size of the delta parameters relative to the advantage of defection increases. At point L, the sum of the delta parameters equals the advantage of defection when the other player cooperates ($\delta^{oi} + \delta^{oe} + \delta^{bi} + \delta^{be} = 1 - c$). Point L' on the horizontal axis represents that point where the internal deltas just equal the advantage of defection ($\delta^{oi} + \delta^{bi} = 1 - c$), and thus the area to the right of L' represents the region where the internal deltas offset the advantage of defecting. When ($c + \delta^{oi}$) > ($1 - \delta^{bi}$), it is clear that both players will choose C (equilibrium region IV in figure 5.5). This is the case in which C is the dominant strategy because the internal costs and rewards for players 1 and 2 are sufficiently high.

Such a norm could be shared in a stable, small community for some time but would be highly vulnerable to immigration from other communities where individuals did not share the same norm. A few instances of individuals taking actions contrary to the norm would generate a cascade of responses. Unless there were a forum in which the importance of keeping the norm could be discussed with newcomers so they could learn the importance of this norm before it disappeared, communities that regulate resources using only norms may find themselves exposed to substantial changes in regularized behavior when exposed to considerable inmigration.

In region III, both players 1 and 2 select a mixed strategy between C and D.[16] As one moves from left to right in region III, the sum of the delta parameters increases and thus the probability that players 1 and 2 assign to selecting C increases. In this region, the Monitor also selects a mixed strategy. The *relative amount* of the Monitor's reward decreases as one moves from north to south. Since the Monitor receives a reward only if defection is detected, the *probability* of obtaining a reward decreases as one moves from west to east because the probability of defection decreases. Thus, as one moves from "northwest to southeast" in this region, the probability assigned to M decreases. The combined effect is that the Monitor has the least incentive to monitor when relative rewards are low and the probability of defection is low (in the southeast corner) and the greatest incentive to monitor when the relative rewards are high and the probability of defection is high (in the northwest corner of this region).

In equilibrium regions I and II of figure 5.5, D remains the dominant strategy for players 1 and 2, as it was in the base game, but for different reasons. In region II, the expenses of monitoring are higher than the expected reward of the Monitor. Thus, the Monitor will choose < M in region II. Since < M is the dominant strategy, players 1 and 2 need not consider the external cost parameters (δ^{oe} and δ^{be}). Given that the internal deltas are relatively low in relation to the advantage of defecting $[(\delta^{oi} + \delta^{bi}) < (1 - c)]$, D is the dominant strategy for players 1 and 2. Region I, on the other hand, represents a socially perverse outcome whereby players 1 and 2 always defect because the advantage of defecting $(1 - c)$ is greater than the sum of all delta parameters. At the same time, the Monitor has a dominant strategy of M because the rewards received from detecting defection exceed the monitoring costs and are guaranteed to occur, assuming perfect detection, because players 1 and 2 face the dominant strategy of D.

This analysis demonstrates that simply introducing norms or monitoring is not sufficient to change predicted results in a PD base game, and that a change in predicted results is not always socially beneficial. The only equilibrium regions where players 1 and 2 select a pure strategy of cooperating is when internal norms generate high internal cost parameters relative to the advantage of defecting. The presence of a Monitor who is motivated to select a mixed strategy boosts the level of cooperation in one region. There is no region where the actions of the Monitor totally prevent defection. Moreover, the lower the probability of defection, the higher the monitoring rewards (R) need to be in order to offset the reduced probability of receiving the reward. These results hold because the reward to the Monitor comes only if there is defection to be reported.

Changes in the assumptions about the rewards to the Monitor substantially affect the outcomes. If the Monitor is rewarded specifically for monitoring, regardless of whether defection is discovered, there are two additional equilibrium regions. In these regions, the reward for simply monitoring is greater than the costs of monitoring. In one of these, the result of the choice of a pure strategy to monitor is to make C a dominant strategy for the two players. In the other, a pure strategy to monitor is combined with players 1 and 2 both adopting mixed strategies.

If one wanted to analyze the incentive structure found in many field settings where monitors are hired as external, disinterested guards, one could change the game so that the Monitor receives a salary regardless of whether he or she detects defection or shirks. In such a setting, the Monitor has little incentive to monitor and thus the rate of cooperation depends heavily on the size of the internal delta parameters for players 1 and 2.

Empirical studies and formal models suggest several other motivational schemes for monitors. Some motivate monitors by embedding them in a series of nested institutions that reward monitors who actively and reliably monitor with positive returns from the increased productivity that the rules generate (see Milgrom, North, and Weingast 1990). Monitors may also be direct participants in ongoing relationships where efforts are made to keep monitoring costs low, to reward one another for monitoring, and to ensure that monitors participate in the greater returns that all achieve when temptations to defect are reduced. In such situations, monitors may achieve sufficient benefits from monitoring that they induce a high level of conformance (but never 100 percent) in an isolated system without recourse to central authorities (Weissing and Ostrom 1991a, 1993).[17]

RULES

Predictions that individuals will select C rather than D in a PD base game based on rules rely upon (1) changes in players' payoffs because of the addition of at least one delta parameter to the players' payoffs, (2) the addition of an institutionally assigned consequence for breaking a rule, (3) the possibility of detection, (4) at least one player who has authority to monitor, (5) at least one player who has authority to impose the OR

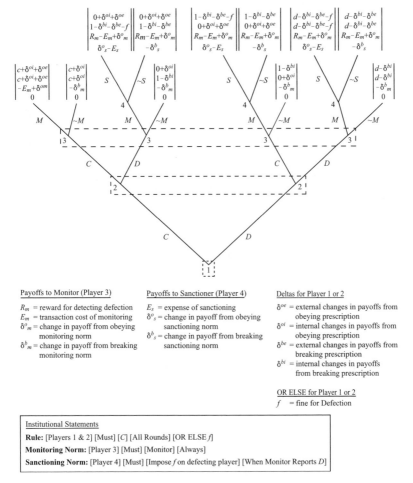

Figure 5.6 Game with a rule. *Source*: Crawford and Ostrom 2000, 146–47.

Payoffs to Monitor (Player 3)

R_m = reward for detecting defection
E_m = transaction cost of monitoring
δ^o_m = change in payoff from obeying monitoring norm
δ^b_m = change in payoff from breaking monitoring norm

Payoffs to Sanctioner (Player 4)

E_s = expense of sanctioning
δ^o_s = change in payoff from obeying sanctioning norm
δ^b_s = change in payoff from breaking sanctioning norm

Deltas for Player 1 or 2

δ^{oe} = external changes in payoffs from obeying prescription
δ^{oi} = internal changes in payoffs from obeying prescription
δ^{be} = external changes in payoffs from breaking prescription
δ^{bi} = internal changes in payoffs from breaking prescription

OR ELSE for Player 1 or 2

f = fine for Defection

Institutional Statements

Rule: [Players 1 & 2] [Must] [*C*] [All Rounds] [OR ELSE *f*]

Monitoring Norm: [Player 3] [Must] [Monitor] [Always]

Sanctioning Norm: [Player 4] [Must] [Impose *f* on defecting player] [When Monitor Reports *D*]

ELSE, and (6) the base game payoffs. In figure 5.6, we present a game that shifts the norm game in figure 5.4 to a game with a rule backed by two norms. The rule that structures this game is: [Players 1 & 2] [must] [Cooperate] [Always] [OR ELSE *f*]. The rule adds a fine (*f*) to the payoffs for players 1 and 2 for *D* if their defection is monitored and sanctioned. This rule is backed by both a monitoring norm ([Player 3] [must] [Monitor] [Always]) and a sanctioning norm ([Player 4] [must] [Impose *f* on a Player] [When Player 3 reports that a Player has defected]). The addition of a monitoring norm adds delta parameters to player 3's payoffs. The sanctioning norm adds another player, player 4. Player 4 (the Sanctioner) faces a cost of sanctioning and receives delta parameters as payoffs.[18] In other words, the Sanctioner in this game is a volunteer who is "rewarded" solely by normative interests.

A wide variety of mixed-strategy equilibria are possible that depend on (1) the relative expected value of the fine and the relative size of the delta parameters originating from external sources for players 1 and 2, (2) the relative strength of the reward and deltas associated with monitoring to the costs of monitoring, and (3) the value of the deltas associated with conforming with the sanctioning norm minus the costs of sanctioning as compared to the value of the delta parameters for not sanctioning. Even in a rule-governed game, if Monitors are not motivated to monitor and Sanctioners are not motivated to sanction, cooperation rests substantially on internalized norms of the players.

We set aside the tasks of analyzing the many possible equilibrium regions and focus here on the simpler task of establishing conditions for equilibria in which players 1 and 2 always cooperate. The rule adds a Fine and a new player, yet the Monitor still plays a crucial role. The parts of the game that come from the OR ELSE (the fine and the sanctioning norm) do not even enter the game on branches in which the Monitor chooses $-M$.[19] As in the norm game, we assume that players 1 and 2 do not see each other's choices, and that the external delta components occur only when player 3 monitors. In order to be sure that the Monitor will choose M when players 1 and 2 are expected to choose C, the sum of the delta parameters for the Monitor must be higher than E, because the Monitor will not expect to receive rewards (R) for detecting defection. As in the base game with norms, in the absence of monitoring, players 1 and 2 will select only C as a pure strategy when their *internal* delta parameters are high enough to offset the advantage of defecting when others cooperate. Thus, the selection of C as a pure strategy depends either entirely on internal sources of normative constraint for players 1 and 2 (δ^{oi} and δ^{bi}), or it depends on the configuration of the size of the normative constraint for the Monitor (o_m and b_m) relative to the monitoring costs, the sum of internal delta parameters for players 1 and 2, the expected value of the external delta parameters, and the expected value of f. This latter configuration matters only when the normative constraint for the Monitor is higher than the monitoring cost. Cooperation can be a pure strategy only when either of the following conditions is met:

1. $\delta^{oi} + \delta^{bi} > 1 - c$
2. $[(\delta^{o}_{m} + \delta^{b}_{m}) / E] > 1$ and
   $[(\delta^{oi} + \delta^{bi}) + (p(M)* (\delta^{oe} + \delta^{be}) + (p(S)* f)) > 1 - c]$.

The first condition is the same as in the game in figure 5.4. The second condition was not possible in the earlier game as the Monitor was not motivated by a norm. Defection by both players continues to be an equilibrium of this game as well as of all the games considered so far.

In settings where players in the base game develop strong internalized norms (high internal delta parameters), the presence of even a low-to-moderate f may be sufficient when combined with Monitors and Sanctioners who are motivated to do their job, to encourage a high rate of cooperation. Consequently, the effect of f depends both on its relative size, the size of the deltas for players 1 and 2, and the behavior of the Monitor and the Sanctioner. If players 1 and 2 expect the Monitor or the Sanctioner to break their respective norms, then the expected probability of S (the Sanctioner choosing to sanction) tends toward zero and f drops out of the decision calculus for players 1 and 2. In order for the Monitor and the Sanctioner to be motivated to do their jobs, their value of following the monitoring and sanctioning norms has to be greater than the relative cost of doing their jobs. In the case of the Sanctioner, the value of the delta parameters needs to be greater than the cost for imposing that sanction: $(\delta^o_s + \delta^b_s) > E_s$.[20] Clearly, recognizing rules in formal analysis of dilemma situations does not automatically "solve" the dilemma and end analysis. Instead, adding rules suggests a whole new set of research questions.

FURTHER RESEARCH QUESTIONS

The game in figure 5.6 is intended to stimulate further formal and empirical research. It suggests questions such as: How do changes in the level of internalization of rules (δ^{bi} and δ^{oi}) affect the levels of monitoring and sanctioning required to bolster cooperation at given levels of social pressure (δ^{oe} and δ^{be})? What size do external delta parameters need to be in order to ensure cooperation at various rates of monitoring and sanctioning with a given value of f that is less than the advantage of defection? How do the incentives to monitor and sanction differ if we assume that players 3 and 4 are the same person? And, what are the empirical equivalents of delta parameters and the external fine in similar situations?

The disjunction between theoretical predictions of complete free-riding in PD situations and the rates of cooperation in case studies and laboratory experiments have provoked much intellectual ferment and development (Udéhn 1993; Camerer 2003; Boyd et al. 2003). The syntax facilitates empirical analysis of the components in institutions that foster cooperation in dilemma situations by providing a language with which to discuss differences between institutions in various settings and changes in institutions over time. When an ADICO component is added to an institutional statement, the statement has changed from one type of institutional statement to another. Similarly, when a component drops out, the type of the institutional statement changes. Key questions then include: What are the processes that lead to such additions or deletions (Burns and Dietz 1991; Opp 1982)? Do the additions or deletions increase or decrease the level of cooperation (Orbell, van de Kragt, and Dawes 1991)? What aspects of the content of the components explain differences in the level of cooperation (e.g., the level of the punishment in the OR ELSE [Rowe 1989], the inclusiveness of the ATTRIBUTE)? A focus on the presence or absence of components, the content of components, and the source of the components promises to be more replicable by scholars than some of our current dialogue that uses the distinctions of "formal and informal" or "internal" and "external."

Using the Grammar for Synthesis

Once we have developed a syntax for expressing institutional statements in a systematic fashion, we can better address a number of important theoretical questions. The above analysis of social dilemmas is just one example. In any science, however, understanding what others have already discovered is an important part of research. Synthesis and discovery go hand in hand.

DISENTANGLING FORMAL LAWS AND INFORMAL INSTITUTIONS

Synthesizing findings from the different subfields that relate to each type of institutional statement is one important task for those interested in institutions. The ADICO syntax and its game applications can be used to help disentangle discussions of formal laws, informal institutions, and ordered behavior. Written laws or procedures often conform to the ADICO syntax requirement for a rule, yet before analyzing the law as a rule in use, one would first examine whether those listed in the ATTRI-BUTES share an understanding of the law, and whether shared understanding also exists for the related monitoring and sanctioning institutional statements. As Cooter (1994) stresses, the complexity of modern economies is so great that centralized law creation cannot effectively cope with the need to achieve normative regulation among communities of individuals who repeatedly face collective-action problems (see also El-lickson 1991). Thus, individuals frequently adopt norms or rules without enacting them as written law. These prescriptions are sometimes called "informal" institutions, but they may well be binding if challenged in a court (Cooter 1994).

We argue that if the prescriptions are shared, then they are either norms or rules. Both formal and informal prescriptions can be classified as shared norms or rules depending on the presence of the OR ELSE compo-nent. Whether or not the formality of an institution influences the level of compliance raises an interesting set of questions that disappear if we use the terms "formal" and "informal" without attention to what those distinctions mean. Do we find differences between situations governed by a similar ADICO statement that arise from the formalization of the institutional statement? Do differences in delta parameters explain the difference in behavior? Do we regularly expect delta parameters to increase or decrease when an institutional statement becomes formalized in some way?

LEGITIMACY AND COMPLIANCE

The language of the syntax enables researchers to address important questions related to the legitimacy of rules (Tyler 1990). If rulers impose rules primarily by force and fiat, individuals subject to these rules are unlikely to develop internal delta parameters associated with breaking the rules. Nor are delta parameters stimulated only by observation by others in such settings likely to enhance the rate of rule conformance. If those who are supposed to follow a rule view it as illegitimate, they may even reward one another for actions that break the rules (a positive b^e) instead of adopting the type of metanorm envisioned by Axelrod (1986) (a negative b^e).

The complementarity of deltas and the OR ELSEs emerges as important in analyses of compliance. When delta parameters are close to zero, the costs of maintaining compliance with the OR ELSE drastically increase (Levi 1988; Margolis 1991; Ayres and Braithwaite 1992). Without a relatively high level of voluntary, contingent compliance to rules, Margaret Levi (1988) explains that rulers can rarely afford the continuing costs involved in hiring enough monitors and sanctioners, motivating them to be efficient, and achieving compliance by the actual imposition of sanctions in a sufficient number of instances that citizens try to conform to the rules rather than risk the chance of detection and punishment. If violators can expect to reap the benefits of violating prescriptions without facing the probability of some established punishment (if there is no OR ELSE), however, then the experience of feeling the "sucker" may erode the value of the delta parameter (Levi 1988, 1990; E. Ostrom 1990; E. Ostrom, Gardner, and Walker 1994; Mansbridge 1994).

BASIC NORMATIVE ASSUMPTIONS

A growing body of work on cooperation and compliance considers the mix of normative and material motivations that individuals consider when faced with choices.[21] These works treat the normative aspects of decisions up-front as a significant part of the analysis. Margolis (1991,

130) argues for the necessity of such an approach: "[i]f we analyze every-thing in terms of strict self-interest and then include some social motiva-tion only if we get stuck or if there is something left over, it is not likely to lead to nearly as powerful a social theory as if the two things are built in at the base of the analysis." Delta parameters provide a conceptual language with which to incorporate explicitly normative considerations into analysis from the beginning and to discuss differences in studies that incorporate normative incentives along with extrinsic payoffs.

In table 5.2, we list studies that have addressed three types of questions about normative motivations. The top section of the table lists different assumptions regarding the meaning and sign of delta parameters. Knack's (1992) analysis of voter turnout, for example, illustrates the insight possi-ble from a careful study of the normative influences captured by the delta parameters. He offers empirical evidence of the substantive content of internal deltas and external deltas associated with a turnout norm and of the influence of these delta parameters on the probability that an individ-ual will vote. Interestingly, his interpretation of the declines in voter turn-out echoes the importance of monitoring and sanctioning discussed ear-lier. He finds that social pressures (external deltas) are a key influence on voting turnout. Social pressure operates, however, only when voters ex-pect to be in situations where someone may ask them if they voted, and may express disapproval if they did not. As the percentage of individuals in organizations, in relationships with neighborhood residents, and in ex-tended family situations drops, this monitoring decreases, and the power of the social sanction (the external delta) diminishes (see also Amaro de Matos and Barros 2004).

The middle section of table 5.2 cites work that addresses the implica-tions of assuming different individual orientations in a situation as dis-cussed in chapter 4. For example, a rational egoist would assign a zero value to praise or blame for obeying or breaking prescriptions. One inter-esting variant of this analysis ties the size of the delta to the number of others who conform to the prescription; conformance is conditional (Els-ter 1989a).

Scholars cited in the last section of table 5.2 discuss variables that in-fluence the creation and maintenance of delta parameters. Offe and Wie-senthal (1980) offer an interesting substantive application. They consider the influence of the costs labor unions face in building and maintaining shared commitment to participation norms as this in turn affects their ability to compete with other interest groups. Several other authors ask whether normative incentives increase or decrease with use. Olson (1991) views the delta parameters as scarce resources that can be dissipated with too much use, while Hirschman (1985) and Mansbridge (1994) come to the opposite conclusion. They argue that the normative constraints in-

TABLE 5.2
Delta parameters and normative concepts used in recent literature

Delta parameters	Concepts used by other authors	Citations
Size, sign, and interpretation of delta parameters		
$+\delta^{oi}$	warm glow	Andreoni 1989; Ledyard 1995
$+\delta^{oe}$	encouragement	Coleman 1988
	status improvement / reputation enhancement	Coleman 1988
	honor	Ullmann-Margalit 1977
$-\delta^{bi}$	duty	Knack 1992
$-\delta^{be}$	cost of being punished (P and P')	Axelrod 1986*
	social sanctions	Knack 1992
	third-party sanctions	Bendor and Mookherjee 1990**
$+\delta^{oi}$ and $-\delta^{bi}$	internalized norms	Coleman 1987
	public-spiritedness	Mansbridge 1994
	moral duty	Etzioni 1988
	duty	Commons [1924] 1968
$+\delta^{oe}$ and $-\delta^{be}$	externally sanctioned norms	Coleman 1987
	reputation	Kreps 1990
	responsibility	Commons [1924] 1968
	moral judgment	Sugden 1986
Types of players		
$+\delta^{oe}$ large	zealot	Coleman 1988
$\Delta = 0$	selfish rational individual	Elster 1989a
$+\delta^{oi}$ and/or $-\delta^{bi}$ large	everyday Kantian	Elster 1989a
$+\delta^{o}$ large when number of cooperators low	elite participationists	Elster 1989a
$+\delta^{o}$ large when number of cooperators high	mass participationists	Elster 1989a
Δ larger when number of cooperators > threshold	people motivated by fairness	Elster 1989a
Creation and maintenance of delta parameters		
Δ affected by labor union activities		Offe and Wiesenthal 1980
Δ are scarce resources that erode with use		Olson 1991
Δ are resources that increase with use		Hirschman 1985; Mansbridge 1994
Δ affected by external fines		Frey and Jegen 2001
Δ lower when rules come from outside authority		Frey 1994

Source: Crawford and Ostrom 2000, 131.

 * In some cases, these sanctions may meet the criteria of an OR ELSE.

 ** As with the P and P' of Axelrod's, the third-party sanctions may at times meet the criteria of an OR ELSE.

crease in size as they are used repeatedly by individuals in a group. Frey and Jegen (2001) contend and provide evidence that external interventions, such as fines, adversely affect the size of delta parameters, particularly the internal deltas. Frey (1994) speculates that the deltas associated with rules will be higher when individuals participate in making their own rules than when rules are made by higher authorities. The other works in this section debate whether deltas increase or decrease with use.

FREEDOM AND CONSTRAINT

By partitioning sets of actions or outcomes into required, forbidden, and permitted subsets, rules both constrain and expand the levels of freedom for actors. Frank Knight reflected on the relationship of institutional rules to freedom through the constraints that they impose. "But freedom is like other traits of human nature, in that it is created by a social situation or, in more technical terms, a complex of institutions. This also sets limits to freedom" (Knight 1965, 304). Freedom is *restricted* by rules that limit the actions an individual can take in an action situation. In a market, for example, an individual is only legally authorized to conduct specific commercial transactions and not to take goods by force. Legislators can vote only on bills presented to them through a formalized set of procedures.

The restrictions on the freedom of one person, however, open up opportunities for creative actions by others. So individual freedom of action is also *expanded* by enforceable rules since rules enhance the predictability of the actions taken by others in a decision situation. A buyer may obtain credit from a seller to buy goods for which the buyer does not yet have sufficient funds because the seller knows that a contract for future payment can be enforced in a court. The capacity to bind oneself to future performance through a set of enforceable rules thus opens opportunities not available without a system of enforceable rules. It is, of course, this relationship of the freedom to accomplish something by being able to constrain oneself that underlies the myth of Ulysses tying himself to the mast in order to resist the call of the sirens and thus safely guide his boat through a rocky passage (Elster 1979; see also V. Ostrom 1996, 1997).

INSTITUTIONAL CONFIGURATIONS

So far, the descriptions of the components of rule and norm statements focus primarily on single statements as if the content of the institutional statements is independent. The focus on single statements is for expository reasons only. When we examine the interactions of individuals in a situation, we expect to find that a configuration of rules, norms, and shared strategies influences the choices of individuals at any one point in time. In fact, we often find nested institutional configurations, professional norms, or agency rules nested within government regulations, for example.

In some cases, the CONDITION component of an institutional statement explicitly states the linkages between statements in a configuration. For example, a rule permitting some action may state as a CONDITION of the rule that the individual follow some procedure outlined in another rule. In other cases, the linkage between statements is implicit. For example, the CONDITION component of a voting rule for legislation may not overtly make reference to the quorum rule, but the specific quorum rule in place strongly influences the effects of the voting rule.[22] A rule stating that a majority must approve before a bill becomes a law affects behavior differently depending upon (1) the quorum rule that states how many members must be present and voting for a vote to be legal and (2) the rule that states what happens if no positive action is taken (e.g., the OR ELSE rule for a collective-choice aggregation rule that states a return to the status quo or an OR ELSE that states some alternative outcome) (see tables 2.2 and 2.3).

A syntax for individual prescriptions serves useful functions in configurational analysis. It provides an initial method for sorting the configuration of institutional statements into rules, norms, and shared strategies. The ability to identify particular parts of the prescriptions and to state all prescriptions in the same DEONTIC makes organizing and comparing the institutional statement in a configuration easier. This facilitates analysis of inconsistencies in configurations, such as instances when institutions simultaneously permit and forbid the same action. The syntax can also be used to help in the organization of types of rules—as we discuss in chapter 7.

Using the Grammar in Empirical Field Research

In empirical field studies, the researcher's task is to discover the linguistic statements that form the institutional basis for shared expectations and potentially for the observed regularity in behavior. Essentially, this entails discovering which of the components exist in these statements and the contents of those components. This frequently requires research employing qualitative methods including in-depth interviews or the reconstruction of historical and case materials.

In explaining established patterns of interaction, the researcher has to decide whether it is reasonable to use an institutional statement that assigns a DEONTIC to an action or outcome. In the field, the researcher listens for normative discourse. Is there an articulated sense of moral or social obligation expressed? If the individuals in a study share only AIC statements, their discussion of why they would follow such advice focuses only on prudence or wise judgment. "The best thing to do when faced with a choice between A and B under condition Y is to choose A because one is usually better off with this choice." When individuals shift to a language of obligation, they use terms such as "must" or "must not" to describe what they and others should do. When social and moral obligations are discussed, an empirical researcher initially assumes that it is appropriate to include a DEONTIC in institutional statements used to explain behavior. "The obligatory action when faced with a choice between A and B under condition Y is to choose A, because this is the proper action." Occasionally, the analyst can directly pick out rules, norms, and strategies from written policy statements such as a law code, written regulations, specific statements in a court decision, or written agreements established by a village or association. It may also be possible to extract clear institutional statements from institutional statements retained through oral traditions. (All of these methods were used to identify the rules discussed in chapter 8.)

For example, if one were analyzing the use of a commons in workplace settings, it would be easy enough in many offices to find a sign taped to the front of the microwave that specifically states "If you use the microwave you must clean up your own mess!" (as in example 4 above, which was observed in the commons of the Complex Systems Group at the University of Michigan in November 2002). In such cases, the institutional statement can be directly parsed using the grammar of institutions. The main operational question here is whether or not that statement found amid the written statements or oral traditions is really a shared institutional statement that participants know and use. The "know and use" conditions here are particularly important for analysis of the influence of the institutions on the outcomes in the action situation, which is the emphasis of this book ("rules in use" as described in chapter 2).

When the institutional statements relating to a specific action situation are clear and shared, *and* when those statements are at an appropriate level of precision for analysis of the question at hand, then extracting them is a relatively straightforward process. The second condition here (appropriate level of precision) returns attention back to the question of scale. Just as different maps are needed depending on the geographic question at hand (e.g., whether one is explaining, for example, where an island is versus explaining to someone how to drive to a specific location on that island), so too different levels of detail or precision may be appropriate to different kinds of policy questions. Sometimes the level of precision of the statements in the empirical setting is quite appropriate for analysis (as is discussed in chapter 8).

Fieldwork will not always lead to easy extraction of simple and clear institutions-in-use occurring exactly at the appropriate level of precision. Consequently, empirical researchers of institutions usually must develop appropriate summaries of the complex morass of legal, written, or oral statements that are relevant to the action situation being analyzed. For some analyses of campaign finance rules, for example, it might be sufficient to summarize volumes of legal code, federal regulations, and court decisions concerning campaign finance in the United States into the set of institutional statements: "Candidates may spend unlimited amounts of money on the condition that disclosure rules are followed. If the spending does not occur in a manner that meets this condition, then the candidate is fined." Another set of institutional statements that could be extracted here would be: "Candidates may spend unlimited amounts of money on the condition that they refuse public financing. If a candidate does not refuse public financing, then the FEC must fine the candidate for exceeding legal spending limits."

The analytical work of identifying the statements that most need to be summarized and identifying the appropriate level of precision are important research design questions in institutional analysis analogous to specifying the appropriate variables and the appropriate precision of variables in statistical analysis. As we have used the syntax, we find that it sometimes takes trial and error to extract a useful summary of institutional statements in an empirical action situation that bring analytical focus to the appropriate questions at the appropriate level of precision.

Some Next Steps

We started this enterprise in an effort to define the concept of rules clearly. We found that in order to do this, we needed to clarify how rules were related to norms and strategies. As a result, we have learned a great deal about norms and strategies. Delving deeper into each of the components brought to light connections among these concepts, and the literature that focuses on them, which had not previously been linked. Moreover, fitting this all into a grammar helped us to catch inconsistencies and to further test and refine our understanding of each type of institutional feature and each component.

A larger question that this research effort must eventually address in order to return to the core concerns of political science is how an institutional grammar relates to a theory of knowledge and a theory of action (see V. Ostrom 1997). Our notion of delta parameters brings normative considerations into the analysis of action and consequences. This is not the same as incorporating concerns about the welfare of other actors into an individual's calculus. The delta parameters arise from commitments to the norms and rules of a community, not from the incorporation of other's payoffs into one's own payoff.[23] Our notion of OR ELSE brings institutional consequences into individual-level decisions. All of the institutional statements affect expectations about others' behavior, which create stability in social life. The ADICO syntax illustrates the potentially cumulative manner in which institutional statements can affect individual expectations. Thus, improving our ability to analyze and to discuss the institutional statements prepares us for a more thorough analysis of institutions and human action. Attending to a grammar of institutions equips us to return to the core issues of institutions and political order with new effectiveness.

Six

Why Classify Generic Rules?

IN CHAPTER 5, Sue Crawford and I use the ADICO grammar to distinguish among three essential components of all institutional analyses: strategies, norms, and rules. Hopefully, the reader has grasped the importance of understanding how individuals adopt strategies in light of the norms they hold and within the rules of the situation within which they are interacting. In chapter 7, we will move forward to discussing a way of consistently grouping rules so that the analysis of rule systems can be made much more cumulative. This chapter is a prologue to chapter 7 in that it addresses why we would introduce still further conceptual tools beyond those of the general Institutional Analysis and Development (IAD) framework and the grammar of institutions discussed in chapter 5.

The approach to classifying rules to be discussed in this and the next two chapters has taken many years to develop. Some of the notes drawn on in writing these chapters were written in the early 1980s. A lecture delivered in Bielefeld in 1982 was my first effort to elucidate how rules were the "hidden" structure underlying games. When I gave a revised version as my Presidential Address to the Public Choice Society meetings in March of 1984 (published two years later as E. Ostrom 1986), and posited the seven types of generic rules that are discussed in this and the next two chapters, several colleagues strongly criticized me for introducing so much complexity. They asked, "Why are you driven to do something so unnecessary?"

Among the answers I have given to these questions is the following list of "needs":

- to work further toward solving babbling equilibrium problems for scholars doing institutional analysis;
- to understand how action situations are constructed so that reasonable reforms can be considered;
- to move beyond slogan words to describe institutions;
- to cope with the immense diversity of rules by clustering them into seven generic rules;
- to look at rules as information-transformation mechanisms; and
- to study the underlying universality of rules.

Solving Babbling Equilibrium Problems

In his book *Convention,* David Lewis (1969) clearly laid out the problems of communicating with one another. Assuming that scholars—as well as anyone else—are better off when successful communication occurs, the problem of communication is that of arriving at a shared convention for the names (or symbols) that we will attach to diverse states of the world. In essence, communicators are engaged in a signaling game. If the senders and receivers of a signal do not understand it the same way, they are unfortunately in a "babbling equilibrium."

The sender of a signal wishes to convey information about states of the world to a receiver of that signal. Since terms are not endowed with some preexisting meaning, the sender could use any of a wide diversity of terms for the particular states of the world being described. If there were, for example, three states of the world that the sender wanted to describe, the sender could use colors to describe the relevant states of the world, such as red for state 1, green for state 2, and orange for state 3. In essence, this is what a traffic signal does when it is appropriately engineered. By sending a green signal to the drivers on one street, it conveys to them the information that the drivers on the cross street have a red signal and will not be crossing the intersection. By sending an orange signal to one street, it is conveying that the signal on the cross street is about to change and drivers there will begin to cross the intersection. By sending a red signal to the drivers on the first street, it is conveying that drivers on the cross street have the right of way and it is dangerous (as well as illegal) to cross the street.

One equilibrium of a signaling game is that everyone uses and understands the signals in the same way. This is obviously the optimal equilibrium. When it comes to traffic signals, the advantage of achieving this equilibrium is obvious! There is nothing inherent in red, green, and orange that means stopping, going, and slowing down. The signals used for stopping and going could easily be different colors (or even the reverse, so that green means stopping and red means going); the crucial problem of optimal communication is that senders and receivers use the same signal to mean the same thing. If they do not, their signals are a form of babbling and the equilibrium outcome is highly undesirable.

In developing the ADICO syntax as a way of sorting out the diverse elements involved in institutional statements, we could just as well have reversed the terms we use for statements containing (or not containing) "or elses." In chapter 5, we proposed that a statement containing four elements of the syntax (ADIC) should be called a norm and five elements of the syntax (ADICO) should be called a rule. Instead, we could have called the first a rule and the second a norm. A quick look at table 6.1 shows that several scholars do exactly this. We even observe some scholars who use the term "norm" at one time for an ADIC statement and at other times for an ADICO statement.

As senders of a signal, they probably know which attributes are present when they use one term or another. As receivers of their signals, however, how are we to know which attributes are present or not? Unless we have access to the *same* materials and spend costly effort determining which attributes are present or absent, we cannot know the meaning of a term when Author Jones uses all five attributes as reference for a norm and four attributes to be a rule as contrasted to Author Smith (or even Author Jones in another text). If senders and receivers have the same attributes of the states of the world in mind, when they use a particular word to describe this state, they reach the optimal equilibrium in a signaling situation.

The similarities between rules, norms, and shared strategies in the ADICO syntax help us to understand why the literature so frequently uses these terms interchangeably. They share several of the same features. Table 6.1 sorts the concepts that other authors use into the types of institutional statements created by our syntax. All of the terms used by other authors, shown in the top section of the table, appear to describe institutional statements that are shared strategies according to the syntax; they contain AIC components. The need for a consensus in the use of terms is vividly illustrated by examining the number of different terms in each section of the table as well as the fact that several terms appear in all three sections. That these terms have been used in so many different ways is not a criticism of past work. Rather, it illustrates the difficulty of untangling key social science concepts that are foundational for institutional analysis.

Lewis proposes that *meaning* occurs when senders and receivers of signals reach such an equilibrium no matter which specific term is being used. There are, of course, other equilibria possible where there is agreement on the attributes of one term but not the others. This appears to characterize the current situation where scholars are more likely to agree on the use of the term *strategy*. This is contrasted to the use of *rules* and *norms* for which there is little agreement. Lewis calls these "babbling" equilibria. Receivers have no reasonable method for imparting meaning to some of the signals they receive, while there is agreed-upon meaning for others (see also Crawford and Sobel 1982; Farrell 1993).

The problem of babble about rules and norms is not confined to scholars who study something other than rules and norms and only occasionally misuse a term whose meaning has become well established by those who work extensively on these concepts. In a recently published book

TABLE 6.1
Shared strategies, norms, and rules as used in ADICO syntax and in recent literature

ADICO components	Terms used by Crawford-Ostrom	Terms used by other authors
AIC	Shared Strategies	Axelrod 1981—Rules, strategies
		Axelrod 1986—Norms
		Bourdieu 1977—Doxic elements of action
		Calvert 1992—Equilibrium strategies
		Hodgson and Knudsen 2004—Conventions
		Levi 1990—Norms
		March and Olsen 1989—Rules
		Meyer and Rowan 1991—Taken-for-granted actions
		Myerson 1991—Rules
		Rowe 1989—Rules of action
		Schank and Abelson 1977—Scripts
		Schelling 1978—Focal points
		Schotter 1981—Institutions
		Ullmann-Margalit 1977—Conventions
ADIC	Norms	Azar 2004—Norms
		Bicchieri 1997—Norms
		Braybrooke 1987—Conventions
		Braybrooke 1996—Rules
		Coleman 1987—Norms
		DiMaggio and Powell 1991—Institutions
		Levi 1990—Norms
		Lewis 1969—Conventions
		March and Olsen 1989—Rules
		McAdams 2001—Normative attitudes
		Meyer and Rowan 1991—Taken-for-granted actions
		North 1981—Ethical codes
		Rowe 1989—Obligations
		Schotter 1981—Institutions
		Sugden 1986—Conventions
		Ullmann-Margalit 1977—Social norms
		Weber 1947—Conventions
ADICO	Rules	Albert 1986—Laws
		Axelrod 1986—Norms backed by metanorms
		Coleman 1987—Norms
		Commons [1924] 1968—Working rules
		Hurwicz 1994—Rules of the game-form
		J. Knight 1992—Rules
		Levi 1990—Legalistic institutions
		North 1990—Rules
		Shepsle 1979a, 1989—Rules
		Ullmann-Margalit 1977—PD norms, decrees
		Weber 1947—Laws

Source: Crawford and Ostrom 2000, 130.

called *Social Norms*, the editors—who had convened several conferences and worked extensively with a group of knowledgeable scholars conducting studies on social norms—introduced the resulting volume by commenting: "These chapters suggest that consensus about social norms is limited both across disciplines and within them. To begin, the concept of social norm clearly means different things to different scholars" (Hechter and Opp 2001, xii). They go on to bemoan the fact that as "there is no common definition of social norms, there can be little agreement about how to measure them" (xiii). Obviously, various authors in the volume did define social norms—many of them in a way that is consistent with the syntactic definition provided in chapter 5. The book contained, however, a multiplicity of definitions of the central concept under study. In an excellent recent review of how the concept of norms is used in the field of law and economics, McAdams and Rasmusen (forthcoming) also bemoan the lack of consensus on the definition of a norm.

The existence of a babbling equilibrium in regard to these terms is a key problem for the social sciences.[1] The concepts of rules and norms are at the heart of many core theoretical questions having to do with how individuals coordinate activities with one another. Lacking agreed-upon definitions of these terms leaves us all in a suboptimal babbling equilibria rather than in a scientific signaling game where general progress is likely. If scholars were to accept the syntax as we have laid it out in chapter 5—or an improved version of it—it would help to solve the babbling equilibrium problem.

At an earlier juncture, Douglass North (1990) dug into another babbling equilibrium problem. Many scholars tended to use the concept of an organization and of an institution interchangeably. North has insisted on a key difference between organizations and institutions. As North described his approach:

> A crucial distinction in this study is made between institutions and organizations. . . . Organizations include political bodies (political parties, the Senate, a city council, a regulatory agency), economic bodies (firms, trade unions, family farms, cooperatives), social bodies (churches, clubs, athletic associations), and educational bodies (schools, universities, vocational training centers). They are groups of individuals bound by some common purpose to achieve objectives. . . . [T]he emphasis in this study is on the institutions that are the underlying rules of the game and the focus on organizations (and their entrepreneurs) is primarily on their role as agents of institutional change; therefore the emphasis is on the interaction between institutions and organizations. (4–5)

We are using terms in a manner consistent with North's distinction. Rules are part of the underlying structure that constitute a single action situation or a series of them. Organizations may be participants in a situation structured by rules and can, in turn, be analyzed by looking at the linked action situations used by the group "bound by some common purpose to achieve outcomes." Most organizations would be composed of multiple simultaneous and sequential action situations—all constituted by rules as well as by the physical world.

Sorting out organizations and institutions, and strategies, norms, and rules is a beginning. It is, however, not enough. The problem becomes even more substantial when one moves beyond the effort to develop a general definition of rules and norms to ways of classifying rules. As soon as one digs below the surface of an action situation to explore the prescriptions partly responsible for their structure, one is struck with the vast array of potential rules. The ADICO framework enables the analyst to classify institutional statements by using their *syntax* to determine the difference between strategies, norms, and rules. Now we need to ask, What is a useful classification based on the *semantics* of rules?

The Policy Analyst's Need to Understand How to Reform Situations

Policy analysts must be able to use the semantics of rules. Elected officials, the staff members of national, state, local governments and citizen interest groups, and many social scientists are asked what rules should be changed to solve a particular kind of problem. The questions may be in regard to problems as global as how to change the incentives facing users of carbon so as to reduce the likelihood and magnitude of global warming or as local as how to change the parking regulations in a small town so as to make it a more attractive location for residents in the region to shop downtown.

The policy analyst stands in relationship to "repairing" single and linked action situations as a doctor stands in relationship to a sick patient, a mechanic in relation to a car that does not run, or a computer technician in relationship to a computer system producing strange symbols on a printer.[2] In attempting to solve all these problems of poor performance, the "Doc" has to dig under the surface, begin to think which subsystem or linkage among systems is most likely to be causing the problem, and begin to do tests to confirm these initial speculations. For physicians and mechanics, the systems they need to understand are primarily biophysical systems and subsystems. The mechanic learns how to take the system totally apart and reconstruct it subsystem by subsystem. The general physician does not have the freedom to take his or her patient's system apart but certainly learned in medical school how to dissect other living beings, witnessed many surgical operations and autopsies, and studied a cumulative body of knowledge about how various parts of the human body should work. The computer technician has both a mechanical system to try to understand as well as multiple layers of software languages. He or she must know what each of the major types of commands does in the most frequently used languages and which types of commands are likely to be compatible or incompatible.

The policy analyst's task is closer to that of the computer technician than to the auto mechanic or physician. A very large proportion of what the policy analyst must understand is language-based. When one is studying rules, after all, the content is entirely language-based. Yet, it is also essential to know key aspects of the relevant biophysical and social world to propose changes that are likely to improve outcomes. When we are asked to propose new rules, however, the request is for something that will be expressed in language, as Vincent Ostrom (1987, 1993, 1997) has so often articulated.

Moving beyond Slogan Words to Describe Institutions

The embarrassment that we face is that policy analysis has yet to develop a coherent understanding of how our subject matter should best be expressed, how rules fit or don't fit together to shape observable behavior and outcomes. All too often, slogan words, such as "privatization," "centralization," and "decentralization," are used as substitutes for careful analysis. What are the specific rules that we are talking about when we talk about a privatization or decentralization policy? What changes in the incentives of participants will occur if we propose a particular set of new rules versus other potential sets? The lack of a disciplined language to be able to analyze, dissect, and propose better reforms was dramatically illustrated for the world after the collapse of the former Soviet Union. Western scholars were asked to help Russia and the other "newly industrializing countries" to create a vigorous and productive private market economy. Many of our proposals were actually accepted and efforts made to implement them. But, instead of an open, competitive market, the rules proposed by policy analysts generated commercial monopolies, massive corruption, and little economic growth. And, this is not the only time that the recommendations of policy analysts were accepted and yet did not produce the predicted results. There is obviously a lot of work to be done.

Coping with the Immense Diversity by Identifying Generic Rules

At the same time as I am committed to digging into and revealing an underlying universality in the components of human action, I am repeatedly challenged and amazed by the multiplicity of rules that colleagues and I have recorded in fieldwork (see chapter 8) and that other scholars have used in their analyses of situations.[3] If one focuses on only the detailed aspects of rules, it is hard to see how they are similar and how they differ. It is then hard to analyze carefully how changes in a particular type of rule (as contrasted to changes in several different types of rules) affect the resulting situations. This recognition and appreciation of variety leads one to have a substantial wariness related to the capacity of humans to design optimal systems without a substantial trial-and-error process so as to learn what works in a particular biophysical environment. I will return to this issue in chapter 8.

The puzzle has been how to develop a language to express rules that enables one to capture in a consistent and cumulative manner the most general characteristics of the basic rules while providing a structure that enables scholars to enumerate and test the impact of changes in a rule type. I remember my surprise when I was working on a draft of my Presidential Address to the Public Choice Society (E. Ostrom 1986) and found that Charles Plott was unaware that his work on "default conditions" (Grether, Isaac, and Plott 1979) was an excellent empirical study related to earlier work by Niskanen (1971) and Romer and Rosenthal (1978) on "reversion levels." I had asked Plott to review my draft paper where I refer to that earlier paper, in which Plott and his colleagues had used the term "default condition" to refer to an ingenious method they had devised to examine what would happen if participants in an experiment were not able to come to an agreement using a unanimity rule.

I thought their "default condition" was the same as the concept referred to as a "reversion level" by Niskanen (1971) and by Romer and Rosenthal (1978). In chapter 7, we discuss the need for all aggregation rules to include a condition stating what decision will hold if multiple participants do not reach an agreement. We call that rule a "lack of agreement" rule. What was neat, I thought, was that Plott and his colleagues had actually tested the impact of changing this rule in the laboratory. They found that the particular "lack of agreement" rule they used "literally determines the outcomes in processes such as these" (Grether, Isaac, and Plott 1979, V-7). Their experimental results thus strongly confirmed Romer and Rosenthal's argument in an earlier "theoretical debate" between them and Niskanen about the likely results when agents did not agree to a proposal under different "reversion levels."[4] Even with Plott's substantial acuity and awareness of the importance of studying rules, he was surprised and pleased when I pointed out the similarity. What I dream of is a method for classifying rules that enables scholars to know when they are talking about the same "variety" of a rule—in this case, the default condition of an aggregation rule.

To illustrate what I mean by a generic rule, let us take an everyday example of the wide variety of a specific rule used in practice—sale of alcoholic beverages. Most state legislatures have passed legislation related to the sale of liquor—particularly related to who can legally hold the position of a Buyer of alcoholic beverages. Using the first generic entry rule enumerated in chapter 7, one would specify a generic entry rule for buying liquor as:

Persons with attributes $a_1, a_2, \ldots a_n$, *Permitted* to hold the position of a Buyer of alcoholic beverages subject to conditions, $c_1, c_2, \ldots c_n$.

What attributes and conditions are used varies widely from one place to another. To buy liquor at a liquor store, the *attributes* usually relate to age and the kind of identity card that may be required. The *conditions* relate primarily to the days of the week and the hours that liquor stores are authorized to be open. To even enter a bar, as contrasted to a liquor store, in some jurisdictions, the attributes of a Buyer must also be held by anyone who enters the facility. Younger siblings can accompany older brothers or sisters when buying liquor at a grocery store, but not at a local pub. If one were to enumerate all of the variations in attributes and conditions just for holding the position of being a Buyer of major types of commodities (bread, prescriptions, pork, liquor, cars, etc.), the list would become incredibly long very fast. For some purposes, such as trying to improve policies related to the issuing of food stamps or reducing adolescent alcoholism, one could identify an important subset of all of these rules to analyze where they have been used, what other factors affect the desired outcomes, and what kind of performance has been achieved.

The specificity of the rules that one studies depends on the question one wants to ask. The generic rules are not specific in terms of identifying the *particular* attributes or conditions that affect a type of rule. When a research team at the Workshop in Political Theory and Policy Analysis was studying the rules used to regulate appropriation from common-pool resources around the world and how they affected behavior and outcomes, we were interested in developing a full enumeration of the specific attributes and conditions described in the case studies that we read and coded. As discussed in chapter 8, we did find a shockingly large number of attributes and conditions used in entry rules. For example, for the first entry rule discussed above, we identified seven ascribed attributes, two acquired attributes, four residency attributes, and thirteen conditions that are used individually or in combination to make an individual eligible to access a common-pool resource (see table 8.1).

The purpose of classifying generic rules in chapter 7, however, is *not* to be exhaustive in regard to detailed attributes and conditions. No general-purpose language for classifying rules can do this! A key task is to provide the equivalent of the components of a general recipe for creating situations. A good cook knows, for example, that to make a cake requires some proportion of flour, sugar, fat, spices, a leavening agent, and time and temperature at which a baking pan should remain in an oven. That is the "general recipe" for making cakes. Pies have quite a different "general" recipe. Grandmother's secret recipe for Chocolate Surprise Cake, on the other hand, lists specific quantities of particular ingredients, the type of pan that should be used, and the temperature and time of baking. What is "secret" is the particular type of spices or sugar, some combination of flours, something about the timing and process of mixing, or any of a wide variety of other details that makes her cake something special that her grandchildren fight over. The purpose of the classification system outlined in chapter 7 is not to get to this level of detail, but rather to provide a general classification system that can be used by multiple scholars who are analyzing a specific question and examining rules in order to address this question.

By identifying the generic structure of entry rules, all of the many ascribed and acquired characteristics that could be used in a specific entry rule are considered together as a diverse set of attributes. Similarly, all of the various relevant events—such as the results of a prior situation—are simply considered as "conditions." Thus, the classification proposed in chapter 7 identifies the most general structure of a rule configuration.

The Role of Rules as Information Transformation Mechanisms

Once we have developed a way of expressing rules in a systematic fashion, we can begin to address a number of quite important and exciting questions. One of these has to do with the generative capacity of rules—their productive and reproductive capacities. If we consider institutional rules to have a broad similarity to grammatical rules, questions concerning the information-processing capabilities of institutional rules are similar to those of a grammar.

Any mechanism that transmits information about how to produce something (a protein, a sentence, or an action situation) is itself subject to noise, to random error, and to distortion. Institutional rules are probably more vulnerable to these problems than either grammatical rules (since humans are motivated to try to make themselves understood and thus to follow grammatical rules) or genetic codes (since these "instructions" do not rely on humans themselves to carry them out, and biologists have ascertained that the mutation rate is actually very low).

Rules that are repeatedly found in many different types of situations are apt to be more reliable "building blocks" than rules that are only infrequently included among the set of rules constructing social arenas. Once we have a systematic way to classify generic rules, we can study diverse institutional arrangements in a manner to identify those rules that are components of a large number of situations but that have a surface appearance of being different. That may begin to give us some clues concerning the use of redundancy and of the iteration and reiteration of a rule to make much more complex structures.

An Underlying Universality?

Another major reason for this effort is my deep conviction, as I state in chapter 1, that underlying the immense variety of surface differences, all repetitive situations faced by human beings are composed of nested layers composed from the same set of elements.

Game theory has already provided us a formal language for expressing the structure of relatively simple and unambiguous action situations. Some of the essential working parts of an action situation—such as positions (as distinct from players) and outcomes (as distinct from payoffs)— are frequently not acknowledged when a game theory textbook lays out the working parts of a game. Expanding these parts—as was accomplished in chapter 2—enables us to be more confident that we have identified the components of a wide diversity of situations found in all sectors of organized life. This improves analysis in several ways. First, it requires the analyst to make hidden or implicit assumptions overt and explicit. Second, it provides clear elements that need to be generated by rules (or by physical laws). By not requiring that all situations must be expressed as a formal game, the concept of an action situation expands the range of situations that can be compared using the same structural variables. The attempt to find a way of expressing the most basic rules that generate action situations will help us illustrate that the generic rules used to constitute a market come from the same set of generic rules used to constitute a legislature, a hierarchy, a self-organized resource governance system, or any of a wide diversity of situations. Having now discussed in some depth the "why," I think it is important to define generic rules. Let us move on to the task of classifying rules by their AIM.

Seven

Classifying Rules

ELINOR OSTROM AND SUE CRAWFORD

THE PURPOSE of this chapter is to develop a useful system for classifying or naming rules. In our effort to group rules into useful classifications, we recognize that no single classification can ever be useful for all purposes. One strategy that is commonly used is to order rules according to the jurisdiction that created them. All national rules are classified together, state or provincial rules are a second group, and local rules are a third group. This is a useful first cut when one is studying the similarities or differences among multiple domains of a legal system, but does not address how to change action situations within a jurisdiction. Another strategy examines how a rule came into being. De jure rules that have been formally authorized by the legitimate form of government in a particular jurisdiction are considered as different from de facto rules that are actually used by participants. Alternatively, some scholars distinguish between rules that have evolved versus those that have been designed. As institutional analysts, however, we need to devise a method that draws on the general Institutional Analysis and Development (IAD) framework to help link rules to the action situations they constitute.

Thus, the core goal that we seek in developing a useful classification system for rules is to devise a nested set of rule-concepts that facilitate building a cumulative body of theoretically and empirically tested research about human behavior and outcomes in diversely structured situations. Current tendencies to use various dichotomies (government versus market, public versus private, formal versus informal) instead of systematic development of empirically supported theories of human behavior in diversely structured situations is, we strongly believe, inadequate to the task.[1] We do not pose our classification system as a universally applicable system, but rather as a useful system for those interested in linking rules and the action situations (games) created by rules, the biophysical world, and communities (see Burns and Gomolińska 1998 for a related effort).

In this chapter, we posit two conceptual approaches that we have found most useful in classifying rules. The first approach—and the one on which we will focus in this chapter—uses the direct *AIM* of a rule (as defined in chapter 5) as a method for classifying rules. This method focuses on one level of action—operational, collective choice, or constitutional choice—and classifies rules by the part of the relevant action situation that is most directly affected. We refer to this as the horizontal approach. The second layer focuses on the level of authority involved in an analysis, which we refer to as the vertical dimension. Here, we are initially inspired by the work of John R. Commons ([1924] 1968), who distinguished between authorized and authoritative relationships. As discussed in chapter 2, the IAD framework further divides authoritative relationships into those with the authority to affect operational action situations, called collective-choice rules, and those with the authority to affect collective-choice situations, called constitutional-choice rules (see figure 2.3).

While analyzing rule sets at multiple levels (the vertical approach) helps us to uncover important authority relationships, to get to a diagnosis for a particular policy situation, we need to sort the rules at any one level into basic categories that clarify the links between specific rules at that level and the structure of the resulting situation (the horizontal approach). Although this chapter focuses on the ways in which rules directly influence the structure of an action situation, we need always to bear in mind that the rules operate alongside the biophysical world and the attributes of the community and that rules can have indirect effects. So, while the discussion in this chapter hones in on the direct link between rules and action-situation components for the sake of sorting rules by their influence on different parts of the action situation, the emphasis on rules should not be taken to imply that rules alone determine these structures.

The Horizontal Approach: Classifying by the A*I*M of a Rule

As we develop in chapter 5, all regulatory rules have the general syntax of:

> ATTRIBUTES of participants who are OBLIGED, FORBIDDEN, OR PERMITTED to ACT (or AFFECT an outcome) under specified CONDITIONS, OR ELSE.

Using this syntax as the basis for classifying rules still leaves multiple ways to sort rules. One could, for example, use the DEONTIC element (must, must not, or may) as the foundation for a classification system. All the rules forbidding something would be classified together. Given that the deontic operators are interdefinable, however, there does not appear to be any particular usefulness to be derived from such a classification system. If a rule were originally classified as a forbidden rule, it could be rewritten using the permitted or obligated operator.

Another possibility would be to classify by the "OR ELSE" part of a rule. For some purposes, this would be useful. One could learn rapidly what kind of rule infractions in a particular jurisdiction carry a life imprisonment sentence, a ten-year sentence, or a one-year sentence. For many purposes, however, classifying by the OR ELSE component of a rule does not get at the substance of the rules.

It would also be possible to organize a classification system using the ATTRIBUTES or CONDITIONS sections of a rule. This would again be useful for some purposes. Young people could potentially look up and find out what they are allowed to do or not do. One could find out what rules apply if you own property versus renting it, or the rules that apply during the period between a party-nominating convention and the general election. The CONDITION does play an important role in assessing which rules apply in a given action situation. Consequently, attention to the CONDITION can help analysts sort out those rules relevant to a given action situation from those that are not. However, it still leaves us with a myriad of relevant rules that need further sorting. It does not get us far enough to solve the policy analyst's need to know how to repair broken action situations!

If one wishes to use the syntax as a foundation, this leaves one with the AIM element of a rule to be used. And this is our plan. Although (as we note in chapter 5) the syntax fits regulatory rules better than generative rules, generative rules still do have an AIM, so a sorting mechanism that uses the AIM works for generative rules too. And, it works for all three levels of the IAD framework.

Chapter 2 identified the components of action situations that are used to construct a wide variety of analytical models of markets, families, hierarchies, legislatures, corporations, neighborhood associations, common-property regimes, as well as all formal games. The elements are participants, positions, actions, outcomes, information, control, and costs/benefits. They are related together in the following manner:

> *Participants* and *actions* are assigned to *positions*.
> *Outcomes* are linked to actions.
> *Information* is available about *action-outcome linkages*.
> *Control* is exercised over action-outcome linkages.
> *Costs and benefits* are assigned to action-outcome linkages.

Participants, who can either be individuals or any of a wide diversity of organized entities, are assigned to positions. In these positions, they choose among actions in light of their information, the control they have over action-outcome linkages, and the benefits and costs assigned to actions and outcomes.

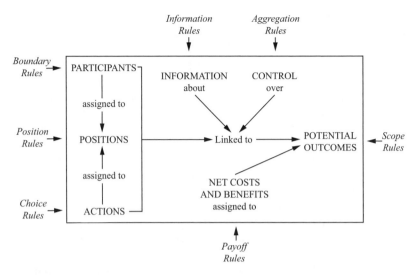

Figure 7.1 Rules as exogenous variables directly affecting the elements of an action situation.

The relationships among the various parts of the action situation are represented within the square on figure 7.1. When an analyst takes each of these working parts as givens, no further inquiry is made as to the cause or source of a particular element. The analyst predicts the likely outcomes based on the model of individual behavior assumed and potentially evaluates the expected pattern of actions and outcomes using such criteria as efficiency, equity, and error proneness.

The analyst examining a one-shot social dilemma among participants who cannot communicate will predict low levels of cooperation (or none at all). To dig under that situation, however, to think about changing it, one needs to know a lot about the underlying structure leading to the social dilemma. Are the participants a set of prisoners who are being held apart by a prosecutor trying to get them to confess? So long as the prosecutor does not use illegal methods and allows the prisoners access to an attorney, what is inefficient for the prisoners is likely to be socially efficient. Better to leave the social dilemma as it stands.

If the participants are harvesters from a common-pool resource, on the other hand, and are led by isolation and individual incentives to over-harvest, the policy analyst needs a coherent scientific language to begin to think about rules that would change this situation. The recommendation simply to create "private property" (Demsetz 1967; R. Smith 1981; L. Anderson 1995) does not tell an analyst anything specific about which rules could be changed to make the situation one of private property (see

Rose 2002 and Tietenberg 2002 for good analyses that dig into this question). Do new positions need to be created—owner versus outsider, for example? How are individuals chosen to become owners? What actions may an owner take, and what actions are forbidden? These are the kinds of questions that we ask at the end of this chapter regarding how to transform the Snatch Game into a more productive game by assigning property rights. It turns out that we have to change seven rules in order to modify this very simple game of nature from one without any rules to one with some property rights defined. Focusing on the direct link between the AIM of a rule and the affected component of the action situation classifies rules in a way that facilitates analysis of structural change.

The action situation mechanism for classifying rules groups rules according to the element in the action situation that they most *directly* impact. Many rules also indirectly affect other components. Figure 7.1 shows the names that we have given to the types of rules based on this coding scheme. The arrows identify the element of the action situation directly affected by that type of rule. We also need to remember that two other major categories of exogenous variables (the biophysical world and attributes of community) also shape these action situation components.

Using the AIM of a rule for classification leads to the specification of seven broad types of rules: position, boundary, choice, aggregation, information, payoff, and scope.[2] Position rules create positions (e.g., member of a legislature or a committee, voter, etc.). Boundary rules affect how individuals are assigned to or leave positions and how one situation is linked to other situations. Choice rules affect the assignment of particular action sets to positions. Aggregation rules affect the level of control that individual participants exercise at a linkage within or across situations. Information rules affect the level of information available in a situation about actions and the link between actions and outcome linkages. Payoff rules affect the benefits and costs assigned to outcomes given the actions chosen. Scope rules affect which outcomes must, must not, or may be affected within a domain.

The direct relationships among rules and the components of an action situation are shown in figure 7.1 as the set of arrows connecting rules to specific parts of an action situation. We can also think of a general verb type that links AIMs directly to different parts of the action situation. These basic verbs assist in sorting out the various types of rules. A first assessment in sorting the rules that affect an action situation can be to determine the general verb that most closely resembles the specific verb in the AIM of the parsed rule. The basic verb can also be used to translate diverse specific verbs in rules to general verb types for the sake of uncovering similarities in rules that, on the surface, look different. Two bound-

TABLE 7.1
The A*I*M component of each type of rule

Type of rule	Basic A*I*M verb	Regulated component of the action situation
Position	Be	Positions
Boundary	Enter or leave	Participants
Choice	Do	Actions
Aggregation	Jointly affect	Control
Information	Send or receive	Information
Payoff	Pay or receive	Costs/Benefits
Scope	Occur	Outcomes

ary rules from two different action situations, for example, might use very different language but may ultimately be identical mechanisms for regulating how a participant exits the position "voting member." Table 7.1 lists the basic A*I*M verb associated with each type of rule.

The discussion of classifying rules by their A*I*M follows the order of the list on table 7.1, which starts with position rules and ends with scope rules.[3] These categories simultaneously sort rules for comparative analysis and identify the immediate link between the rule and a component of the action situation. However, rules operate together as a *configuration*. The clean arrows from one type of rules to one part of the action situation in figure 7.1 should not be taken as an assumption that these rules operate *independently* of one another, or that boundary rules influence only who enters positions, or that payoff rules influence only net costs and benefits. While the A*I*M may hit one element of the action situation, other components of the rules—particularly the CONDITION and the OR ELSE component—may impact another component.[4] And, one rule may eventually affect other components of the action situation in addition to the component directly affected.

An example of a boundary rule that influences many other action situation components of an "urban taxi game" is a local medallion ordinance. Such a boundary rule requires that a taxicab display a purchased medallion from the city before it can legally use the city streets to attract customers. It has been used in New York City for decades. When a city limits the number of medallions it will authorize, the entry costs for putting a taxi on the streets rise substantially, but if the medallions are strictly limited, the potential returns per unit of time also increase substantially. And the time that a traveler has to wait before getting a taxi ride may increase substantially. Thus, one rule can have very substantial impact on the entire structure of resulting action situations through its direct impact on one of the working components of an action situation. This example also illustrates another advantage of a systematic method for classifying rules, namely, to help in identifying rules that are similar in function in widely diverse settings. The medallion entry rule is a specific example of a generic boundary rule used in a variety of action situations to limit entry. As we will discuss in chapter 8, it is one of the entry rules used in some locations to regulate fisheries—requiring fishing boats to purchase fishing permits.

In fact, all rules indirectly impact net costs and benefits since all rules include DEONTICS that translate into deltas and OR ELSES that generally have payoff consequences. This complexity does not invalidate the analytical goal of sorting rules by types in order to get a better handle on the influence of rules on the action situation components. It does, however, mean that the initial sorting does not identify all of the rules that indirectly influence each component. Finding the rules that indirectly influence each component involves a next step of looking at the other rule components to find ATTRIBUTES, CONDITIONS, or OR ELSES that link to that particular component.

Thus, classifying rules by their direct effect on an AIM offers an important tool for sorting rules into basic types based on their immediate impact on the action situation, but it does not cleanly classify all rules into mutually exclusive categories based on the component of the action situation that is eventually affected. Since rules can often influence more than one part of an action situation, this simply cannot be done at this level of sorting. This classification scheme sorts rules into useful categories for policy analysis by focusing on the AIM first, while recognizing that further sorting may be necessary for more complete specification of the rules linked to particular components of the action situation.

With caveats aside, we now turn to an overview of each of these seven types of rules. We concentrate here on identifying the most general aspects of each type of rule since so many specific examples of each type of rule are found in practice. We thus focus on what appear to be the most basic or generic forms of each type of rule affecting diverse action situations. The language of rules is, like all of the analytical concepts discussed in this book, hierarchical in structure. The generic rule forms are special cases of the seven basic types of rules, and finer rules are elaborations and special cases of these generic rule forms that we lay out here. Chapter 8 provides examples that illustrate the immense variety of specific rules by drawing on empirical studies of rules related to common-pool resources to elaborate the immense variety of specific rules found to exist in a study of the governance and management of irrigation, inshore fisheries, and forest institutions around the world.

Position Rules

An initial building block of an action situation is the set of positions or anonymous slots that are filled by participants and to which specific action sets are assigned at junctures in a decision process. Position rules create these positions. Position rules are often not by themselves intrinsically interesting, as they merely create "holders" for participants to enter and for the specification of actions that participants in positions can take at specific nodes in a process.[5] As discussed in chapter 2, positions are the connecting link between participants and authorized actions. Thus, they create the scaffolding for a wide diversity of situations that can vary significantly in terms of the number of positions and the relative authority assigned to each position.

A minimal position rule names a single position or slot—such as "member"—as the most inclusive position to be held by all participants in a situation. In the initial Commons Dilemma experiments described in chapter 3, the experimenters generated only one position, even though there were eight participants holding that position. A situation with one and only one position held by all participants is an internally egalitarian situation even though entry into the position may be difficult. Most situations contain more than a single position, and sets of rules assign different kinds of authority to those in different positions. The Trust games also explored in chapter 3 all had at least two positions: Investor and Trustee. Differentiation of authority to act or to effect outcomes depends upon the establishment of multiple positions within a situation.

Number of Participants in a Position

A position rule may also state whether there is a defined number, no limit, a lower limit, or an upper limit on the number of participants who hold a position. If all positions in a situation have a defined number of participants, the maximum number of participants is thus also defined. A defined number of participants in positions is used in most recreational games or competitive sports. It is not legal to play with more or less than the defined number of participants in each position on the field. The position of a member of a jury must be filled by a defined number of participants (defined by law, it is frequently twelve jurors, but it varies from jurisdiction to jurisdiction and according to the type of case involved).

Sometimes a rule states only a lower bound or an upper bound on the number of participants in a position. Either bound may be left undefined. When the lower bound is defined and the upper bound is left unspecified, a minimum number of participants must be present, but not a maximum. Most quorum rules define a minimum number of participants who must occupy a particular position before particular actions must be taken.

When a lower bound is not defined, action can occur without any participants in a particular position. When the upper bound is defined and the lower bound is left unspecified, a "lid" is placed on the total number of participants that can hold a particular position. An operational example of this type of rule is found in the authorizations given to many public agencies that they can hire up to a specified number of participants in a particular position (state trooper, for example). Such rules may or may not specify whether there is a lower bound. When both bounds are specified, action may not take place until at least the minimum participants are in their position and no more than the maximum are present. Most position rules do not specify conditions, which means that the position rule holds under any of the likely conditions to be found in the situations. It is certainly possible that there may be conditions added to a specific position rule. For example, a position rule in a school district may raise the number of teacher aides who may be hired by a school in the condition that the number of students per teacher rises above twenty.

Where position rules do not exactly specify the number of participants, it is entirely the operation of the boundary rules over time in conjunction with the type of goods and attributes of a community that affect the number of participants, their characteristics, and their ease of entry or exit.

Boundary Rules

Boundary rules—frequently called entry and exit rules—define (1) who is eligible to enter a position, (2) the process that determines which eligible participants may enter (or must enter) positions, and (3) how an individual may leave (or must leave) a position. Some entry rules, then, specify the criteria to be used to determine whether an actor is eligible to fill a particular position. Ascribed and acquired attributes are frequently used in this type of entry rule. Individuals may have to meet certain physical standards, such as height and weight. They may have to meet a certain wealth standard or pay an entry fee. Individuals may be required to possess a certain range of experiences, to be above a minimum age, to have graduated from certain schools, to be the descendants of a particular group, to possess certain abilities, or to live in certain geographic areas. Public employment under civil service systems and patronage systems differs substantially in the entry rules that are applicable.

When those crafting a rule hope to increase the skills and knowledge held by those in a position, they may list one or more acquired characteristics, such as holding a college degree or passing a test. Exclusive country clubs may require that a family own a fortune in liquid assets and have sent their children to Ivy League schools to be eligible to be members. Immense and important issues have and will continue to erupt over whether one or another attribute should be included in a rule. Whether race should be used in an entry rule—biased either for, or against, individuals of a particular race—has been a major controversy in the United States for multiple decades (see Greve 2001).

First-order boundary rules define the eligibility of individuals to hold the position of member. These rules include a set of transformations that partition a defined set of individuals, usually bounded in space and time, into subsets of individuals who are eligible and ineligible to hold the position of member. A simple rule to partition the set is that a participant *must* be eligible if the set of ATTRIBUTES of the participant equals the required set of ATTRIBUTES and the participant meets specified CONDITIONS. The ATTRIBUTES that may be specified can include ascribed or acquired characteristics (see chapter 8 for examples). An alternative formulation of the *same* rule is that it is forbidden to keep a person who has certain defining ATTRIBUTES and has met required CONDITIONS from being eligible to be a member. Since the deontic operators are interdefinable, the same rule can be stated with any of the deontic operators. Alternatively, one can state that an individual must not be eligible unless they have certain ATTRIBUTES and have met defined CONDITIONS. An example of a rule stated in this manner is the rule in the U.S. Constitution (article 1, section 2, paragraph 2) regarding the eligibility of citizens to be a Member of Congress: "No Person shall be a Representative who shall not have attained to the age of twenty five Years, and been seven Years a Citizen of the United States, and who shall not, when elected, be an Inhabitant of that State in which he shall be chosen."

Second-order entry rules define how the set of eligibles are further partitioned into subsets of position-holders and nonholders. Nonholders here are narrowly defined to include those individuals who would be eligible to hold the position of a member in a particular situation but do not hold that position. Boundary rules are open when they allow eligibles full control over the decision whether or not they wish to hold a position. Most election laws within the United States, for example, are open and allow eligible voters (those who are above a defined age and have registered, etc.) to decide whether or not to come to the polls to vote. All eligible voters who appear at designated places and times are authorized to participate in an election. Variables such as the length of residency required for eligibility, registration procedures, absentee voting rules, and number of hours allowed for voting on election day combine to make the act of voting more or less expensive in terms of the amount of time, effort, and knowledge required to be legally registered prior to election day.

Boundary rules are invitational when they authorize holders of a position to select future holders from the set of those who are eligible. Thus, eligibles are divided into two sets—those who have been invited and those who have not been invited. Entry requires an invitation. Many private clubs use a rule of this type. Most businesses and public bureaus also use rules of this type with invitations taking the form of job offers.

Closely related to an invitational entry rule is a competitive rule where participants are selected as an outcome of another action situation in which potential members compete against each other to gain entry. In a competitive election, entry requires receiving the most votes (or some other definition, depending upon the aggregation rule used in the election situation). The selection of legislators is normally the outcome of a separate election in which members are selected by voters from among candidates who are running in this election.

Boundary rules are compulsory when eligibles have no control over whether they fill a position or not. When focusing on broad jurisdictions, the most inclusive class of individuals within a jurisdiction is its subjects—those subject to its rules. The status of being a subject is not conferred by choice when the jurisdiction is a general-purpose governmental unit such as a city, county, state, or province, or the largest, general-purpose jurisdiction, a nation. Subjects are nonvoluntary members of a public instrumentality. A voluntary member of an organization in the private domain of life exercises choice concerning whether or not to join (subject to eligibility criteria) but is subject to the rules of the arrangement while remaining a member.

A suspect arrested by the police has no choice as to whether to participate or not in court proceedings concerning charges made by the state. The suspect has limited choices: what to plead, whether to hire a lawyer, whether or not to testify on his or her own behalf. A suspect in a criminal case cannot take any action independently to exit from the process.[6] Compulsory rules oblige anyone who meets certain CONDITIONS to hold a position. Being drafted into the army or subpoenaed to serve on a jury involves the selection of a member by a formal process outside the control of any individual draftee. A person selected as a defendant in a criminal trial has entered this position through a compulsory process. Under universal compulsory entry rules, participation is required for all those who are eligible to participate. All eligible taxpayers, for example, must complete tax forms and pay any taxes they owe. A compulsory entry rule is particular when only a subset of eligibles must become members at any one time period. Both the draft and jury duty are particular entry rules.

Boundary rules may also assign fees for entry and/or exit. Entry rules that are open, invitational, or competitive may assign a fee or inducement to any eligible individual who wishes to enter a position. An example is an application fee or reward. Poll taxes are fees that eligible voters had to pay in order to vote at an earlier juncture in the United States. An example of the second is a membership fee or reward. Many competitions also require a fee before entry.

Boundary rules may define high licensing fees or large bonding requirements for entry or exit. These rules also interact with the physical world and attributes of the community to shape the dynamics of entry and exit into positions. A fee of $1 per hour to use a tennis court may be considered a low entry cost in a middle- or upper-class community, while in a poor community such a fee may preclude the entry of many potential users. The level or strictness of entry and exit costs is relative to the availability of an attribute or a resource in a community.

Governmental jurisdictions can also increase entry and exit costs via other kinds of boundary rules such as certification procedures with many requirements imposed on all potential entrants, or a limitation on the number of enterprises licensed (which makes the license itself a very valuable good like a liquor license or taxi cab medallion). So, one way of increasing strictness involves more stringent requirements. However, entry costs are also affected by the production technology of particular goods. When a high fixed investment is required to produce any quantity of the good at all, entry costs are relatively high, and the conditions of a competitive market are rarely met.

Rules Related to Multiple Positions

When situations involve more than a single position, a mix of position and boundary rules together define relationships between those positions. Some rules create multiple positions (position rule), require each participant to hold one of them (boundary rule), and forbid the holding of more than one position (boundary rule). Such a rule set is used in many recreational sports. Positions such as pitcher and hitter are defined. Each position is filled by at least one member. All members hold one, and only one, position. Such a rule set covers and partitions the set of participants in the situation. Another rule set is used in many committee settings to assign one and only one member a unique position, such as the chair of the committee, and to assign all other members to the other position. The U.S. Constitution provides an example in article 1, section 6, paragraph 2: "No Senator or Representative shall, during the Time for which he was elected, be appointed to any civil Office under the Authority of the United States, which shall have been created, or the Emoluments whereof shall have been encreased during such time; and no Person holding any Office under the United States, shall be a Member of either House during his Continuance in Office."

Alternatively, the rule set may assign a member to at least one position and permit members to hold multiple positions. Such a rule is used in many organizations when members may hold several different positions simultaneously. A member of a firm may hold a position as a particular worker (secretary, foreman, president) as well as a position related to tenure in office (a probationary versus permanent staff member). This rule set covers, but does not partition, the set of participants.

Succession Rules

Boundary rules may also define eligibility for entry to positions in terms of rules that define who is eligible to move from one position to another and what criteria must be met, often called succession rules. Civil service, seniority, and patronage institutional rules differ primarily in the procedures used and criteria applied in regard to succession of individuals into higher-level positions. In a civil service or "merit" system, those who are already employees must serve specified periods of time at lower-level positions and pass examinations in order to be placed on an eligible list for promotion to higher-level positions. When a seniority rule is used, individuals who have been in a particular position for the longest period of time are selected to move into higher-level positions when vacancies occur. Decisions about upward mobility in a patronage system are made by individuals who hold the position of "patrons."

Exit Rules

While entry rules define who is eligible to enter a position and who has control over entry, exit rules define the conditions under which a participant must, must not, or may leave a position. In two-player repeated social dilemma games, the capability to exit—leave the situation and the position of player—has consistently been shown to make a big difference in the rate of cooperation reached over time (Orbell, Schwarz-Shea, and Simmons 1984; Schuessler 1989; Vanberg and Congleton 1992). Exit allows a participant to extract themselves from having to make a choice between defecting on someone else or being a sucker when the other participants defect. Defendants in a criminal trial or a prisoner may not leave such a position at their own initiative. The results of a trial may be to release the defendant (allowing the participant in this position to get out of this position). After a defined period of time has passed, a prisoner may be released from this position by a parole board or may have simply served a set term and be automatically released. A citizen of a nation may not have full control over leaving this position. Many countries have placed severe constraints on the capabilities of citizens to exit voluntarily.

Rules sometimes set fixed terms of office with stringent rules concerning the eligibility of a past position holder to be eligible to hold the same position again. Governors of some states and mayors in some cities may hold these positions for one term only or may not be eligible to succeed themselves (even though they may later be eligible after someone else has served in the office). Under such circumstances, the person in the position has no control over retaining the position after the fixed term has expired. For most elected positions, voters have full control over a participant's continuation in office. Positions like those of judges, however, may be for life, subject only to removal for illegal or immoral behavior. Participants in such positions are assigned very high levels of control over when and under what conditions they leave office.

The rules related to many positions, however, give both the occupant and others partial control over whether the occupant continues. Except under slavery or imprisonment, occupants of most positions are allowed to exit or resign from positions at their own initiative.[7] (Particular rules may set a limit on the amount of time that must elapse from announcing a decision to leave and actually leaving or may set a charge associated with leaving a position prior to fulfilling some aspects of a contract.) The capability of a participant to leave a position is a fundamental limit on the power that other participants can exert over a participant.

In regard to civil proceedings, the plaintiff has an initial voice regarding the instigation of legal proceedings and also a choice concerning their termination. If the plaintiff wishes to terminate the case by dropping the charges, the plaintiff will probably have to pay court charges, attorney fees, and other costs, but can otherwise freely exit. Upon termination of many civil cases, one or all of the parties are usually assigned court and attorney fees as part of the costs of the use of the institutional arrangements. The costs of exit here may be very high. Litigants may use the potential costs of a trial as a threat to reach a negotiated settlement in the shadow of the court. When there is sufficient ambiguity as to the outcome of the trial, both sides may be willing to negotiate outside the courtroom in order to reduce the possibility of losing in court and paying the exit costs.

While the holder of a position in most situations may be able to exit voluntarily, others may also have greater or lesser control over whether the person continues in or leaves the position. Prior to the establishment of civil service legislation in many states, appointed local public employees could be easily removed from office by elected officials. Changes in the party of locally elected officials frequently meant that public employees hired by the other party were fired and new workers loyal to the incoming party were hired. Civil service legislation changed the relative "rights" of public employees to their positions. No longer could they be fired at will or for lack of political loyalty and activity. After an initial probationary period had expired, a public employee could not be fired except for "cause."

Collective bargaining agreements also affect the relative control that various participants have over exit from positions. Under such contracts, the terms and conditions of employment and firing for an entire set of positions are negotiated at the same time. Grievance procedures may be instituted to provide a forum and procedure for a participant who wishes to appeal an involuntary termination. A participant holding the position of a boss may be forced to reemploy an employee (or provide compensation) if a termination is not considered by the grievance panel to have been within the power of the boss. Contracts often specify rights to positions according to seniority, which limits the power of a boss to select which employees will be terminated during times of financial restrictions. Under seniority rules, the last person hired into a position is the first to be laid off, regardless of work performance.

Choice Rules

Choice[8] rules specify what a participant occupying a position must, must not, or may do at a particular point in a decision process in light of conditions that have, or have not, been met at that point in the process. The actions that participants must, must not, or may do are dependent both on the position they hold, prior actions taken by others and/or themselves, and attributes of relevant state variables.

Rules with action AIM's partition possible actions in an action situation into required, permitted, and forbidden acts dependent upon the path of past actions taken by participants and others and readings on relevant state variables. Since the classification system focuses on the most direct link between the AIM of a rule and the components of an action situation, not all rules with action AIMs fall into the choice rule category. When the action of an AIM relates directly to entry or exit from a position, giving or receiving information, joint control over a decision, or giving or receiving payoffs, then the rule is a boundary rule, information rule, aggregation rule, or payoff rule, respectively. Choice rules partition all other actions that do not fit into those specific parts of the action situation. In complex situations structured by complex systems of rules, however, a system of choice rules may not completely partition all other possible actions into required, permitted, or forbidden actions. The partitioning of actions can also be complicated by complex sets of rules that may be inconsistent in their ordering of actions with different rules assigning different DEONTICS to the same action. One rule may forbid an action, while another rule requires that same action.

Reference to a jurisdiction usually occurs in either the CONDITION of the rule that states when a particular action is forbidden, required, or permitted or in the ATTRIBUTES of a rule that define to whom a particular rule applies. CONDITIONS may specify where and at what time actions taken by individuals are considered to be within the boundaries of a particular jurisdiction with the attendant benefits or sanctions that might result. If a carpenter injures a hand while hammering a nail on the job, the carpenter may be eligible for Worker's Compensation because of the institutional arrangements encompassing the activities of the workplace. Other individuals have a duty to pay the worker for his injury. The same injury inflicted at home on an evening hobby project will not entitle the carpenter to any compensation. Similarly, the penalty for some acts, such as theft, varies radically from jurisdiction to jurisdiction. Convictions for stealing property owned by the federal government in the United States may carry a much stiffer sentence than conviction for stealing private property.

In many bureaucratic action situations, no one participant is authorized to take particular positive actions unless specific state variables are above some minimum or below some maximum. A power-plant employee, for example, may not be authorized to open a turbine unless water levels are above a minimum. A social worker cannot authorize food stamps or welfare payments unless an applicant's income is below some defined level given the size of the family and other conditions. Further, specific procedures must be completed prior to any determination of the eligibility of a family for welfare payments of any kind.

By widening or narrowing the range of actions assigned to participants, choice rules affect the basic rights, duties, liberties, and exposures of members and the relative distribution of these to all. Choice rules may allocate to positions high levels of control over many different state variables; in other words, authorize powerful positions. Choice rules empower, but the power so created can be distributed in a relatively equal manner or a grossly unequal manner. Choice rules thus affect the total power created in action situations and the distribution of this power.

One particular type of choice rules, agenda control rules, proves to be quite important in legislative games. Such agenda rules limit or expand the authority of participants in particular positions to propose particular actions (see Shepsle 1979b; Plott and Levine 1978). A closed agenda control rule limits the number of alternative actions that can be decided upon. An open rule, on the other hand, allows any feasible action to be considered. A "germaneness rule" restricts alternatives to those that affect the same set of state variables (see Shepsle 1979b for further discussion of these rules).

Aggregation Rules

Aggregation rules determine whether a decision of a single participant or of multiple participants is needed prior to an action at a node in a decision process. In many social games, particularly board games, each participant is authorized to make a move when it is his or her turn. The player's action set at that juncture includes the specific physical moves to be made. While no single player fully controls the final outcome, individual players do control the decisions to be made at individual nodes. However, in legislative and other group action situations, multiple participants jointly control which actions will be taken at nodes in the decision tree. The decision whether to amend or not amend a bill is subject to the joint control of the members of a legislature. Individual participants affect that decision by casting votes that are then aggregated by an aggregation rule. No single participant has full control over the move to amend or not amend the bill.

Aggregation rules are necessary whenever choice rules assign multiple positions partial control over the same set of action variables. The problem that aggregation rules must clarify for a group is "who is to decide" which action or set of activities is to be undertaken. Thus, in any action situation in which multiple members could each potentially have partial or total control over the selection of an action at a decision node, aggregation rules are used to determine who will participate in the choice, how much weight each participant will have relative to others, and the specific formula to be used in adding up the contribution of each person's decision to a final decision about the action. There are many different types of aggregation rules. Levin and Nalebuff (1995) identified sixteen distinct methods for aggregating individual decisions into final electoral decisions. Three major generic forms of these rules are nonsymmetric aggregation rules, symmetric aggregation rules, and rules that define outcomes in cases of nonagreement.

Nonsymmetric Aggregation Rules

All nonsymmetric aggregation rules treat the participants in a situation differently in regard to some decision to be made at some point in a decision process (Straffin 1977). Some named individual or named subgroup is designated as the participant(s) who make the decision for the group. Karotkin and Paroush (1994) analyze nonsymmetric aggregation rules for a group of four participants and analyze six different nonsymmetric rules that vary in regard to the weights given to players. When only a single person is assigned full authority to select the action, the person can be called an "expert" (or a dictator) for that decision. The dictator picks which action will be taken by the group. Such a rule gives a single named individual the capacity to select any of the feasible actions as well as to avoid any of the feasible actions—full active and blocking capacity. The individual holding that position can act or make an authoritative decision without gaining the prior agreement of others. An individual holding such a position may, of course, consult with others prior to action. Unless regular expectations have been established about the rules used to aggregate the expressed preferences of others, such consultation is not required by the aggregation rule. A single player with veto power may not be able to direct choice as fully as a player with expert power, but the power of such a participant is very substantial (Tsebelis 2002; Herzberg and Ostrom 2000).

A subgroup may be named from the full group and assigned the capacity to make a decision about actions for the entire group. The subgroup will need an aggregation rule of its own in order to make its decision. Such a decision rule may be called an oligarchy rule. The full set of participants may participate in the decision, but each individual participant may be assigned a "weighted vote." This type of nonsymmetric aggregation rule is used in some types of special districts where each member of a council votes, but each is assigned a set of votes depending upon some formula. A subgroup may be named from the full group and a decision must be agreed to by this subgroup, as well as by the full group, using one or more aggregation rules. Such a rule would be associated with many "committee" arrangements wherein committees must approve legislation before the full body gets a chance to approve the legislation. Members of such a committee have greater voice in determining group actions.

On the other hand, an aggregation rule may grant certain positions less voice in group decisions. In most legislative action situations, a presiding officer is not given the authority to vote on most decisions. Thus, the act of voting is not among the presiding officer's set of permitted actions at many points in a decision process, and so his or her vote does not count in the aggregation of a regular voting process. However, if a tie occurs in a vote by regular members, the presiding officer is then authorized to vote in order to break the tie.

Symmetric Aggregation Rules

Symmetric aggregation rules assign joint control over an action to multiple participants so that all are treated alike. One symmetric aggregation rule is that of unanimity—everyone must agree prior to action. A unanimity rule may be built into a process in such a manner that participants do not self-consciously "vote," but each is required to agree before an action can be taken. A bank clerk, for example, is not authorized to open safety deposit boxes unless the owner of the box or an authorized agent signs a registration form and produces a second key to fit the box. The dual and equal authority and unanimous aggregation rule are built into the locking mechanism that requires two keys assigned to different individuals to open the box. Similar conjunctive authority to act and unanimous aggregation rules occur in the military when the results of action could be extremely serious for national security. In addition to the necessity of receiving positive approval from positions higher in the military hierarchy, taking some actions—such as launching an intercontinental missile—cannot physically be undertaken unless multiple persons are present and all agree.

Once the votes are cast, rules specify what proportion of the total must be in agreement before an authoritative decision can be made and what happens if the minimal agreement is not reached. For votes that are weighted equally, it is possible to conceptualize a simple voting rule as ranging from allowing any one member of those given joint authority to make the decision for the collectivity (the anyone rule—used in calling out public emergency vehicles) to requiring all those given joint authority to agree prior to a decision (the unanimity rule) (Buchanan and Tullock 1962). Between the two extremes of the anyone rule and the unanimity rule lies a variety of other specific rules, the most familiar being the requirement that 50 percent plus 1 person agree (majority rule) or some large percentage, such as two-thirds or three-quarters (an extraordinary majority rule). The array of decision rules between these two extremes can be thought of as the proportions of the persons in the group required to agree prior to a decision with the most common being majority rule.

Scholars have puzzled why participants in some jurisdictions or legislative bodies have used a simple majority voting rule to create a new situation—for example, to approve or not approve a municipal bond—while others use a supramajority vote rule such as two-thirds of those voting. Messner and Polborn (2004) attack this problem using the example of bond issues and show that the voters who may form a simple majority at time one may not be in the majority five years, ten years, or twenty years later. Voters who expect a change in population composition and preferences related to policy issues over time may well use their simple majority vote at one time to ensure that the size of the winning coalition in the future requires a supramajority, precisely because this is a more conservative voting formula. Looking ahead, they fear that their preferences will be overwhelmed in future votes on costly bond issues if a simple majority rule is retained.

Lack of Agreement Rules

The formula for determining a joint decision (for either symmetric or nonsymmetric rules) must also include a "no agreement" condition stating what decision will happen if no agreement is reached under a rule. Whenever a decision depends on the approval of more than one participant, the possibility of no agreement is always present. The no agreement condition is the reference point for the proposed decision. It states what will happen if a certain proportion of the participants does not agree to a proposed action.[9]

Several types of no agreement rules are possible. One type continues the status quo distribution of outcome variables. A second presumes that no one receives any outcome variables if participants cannot agree (all relevant outcome variables are reduced to zero). A third no agreement rule is to assign state variables randomly. A fourth type of rule is to apply some external rule (or turn to some external decision maker) to allocate outcome variables.

As mentioned in chapter 6, Grether, Isaac, and Plott (1979) used three "no agreement rules"—which they called default conditions—in a series of laboratory experiments simulating the allocation of landing slots at airports. The first rule was the continuation of the status quo allocation of slots. The second rule was a random assignment of slots. The third rule was the application of an external rule that would take slots from those who had the most and give them to those who had none or only a few (a Robin Hood rule!). These three no agreement rules were combined with a unanimity rule. What is interesting about the findings from a set of experiments using each of these no agreement rules, combined with unanimity, is that the results of the experiment were strongly determined by which no agreement rule was in use. The committee outcomes were substantially influenced by the specific lack of agreement rules used in an experiment (V-7).

That the specific lack of agreement rules that Grether, Isaac, and Plott used had such an important impact on the outcomes achieved is another illustration of how one small part of a rule configuration can strongly affect how the other rules impact the action situations. Scholars need to study the effects of a full rule configuration rather than assume they can study the impact of one rule at a time—while assuming that the other rules are "randomly distributed." A considerable literature has been generated about the likely effects of using unanimity rules in different situations. Very few theorists have explicitly stated the no agreement rule they are assuming. Yet, one might speculate that once an analyst assumes a unanimity rule, that the most important assumption driving analysis is the aggregation no agreement rule presumed in operation. Implicit assumptions about rules, rather than the explicit rules studied, may have been the most important drivers of the results in earlier analyses of institutional arrangements.

Information Rules

An important part of any action situation is the information available to participants about the overall structure of that situation, the current state of individual state variables, the previous and current moves of other participants in positions, and their own past moves. Information rules affect the level of information available to participants. Information rules authorize channels of information flow among participants, assign the obligation, permission, or prohibition to communicate to participants in positions at particular decision nodes, and the language and form in which communication will take place. Information rules are particularly important in generating information about past actions of participants so that other participants can know who is, or is not, trustworthy (see Janssen 2004).

Channels of Information Flow

Rules concerning the establishment of information channels relate to the set of all possible channels connecting all participants in a situation. The connections can be represented as a perfectly connected polygon of whatever dimension equals the number of participants. If there are five participants, there are nine possible connections between these participants. Information rules partition this set of possible connections into subsets of required (a channel must exist), forbidden (a channel must not exist), and permitted (a channel may exist). In a paper by Mueller, Chanowitz, and Langer (1983), for example, they conduct several experiments (at the action situation level) of communication patterns under different structures connecting five subjects.

Given that the number of potential communication channels among any large group is very large and the set of possible rules requiring, permitting, or forbidding channels is also very large, it will be necessary to identify specific types of channel rules if one wishes to devise a finer classification scheme for this aspect of information rules.

Frequency and Accuracy of Communication

In addition to specifying which channels of communication may or may not exist between positions in a situation, information rules also regulate the frequency of exchange of information and the accuracy of information. In many action situations, regular reports must be filed containing certain types of information on either a regular basis or at any time that a participant wishes to obtain certain actions or rewards from others. A person who is on probation is supposed to report to a probation officer on a regular basis and provide a report about their conformance or non-conformance to a set of rules about the actions that they can or must not do. Most bureaucratic life is filled with requirements to complete regular reports about recurrent events in these organized settings. The accuracy rules affect what type of indicators may or must be used as evidence about the state of the world. Rules establishing audit procedures are intended to enforce the accuracy of financial information available to top management and shareholders of a firm.

Subject of Communication

Information rules often limit the topics that can be discussed among participants. In a courtroom, a witness is forbidden to refer to "hearsay" evidence. In industrial meetings, participants are not supposed to discuss price-setting decisions. In many laboratory experimental sessions, rules frequently limit the subjects that participants can discuss with instructions like the following: "Some participants in experiments like this have found it useful to have the opportunity to discuss the decision problem you face. You will be given 10 minutes to hold such a discussion. You may discuss anything you wish during your 10-minute discussion period, with the following restrictions: (1) you are not allowed to discuss side payments (2) you are not allowed to make physical threats (3) you are not allowed to see the private information on anyone's monitor" (E. Ostrom, Gardner, and Walker 1994, 150–51).

Official Language

Information rules also often specify the official language for communication in a situation. These types of rules are quite familiar to us in international settings where there is always an official language in which the business of an international organization or conference will be conducted. All nations also have their official languages. But organizations also establish official languages, including coding systems assigned to products, customers, order numbers, invoices, and the like.

Payoff Rules

Payoff rules assign external rewards or sanctions to particular actions that have been taken or to particular readings on outcome state variables. An example of a set of payoff rules is the pay schedule that is used by a government agency or by a private firm to assign salaries to participants in particular positions. This payoff schedule will vary in terms of the variables taken into account and the complexity of the schedule. Hourly wage payoff rules frequently are very simple and specify a computation of a wage for a certain number of hours considered to be the official working hours of an employee during a set period. Someone being paid according to piecework will, on the other hand, be paid by formula, attaching a weight to a quantity of intermediate or final goods attributed to the work of the participant. Performance contracts for corporations frequently are very much more complex. A contract may state that a corporation will receive x amount if some physical transformation in the world (like a particular apartment building) is completed to someone else's satisfaction by a set date. If the time period is greater than x, then the payment is reduced according to a formula including the amount of time of delay. In the field, many payoff rules that involve costs assigned to a forbidden action (sanctions) involve a low cost for the first infraction, a higher cost for the second, and further graduated sanctions leading to large costs assigned for repeated infractions.

Payoff rules have an AIM that involves paying or receiving something of potential value. As figure 7.1 shows, payoff rules directly impact the net costs and benefits of action or outcomes for actors in an action situation. However, payoff rules often are not the only rules that shape costs and benefits. One could discuss payoff consequences of boundary rules tied to assignment of actions to positions, payoff consequences of information rules, as well as payoff consequences tied to choice and scope rules.

Scope Rules

The above sections have focused on the rules that affect the deontic status of the actions that could physically be taken by a participant in a situation. Scope rules affect a known outcome variable that must, must not, or may be affected as a result of actions taken within the situation. Scope rules define this set, affect the width of the outcome space (number of state variables affected), and specify the range on each outcome variable included in that space. The AIM component in scope rules describes an outcome rather than an action. Since our classification scheme focuses on the most direct link between the AIM and a component of the action situation, rules with outcome AIMs directly tied to positions, boundaries, information, payoffs, or aggregation would be classified as position, boundary, information, payoff, and aggregation rules, respectively, leaving all other rules with outcome AIMs in the scope rules category. Thus, the scope rule category and the choice rule category both work as "all other" categories. If a rule is not a position, boundary, information, pay-off, or aggregation rule, then it is either a choice rule (if the A*I*M is an action) or a scope rule (if the A*I*M is an outcome). Heiner (1990) focuses entirely on rules that place constraints on the production possibility frontier and not on actions in his "Rule-Governed Behavior in Evolution and Human Society." Thus, implicitly his analysis of rules constraining the range of outcomes relates to what we are calling here scope rules.

Because scope rules affect action sets through their effect on outcome variables, they do not directly enumerate action sets. Rules related to the operations of cable television stations have frequently listed upper and lower bounds on particular state variables that a station is forbidden to exceed. In some situations, the physical world or attributes of the community may make monitoring of actions more difficult or sensitive than monitoring outcomes, which would then likely make scope rules more appropriate than choice rules. The attributes of community may stress autonomy and liberty, which may make it easier to gain legitimacy for scope rules than choice rules.

For example, strong norms and rules governing academic freedom render many university rules governing specific teaching and research activities suspect, while rules that base promotions on outcomes for professors may be seen as much more legitimate. Rules generally tie tenure and promotion most heavily to outcome measures (quantity and quality of publications, quality of teaching overall), with less evaluative attention given to choices of actions. Similarly, gaining legitimacy for government regulation from business communities with strong antiregulation views may be easier with scope rules that allow firms to choose how to comply.

A recent workshop was held in Washington, D.C., to examine when scope rules are most likely to be effective regulatory tools. The organizers identified two basic types of rules that can be used in regulating industry: "Regulators can direct those they govern to improve their performance in at least two basic ways. They can prescribe exactly what actions regulated entities must take to improve their performance. Or they can incorporate the regulation's goal into the language of the rule, specifying the desired level of performance and allowing the targets of regulation to achieve that level" (Coglianese, Nash, and Olmstead 2003, 706).

The first alternative focuses on regulation via choice rules. The second alternative—and the one that was examined in some depth at the workshop described above—is via scope rules. Even though considerable emphasis in Washington has been on using scope rules rather than choice rules,[10] Coglianese, Nash, and Olmstead point out that there has been relatively little empirical study of the impact of setting performance targets. This may be related to lower numbers of scope rules in the real world because of the difficulty that regulators face in measuring performance rather than in determining whether forbidden actions were indeed taken. Many of the agency officials participating in the discussion were attracted to the idea of performance-based regulation, but pointed out that it was difficult to move away from regulation focusing on permitted or forbidden actions.

In problematic situations, the most immediate questions raised frequently focus on the behaviors (the actions) that need to change in order to improve the situation, and so choice rules would tend to be the most obvious direct response. However, growing emphasis on outcome measurement in industries, in foundation grants, and in government programs may well lead to more attention to reforms that use scope rules. Experience in the field and in formal theory has focused less on scope rules than on choice rules.[11] At this point, we find many fewer instances of explicit scope rules and thus less need to further divide scope rules into specific types. If outcome regulation continues to expand, and thereby increases the need for policy scholars to study scope rules, more attention will need to be paid to the types of scope rules that exist.

Default Conditions: What Happens if No Rules Exist Related to Components of an Action Situation?

Rules do not always exist related to all elements of an action situation. What should a participant—or an observer—deduce about the structure of a game in the absence of rules affecting all seven parts of an action situation? This is particularly important due to the configurational nature of rules. One needs to know the basic rules related to a full rule configuration, rather than to a single rule, to infer both the structure of the resulting situation and the likely outcome of any particular rule.

In chapter 5, we identify the default conditions for the internal components of a rule. A rule that does not list any specific attribute or condition, for example, applies to all attributes and conditions that the physical world and the community make possible. It is also useful—and even necessary—to define the default rules for each of the seven types of rules. The notion of default conditions allows us to address the question of what happens if *no* rules exist related to a specific component of an action situation (see E. Ostrom, Gardner, and Walker 1994 for an earlier exploration of this question).

The seven default conditions that we specify in table 7.2 are those that would be used by a participant or an observer in a general legal system that presumed general freedom unless a rule specifically prohibited or mandated an act or event. These are the broadest default conditions that

TABLE 7.2
Default conditions

Default Position Condition	One position exists.
Default Boundary Condition	Anyone can hold this position.
Default Choice Condition	Each player can take any physically possible action.
Default Aggregation Condition	Players act independently. Physical relationships present in the situation determine the aggregation of individual moves into outcomes.*
Default Information Condition	Each player can communicate any information via any channel available to the player.
Default Payoff Condition	Any player can retain any outcome that the player can physically obtain and defend.
Default Scope Condition	Each player can affect any state of world that is physically possible.

* If a rule configuration contains only a default choice condition, the default aggregation condition *must* be present.

would be used in a common-law legal system as contrasted to a Roman Law system that presumes that most things are forbidden unless specifically permitted. These default conditions are listed in table 7.2.[12] If one were to analyze a situation where there were no rules—and thus the rule configuration would contain only the default conditions—the resulting configuration constitutes a Hobbesian state of nature.

One way of representing such a game of nature is the Snatch Game presented in chapter 2 (figure 2.2). The predicted equilibrium of this game is grossly inefficient—no exchanges. If the players do adopt internal norms, as discussed in chapter 4, they may be able to achieve an efficient outcome of an exchange. But the value of the negative delta parameter assigned to snatching the offered goods has to be larger than the value of the goods snatched. Otherwise, even individuals who hold norms against snatching goods from others may end up doing so when the value of goods is very high.

Some analysts might respond that it is easy to fix this situation—simply impose private property rights! But the question is, How does one create private property? What rules need to be changed to create "private property"? If all the households in a region were to get together and create a legal system defining their ownership of goods and the punishment for stealing, they would need to establish at least four kinds of rules: position, boundary, choice, and aggregation. A brief summary of one possible set of these rules is shown in table 7.3.

TABLE 7.3
Rules changed to create elementary property rights for agricultural commodities

Position Rules	There exist two positions: (1) an eligible exchange participant and (2) a judge.
Boundary Rules	(1) All farmer households are permitted to become exchange participants or else those refusing their entry may be punished. (2) The judge must be selected on the basis of merit and integrity by the households in the community or else the other rules will not be in effect.
Choice Rules	(1) All exchange participants are permitted to offer to exchange goods they own for goods owned by others or else those forbidding the exchange may be punished. (2) If a household's goods are snatched, the household can report to a judge or else those preventing the report may be punished. (3) If a judge finds that a household has snatched goods illegally,* the judge must ensure that the illegal household returns the goods and forfeits its own commodities or else the judge will be sanctioned.
Aggregation Rules	All parties to an exchange must agree before a legal exchange can occur or else the exchange does not occur.

* Now we could use the term *stealing* instead of simply snatching.

With these multiple changes of seven rules from their default status to the simple rules stated above, combined with the remaining default conditions, a new operational-level game—shown in figure 7.2—is created. In this game, a new move has been created. If Household 2 snatches Household 1's goods, Household 1 has the option of going to a judge (who is not modeled here as a player since this simple game assumes the judge complies with the rule that requires him to return the commodities to their rightful owner and to make the household who stole the goods forfeit their own commodities as well). Given this option now made available to Household 1, Household 2 is unlikely to snatch the goods since Household 1 would be motivated to use this option if they reached this part of the game. Instead, Household 2 will select the exchange option where both players are better off.

Of course, this is a highly simplified version of both the action situation and the rule configuration that could be adopted to avoid the deficient outcome of the Snatch Game in a State of Nature.[13] However, even in this highly simplified example, several important points have been illustrated. These are:

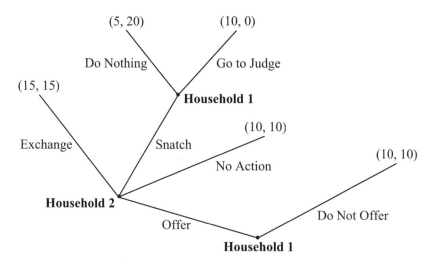

Figure 7.2 The Snatch Game with minimal property rights.

   1. In the absence of any rule directly affecting an element of an action situation, the relevant rule in place can be described by a default rule.

   2. When all rules are in their default, the attributes of the physical world generate all aspects of the structure of the action situation. This is the Hobbesian "state of nature."

   3. Rules operate together with the attributes of a physical world to create a structure.

To change the game from the one shown in figure 2.2 requires changes in at least seven rules. If the choice rule mandating the action of the judge had only given the judge *permission* to return goods to those from whom they were stolen and to confiscate the goods of an offender, a different predicted outcome would be likely. It would depend on whether Household 2 thought there were any factors that would affect the likelihood that the judge would not impose the punishment if they snatched the goods. If the head of Household 2, for example, was the brother of the judge, and the choice rule of the judge stated only a permission to impose a punishment rather than a requirement, a different calculation would be made by Household 2. And, it needs to be stressed, the default conditions jointly create the structure of the situation along with the rules (as well as the relevant characteristics of the biophysical world and relevant community).

To keep the initial analysis as simple and clear as possible, the Snatch Game has been represented as a game between households living in the same region. The problem of gaining a commitment that goods—once presented for trade—would not be snatched is a widespread problem un-derlying the development of commercial relationships in general and long-distance trade in particular. When the presumption is made that you solve this problem by creating property rights and then judges and police to enforce these rights, the judges and police are viewed as outside the situa-tion (as shown above by not viewing the judge as a player). These are automatic agents assigned to do a job reliably and not viewed as strategic actors in many analyses.

A key problem is that once you have created private property, markets, and the role of a judge or "ruler," how is the holder of this position going to undertake the assigned duties?[14] The judge or ruler will need to obtain funds to organize the court, keep records, maintain a police force to pro-vide patrols in the marketplace, search the storehouse of merchants sus-pected of stealing, and so forth. One way to do this is to impose a fee on the merchants who want to use a market. Both rulers and merchants have a mutual interest in the evolution of a safe place for trading goods. The greater the number of merchants that come to a market and the more diverse the goods they bring with them, the more valuable the market becomes both for the merchants and for the ruler. This is especially so if merchants from far away can be lured who bring goods that are not lo-cally available. Now the ruler faces a substantial temptation to pledge security to traders from other regions and get them to come. Once a lucra-tive trade is established, however, a ruler also faces a temptation to renege on that costly promise or even use his or her own military forces to obtain the valuable goods for the ruler's household.[15] So life goes on. No change in a set of rules is ever sufficient to solve the next set of problems created by new opportunities and constraints that continually arise in an evolving human community.

The Vertical Approach: Operational, Collective-Choice, and Constitutional-Choice Levels of Analysis

In the IAD framework, authoritative relationships occur in collective-choice and constitutional-choice situations. Using the IAD framework, we focus on operational rules that affect authorized relationships and on collective-choice rules and constitutional-choice rules (both of which Commons and Hohfeld considered to be authoritative relationships). This vertical approach recognizes that rule sets are themselves nested in hierar-chical levels. The participants in operational situations are directly af-fected by the operational rules structuring what they must, must not, or may do. These rules were crafted in a collective-choice situation struc-tured by collective-choice rules (which participants, in what positions, chosen how, given information, and an assessment of benefits and costs can make operational rules). The collective-choice rules were themselves crafted in a constitutional situation.

Vertical arrangements do not exist just within government. These relationships also exist in the contractual arrangements among private individuals as well as within a variety of governmental decision-making arrangements for determining, enforcing, and altering authorized legal relationships (operational decisions). Under contractual arrangements, people may participate in a mutually agreeable arrangement in redefining and altering legal relationships in order to accomplish the objectives of some undertaking of mutual interest. A large literature drawing on the work of Coase (1937), Milgrom and Roberts (1992), Williamson (1985, 2000), and Schmid (2004) has explored a variety of conditions under which individuals voluntarily move from horizontal to vertical relationships. Governmental arrangements, inherent in the operations of courts, executive agencies, and legislative bodies, enable people to sustain efforts to determine, enforce, and alter legal relationships. Each particular decision-making structure or decision-making arrangement, then, involves a complex set of rules regarding the variety of participants who may wish to pursue their strategic opportunities in order to realize some outcomes that may be made through those decision structures.

Using Rules as Tools to Change Outcomes

Changing the Snatch Game into a game with property rights demonstrates how even a relatively simple policy reform requires multiple rule changes. The AIM classification system introduced here provides a rough mechanism for simplifying the complex array of rules in any situation. Even with this system, complexity remains. We cannot just assume that boundary rules affect only who fills positions, for example, without examining how restricting or opening entry affect the other components of an action situation. So, while the tools in chapters 5 and 7 allow us to sort institutional statements and define default conditions, there is still much to be learned from the diversity of institutional structures in field settings. What kinds of institutional structures do participants in field settings use? How do these participants use rules to change the structure of the situations that they face? Chapter 8 demonstrates the widely diverse rules that resource appropriators use to craft institutions for governing and managing common-pool resources.

Part III

WORKING WITH RULES

Eight

Using Rules as Tools to Cope with the Commons

IN CHAPTER 7, we described the seven generic rules that individuals use when establishing or changing action situations they confront in everyday life. Chapter 7, hopefully, provided the reader with a useful overview of the tools that individuals use in creating structure in the multiple action situations they face in life. Chapters 8 and 9 will apply these tools, and the framework developed in the earlier chapters of this book, to a focused study of common-pool resource problems.

Common-pool resource problems are among the core social dilemmas facing all peoples (see discussion in chapters 1 and 3). Collective action is required to establish and enforce rules limiting the appropriation of water, fish, forest products, pasturage, and other resource products. These problems are portrayed in many contemporary policy textbooks as relatively simple problems that can be solved analytically to achieve optimal outcomes. Empirical research over the past decades has led to a realization of their complexity. Applying the Institutional Analysis and Development (IAD) framework developed in the first part of this book helps one to recognize the source of this complexity. The many variables of the biophysical/material world, the communities involved, and the rules-in-use combine to affect the structure of appropriation situations, the patterns of interactions among appropriators from a common-pool resource, and the outcomes achieved. Those who try to solve these problems have to cope with complexity as well as coping with the commons.

In the first section of this chapter, we will briefly review the empirical literature that documents many successes as well as failures of the diverse ways that resource appropriators have coped with the commons. In light of a general overview of empirical evidence, we will then apply the classification system developed in chapter 7 to examine the diversity of rules that are used in efforts to govern and manage common-pool resources all over the world.

After explicating the specific rules discovered in extensive field research by many scholars, the third section of this chapter will examine the disjuncture that exists between the policy recommendations frequently made to overcome commons dilemmas and the types of interventions that appropriators themselves have adopted. Three broad assumptions underlie many contemporary policy recommendations that are challenged by evidence from the field. One is that resources are so interconnected that they all need to be managed centrally. A second of the challenged beliefs is that resource appropriators are not themselves capable of designing rules to sustain resources over time. Somehow, public officials are presumed to have the capabilities that the resource appropriators themselves lack. Third, it is presumed that designing rules to improve outcomes is a relatively simple analytical task that is best done by objective analysts.

In light of the diversity of rules actually used to cope with common-pool resource problems, one must conclude that conducting an analytical search for *the optimal* combination of rules is an impossible task for appropriators, officials, or policy analysts. No one can do a full analysis of the combination of rules potentially available and how they might interact with attributes of the biophysical world and the relevant community. All efforts to solve resource problems need to be viewed as experiments based on partial analyses of specific problems. Theory and evidence play a key role in increasing the probability of selecting rules leading to better as contrasted to worse outcomes. Theory cannot, however, eliminate the need to view all policies as ongoing experiments that need to be monitored, evaluated, and adapted over time.

What factors lead appropriators to think about experimenting with rules and what calculations do they use in making such decisions? Most of the policy literature is silent on these questions since the general presumption is made in this literature that making policies is what government officials, rather than those who are directly affected by problems, do. Fortunately, many field researchers have identified variables that are related to local efforts to self-organize and craft better rules related to local settings. In light of this research, the last section of the chapter examines the attributes of resources and of appropriators that affect the likelihood of collective action and develops a theoretical structure for analyzing how appropriators may be led to change one or more of the rules they use in relation to a resource. The analysis does not lead to the conclusion that if left alone, resource appropriators will always, or even most frequently, undertake the difficult task of experimenting with rules. Instead, we will posit a set of conditions of a resource and of the resource appropriators that are *most* conducive to self-organization. The absence of these attributes leads to situations that are the *least* conducive to self-organization.

Local self-organization can also be dominated by local elites to use rules as tools to advantage themselves. That problem leads to a discussion in the final chapter of the book of the design principles that characterize robust institutions for governing and managing common-pool resources, the factors that threaten the long-term sustainability of any such system, and the need for polycentric institutions at multiple levels to cope with poorly performing systems at any level through redundant, multitier governance systems.

Field Research on Common-Pool Resources

A large number of field studies have found that local groups of resource users, sometimes by themselves and sometimes with the assistance of external actors, have managed to create viable institutional arrangements for coping with common-pool resource problems.[1] These empirical studies document successful self-organized resource governance systems in diverse sectors in many parts of the world. At the same time, some commons dilemmas have continued unabated (see, for example, Finlayson and McCay 1998; Berkes et al. 2001), and some common-property institutions have experienced drastic negative changes during the last century (Seixas and Berkes 2003). Further, some common-property institutions have been converted by local leaders into private property institutions enforced by governmental officials (Ensminger and Knight 1997; Mwangi 2003).

Another important set of findings is that national governmental agencies have been notably unsuccessful in their efforts to design effective and uniform sets of rules to regulate important common-pool resources across a broad domain (Ascher 1995). The harmful effects of nationalizing forests that had earlier been governed by local user-groups have been well documented for Thailand (Feeny 1988), Africa (Shepherd 1992; Thomson 1977; Thomson, Feeny, and Oakerson 1992), Nepal (Arnold and Campbell 1986), and India (Gadgil and Iyer 1989; Grafton 2000; Jodha 1990, 1996). Similar results have occurred in regard to inshore fisheries taken over by state or national agencies from local control by the inshore fishers themselves (Cordell and McKean 1992; Cruz 1986; Dasgupta 1982; Higgs 1996; Pinkerton 1989).

Many developing countries nationalized their land and water resources between the 1950s and 1970s. The institutional arrangements that local resource users had devised to limit entry and use lost their legal standing. The national governments that assumed these new and difficult tasks lacked adequate funds and personnel to monitor resource use effectively. They frequently turned to private forestry firms to gain revenue from these resources. Governments in these countries wanted to convert common-pool resources to a de jure government-property regime, but their actions frequently resulted in de facto open-access regimes (Arnold 1998; Arnold and Stewart 1991). The incentives of an open-access commons were accentuated since local users had specifically been told that they would not receive the long-term benefits of their own costly stewardship efforts. Johnson and Forsyth (2002) illustrate the longer-term problem that these earlier interventions generated by examining the efforts of the Thai government to establish communal rights to forest access through legislation. The potential effectiveness of the legislation has, however, been effectively undermined by the earlier state interventions that supported commercial interests against local interests.

Tang (1992), Lam (1998), and Joshi et al. (2000) have all found that large-scale government irrigation systems do not tend to perform at the same level as smaller-scale, farmer-managed systems (see also Mehra 1981; Levine 1980; Bromley 1982; Hilton 1992). In a study of over one hundred irrigation systems in Nepal, Lam (1998) found that in terms of cropping intensity and agricultural yield, crudely constructed irrigation systems using mud, rock, timber, and sticks significantly outperform systems built with modern concrete and iron headworks operated by national agencies.

Extensive empirical research has thus found resource appropriators potentially capable of self-organizing to manage common-pool resources sustainably while many centralized government systems have performed less effectively than presumed according to much of the policy literature. One cannot assert, however, that all local efforts work well and all large-scale efforts work poorly. From the empirical literature only one conclusion is tenable: averting the overuse and destruction of common-pool resources used by many individuals is a challenge. It cannot be assumed that these problems will be solved by an automatic process. Overcoming commons dilemmas is always a struggle (Dietz, Ostrom, and Stern 2003).

What Rules Are Found in Self-Organized Common-Pool Resource Regimes?

A team of researchers at the Workshop in Political Theory and Policy Analysis has read and archived much of the extensive case study literature on local common-pool resources written by anthropologists, agricultural economists, ecologists, historians, political scientists, and sociologists (see <http://www.indiana.edu/~workshop/wsl/wsl.html>; Hess 1999). Using the Institutional Analysis and Development (IAD) framework elucidated in chapters 1 and 2, we developed structured coding forms to help us identify the specific kinds of action situations faced in the field as well as the types of rules that users have evolved over time to try to govern and manage their resource effectively (E. Ostrom et al. 1989; E. Ostrom, Gardner, and Walker 1994). In order to develop standardized coding forms, we read hundreds of cases describing how local common-pool resources were or were not regulated by a government agency, by the users themselves, or by a nongovernmental organization (NGO).

This section provides an overview of the diversity of specific rules that we recorded using the general classification described in chapter 7. I do this for several purposes:

1. To illustrate the immense creativity of individuals coming from all stations of life living in all parts of the world. Their creativity and entrepreneurship are frequently unrecognized since many resource appropriators engaged in problem solving are not well educated and have only local reputations.

2. To show the incredible diversity of rules that individuals have adopted in one or more settings.

3. To challenge the assumption frequently made by policy analysts that it is routinely feasible to conduct complete analysis of a problem and develop "the optimal" set of rules for solving that problem.[2]

4. To illustrate the benefit of classifying rules by their AIM. While we cannot point to an optimal set of rules usable in most commons dilemma situations, we can now use a common language for identifying rules that is functional for academics as well as those directly involved in solving problems.

To understand the tools that appropriators use in the field, let us examine the specific boundary, position, choice, and payoff rules used in common-pool resource situations around the world initially identified in a meta-analysis conducted by Arun Agrawal, William Blomquist, Edella Schlager, Shui Yan Tang, and myself (see E. Ostrom et al. 1989). These four clusters of rules are the major tools used everywhere to affect commons dilemmas. Information, scope, and aggregation rules are additional tools used to complement changes induced by these four types of rules.

Affecting the Attributes of Users through Boundary Rules

As discussed in chapter 7, boundary rules define the attributes and conditions required of those who enter a position in an action situation. In field settings, many action situations are involved but I will focus attention on the appropriation situation: Who appropriates (harvests) how many resource units from which common-pool resource? Boundary rules, thus, define who has a right to enter and use a resource as an "authorized appropriator"—the term we will use for this most general position that exists in multiple settings. Boundary rules affect the types of participants with whom other participants will be interacting related to a particular resource.

If contingent cooperation is perceived to be a possibility, then an important way to enhance the likelihood of using reciprocity norms is to increase the proportion of appropriators who are well known in a com-

TABLE 8.1
Attributes and conditions used in boundary rules to define who is authorized to appropriate from a common-pool resource

Attributes		Conditions
Residency or Membership	**Personal characteristics**	**Relationship with resource**
National	Ascribed	Use of specified technology
Regional	Age	Continued use of resource
Local community	Caste	Long-term rights based on
Organization (e.g., co-op)	Clan	Ownership of a proportion of
	Class	annual flow of resource
	Ethnicity	units
	Gender	Ownership of land
	Race	Ownership of nonland asset
	Acquired	(e.g., berth)
	Education level	Ownership of shares in a
	Skill test	private organization
		Ownership of a share of the
		resource system
		Temporary use-rights acquired
		through
		Auction
		Per-use fee
		Licenses
		Lottery
		Registration
		Seasonal fees

munity. These participants have a long-term stake in that community and would find it costly to have their reputation for trustworthiness harmed in that community. Reducing the number of users, but opening the resource to strangers willing to pay a license fee, as is frequently recommended in the policy literature, introduces appropriators who lack a long-term interest in the sustainability of a particular resource. Using licenses to regulate entry increases the number of strangers using the resource and may reduce the level of trust among participants and their willingness to use reciprocity and thus increase enforcement costs substantially.

From our initial reading and our own fieldwork, we expected to find boundary rules that focused on local residency as a way of increasing the opportunity for reciprocity, and these rules were used extensively. What amazed us, however, as we read the extensive number of case studies describing field settings, was the variety of attributes and conditions used to define who could be an authorized appropriator from diverse inshore fisheries, irrigation systems, and forests. As shown in table 8.1, we identified twenty-three attributes of individuals and thirteen conditions described by case-study authors as having been used in at least one common-pool resource somewhere in the world (E. Ostrom et al. 1989). While some systems use only a single attribute or condition, many use two or three of these rules in combination.

Boundary rules that are used in the field can be broadly grouped in three general classes related to how individuals gain authority to enter and appropriate resource units from a common-pool resource. The first type of boundary rule focuses on residency or membership requirements. These include an individual's citizenship, residency, or membership in a particular organization. Many forestry and fishery user groups require members to have been born in a particular location. A second broad group of attributes relates to ascribed or acquired personal attributes. User groups may require that appropriation depends on age, ethnicity, clan, caste, and/or education. A third group of boundary rules relates to the conditions of use relating an appropriator with the resource itself. Using a particular technology or acquiring appropriation rights through an auction, a lottery, or purchases of land or livestock are examples of this type of condition.

For the forty-four case studies of inshore fisheries in many parts of the world for which sufficient information existed, Schlager (1994, 258) identified thirty-three user groups as having at least one boundary rule regarding the use of the resource. All thirty-three groups depended on some combination of fourteen attributes or conditions. None of these groups relied on a single attribute or condition. Thirty out of thirty-three groups limited fishing to those individuals who lived in a nearby community, while thirteen groups also required membership in a local organization. Consequently, most inshore fisheries organized by the users themselves restrict fishing to those individuals who are well known to each other, have a relatively long-term time horizon, and are connected to one another in multiple ways (see Taylor 1982; Singleton and Taylor 1992; Berkes et al. 2001).

After residency, the next most frequent attribute or condition, used in two-thirds of the organized subgroups, is that appropriators use a particular type of technology. These rules are often criticized by policy analysts, since gear restrictions are thought to reduce the "efficiency" of fishing. Gear restrictions, however, have many other consequences as well. Used in combination with choice rules that assign fishers that use one type of gear to one area of the grounds they use, and fishers using a second type of gear to a separate area, these rules solve conflicts among incompatible technologies. Many gear restrictions also place a reduced load on the fishery itself and thus help to sustain longer-term use of the resource (Acheson 2003; Corson 2002).

Consider other boundary rules in use. A scattering of groups used ascribed characteristics (age—two groups; ethnicity—three groups; race—five groups). Three types of temporary use rights included government licenses (three groups), lottery (five groups), and registration (four groups). Seven groups required participants to have purchased an asset such as a fishing berth, while three groups required ownership of nearby land as a condition of appropriation. Schlager (1994) did not find that any particular attribute or condition was correlated with higher performance levels, but she did find that the thirty-three groups, who had at least one boundary rule, tended to be able to solve common-pool problems more effectively than the eleven groups who had not crafted boundary rules.

In a study of forty-three small- to medium-sized irrigation systems managed by farmers or by government agencies, Tang (1992) found that the variety of attributes or conditions used in irrigation was smaller than among inshore fisheries. The single most frequently used boundary rule, used in thirty-two of the forty-three systems (74 percent), was that an irrigator must own land in the service area of an irrigation system (84–85). All of the government-owned and -operated irrigation systems relied on this attribute and *only* this attribute. Many of the user-organized systems relied on other attributes and conditions or land ownership combined with other rules. Among the other rules used were ownership of a proportion of the flow of the resource (e.g., fish, water, forest products), membership in a local organization, and a per-use fee.

Tang found a strong negative relationship between reliance on land as the *sole* boundary requirement and performance (87). Over 90 percent of the systems using other boundary rules or a combination of rules including land ownership were rated positively in the level of maintenance achieved and in the level of rule conformance, while fewer than 40 percent of those systems relying solely on land ownership were rated at a higher performance level ($p = .001$).

Many of the boundary rules used by appropriators in the field are a mechanism to ensure that appropriators will interact with others who live nearby and have a long-term interest in sustaining the productivity of the resource. One way that the rules devised by appropriators increase the sustainability of a resource is to change the composition of the group that uses a common-pool resource. Their rules tend to increase the proportion of participants who have a long-term interest in the resource, who are more likely to use reciprocity, and who can be trusted. Central governments tend to use a smaller set of rules. Some of these may open up a resource to strangers without a long-term commitment to the resource, create too large a geographic domain, generate conflict among users, and lead to an unwillingness to abide by any rules.[3]

Position Rules Creating Monitors

In the discussion above, we focused on how boundary rules create the general position of authorized appropriator. In some self-organized resource governance systems, a second position of guard or monitor is also created. Many different names are used.

Among self-organizing forest governance systems, creating and supporting a position as guard is frequently essential when resource units are highly valuable and a few hours of stealth generates substantial illicit income. Monitoring rule conformance among forest users by officially designated and paid guards may make the difference between a resource in good condition and one that has become totally degraded. In a study of 279 local forest councils in the Kumaon region of India, Agrawal and Yadama (1997), for example, found that the number of months a guard was hired was the most important variable affecting forest conditions. The other variables that affected forest conditions in their study included the number of meetings held by the forest council (this is usually a time when infractions are discussed) and the number of residents in the village.

> It is evident from the analysis that the capacity of a forest council to monitor and impose sanctions on rule-breakers is paramount to maintaining the forest in good condition. Nor should the presence of a guard be taken simply as a formal mechanism that ensures greater protection. It is also an indication of the informal commitment of the *panchayat* and the village community to protect their forests. Hiring a guard costs money. The funds have to be generated within the village and earmarked for protection of the resource. If there was scant interest in protecting the forest, villagers would have little interest in setting aside the money necessary to hire a guard. (455)

Many self-organized fisheries rely on self-monitoring more than the creation of a formal position of guard. Most inshore fishers now use short-wave radios as a routine part of their day-to-day operations allowing a form of instant monitoring to occur. An official of a West Coast Indian tribe reports, for example, that "it is not uncommon to hear messages such as 'Did you see so-and-so flying all that net?' over the short-wave frequency—a clear reference to a violation of specified gear limits" (cited in Singleton 1998, 134). Given that most fishers will be listening to their short-wave radios, "such publicity is tantamount to creating a flashing neon sign over the boat of the offender. Such treatment might be preceded or followed by a direct approach to the rule violator, advising him to resolve the problem. In some tribes, a group of fishermen might delegate themselves to speak to the person" (134).

Whether irrigation systems create a formal position as guard depends both on the type of governance of the system and on its size. Of the fifteen government-owned irrigation systems included in Tang (1992), twelve (80 percent) have established a position of guard. Stealing water was a problem on most government-owned systems, but it was endemic on the three government systems without guards. Of the twenty-eight farmer-organized systems, seventeen (61 percent) utilize the position of water distributor or guard. Eleven farmer-organized systems do not employ a guard. Farmers are vigilant enough in monitoring each other's activities on five systems (45 percent) that rule conformance is high. This means, of course, that self-monitoring is not high enough on the other six systems to support routine conformance with their own rules.

An earlier study by Romana de los Reyes (1980) of fifty-one communal irrigation systems in the Philippines illustrates the effect of size. Of the thirty systems that were less than fifty hectares, only six (20 percent) had established a position as guard; of the eleven systems that served between fifty to one hundred hectares, five (45 percent) had established guards; and of the ten systems over one hundred hectares, seven (70 percent) had created guards. In a survey of over six hundred farmers served by these communal irrigation systems, she also found that most farmers also patrolled their own canals even when they were patrolled by guards accountable to the farmers for distributing water. Further, the proportion of farmers who reported patrolling the canals serving their farms increases to 80 percent on the largest self-organized systems compared to 60 percent on the smallest systems.

Considerable variation thus exists in the kind of monitoring positions created in self-organized systems. Regardless of the rules creating such positions, we have consistently found that higher levels of local monitoring are positively related to resource conditions (see Gibson, Williams, and Ostrom 2005).

Affecting the Set of Allowable Actions through Choice Rules

Choice rules are also a major type of rule used to regulate common-pool resources. Some irrigation systems allocate water simply on the basis of the crops that a farmer grows.[4] Some rules involve a simple formula as a way of devising how many resource units appropriators may obtain. Others simply choose the resource for a defined period(s) and then allow harvesting during a particular season. Many forest resources, for example, are closed to all forms of harvesting during one portion of the year and open for extraction by all who meet the boundary rules during an open season. Most choice rules, however, have two components: an allocation formula and the assets on which the formula is based.

In table 8.2, the eight allocation formulas used in the field are shown in the left column. A fisher might be assigned to a fixed location (a fishing

TABLE 8.2
Choice rules used to allocate common-pool resources

Allocation formula for appropriation rights	Basis for allocation formula
Percentage of total available units per period	Amount of land held
Quantity of resource units per period	Amount of historical use
Appropriate only from a specific location	Location of appropriator
Appropriate only from a specific time slot	Quantity of shares of resource owned
Rotate in time or space	Proportion of resource flow owned
Appropriate only during open seasons	Purchase of periodic rights at auction
Appropriate only resource units meeting criteria	Rights acquired through periodic lottery
Appropriate whenever and wherever	Technology used
	License issued by a governmental authority
	Equal division to all appropriators
	Needs of appropriators (e.g., type of crop)
	Ascribed characteristic of appropriator
	Membership in organization
	Assessment of resource condition

spot) or to a fixed rotational schedule, a member of the founding clan may be authorized to cut timber anywhere in a forest, while an irrigator might be assigned to a fixed percentage of the total water available during a season or to a fixed time slot. In addition to the formula used in a choice rule, most also attach a condition as a basis for the assignment. For example, a fisher might be assigned to a fixed location *based on* a number drawn in a lottery, on the purchase of that spot in an auction, or on the basis of his or her historical use.[5] An irrigator might be assigned to a fixed rotation *based on* the amount of land owned, the amount of water used historically, or the specific location of the irrigator.

If all of the conditions were equally likely to be combined with all of the formula, there would be 112 different choice rules (8 allocation formulas × 14 bases). A further complication is that the rules for one product may differ from those of another product harvested from the same resource. In regard to forest resources, for example, children may be authorized to pick fruit from any tree located in a forest so long as it is for their own consumption, women may be authorized to collect so many headloads of dead wood for domestic firewood and certain plants for making crafts, while shaman are the only ones authorized to collect medicinal plants from a particular location in a forest (Fortmann and Bruce 1988). Appropriation rights to fish are frequently related to a specific species. A still further complication is that the rules may regularly change over the course of a year depending on resource conditions. Thus, the exact number of rules that are actually used in the field is difficult to compute.

Schlager (1994, 259–60) found that user groups included in her study frequently assigned fishers to fixed locations using a diversity of bases including technology, lottery, or historical use. Seven groups allocated fishers to fishing spots using a rotation system, and seven other groups allowed fishing locations to be used only during a specific season. Four groups allocated fishing spots for a particular time period (a fishing day or a fishing season). On the other hand, nine user groups required fishers to limit their harvest to fish that met a specific size requirement.

An important finding—given the puzzles addressed in this chapter—is that the choice rule most frequently recommended by policy analysts (see L. Anderson 1986; Arnason and Gissurarson 1999; Copes 1986) was *not* used in any of the coastal fisheries included in Schlager's study. In none of the fisheries coded by Schlager was an attempt made to regulate the quantity of fish harvested per year based on an estimate of the yield. "This is particularly surprising given that the most frequently recommended policy prescription made by fishery economists is the use of individual transferable quotas based on estimates on the economically optimal quantity of fish to be harvested over the long run" (397).

In an independent study of thirty traditional fishery societies, Acheson, Wilson, and Steneck also noted the surprising absence of quota rules: "All of the rules and practices we found in these 30 societies regulate 'how' fishing is done. That is, they limit the times fish may be caught, the locations where fishing is allowed, the technology permitted, and the stage of the life cycle during which fish may be taken. None of these societies limits the 'amount' of various species that can be caught. Quotas—the single most important concept and tools of scientific management—is conspicuous by its absence" (1998, 397; see Wilson et al. 1994). Many local inshore fishers, when allowed to self-organize, appear to use rules that differ substantially from those recommended by advocates of scientific management (Berkes et al. 2001, 177–79). Fishers have to know a great deal about the ecology of their inshore region including spawning areas, nursery areas, the migration routes of different species, and seasonable patterns just in order to succeed as fishers. Those inshore fisheries that have survived the threat of rapid technological change have learned how "to maintain these critical life-cycle processes with rules controlling technology, fishing locations, and fishing times. Such rules in their view are based on biological reality" (Acheson, Wilson, and Steneck 1998, 405). Lobe and Berkes (2004) also illustrate how a combination of these three types of rules sustains contemporary coastal shrimp fisheries in Kerala, India.

In the irrigation systems studied by Tang (1992, 90–91), three types of choice rules are used most frequently: (1) a fixed time slot is assigned to each irrigator (nineteen out of the thirty-seven cases for which data are available, and in ten out of twelve government-owned systems), (2) a fixed order for a rotation system among irrigators (thirteen cases), and (3) a fixed percentage of the total water available during a period of time (five cases). A variety of conditions were used in these rules such as "amount of land held, amount of water needed to cultivate existing crops, number of shares held, location of field, or official discretion" (Tang 1994, 233). Three poorly performing systems with high levels of conflict had not crafted any choice rule at all. Farmers also do not use rules that assign a specific quantity of water to irrigators other than in the rare circumstances where they control substantial amounts of water in storage (see Maass and Anderson 1986).

Fixed time slot rules allow farmers considerable certainty as to when they will receive water without an equivalent certainty about the quantity of water that will be available in the canal. Fixed time allocation systems are criticized as inefficient since water is not allocated to the farmers with the highest productivity. This condition does, however, economize greatly on the amount of knowledge farmers have to have about the entire system and on monitoring costs. Spooner (1974) and Netting (1974) described long-lived irrigation systems in Iran and in Switzerland where there was full agreement on the order and time allotted to all farmers located on a segment of the system, but no one knew the entire sequence for the system as a whole.

In a study of 248 irrigation systems in Nepal, colleagues associated with the Irrigation Management Systems Study Group (IMSSG) at the Institute of Agriculture and Animal Sciences in Rampur, Nepal, found a substantial variety of choice rules used depending largely on the elevation of the district in which the system was located *and* the time of year involved. Thus, not only is a variety of rules used—but the rules chosen by farmers tend to depend on ecological conditions. As shown in table 8.3, the systems included in the study were located in two districts of Nepal: (1) Chitwan—a district in the flatlands of Nepal that has larger river systems with substantially higher volume of water during the monsoon seasons than (2) Tanahun—a district in the middle hills with few large rivers.[6] Since water is more abundant during the monsoon season in Chitwan, a larger proportion (43 percent) of the systems in this district relies on a "free flow rule" that authorizes a continuous supply in channel than in Tanahun (33 percent). In Tanahun during the water surplus, monsoon season, the most frequently used rule is "rotational" (52 percent), but this rule is hardly used in Chitwan during the monsoon season (6 percent).

Rules are different in both districts during the spring—or the water deficit time—of the year. The proportion of systems that allow farmers to appropriate whenever they desire in the dry months is less than 10

TABLE 8.3
Water allocation rules in Chitwan and Tanahun districts

	Water surplus time of year		Water deficit time of year	
	Chitwan	Tanahun	Chitwan	Tanahun
Free flow/continuous supply	38 (43%)	52 (33%)	1 (1%)	14 (9%)
Demand/first in time	43 (49%)	4 (3%)	0 (0%)	4 (3%)
Rotational	5 (6%)	83 (52%)	79 (90%)	103 (64%)
No specific methods (consensus)	2 (2%)	35 (22%)	8 (9%)	39 (24%)
Number of irrigation systems	88	160	88	160

Sources: Adapted from Shukla et al. 1993; Poudel et al. 1994.

percent in both districts (see table 8.3). In the water deficit time of the year, nine out of ten systems in Chitwan and over six out of ten systems in Tanahun use some form of a rotation system. This movement back and forth between rules depending on the season is very typical for self-organized resource systems around the world.[7]

Tang (1992) also found that many irrigation systems use different sets of rules depending on the availability of water. During the most abundant season, for example, irrigators may be authorized to take water whenever they need it. During a season when water is moderately available, farmers may use a rotation system where every farmer is authorized to take water for a fixed amount of time during the week based on the amount of land to be irrigated. During scarcity, the irrigation system may employ a special water distributor who is authorized to allocate water to those farmers who are growing crops authorized by the irrigation system and are most in need.

In addition to devising choice rules specifying how resource units may be harvested, many systems also have to devise rules for how resources will be mobilized. These types of choice rules specify duties as contrasted to rights. As discussed in chapter 9, robust common-property regimes tend to rely on a close match between the formulas used for harvesting and the formulas used for input requirements. In regard to irrigation, farmers may even craft different rules related to maintenance according to the part of the canal needing attention—such as the headworks, the main canal, secondary canals, or areas that need emergency repair. In Chitwan, most systems tend to rely on mobilizing labor for repairing the headworks on an irrigation system on a per household basis (also for emergency repair anywhere on the system) but use the amount of land owned and served by a particular part of a canal in cleaning of weeds and other impediments to the flow of water in the main or secondary canals (see summary of these findings in Shivakoti and Ostrom 2002, 14–15). In Tanahun—where the systems tend to be much smaller than in Chitwan, and thus smaller differences between farmers located at the head and the tail—different rules tend to be used. About half of the 160 systems for which the IMSSG group of researchers gathered data relied on landholding anywhere in the system and a per household basis for mobilizing regular repairs on all parts of the system.

The diversity of choice rules devised by users greatly exceeds the few rules recommended in textbook treatments of this problem. Appropriators thus cope with the commons by crafting a wide variety of rules affecting the actions available to participants and thus their basic set of strategies. Given this wide diversity of rules, it is particularly noteworthy that rules assigning appropriators a right to a specific quantity of a resource are used so infrequently in inshore fisheries and irrigation systems. They are used more frequently when allocating forest products where the quantity available, as well as the quantity harvested, are much easier to measure (Agrawal 1994). To assign an appropriator a specific quantity of a resource unit requires that those making the assignment know the total available units. In water resources, only when water is stored from one season to another in a groundwater basin or dam, and reliable information about the quantity of water is available, are rules that allocate a quantity of water to an authorized appropriator utilized (Blomquist 1992; Schlager, Blomquist, and Tang 1994).

Affecting Outcomes through Payoff and Position Rules

One way to reduce or redirect the appropriations made from a common-pool resource is to change payoff rules so as to add a penalty to actions that are prohibited. Many user groups also adopt norms that those who are rule breakers should be socially ostracized or shunned, and individual appropriators tend to monitor each other's behavior rather intensively. Three broad types of payoff rules are used extensively in the field: (1) the imposition of a fine, (2) the loss of appropriation rights, and (3) incarceration. The severity of each of these types of sanctions can range from very low to very high and tends to start out on the low end of the scale.

Inshore fisheries studied by Schlager relied heavily on shunning and other social norms and less on formal sanctions. Thirty-six of the forty-three irrigation systems studied by Tang used one of these three rules and also relied on vigorous monitoring of one another's behavior and shunning of rule breakers. The seven systems that did not self-consciously punish rule infractions were all rated as having poor performance. Fines were most typically used (in twenty-one cases) and incarceration the least (in only two cases). Fines tend to be graduated depending on the seriousness of the infractions and the number of prior infractions. The fines used for a first or second offense tend to be very low.

Once a position of a paid guard is created, payoff rules must also change so as to mobilize resources to remunerate a guard. Several formulas are used. On government-owned irrigation systems, guards are normally paid a monthly wage that is not dependent on the performance of a system or farmers' satisfaction. Agrawal (2005) describes four different payment methods for forest guards that users select: by each household in kind (grains, services), by each household in cash, by the local forest user organizations out of general funds, and by the local forest organization out of central government distributed funds. In South India, Wade (1994) describes self-organized systems where the water distributor-guard is paid in kind based on a proportion of the yield. As the harvest is reaped, the guard must go to each farmer to collect his share based on the harvest level and the amount of land owned by the farmer. Sengupta (1991, 104) describes another system where immediately after appointment, the guards "are taken to the temple for oath taking to remain impartial. With this vow, they break a coconut. They are paid in cash at the rate of Rs 10 per acres . . . per month by the cultivators. The *neerpaichys* (guards) themselves collect the money." Having the farmers pay the guards directly in kind or in cash enables the farmers to "monitor" the monitor more effectively and ensure that there is a rough proportionality between benefits received and the costs of the system.

Boundary and choice rules also affect how easy or difficult it is to monitor activities and impose sanctions on rule infractions. Closing a forest or an inshore fishery for a substantial amount of time, for example, has multiple impacts. It protects particular plants or fish during critical growing periods and allows the entire system time to regenerate without disturbance. Further, during the closed season, rule infractions are highly obvious. *Any* person in the resource during the closed season is almost certainly breaking the rules. Similarly, requiring appropriators to use a particular technology may reduce the pressure on the resource, help to solve conflicts among users of incompatible technologies, and also make it very easy to ascertain if rules are being followed. Many irrigation systems set up rotation systems so that only two persons need to monitor actions at any one time. The farmers whose "turn" it is watch to be sure the next farmer does not start a turn early, and the next farmer watches to be sure the turn-taker stops at the specified time. This keeps monitoring costs low.

In general, self-organized governance systems need to match the rules that impose costs in a rough proportion to the likely positive payoffs that appropriators are likely to obtain over time. If the appropriators do not view the requirements placed on them to provide funds, time, or materials to be equitable, they are much less willing to conform. Since self-governed systems must rely more on willing consent as contrasted to coerced contributions, they need to pay more attention to the relationship between positive and negative payoffs than systems that can easily mobilize police to extract contributions from participants.

Affecting Outcomes through Changes in Information, Scope, and Aggregation Rules

Information, scope, and aggregation rules tend to be used in ways that complement boundary, position, choice, and payoff rules. Individual systems vary radically in regard to the mandatory information that they require. Many smaller and informal systems rely entirely on a voluntary exchange of information and on mutual monitoring. Where resource units are very valuable and the size of the group is larger, more and more requirements are added regarding the information that must be kept by appropriators or their officials. Blomquist (1992, 1994) examined the information rules for eight groundwater basins in southern California. He found that the groundwater basins that had overcome severe overdraft problems had information rules that differed from those used in the one basin that had not overcome these problems. For example, in the "successful" basins, all groundwater producers were required to report the amount of water they produced each year, and various methods were implemented to verify the accuracy of these records. Producers were entitled to receive annual reports providing data about the activities of their monitors, basin conditions, and the production records of others. The basin that still faced overdraft conditions did not have the same information rules (Blomquist 1994, 292).

Scope rules are used to limit harvesting activities in some resources by creating refugia, where actions that are permitted in other areas of a resource are forbidden in the refugia. By not allowing any appropriation from these locations, the regenerative capacity of a system can be enhanced. Sacred groves are probably the most well-known form of refugia. The ancient sacred groves of India, Africa, and the Mediterranean are well documented in history. Modern sacred groves are known to exist in modern times in China, Ghana, India, Mexico, Nepal, Thailand, Uganda, and Zimbabwe (Gadgil, Hemam, and Reddy 1998, 37; Gombya-Ssembajjwe 1995). Many locally controlled fisheries also protect breeding grounds as off-limits for harvesting to enable the eggs and small fish to mature successfully before being subject to harvest (see Folke, Berkes, and Colding 1998).

Aggregation rules are used extensively in collective-choice processes and less extensively in appropriation situations. One aggregation rule that is found in diverse resource systems is a requirement that harvesting activities be done in teams. This increases the opportunity for mutual monitoring and reduces the need to hire special guards. We will return to a discussion of aggregation rules later in this chapter when we analyze the factors affecting appropriators' choice of rules. The aggregation rules used in making collective choices are crucial rules affecting whose interests are taken into account when decisions are made to change the operational rules of an appropriation situation.

It is important to note that we have not yet found any *particular* rules to have a statistically positive relationship to performance across resource types, ecological zones, and communities. On the other hand, the absence of *any* boundary or choice rule *is* consistently associated with poor performance. Relying on the use of a single type of rule for an entire set of common-pool resources in a large region is also negatively related to performance.

Contemporary Approaches to Resource Policy

Instead of studying the literature describing the successful and unsuccessful efforts of local users or public officials to devise rules for coping with common-pool resource problems, which is briefly presented above, many students of public policy read only textbooks that elucidate an approach that can broadly be called "the scientific management of natural resources." This approach teaches future policy analysts to consider fisheries, forests, pasture lands, and water resources as relatively homogeneous systems that are closely interrelated across a vast domain (see Sherman and Laughlin 1992). Irrigation systems are interlinked along watersheds of major river systems. Fish and wildlife species tend to migrate over a large range. By implication, uniform systems of rules are usually prescribed as the best solution. Acheson, Wilson, and Steneck (1998, 391–92) describe this approach as applied to fisheries management:

> For those trained in scientific management, it is also an anathema to manage a species over only part of its range. From the view of fisheries scientists and administrators, it is not rational to protect a species in one zone only to have it migrate into another area where it can be taken by other people due to a difference in regulations. As a result, the units to be managed range along hundreds of miles of coast and can *only be managed by central governments with jurisdiction over the entire area.* . . . From the point of view of the National Marine Fisheries Service, it makes sense to have a set of uniform regulations for the entire US coast rather than one for each state. (italics added)

Many policy analysts share a belief in the feasibility of central authorities to design close-to-optimal rules for governing and managing common-pool resources existing in a large domain.[8] Since common-pool resources are viewed as relatively homogeneous and interlinked and since simple models have been developed of how they are thought to work (Gordon 1954; Heal 1998), officials acting in the public interest are considered capable of devising uniform and effective rules for an entire region.

Recommendations calling for central governments to impose uniform regulations over natural resources within a country's boundary are frequent and strident. After reviewing the problems of deforestation in many countries, Grainger (1993, 224) urges the different departments whose policies affect forests to come together and "agree on an integrated land use policy for the whole country." As his first priority in controlling deforestation, Grainger recommends directing "more funds into forestry departments so they have sufficient personnel and technology to monitor forests and logging operations, prevent illegal deforestation by improving protection, and ensure that logging operations take place in accordance with government regulations" (225). As Blomquist and Ingram (2003) point out, some analysts even call for central administrative control over transboundary resources. Fortunately, there are now some strong voices challenging the presumed superiority of central authorities to solve smaller-scale appropriation problems (see Karkkainen 2001/2; Holling, Gunderson, and Ludwig 2001).

As an alternative to central control, other policy analysts call for the imposition of a market system related to resources at various scales. Carson, Marinova, and Zilberman (1999, 1), in addressing transboundary water problems in the Middle East, conclude that "the current water allocation structure has proven inadequate. It should be replaced with some form of a water market." Further, they declare that considerations of different ways to create markets are irrelevant and that the *first* step for a dramatic change is: "Replace the current water institutions and allocation structure with a water market" (1).

Challenging Three Basic Assumptions of Contemporary Policy Analysis

Based on evidence, it is important to challenge three basic assumptions underlying the study of contemporary resource policies: (1) the view that resource appropriators are helpless to overcome their temptations to harvest excessively from a resource; (2) the assumption that designing rules to change the incentives of participants is a relatively simple analytical task; and (3) the view that organization itself requires *central direction*.

The first foundation that can be disputed is the model of the human actor. Resource users are explicitly thought of as rational egoists who plunder local resources so as to maximize their own short-term benefits. Government officials are implicitly depicted, on the other hand, as seeking the more general public interest, having the relevant information at hand, and the capability of designing optimal policies. As discussed in chapter 4, the rational egoist used in conventional noncooperative game theory is an appropriate model to use for all participants in open competitive markets and other settings where participants are relatively anonymous and have little opportunities to develop norms and longer time horizons. Outside of these settings, however, one needs to assume a mix of participants ranging from those with strong norms of reciprocity to those with weak or few shared intrinsic values. Assuming a multiplicity of orientations is more appropriate in these settings in which individuals can communicate and come to know and potentially trust one another. Rational egoists may come to dominate in any situation in which conflicts are left unresolved and participants lose trust in one another.

One should not, however, presume that all government officials are "saints" while assuming that all resource users are "sinners." Nor should we presume that officials have all the relevant knowledge to manage complex dynamic systems while local appropriators are ignorant. The knowledge base of government officials may not, in reality, be better than that of local appropriators who have used a particular resource for years and know its characteristics in considerable detail. Even when the knowledge base is similar, no guarantee exists that government officials (or the researchers who advise them) will use available information to make efficient and/or sustainable decisions.

For example, Moxnes (1998) conducted a series of experiments examining the capacity of eighty-two subjects who were Norwegian fishers, officials working for government resource agencies, or researchers familiar with resource problems to make economically efficient and resource-sustaining decisions related to a simulated dynamic model of a fishery. All subjects were assigned the equivalent of private property rights over a fishery and asked to make decisions about the purchase of vessels and harvesting rates over a twenty "vertical" year period. On average, all subjects substantially overinvested in the fishery. Many subjects reported using heuristics of the type: "Things seem to be going well; I'll order another vessel" (1241) similar to the heuristic used in the commons dilemma experiments with no communication described in chapter 3. Government officials and researchers did *no* better than the fishers in solving this problem.

A second foundational belief of contemporary resource policy is that designing rules to change the incentives of participants is a relatively simple analytical task best done by objective analysts not specifically related to any specific resource. As Acheson, Wilson, and Steneck (1998) describe above, analysts frequently view most resources in a particular sector as relatively similar and sufficiently interrelated that they need to be governed by the same set of rules.

It should now be obvious that the search for rules that improve the outcomes obtained in commons dilemmas is an incredibly complex task involving a potentially infinite combination of specific rules that could be adopted. To ascertain whether one has found an optimal set of rules to improve the outcomes achieved in a single situation, one would need to analyze how diverse rules affect the components of such a situation and as a result, the likely effect of a reformed structure on incentives, strategies, and outcomes. Since multiple rules directly or indirectly affect each of the seven components of action situations, conducting such an analysis would be an incredibly time- and resource-consuming process.

If only five changes in rules per component were considered, for example, there would be 5^7 or 75,525 different situations to analyze. This is a gross simplification, however, since some of the important rules used in field settings include more than twenty-five rules (in the case of boundary rules) and even over one hundred variants (in the case of choice rules). Further, how these changes affect the outcomes achieved in a particular location depends on the biophysical characteristics of that location and the type of community relationships that already exist. No set of policy analysts (or even all of the game theorists in the world today) would ever have sufficient time or resources to analyze over 75,000 combinations of rule changes and resulting situations, let alone all of the variance in these situations due to biophysical community differences.

Those directly involved would also not be able to do a complete analysis. They would know a lot about local biophysical processes, but not necessarily how that resource system might be linked with biophysical processes occurring at a somewhat larger scale or even how complex biophysical systems were operating. They would also know a great deal about local community norms and the distribution of resources and interests within a community. Given the nonlinearity and complexity of many action situations, it is challenging to predict the precise effect of a change in a particular rule.

For example, a change in a boundary rule to restrict who is authorized to enter and harvest from a resource reduces the number of individuals who are entitled to appropriate from a resource. It also reduces the number of individuals who are interested in monitoring what is happening or contributing funds toward hiring a guard (Agrawal 2000; Agrawal and Goyal 2001). Thus, the opportunities for rule breaking may increase. Further, the cost of a rule infraction will be spread over a smaller group of appropriators. Thus, the harm to any individual may be greater. Assessing the overall effects of a change in boundary rules is a nontrivial analytical task (for examples, see Weissing and Ostrom 1991a, 1991b). Instead of conducting such a complete analysis, appropriators are more apt to use their intuitive understanding of the resource and of one another's norms and preferences to experiment with different rule changes and assess the effects of rules with which experiment until they find a combination that seems to work in their setting.

Local appropriators would receive feedback from their own experiments over time and could then improve how their rules worked over time. If they had good communication with other communities who had experience with multiple rules related to similar resources, they would be able to make informed judgments about the likely impact of some rules, but certainly not all of the rules that they might contemplate adopting or changing. Greater attention to the ways that local experiments are monitored and the mechanisms available for sharing information could improve the likelihood of improving performance over time.

The third foundational belief of much contemporary policy analysis is the view that organization itself requires *central direction*. Consequently, the multitudes of self-organized resource governance systems are viewed as mere collections of individual agents each out to maximize her own short-term returns. The groups who have actually organized themselves are invisible to those who cannot imagine organization without rules and regulations issued by a central authority (see, for example, Lansing 1991). A more appropriate foundation is to assume that governments at multiple levels could, but do not always, adopt policies that enhance effective problem-solving and resource sustainability. Instead of central direction, what is needed are policies that enhance the accuracy and reliability of information, that provide low-cost conflict resolution, and that develop the authority to govern resources at multiple levels.

Useful (but Partial) Analyses of Rule Configurations

I do not wish to argue that analysts as well as participants are unable or should not examine interesting combinations of rules under specified conditions. Analyzing specific situations and how diverse rules would affect the likely incentives, behavior, and outcomes of participants is an extremely important and useful endeavor that social scientists should and do perform.

Scholars at the California Institute of Technology, for example, took on an important assignment for the Civil Aeronautics Board (CAB) to examine how several rules they were considering for the allocation of airport slots would work (Grether, Isaac, and Plott 1979, 1981). Not only did they develop a formal analysis of how alternative rules would affect the incentives of airline carriers and the likely resulting behavior, they also implemented a version of the decision setting in an experimental laboratory. They were interested in predicting the level of efficiency likely from alternative decision rules at multiple levels, but also the responsiveness that was likely due to changed economic conditions and the susceptibility of alternative rules to collusion. In light of their modeling and their experimentation, they recommended the establishment of a "one-price sealed bid auction" as the best method they could recommend for allocating landing slots. Their recommendations came after they developed a model of this specific situation *and* after they had undertaken a trial run process in an experimental lab to see if their theory did predict behavior in this particular situation.[9]

For a paper that I presented at the Annual Bank Conference on Development Economics (called the ABCDE conference!), I also undertook a comparative analysis of a set of rules as they would affect the structure of an action situation—in this case, a formal game—and the net benefits that would be likely at the equilibria of such a game. In that paper (E. Ostrom 1996), I assumed an environment of ten farmers who all owned about the same amount of land on a relatively flat but rich alluvial plain. The farmers were hypothesized to be interested in constructing and then managing their own small irrigation system. I explored a series of games that would be created by using several combinations of rules for allocating benefits and costs. Given my assumptions about the farmers, the environment, and the costs of maintenance, I could show that the farmers would gain the most out of two different combinations of rules.

The ABCDE paper was useful for several reasons. First, it was fun. It is a delight to work with formal worlds and be able to demonstrate clearly how rules would affect the structure of a formal game. Second, I was able to demonstrate overtly the link between changes in the set of rules and how these affect the structure of the action situation itself (see also E. Ostrom, Gardner, and Walker 1994, chap. 4, where we undertake similar efforts). Since I think there is a strong connection between rule configurations and action situations, it is always helpful to demonstrate the linkage between rules and games clearly. Third, the paper demonstrates that in order to undertake such a formal analysis of rules and game structures, I had to make multiple assumptions about the participants and the environment they were in. These included:

Assumptions about the participants:
1. the number of farmers (ten);
2. the relative equality of their holdings;
3. the value of the water for farming to all of the farmers;

4. the engineering knowledge and skills of the farmers;

5. the rights of the participants to use the source of water without contest by other farmers;

6. the rights of the farmers to organize for joint benefit and create rules which they themselves would enforce; and

7. the rational egoistic behavior of farmers.

Assumptions about the environments:

1. the existence of a flat plain;

2. the existence of a nearby water source that was not currently used by other farmers;

3. relatively similar soil conditions across the plain;

4. the layout of the parcels; and

5. the feasibility of two different canal layouts.

Further, I considered the impact of only a total of seven rules—an extremely small set, when one considers the multiplicity of rules arrayed above. Any major change in the variables that I assumed could have led to an entirely different outcome. Thus, the exercise in no way demonstrated an optimal rule configuration at a more general level. Any effort to examine the impact of alternative rules on some specific kind of action situation will always have to make a large number of assumptions as I did in this effort. We should not fool ourselves into thinking that the results of these useful exercises are a full analysis showing one rule configuration producing more net benefits than others.

Coping with Complexity: A General Problem

The complexity we have found in regard to common-pool resources in the field is not in any way unique to natural resources. For far too long, social scientists have viewed the physics of static, simple systems as the model of science we should try to emulate. Those who want to emulate the science of static, simple systems are grossly out-of-date when it comes to understanding contemporary science and particularly contemporary engineering. The engineers responsible for the design of airplanes and bridges—and now computers—have long coped with complex dynamic systems. The Boeing 777, for example, has 150,000 distinct subsystems that are composed, in some instances, of highly complex components.

Design engineers of complex systems long ago gave up hope of ever doing complete analyses of all combinations of subsystems under all combinations of external environmental conditions. Obviously, they invest heavily in trying out diverse design elements under a variety of conditions. Testing designs by building models, using wind tunnels and computer simulations, increases the likelihood that engineers can produce a viable combination of design elements that are robust under many conditions. They also invest in complex backup systems that enable these designed systems to achieve a high degree of robustness—meaning the capacity to maintain some desired system characteristics under changing circumstances. All such robust systems are, however, fragile to a variety of small perturbations (Carlson and Doyle 2002). Small, rare disturbances can cause a disastrous cascade of failure in any highly complex designed system.

Instead of assuming that designing rules that approach optimality, or even improve performance, is a relatively simple analytical task that can be undertaken by distant, objective analysts, we need to understand the policy design process as involving an effort to tinker with a large number of component parts (see Jacob 1977). Those who tinker with any tools— including rules—are trying to find combinations that work together more effectively than other combinations. Policy changes are experiments based on more or less informed expectations about potential outcomes and the distribution of these outcomes for participants across time and space (Campbell 1969, 1975). Whenever individuals decide to add a rule, change a rule, or adopt someone else's proposed rule set, they are conducting a policy experiment. Further, the complexity of the ever-changing biophysical and socioeconomic world combined with the complexity of rule systems means that any proposed rule change faces a nontrivial probability of error.

Changing Rules as an Adaptive Process

Given the logic of combinatorics, it is not possible for anyone to conduct a complete analysis of the expected performance of all the potential rule changes that could be made in an effort to improve the outcomes achieved. When we study rules used by appropriators from common-pool resources in the field, we can think of appropriators trying to understand the biophysical structure of their resource and how they can develop a set of rules consistent with the time and place exigencies and the norms shared in their community. Instead of being given a set of instructions with a fully specified transformation function (as is the case for subjects in experimental settings discussed in chapter 3), appropriators in the field have to explore and discover the biophysical structure of a particular resource. It will usually differ on key parameters from similar resources in the same region. Further, they have to cope with considerable uncertainty related to the weather, complicated growth patterns of biological systems that may be characterized by multiple equilibria, and external price fluctuations affecting the costs of inputs and value of outcomes (see Baker 2005; Wilson et al. 1994; Wilson 2002). One of their first challenges will be to convince those who doubt that the resource is limited or that they will benefit from cooperation, and thus that they need to constrain use in a manner that they agree is workable and fair (Gibson 2001).

Officials and/or the appropriators themselves may try to improve performance by changing one or more rules in an adaptive process. Participants adapt the rules, norms, and strategies of their parents and elders as well as those who are viewed as highly successful in a particular culture. They learn about neighboring systems that work better than theirs and try to discern which rules are helping their neighbors to do better. Human agents try to use reason and persuasion in their efforts to devise better rules, but the process of choice from the vast array of rules they might use always involves experimentation. Self-organized resource governance systems use many types of decision rules to make collective choices ranging from deferring to the judgment of one person or elders to using majority voting to relying on unanimity.

Scholars familiar with the results of field research do substantially agree on a set of variables that enhance the likelihood of appropriators organizing themselves to try to avoid the social losses associated with open access or rules that are not yet working well.[10] Considerable consensus exists that the following attributes of resources and of appropriators are conducive to an increased likelihood that self-governing associations will form.

Attributes of the Resource

R1. Feasible improvement: Resource conditions are not at a point of deterioration such that it is useless to organize or so underutilized that little advantage results from organizing.

R2. Indicators: Reliable and valid indicators of the condition of the resource system are frequently available at a relatively low cost.

R3. Predictability: The flow of resource units is relatively predictable.

R4. Spatial extent: The resource system is sufficiently small, given the transportation and communication technology in use, that appropriators can develop accurate knowledge of external boundaries and internal micro-environments.

Attributes of the Appropriators

A1. Salience: Appropriators depend on the resource system for a major portion of their livelihood or the achievement of important social or religious values.

A2. Common understanding: Appropriators have a shared image of how the resource system operates (attributes R1, 2, 3, and 4 above) and how their actions affect each other and the resource system.

A3. Low discount rate: Appropriators use a sufficiently low discount rate in relation to future benefits to be achieved from the resource.

A4. Trust and reciprocity: Appropriators trust one another to keep promises and relate to one another with reciprocity.

A5. Autonomy: Appropriators are able to determine access and harvesting rules without external authorities countermanding them.

A6. Prior organizational experience and local leadership: Appropriators have learned at least minimal skills of organization and leadership through participation in other local associations or learning about ways that neighboring groups have organized.

Many of these variables are affected by the larger regime in which a resource and its appropriators are embedded. Larger regimes can facilitate local self-organization by providing accurate information about natural resource systems, providing arenas in which participants can engage in discovery and conflict-resolution processes, allowing for autonomy, and providing mechanisms to back up local monitoring and sanctioning efforts. The probability of participants adapting more effective rules in macroregimes that facilitate their efforts over time is higher than in regimes that ignore resource problems entirely or, at the other extreme, presume that all decisions about governance and management must be made by central authorities.

A Rule Change Calculus

Now, why are these attributes of a resource and of appropriator likely to be associated with solving collective-action problems? These attributes combine to affect the perceived net benefits of a set of appropriators (A) using a resource under a particular set of rules. The benefits and costs involved in this calculus involve both extrinsic and intrinsic valuations as discussed in chapter 4. Each appropriator i $(i \in A)$ has to compare his or her perception of the expected net benefits of harvesting while continuing to use an old set of rules (R_{old}) to the benefits he or she expects to achieve with a new set of rules (R_{new}). Each appropriator i must ask whether his or her incentive to change (Γ_i) is positive or negative.

$$\Gamma_i = R_{new} - R_{old}.$$

If Γ_i is negative for all appropriators, no one has an incentive to change. If Γ_i is positive for some appropriators, they then need to estimate three types of costs:

C1—the up-front costs of time and effort spent devising and agreeing upon new rules;

C2—the short-term costs of adopting new appropriation strategies; and

C3—the long-term costs of monitoring and maintaining a self-governed system over time.

If the sum of these expected costs for each appropriator exceeds the incentive to change, no appropriator will invest the time and resources needed to create new institutions. Thus, if

$$\Gamma_i < (C1_i + C2_i + C3_i)$$

for all $i \in A$, no change occurs.

In field settings, appropriators are not likely to expect the same costs and benefits from a proposed change. Some may expect positive net benefits. Others may expect net losses from the same proposed rule change. Consequently, the collective-choice rules used for changing operational rules related to appropriation affect whether an institutional change favored by some and opposed by others will be adopted. For any collective-choice rule, such as unanimity, majority, ruling elite, or one-person rule, a minimum coalition of appropriators, $M \subset A$, must agree prior to the adoption of new rules. If for all coalitions,

$$\Gamma_m \leq (C1_m + C2_m + C3_m),$$

no new rules will be adopted. And if for at least one coalition $M \subset A$,

$$\Gamma_m > (C1_m + C2_m + C3_m),$$

for all members of M, a new set of rules may be adopted. If there are several such coalitions, the question of which coalition will form, and thus which rules will result, depends on the relative resources of the coalitions and their bargaining strength (see J. Knight 1992; Ensminger and Knight 1997). This analysis is applicable to a situation where a set of appropriators starts with only default conditions—open access—and contemplates adopting its first rules limiting access. Appropriators considering changing operational rules over time would also use such a general calculus.[11]

The collective-choice rule used in field settings varies from reliance on the decision of one chief or a few members of an elite, to a reliance on majority or supermajority vote, all the way to reliance on consensus or close to unanimity (Buchanan and Tullock 1962). If there are substantial differences in the perceived benefits and costs of appropriators, it is possible that M appropriators will impose a new set of rules on the $A-M$ other appropriators that strongly favor those in the winning coalition and impose losses or lower benefits on those in the losing coalition (Thompson, Mannix, and Bazerman 1988). If expected benefits from a change in institutional arrangements are not greater than expected costs for many appropriators, however, the costs of enforcing a change in institutions will be much higher than when most participants expect to benefit from a change in rules over time.

Where the enforcement costs are fully borne by the members of M, operational rules that benefit the $A-M$ other appropriators lower the long-term costs of monitoring and sanctioning for a governing coalition. Where external authorities enforce the rules agreed upon by M appropriators, the distribution of costs and benefits are more likely to benefit M and may impose costs on the $A-M$ other appropriators (Ensminger and Knight 1997; Mwangi 2003).

RESOURCE ATTRIBUTES AND CALCULATING COSTS AND BENEFITS

The attributes of a resource (listed above) affect both the benefits and costs of institutional change. Linking these attributes of the biophysical world to the perception of appropriators enables one to develop an underlying metric of perceived net benefits to explain why self-organization occurs in some locations and not in others. If resource units are relatively abundant (R1), little reason exists for appropriators to invest costly time and effort in organizing. If the resource is already substantially destroyed, the high costs of organizing may not generate sufficient benefits. Self-organization is likely to occur only after appropriators observe substantial scarcity. The danger here, however, is that exogenous shocks leading to a change in relative abundance of the resource units may occur rapidly, and appropriators may not adapt quickly enough to the new circumstances (Libecap and Wiggins 1985; Baker 2005).

The presence of reliable indicators about the conditions of a resource (R2) affects the capacity of appropriators to adapt relatively soon to changes that could adversely affect their long-term benefit stream (Moxnes 1996). A resource flow that is highly predictable (R3) is much easier to understand and manage than one that is erratic (Schlager, Blomquist, and Tang 1994). In the latter case, it is always difficult for appropriators (or, for that matter, for scientists and government officials) to judge whether changes in the resource stock or flow are due to overharvesting or to random exogenous variables.[12] Unpredictability of resource units in smaller locations, such as private pastures, may lead appropriators to create a larger common-property unit to increase the predictability of resource availability somewhere in the larger unit (Netting 1972;

Wilson and Thompson 1993). The spatial extent of a resource (R4) affects the costs of defining reasonable boundaries and then of monitoring them over time.

Appropriators' attributes also affect expected extrinsic and intrinsic benefits and costs. If appropriators do not obtain a major part of their income from a resource or value it highly for some other purpose (A1), the high costs of organizing and maintaining a self-governing system may not be worth their effort (Lawry 1990; Gibson 2001). If appropriators do not share a common understanding of how complex resource systems operate (A2), they will find it extremely difficult to agree on future joint strategies. As Libecap and Wiggins (1985) argue, asymmetric private information about heterogeneous assets may adversely affect the willingness of participants to agree to a reduction in their use patterns before considerable damage is done to a resource. Given the complexity of many common-pool resources—especially multispecies or multiproduct resources—understanding how these systems work may be counterintuitive even for those who make daily contacts with the resource.

Appropriators with many other viable and attractive options, who thus discount the importance of future income from a particular resource (A3), may prefer to "mine" a resource without spending resources to regulate it. In light of his study of many fisheries, Berkes (1985, 201) noted that "community control over the fishing effort appears to be very difficult to achieve in commercial fisheries in general." He was pessimistic enough about the likelihood of local organization to reflect that if a "given stock is not overexploited, this is probably related to insufficient market demand rather than to community-level controls" (201). We will discuss a more optimistic picture in chapter 9, however, of the Maine lobster fishery. Maine lobster fishers are embedded in a polycentric system where small-scale commercial interests are centered in communities that have considerable autonomy to craft rules that have enabled the fishery to flourish. In many other cases, commercial fishing firms simply move on to another resource once one is destroyed, assuming there will always be other resources available to them. Berkes and colleagues (2001) also discuss how comanagement strategies involving organizing at a local level along with an active role for a larger-scale government are challenging to create but are an effective way to slowly increase the time horizon of fishers in these systems.

Appropriators who trust one another (A4) to keep agreements and use reciprocity in their relationships with one another face lower expected costs involved in monitoring and sanctioning one another over time. Appropriators who lack trust at the beginning of a process of organizing may be able to build this form of social capital (Coleman 1988; E. Ostrom and Ahn 2003) if they initially adopt small changes that most appropriators follow before trying to make major institutional changes. Autonomy (A5) tends to lower the costs of organizing. A group that has little autonomy may find that those who disagree with locally developed rules seek contacts with higher-level officials to undo the efforts of appropriators to achieve regulation.[13] Prior experience with other forms of local organization (A6) greatly enhances the repertoire of rules and strategies known by local participants as potentially useful to achieve various forms of regulation. Further, appropriators are more likely to agree upon rules whose operation they understand from prior experience, rather than rules that are introduced by external actors and are new to their experience. Given the complexity of many field settings, appropriators face a difficult task in evaluating how diverse variables affect expected benefits and costs over a long time horizon.

Attributes of the resource also affect the attributes of appropriators. In highly variable resources (R3), for example, it may be particularly difficult to understand and to sort out outcomes stemming from exogenous factors and those resulting from the actions of appropriators (McKean 2000). Brander and Taylor (1998) have argued that when the resource base itself grows very slowly, population growth may exceed the carrying capacity before participants have achieved a common understanding of the problem they face (see also Reuveny and Maxwell 2001; Decker and Reuveny 2005). Rolett and Diamond (2004) identify nine biophysical variables that are significant predictors of the historical deforestation of Pacific islands, irrespective of the culture and traditions of the pre-European settlers.

Many aspects of the macroinstitutional structure surrounding a particular setting affect the perceived costs and benefits. Thus, external authorities can do a lot to enhance the likelihood and performance of self-governing institutions (Shivakumar 2005). The availability of open and fair courts for resolving conflicts is one important facility that larger governance units can provide to increase the capability of smaller units. The actions of external authorities can also seriously impede these developments as well. Further, when the activities of one set of appropriators, A, have "spillover effects" on others beyond A, external authorities can either facilitate processes that allow multiple groups to solve conflicts arising from negative spillovers or take a more active role in governing particular resources themselves.

Appropriators in the field rarely face a setting that generates clear-cut, expected benefit-cost ratios. The collective-choice rules in some settings give a small elite substantial power to block suggested changes that may generate positive gains for most appropriators but some losses for those in power. Consequently, we cannot conclude that most appropriators using common-pool resources will undertake self-governed regulation. Many settings exist where the theoretical expectation should be the opposite: Appropriators will overuse the resource unless efforts are made to change one or more of the variables affecting perceived costs or benefits. Given the number of variables that affect these costs and benefits, many points of external intervention can enhance or reduce the probability of appropriators' agreeing upon and following rules that generate higher social returns. Both social scientists and policymakers have a lot to learn about how these variables operate interactively in field settings and even how to measure them so as to conduct well-crafted empirical studies to test the warrantability and usefulness of this calculus.

Researchers and public officials need to recognize the multiple manifestations of these theoretical variables in the field. Appropriators may be highly dependent on a resource (A1), for example, because they are in a remote location and few roads exist to enable them to leave. Alternatively, they may be located in a central location, but other opportunities are not open to them due to lack of training or a discriminatory labor market. Appropriator's discount rates (A3) in relation to a particular resource may be low because they have lived for a long time in a particular location and expect that they and their grandchildren will remain in that location or because they possess a secure and well-defined bundle of property rights to this resource (see Schlager and Ostrom 1992).

Reliable indicators of the condition of a resource (R2) may result from activities that the appropriators themselves do—such as regularly shearing the wool from sheep (see Gilles and Jamtgaard 1981) or because of efforts to gather reliable information by appropriators or by external authorities (Blomquist 1992). Predictability of resource units (R3) may result from a clear regularity in the natural environment of the resource or because storage has been constructed in order to even out the flow of resource units over both good and bad years. They may have autonomy to make their own rules (A5) because a national government is weak and unable to exert authority over resources that it formally owns, or because national law formally legitimates self-governance—as is the case with Japanese inshore fisheries.

When the benefits of organizing are commonly understood by participants to be very high, appropriators lacking many of the attributes conducive to the development of self-governing institutions may be able to overcome their liabilities and still develop effective agreements. Libecap (1995, 166) reflects that "the larger the expected aggregate gains, the more likely an acceptable share arrangement can be devised." The crucial factor is not, however, whether *all* attributes are favorable but the relative size of the expected extrinsic and intrinsic benefits and costs they generate as perceived by participants. All of the resource and appropriator variables listed above affect their expected benefits and costs. It is difficult, however, particularly for outsiders to estimate their specific impact on expected benefits and costs given the difficulty of making precise measures of many of these variables and weighing them on a cumulative scale.

Theoretical Puzzles

In addition to the growing consensus concerning the variables most likely to be associated with self-organization, many unresolved theoretical issues still exist. Two major theoretical questions relate to the effect of the number of appropriators involved and their heterogeneity on the likelihood of self-organization and the type of rules designed.

Size

Many theorists argue that the size of a group is negatively related to solving collective-action problems in general. Many results from game-theoretical analysis of repeated games conclude that cooperative strategies are more likely to emerge and be sustained in smaller rather than larger groups (see synthesis of this literature in Baland and Platteau 1996). Scholars who have studied self-organized resource systems in the field point to the increased transaction costs of larger groups and tend to conclude that success will more likely happen in smaller groups (see, for example, Barker et al. 1984; Cernea 1989; Wilson and Thompson 1993; Meinzen-Dick, Raju, and Gulati 2002). Libecap (1995) reflects that the common-pool resource experiments without communication, discussed in chapter 3, are closer to his experience of studying large groups of oil producers, fishers, and orange producers than the experiments with communication.

On the other hand, Tang (1992, 68) did not find a statistical relationship within the 37 farmer-governed systems he studied (which varied from 7 to 300 farmers) between the number of appropriators or the amount of land being irrigated and performance variables. In Lam's (1998, 115) analysis of the performance of a much larger set of irrigation systems in Nepal ranging in size up to 475 irrigators, he also did not find any significant relationship between either the number of appropriators or the amount of land included in the service area with any of the three performance variables he studied. On the other hand, in a systematic study of forest institutions, Agrawal (2000) found a curvilinear pattern. Both smaller and much larger forest user groups were not as able to undertake the level of monitoring needed to protect forest resources as moderately sized groups.

One of the problems with a focus on size of group as a key determining factor is that many other variables change as group size increases (Chamberlin 1974; R. Hardin 1982). If the costs of providing a public good related to the use of a common-pool resource, say a sanctioning system, remain relatively constant as group size increases, then increasing the number of participants brings additional resources that could be drawn upon to provide the benefit enjoyed by all (see Isaac, Walker, and Williams 1994). Marwell and Oliver (1993, 45) conclude that when a "good has pure jointness of supply, group size has a *positive* effect on the probability that it will be provided." On the other hand, if one is analyzing the conflict levels over a subtractable good and the transaction costs of arriving at acceptable allocation formulas, group size may well exacerbate the problems of self-governing systems. Since there are trade-offs among various impacts of size on other variables, a better working hypothesis is that group size has a curvilinear relationship to performance.

Heterogeneity

Heterogeneity is also a highly contested variable. For one thing, groups can differ along a diversity of dimensions including their cultural backgrounds, interests, and endowments (see Baland and Platteau 1996; Platteau 2004). Each may operate differently. If groups coming from diverse cultural backgrounds share access to a common resource, the key question affecting the likelihood of self-organized solutions is whether the views of the multiple groups concerning the structure of the resource, authority, interpretation of rules, trust, and reciprocity differ or are similar. New settlers to a region may simply learn and accept the rules of the established group, and their cultural differences on other fronts do not affect their participation in governing a resource. On the other hand, new settlers are frequently highly disruptive to the sustenance of a self-governing enterprise. They may not recognize the legitimacy of the local rules and may place heavy demands on a resource.

When the interests of appropriators differ, achieving a self-governing solution to common-pool resource problems is particularly challenging (Libecap 1995). Appropriators who possess more substantial economic and political assets may have similar interests to those with fewer assets or they may differ substantially on multiple attributes. When the more powerful have similar interests, they may greatly enhance the probability of successful organization if they invest their resources in organizing a group and devising rules to govern that group. Those with substantial economic and political assets are more likely to be a member of a minimal winning coalition—and thus have a bigger impact on decisions about institutional changes. Mancur Olson (1965) long ago recognized the possibility of a privileged group whereby some of those possessing a large share of political and economic assets were sufficiently affected to bear a disproportionate share of the costs of organizing to provide public goods (such as the organization of a collectivity). On the other hand, if those with more assets also have low discount rates (A3) related to a particular resource and lower salience (A1), they may simply be unwilling to expend inputs or actually impede organizational efforts that might lead to their having to cut back on their productive activities.

Appropriators may also design institutions that cope effectively with heterogeneities. In a study of eighteen forestry user groups in Nepal, Varughese and Ostrom (2001) found that wealth disparities and locational or sociocultural differences had no impact on the measured level of collective action and forest conditions. When groups adopted rules that allocate benefits using the same formulas used to allocate duties and responsibilities, appropriators who differ significantly in terms of assets will tend to agree and follow such rules. Poteete and Ostrom (2004) reviewed the findings from five studies conducted by scholars associated with the International Forestry Resources and Institutions (IFRI) research network, who used the same research protocols to measure group and forest characteristics and the rules crafted by these groups. In these studies, heterogeneity was not consistently a negative factor affecting forest conditions. In many cases, appropriators had designed rules that took into account the diverse forms of heterogeneity found in a user group. These ingenious rules enabled a group to overcome the potential resentment and injustices associated with heterogeneity. On the other hand, when heterogeneity is accentuated by rules rather than counteracted by rules, Platteau (2003) has documented how inequalities can lead to further inequalities.

Summing Up

Even in a group that differs on many variables, if at least a minimally winning subset of M appropriators harvesting an endangered but valuable resource are dependent on it (A1), share a common understanding of their situations (A2), have a low discount rate (A3), trust one another (A4), and have autonomy to make their own rules (A5), it is more likely that they will estimate the expected benefits of governing their resource greater than the expected costs. Whether the rules agreed upon distribute benefits and costs fairly depends both on the collective-choice rule used and the type of heterogeneity existing in the community. Neither size nor heterogeneity are variables with a uniform effect on the likelihood of organizing and sustaining self-governing enterprises. The debate about their effect is focusing on the wrong variables. Instead of focusing on size or the various kinds of heterogeneity by themselves, it is important to ask how these variables interact with other variables as they impact the benefit-cost calculus of those involved in negotiating and sustaining agreements. Their impact on costs of producing and distributing information (Scott 1993, forthcoming) is particularly important.

For appropriators to cope with the complexity of experimenting with the rules that they could use to sustain a common-pool resource, they have to conclude that the expected benefits from an institutional change will exceed the immediate and long-term expected costs. When appropriators cannot communicate and have no way of gaining trust through their own efforts or with the help of the macroinstitutional system within which they are embedded, the prediction of an incapacity to extract themselves from a pattern of overuse is likely to be empirically supported. Ocean fisheries, the stratosphere, and other global commons come closest to the appropriate empirical referents (E. Ostrom et al. 1999).

If appropriators can engage in face-to-face bargaining and have autonomy to change their rules, they may well attempt to organize themselves. Whether they organize depends on attributes of the resource system and the appropriators themselves that affect the benefits to be achieved and the costs of achieving them. Whether their self-governed enterprise succeeds over the long term depends on whether they can successfully experiment with a subset of the rules that are used to govern common-pool resources and a configuration of rules that are easy to understand and monitor, keep harvesting levels within bounds, and are considered equitable by most appropriators.

Once one adopts the view that one cannot create the perfect set of rules and that all efforts at reform must be viewed as experiments, one recognizes that policy analysis can never find "the" answer. We can analyze the effect of rules in highly simplified game-theoretic analyses. We can certainly expand knowledge about the rich diversity of rules used in practice. Appropriators in field settings across time and space have already devised an incredible richness in the rules they use. We need to learn more about this heritage so as to be better facilitators of building adaptive institutional designs—in contrast to presuming we are the experts who can devise *the* optimal design to solve a complex problem. All analyses of potential institutional reforms are partial analyses. We can improve their quality by carefully studying rules-in-use and the incentives, interactions, and outcomes they generate in light of the biophysical and social world in which they exist.

Nine

Robust Resource Governance in Polycentric Institutions

THE STUDY OF the rules actually used in many field settings across the world to regulate the use of common-pool resources leads to an unsettling conclusion. We must conclude that those making rules in efforts to improve outcomes in this policy domain can undertake only partial analyses of a limited set of potential rules and their impact on actions and outcomes in specific environments. No one can undertake a *complete* analysis of all of the potential rules that they might use and analytically determine which set of rules will be optimal for the outcomes they value in a particular ecological, economic, social, and political setting. One must recognize that policies involving rule changes must be viewed as experiments. Further, since ecological, economic, social, and political settings are always changing over time, no specific set of rules will produce the same distribution of benefits and costs over time.

For some readers, this is a depressing lesson. They are looking for "the" answer of how best to solve commons dilemmas and other policy problems. We all recognize that some efforts at designing or reforming rules have had disastrous results. Developing a "sure-fire" method to avoid all disasters stemming from rules that generate perverse incentives in a particular environment sounds like a great advance. I am sure that the designers of modern airplanes would also like to have a sure-fire method to test out *all* contingencies before sending planes into the air. Similarly, the designers of high-speed computers and software would appreciate having a method that would enable them to produce a "crash-proof" computer system.

The contemporary levels of knowledge related to designing new institutions for governing complex resource systems, airplanes to fly through uncertain weather, and computers subject to diverse exigencies, are substantial, but not complete (H. Simon 1981). And, I am willing to predict given the large number of components that combine in a nonadditive fashion, that our knowledge of how to design these systems will continue to grow but will never be complete. As soon as one design has proved itself in one environment, innovations in strategies adopted by participants or changes in the environment in which a humanly designed system is in operation will produce unexpected results.

We are not, however, helpless in finding ways to improve the performance of complex social-ecological systems. We cannot conduct full analyses of the consequences of changing *all* possible parts of a complex system interacting itself with a complex and changing environment. Further, officials and policy analysts who presume that they have the right design can be dangerous. They are likely to assume that citizens are short-sighted and motivated only by extrinsic benefits and costs. Somehow, the officials and policy analysts assume that they have different motivations and can find the optimal policy because they are not directly involved in the problem (Moore 1995). They are indeed isolated from the problems. This leaves them with little capability to adapt and learn in light of information about outcomes resulting from their policies.[1] All too often, these "optimal" policies have Leviathan-like characteristics to them.[2]

Continuing to presume that complex policy problems are simple problems that can be solved through the adoption of simple designs that are given general names, such as private property, government ownership, or community organization, is a dangerous academic approach. Dichotomizing the institutional world into "the market" as contrasted to "the state" is so grossly inadequate and barren that it is surprising how the dichotomy survives as a basic way of organizing academic studies and policy advice. Oversimplification of our design options is dangerous since it hides more of the working parts needed to design effective, sustainable institutions than it reveals (Seabright 1993). And, it reduces our awareness of the need to monitor outcomes and improve them over time through better processes of learning and adaptation.

The language developed in this book to identify the working components of action arenas that exist everywhere (chapters 1 through 4); to analyze the similarities and differences in rules, norms, and strategies (chapter 5); and then to group similar rules together by the component of an action situation they directly affect (chapters 6 through 8), is undoubtedly more complex than many contemporary scholars would prefer. This complexity of language has not been introduced lightly. A scholar should also keep analysis as simple as possible—given the problems to be analyzed. Just as important, however, is developing a mode of analysis that enables scholars, policymakers, and participants in ongoing processes to grapple with the problems they face by digging through the layers of nested systems in which these processes exist. When one is analyzing what is operationally a relatively simple system using a relatively simple language for analysis, one may not need the full language system developed in this volume. Most common-pool resources, and many other policy fields, however, are complex systems and not simple systems. Thus, we need a consistent, nested set of concepts that can be used in our analysis, research, and policy advice in a cumulative manner. The concepts developed in this book do, I hope, form the foundation for such an endeavor. They are derived from a commitment to use theory to observe the institutional world and to learn from that observation and measurement. And, of course, given the central lesson just discussed, institutional analysts will improve on these concepts over time as further research and policy advice uses these concepts.

In chapter 8, after examining the kinds of rules used in the field for coping with common-pool resources in many settings, I stressed the impossibility of conducting a full analysis of all options available to officials, appropriators, scholars, and others interested in improving the performance of resource governance institutions. The question to be examined in this final chapter is whether methods exist that can be used to learn more effectively from the experience of engaging in "reforms as experiments" (Campbell 1969). Are there ways that we can avoid some of the disastrous results that have been produced by systems of governance in the contemporary world? My answer is yes. While no "sure-fire" methods exist, I will argue that there are approaches to speed up and share the learning that can result from tinkering with rules and gaining experience with outcomes. E. Jones (2003), for example, developed a graphical method for analyzing relationships in these complex systems.

First, instead of trying to search for the single set of rules that is the optimal set for every type of problem, I will again urge the importance of studying the underlying designs of those real-world experiments that have proved to be robust over time as I did in *Governing the Commons* (see E. Ostrom 1990). In the first part of this chapter, I will review what we have learned since 1990 about design principles related to robust, common-pool resource institutions. In light of still further evidence about the performance of self-organized systems that are consistent with the earlier derived design principles, we can conclude that there are ways of organizing governance that increase the opportunities for adaptation and learning in a changing and uncertain world with continuing advances in knowledge and technologies.

The design principles are not blueprints, however! They describe the broad structural similarities among those self-organized systems that have been able to adapt and learn so as to be robust to the many social, economic, and ecological disturbances that occur over time. Threats always challenge the robustness of any system—no matter how well it fits the best design principles known for a particular problem Thus, the second topic of this chapter is a discussion of the threats that exist to any set of self-organized, resource governance systems. Since one of the important threats is the effort to impose uniform rules and large boundaries on systems so they are more comprehensible to academics and policymakers, I will conclude this chapter by urging readers to think more positively about the complex, polycentric systems of governance that are created by individuals who have considerable autonomy to engage in self-governance. Given the wide variety of ecological problems that individuals face at diverse scales, an important design principle is getting the boundaries of any one system roughly to fit the ecological boundaries of the problem it is designed to address. Since most ecological problems are nested from very small local ecologies to those of global proportions, following this principle requires a substantial investment in governance systems at multiple levels—each with some autonomy but each exposed to information, sanctioning, and actions from below and above (Low et al. 2003; Folke, Berkes, and Colding 1998; Moran and Ostrom 2005).

Design Principles and Robust Social-Ecological Systems

The findings briefly reviewed in chapter 8—that self-organized systems have frequently solved many Commons Dilemmas—have surprised many scholars. These findings differ from the grim predictions made in the 1970s and 1980s that individuals were trapped in unproductive situations and could not themselves restructure their perverse incentives. One cannot, of course, now substitute for the earlier grim predictions a presumption of a uniformly successful conquering of collective-action problems. As social scientists, we have to use one of our favorite slogans once again—it depends!

In my earlier effort to understand the governance systems that had been identified during the last half of the 1980s as long-surviving systems, I first tried to identify the specific rules used by the systems that had survived for a long period of time using Kenneth Shepsle's (1989) definition of a robust institution. Shepsle considered a system to be robust if it was long-lasting and the operational rules had been devised and modified over time according to a set of collective-choice rules (which themselves might be modified more slowly over time within a set of constitutional-choice rules, which were modified, if at all, very infrequently). The contemporary use of the term *robustness* in regard to complex systems focuses on adaptability to disturbances: "the maintenance of some desired system characteristics despite fluctuations in the behavior of its component parts or its environment" (Carlson and Doyle 2002, 2538; see also Anderies, Janssen, and Ostrom 2004).

Among the many governance systems that met Shepsle's criteria for robustness—as well as the criteria specified by Carlson and Doyle—the specific operational and collective-choice rules that were observed varied dramatically from one system to the next. It was frustrating that I could not identify any particular rules consistently associated with robust governance of common-pool resources. Instead of focusing on specific rules, my effort turned to identifying eight underlying design principles that characterized robust common-property institutions. No assertion was made that those crafting these institutions self-consciously used the design principles. Rather, it was my thought that robust systems had simply met most of these principles and that those systems that had collapsed or were performing ineffectively were not so structured.

Design principles derived from studies of long-enduring institutions for governing sustainable resources:

1. *Clearly defined boundaries.* The boundaries of the resource system (e.g., irrigation system or fishery) and the individuals or households with rights to harvest resource units are clearly defined.

2. *Proportional equivalence between benefits and costs.* Rules specifying the amount of resource products that a user is allocated are related to local conditions and to rules requiring labor, materials, and/or money inputs.

3. *Collective-choice arrangements.* Many of the individuals affected by harvesting and protection rules are included in the group who can modify these rules.

4. *Monitoring.* Monitors, who actively audit biophysical conditions and user behavior, are at least partially accountable to the users and/or are the users themselves.

5. *Graduated sanctions.* Users who violate rules-in-use are likely to receive graduated sanctions (depending on the seriousness and context of the offense) from other users, from officials accountable to these users, or from both.

6. *Conflict-resolution mechanisms.* Users and their officials have rapid access to low-cost, local arenas to resolve conflict among users or between users and officials.

7. *Minimal recognition of rights to organize.* The rights of users to devise their own institutions are not challenged by external governmental authorities, and users have long-term tenure rights to the resource.

For resources that are parts of larger systems:

8. *Nestled enterprises.* Appropriation, provision, monitoring, enforcement, conflict resolution, and governance activities are organized in multiple layers of nested enterprises (based on E. Ostrom 1990, 90).

When I first speculated about these design principles (E. Ostrom 1990), I stressed the speculative nature of my efforts and urged others to test out these tentative conclusions through further empirical research that would help ascertain if these principles distinguished between robust and failed systems. Since *Governing the Commons* was published, other scholars have responded to the challenge and examined the relevance of these principles for helping to explain the performance of resource governance systems (such as fisheries, irrigation systems, pastures, and forests) throughout the world (see Dietz, Ostrom, and Stern 2003).[3]

Martin S. Weinstein (2000), for example, examined indigenous inshore fishery institutions in Canada and Japan and found that these extremely long-lived institutions were characterized to a large extent by the design principles that I had earlier proposed. Abernathy and Sally (2000) studied nine small but long-surviving irrigation systems in the dry areas of Burkina Faso and Niger. They measured system performance using both physical and nonphysical factors and did not find a single indicator that could systematically be used to measure system performance. They found that an average measure of performance based on six indicators, on the other hand, was highly correlated with governance arrangements conforming to the design principles listed above. Other studies of irrigation systems that found systems that were characterized by the design principles to exhibit robustness include works by Crook and Jones (1999), Guillet (1992a, 1992b), Gupta and Tiwari (2002), and Merrey (1996).

Haley (2002) examined a somewhat different question using the design principles: the performance of the same private oil corporation—Arco—related to the exploitation of two different oil fields located in indigenous territories. Arco discovered oil in 1992 in the Pastaza Province in Eastern Ecuador near a Quichua indigenous community (the Villano field) and in 1994 in the Colville Delta in northern Alaska on land owned by an Inupiat Eskimo community (the Alpine field). Both communities have received benefits from the oil revenues generated. Haley estimated that the indigenous community received around 3.2 percent of the total government and resource owner take for the Alpine field, but less than 1 percent of the government share (and not even the total return) related to the Villano field. Haley appraised each case for the presence or absence of the design principles and found that the governance arrangements for the Alpine field were consistent with all of the design principles. For the first decade, the arrangements for the Villano field were not consistent with any of the design principles. Recently, the Villano field has developed some ad hoc arrangements that are consistent with two of the principles.

In light of the positive reaction to these design principles, let us briefly review some of the research that has focused specifically on each of them.

Well-Defined Boundaries

The first principle is that the boundaries of the resource system, as well as the individuals or households with rights to harvest resource units, are clearly defined. The problem that is addressed by systems that do define their boundaries is clearly free-riding. If a group of users can determine their own membership—including those who agree to use the resource according to their agreed-upon rules and excluding those who do not agree to these rules—the group has made an important first step toward limiting access and developing greater trust and reciprocity. Using this principle enables participants to know who is in and who is out of a defined set of relationships and, thus, with whom to cooperate. Smaller resource governance systems do not always have extensively developed rule systems, but those that are robust do demark their boundaries (see, for example, Schlager 1994; Berkes et al. 2001).

Group boundaries are frequently marked by well-understood attributes, such as residing in a particular community or joining a specific local cooperative (as shown in table 8.1 in chapter 8). Further, membership may be marked by various "tags"—symbolic boundaries—and involve complex rituals and beliefs that help solidify individual beliefs about the trustworthiness of others. Contemporary developments in evolutionary theory applied to cultural systems and processes of adaptation help to explain how these design principles work to help groups sustain and build their cooperation over long periods of time (Janssen and Ostrom forthcoming b).

. Just defining the resource boundaries carefully, however, may not be sufficient in and of itself! In a study of irrigation systems in Nepal, Shukla (2002) found that almost all of these systems have well-demarked boundaries. A substantial difference exists, however, between the systems that have been designed, built, and maintained by farmers as contrasted to the systems designed by government engineers. On the farmer-designed systems, the farmers themselves determine how large the area to be served should be. The farmers who demark the boundary will also have to participate in the construction of the system and its maintenance by contributing time, materials, and potentially some funds. Thus, the boundaries of irrigation systems developed by farmers tend to be conservative so that those who make the system work are more assured of getting water. Farmers on these systems—even at the tail end—tend to receive water in the dry season as a consequence of keeping their systems small and the other elements of the physical and institutional structures they build.

The boundaries of those systems constructed by government agencies, by contrast, are frequently demarked as part of donor-funded projects. Irrigation engineers are strongly motivated to show a positive benefit-cost ratio. The more farmers placed within the service boundary of a system, the higher the benefits that can be reported in the plans submitted to donors for funding (Palanisami 1982; R. Repetto 1986). Once funding is granted, few efforts are made to check the reliability of earlier estimates. Farmers in the larger service area are promised water but may not receive a reliable supply. Farmers on these systems are more likely to steal water and less likely to contribute resources to maintenance. Thus, appropriator-defined boundaries tend to include a clear set of participants who know that they have mutual responsibilities as well as benefits.

Externally imposed boundaries may not be viewed as legitimate by those who have cared for a resource for long periods of time. If imposed boundaries are enforced, they generate substantial costs for local peoples (Ghate 2003). On the other hand, the boundaries may not even be known to local appropriators. Paper parks have been created in the capitals of many countries that look clear on the official maps but are not demarked or enforced locally (Hayes 2004; Dietz, Ostrom, and Stern 2003).

Some governmental reserves have had remarkable stability over time. Vogt and colleagues (2005) have dug into archives and talked with older residents and officials to determine why remotely sensed images of forest reserves in one region of Uganda show remarkably stable boundaries when so many forest reserves have failed to reduce deforestation within their boundaries. In this case, Vogt and colleagues determined that the boundaries were negotiated as part of the 1900 agreement between the Regents of the Buganda Kingdom and the British colonial government—and have thus had legitimacy for more than a century. Further, the boundaries have been clearly demarked with stone-covered cairns, and specific tree species were planted in the cairns. Local clan elders and traditional administrators participated in the original demarcation, and local residents continue to participate in the renewal of these boundaries every two decades or so. Strict enforcement of the boundaries backed by legitimate and well-known boundaries have led to a remarkable stability in a region of Africa where many government forests have been extensively deforested by local residents (see also Dietz, Ostrom, and Stern 2003).

In a thoughtful analysis of the usefulness of the design principles for analyzing why some donor-sponsored conservation projects have failed while others have succeeded, Morrow and Hull (1996) pointed out that many donor projects formally met the first design principle. Formal congruence with the first principle is not enough, however, to enable appropriators to defend their borders from free riders. Morrow and Hull suggested a rephrasing for the first design principle to be: "The resource itself and the users of the resources are clearly defined, and the appropriators are able to effectively defend the resource from outsiders" (1643). Given our own research on the importance of defending the boundaries that are demarked, this rephrasing is a positive step forward (Dietz, Ostrom, and Stern 2003; Gibson, Williams, and Ostrom 2005).

Proportional Equivalence between Benefits and Costs

The second design principle is that the rules-in-use allocate benefits proportional to inputs that are required. If a group of users is going to harvest from a resource over the long run, they must devise rules related to how much, when, and how different products are to be harvested. They also need to assess the costs of operating a system on users. When the rules related to the distribution of benefits are made broadly consistent with the distribution of costs, participants are more willing to pitch in to keep a resource well-maintained and sustainable (see, for example, Nemarundwe and Kozanayi 2003). Relating user inputs to the benefits they obtain is a crucial element of establishing a fair system (Trawick 2001). If some users get all the benefits and pay few of the costs, others are not willing to follow rules over time (Ensminger 2000). Thus, fairness is a crucial attribute of the rules of robust systems (Chakraborty 2004).

The Chisasibi Cree have devised a complex set of entry and authority rules related to the coastal fish stocks of James Bay, as well as the beaver stock located in their defined hunting territory. Fikret Berkes (1987, 87) explains that these resource systems and the rules used to regulate them have survived and prospered for so long because effective "social mechanisms ensure adherence to rules which exist by virtue of mutual consent within the community. People who violate these rules suffer not only a loss of favour from the animals (important in the Cree ideology of hunting) but also social disgrace." Fair rules of distribution help to build trusting relationships since more individuals are willing to abide by these rules because they participated in their design and also because they meet shared concepts of fairness (Bowles 1998; Trosper 2002).

In long-surviving irrigation systems, for example, subtly different rules are used in each system for assessing water fees used to pay for maintenance activities, but water tends to be allocated proportional to fees or other required inputs (Bardhan 2000; Bardhan and Dayton-Johnson 2002). Sometimes water and responsibilities for resource inputs are distributed on a share basis, sometimes on the order in which water is taken, and sometimes strictly on the amount of land irrigated. No single set of rules defined for all irrigation systems in a region would satisfy the particular problems in managing each of these broadly similar, but distinctly different, systems (Tang 1992; Lam 1998).

Collective-Choice Arrangements

The third design principle is that most of the individuals affected by a resource regime are authorized to participate in making and modifying their rules. Resource regimes that use this principle are both better able to tailor rules to local circumstances and to devise rules that are considered fair by participants. As environments change over time, being able to craft local rules is particularly important as officials located far away do not know of the change. When a local elite is empowered at the collective-choice level, policies that primarily benefit them can be expected (Platteau 2003, 2004; Ensminger 1990).

In a study of forty-eight irrigation systems in India, Bardhan (2000) finds that the quality of maintenance of irrigation canals is significantly lower on those systems where farmers perceive the rules to have been made by a local elite. On the other hand, those farmers (of the 480 interviewed) who responded that the rules for their system have been crafted by most of the farmers, as contrasted to the elite or the government, have a more positive attitude about the water allocation rules and the rule compliance of other farmers. Further, in all of the villages where a government agency decides how water is to be allocated and distributed, frequent rule violations are reported, and farmers tend to contribute less to the local village fund. Consistent with this is the finding by Ray and Williams (1999) that the deadweight loss from upstream farmers stealing water on government-owned irrigation systems in Maharashtra, India, approaches one-fourth of the revenues that could be earned in an efficient water allocation and pricing regime.

Knox and Meinzen-Dick (2001, 22) note that property rights "are significantly more likely to address the interests and needs of local people when they are not imposed from the outside but rather are based on existing rights and reflect local values and norms." As they point out, these rules take time and effort to develop, try out, modify, and then experiment with again. Users who have been engaged in this process for some time understand the rules that they have crafted, agree on why they are using one rule rather than another, and tend to follow their own rules to a greater extent than those that are imposed on them. Sekher (2000) conducted a study of villages in Orissa, India, that varied in regard to the extent of participation of local villagers in making rules related to nearby forests that they used. He found that the "wider the representation of the community in the organization, the better are its chances of securing local cooperation and rule confirmation for managing and preserving the resource" (8).

In a comparative study of farmer-designed and governed irrigation systems (FMIS), as contrasted to those designed and operated by engineers without involvement of the farmers in making rules to govern these systems, Shukla (2002, 83), a water engineer himself, is relatively critical of the "unrealistic planning and design, incomplete development, a nonsystematic and inadequate maintenance program, deficit operation, and lack of participation of the users" that characterized many of these systems in Nepal. Drawing on the earlier research of Pant and Lohani (1983), Yoder (1994), Lam (1998), and Pradhan (1989), Shukla identifies the following as the strengths of the farmer-designed systems: "(1) Their technical deficiencies are compensated by management inputs; (2) they are low cost and based on local resources; (3) effective irrigation organizations exist in most FMIS; (4) most FMIS have well-defined rules and roles for water allocation, distribution, resource mobilization, and conflict resolution; and (5) the leaders of these systems are accountable to the users" (2002, 83).

Monitoring

Few long-surviving resource regimes rely primarily on endogenous levels of trust and reciprocity among appropriators to keep rule breaking levels down. Evidence of the consequence of inadequate monitoring is convincingly presented by Schweik (2000). It is obvious to most institutional analysts that rules must be enforced in some manner to achieve robust governance; the question of how rules will *actually* be enforced is frequently ignored when proposed institutional changes are analyzed and a reform is proposed. All too many "comanaged paper parks" have been drafted in the home office of an overseas donor or even in a country's capital city only to be destroyed by illegal harvesting in the specified territory. While many agree that rule enforcement is necessary for creating a sustainable resource over time, a vigorous debate is raging about who should be the monitors (Bruner et al. 2001; Igoe 2004; Hockings and Phillips 1999; Stevens 1997; Wells and Brandon 1992).

Most long-surviving resource regimes select their own monitors, who are accountable to the appropriators or are appropriators themselves and who keep an eye on resource conditions as well as on harvesting activities (design principle 4). By creating official positions for local monitors, a resource regime does not have to rely only on the norms of local appropriators to impose personal costs on those who break a rule. The community creates an official position. In some systems, appropriators rotate into this position so everyone has a duty to be a monitor. In other systems, all participants contribute resources and they jointly hire monitors. With local monitors, conditional cooperators are assured that someone is generally checking on the conformance of others to local rules. Thus, they can continue their own cooperation without constant fear that others are taking advantage of them.

Some government-owned forests have successfully adopted monitoring arrangements similar to those of self-organized systems. Banana and Gombya-Ssembajjwe (2000) compare the Echuya Forest in Uganda with three other government-owned forests and one private forest. In the three other government-owned forests, they found extensive illegal harvesting—charcoal burning, pit-sawing, grazing, and cutting commercial firewood—in the forest plots they had randomly selected for observation and measurement. Over 70 percent of the sample forest plots in the three other government forests contained evidence of illegal harvesting (90). In the Echuya Forest and the private forest, the level of illegal harvest was relatively minor—only 20 percent of the sample plots showed any evidence of illegal harvesting (90). In Echuya, members of an Abayanda pygmy community, who live in the forest itself, have been asked by the government to monitor local harvesting from the predominately bamboo forest that is officially limited to one day a week. Even though the Echuya Forest is quite large, local monitors have made a significant difference in the level of illegal harvesting. A similar system drawing on local appropriators to monitor government reserves has evolved the State of Rondônia in Brazil. In a series of forest reserves located near to a large area devoted to colonist settlements, Batistella (2001) has documented the positive impact of the government using local rubber tappers to monitor forest use (see online supplement to Dietz, Ostrom, and Stern 2003).

In a study of the forest conditions used by 178 forest user groups located in twelve countries studied by the International Forestry Resources and Institutions (IFRI) research network, Gibson, Williams, and Ostrom (2005) found that the level of local monitoring varies substantially across groups. One of the measures obtained in this study is the frequency with which a local group monitors and sanctions rule breaking behavior in the forest.[4] We examined the impact of this variable on appropriators' assessment of forest conditions (as well as on a forester's assessment). We also examined the impact of a group's social capital, the group's dependence of forest resources, and whether the group was formally organized or not. The result of the analysis is that regular monitoring by a local group is more important than the other three variables in enhancing forest conditions. Regardless of the levels of social capital, forest dependence and formal organization, regular monitoring and sanctioning is strongly and statistically associated with better forest conditions (Gibson, Williams, and Ostrom 2005).

Graduated Sanctions

The fifth design principle identified earlier was the use of graduated sanctions by robust governance arrangements. In many self-organized systems, the first sanction imposed by a local monitor is so low as to have *no* impact on the expected benefit-cost ratio of breaking local rules (given the substantial temptations frequently involved). Rather, the initial sanction needs to be considered more as information to the person who is "caught" as well as to others in the community. Everyone can make an error or can face difficult problems leading them to break a rule. A few rule infractions, however, can generate a downward cascade of cooperation in a group that relies only on conditional cooperation and has no capacity to sanction (see, for example, Kikuchi et al. 1998). In a regime that uses graduated punishments, however, a person who purposely or by error breaks a rule is notified that others notice the infraction (thereby increasing the individual's confidence that others would also be caught). Further, the individual learns that others basically continue to extend their trust and want only a small token to convey a recognition that the mishap occurred. Self-organized regimes rely more on what Margaret Levi (1988) calls "quasi-voluntary" cooperation than either strictly voluntary or coerced cooperation. A real threat to the continuance of self-organized regimes occurs, however, if some participants break rules repeatedly. The capability to escalate sanctions enables such a regime to warn members that if they do not conform, they will have to pay ever higher sanctions and may eventually be forced to leave the community.

Let me summarize the argument to this point. When the users of a resource design their own rules (design principle 3) that are enforced by local users or accountable to them (design principle 4) using graduated sanctions (design principle 5) that clearly define who has rights to withdraw from a well-defined resource (design principle 1) and that effectively assign costs proportionate to benefits (design principle 2), collective action and monitoring problems tend to be solved in a reinforcing manner.

Individuals who think a set of rules will be effective in producing higher joint benefits and that monitoring (including their own) will protect them against being a sucker, are willing to undertake conditional cooperation. Once some users have made contingent self-commitments, they are then motivated to monitor other people's behavior, at least from time to time, in order to assure themselves that others are following the rules most of the time. Conditional cooperation and mutual monitoring reinforce one another especially in regimes where the rules are designed to reduce monitoring costs (Kameda, Takezawa, and Hastie 2003). Over time, further adherence to shared norms evolves and high levels of cooperation are achieved without the need to engage in extensive monitoring and the imposition of costly sanctions in all cases of observed infractions in order to achieve rule conformance.

Conflict-Resolution Mechanisms

The operation of the above principles is bolstered by the sixth principle, which points to the importance of access to rapid, low-cost, local arenas to resolve conflict among users or between users and officials. Rules, unlike physical constraints, have to be understood in order to be effective. There are always situations in which participants can interpret a rule that they have jointly made in different ways. By devising simple, local mechanisms to get conflicts aired immediately and resolutions that are generally known in the community, the number of conflicts that reduce trust can be reduced. If individuals are going to follow rules over a long period of time, some mechanism for discussing and resolving what is or is not a rule infraction is quite necessary to the continuance of rule conformance itself. Further, one way of reducing the problem of elite capture of a local resource is the availability of arenas for conflict resolution at levels above that of a local resource.

Minimal Recognition of Rights

The capability of local users to develop an ever more effective regime over time is affected by whether they have at least minimal recognition of the right to organize by a national or local government (design principle 7). While some resource regimes have operated for relatively long times without such rights (see Ghate 2000), participants have had to rely almost entirely on unanimity as the rule used to change rules. Otherwise, any temporarily disgruntled participant who voted against a rule change could go to the external authorities to threaten the regime itself! Unanimity as a decision rule for changing rules imposes high transaction costs and prevents a group from searching for better matched rules at relatively lower costs. Lobe and Berkes (2004) do describe a remarkable system, however, designed by a set of fishers in Bengal who have no legal rights and who call themselves illicit fishers, that is enforced locally without any recognition by government officials.

Some users do devise their own rules without creating formal, governmental jurisdictions for this purpose. In many inshore fisheries, for example, local fishers devise extensive rules defining who can use a fishing ground and what kind of equipment can be used (Acheson 2003; Schlager 2004). So long as external governmental officials give at least minimal recognition to the legitimacy of such rules, the fishers themselves may be effective enforcers of these rules when government agencies do not have the staff to enforce them. When external governmental officials presume that *only* they can make authoritative rules, then it is difficult, but not impossible, for local users to sustain a self-organized regime (Johnson and Libecap 1982).

Communities that have the authority to craft their own rules, however, are frequently able to overcome the lack of local scientific knowledge if and when reliable information is made available about complex relationships and is understood locally. When a study was first conducted by Workshop colleagues in the Loma Alta *comuna* in 1995, they found that the comuna owned almost seven thousand hectares of land in western Ecuador (Gibson and Becker 2000). Further, the comuna had full authority to allocate land—including land in a high altitude fog forest—to members of the community for their use. At the time of the initial study, our team found that the comuna had allocated a substantial portion of their land to community members who cut down the indigenous trees in order to grow *paja toquilla* to generate fiber to make hats and other handicrafts for income.

Members of the comuna had not recognized that the indigenous trees growing in this fog forest were extremely efficient in capturing water from the fog and allowing water to precipitate into the ground. The water so captured eventually emerged as a stream many miles away. Members of the community relied heavily on this stream to water their agricultural plots. Given the distance involved, it would be a challenge to discover that connection even though farmers in the community had increasing concerns about the reduced flow of water in this stream. In other words, the community did not recognize the "ecosystem services" that the indigenous forest generated for their own agricultural lands.

Fortunately, one of the coleaders of our initial research team, Dusty Becker, was able to return to Loma Alta in 1996 with a group of Earthwatch volunteers. They spent a summer carefully monitoring the amount of water captured by the indigenous trees in the high altitude forest as compared to the trees planted for commercial purposes. They also recruited some of the high school students from Loma Alta to work with them collecting data on a daily basis. By the end of the summer, it was clear from the data they had collected that the indigenous trees collected substantially more water than the trees planted for commercial purposes. Becker (2003) estimated that the community lost 2 million liters of water per hectare per year in those sections of the forest converted to agroforestry. The students from Loma Alta were so motivated by participating in this summer project that they proposed making a video for their parents that demonstrated the value of keeping the indigenous trees in their own forest. Once the knowledge was generally available to the citizens of Loma Alta, they voted to create a forest reserve of one thousand hectares in the highlands of their own forest (ibid.).

Nested Enterprises

When common-pool resources are larger, an eighth design principle tends to characterize robust systems—the presence of governance activities organized in multiple layers of nested enterprises. The rules appropriate for allocating water among major branches of an irrigation system, for example, may not be appropriate for allocating water among farmers along a single distributory channel (Yoder 1994). Consequently, among long-enduring self-governed regimes, smaller-scale organizations tend to be nested in ever larger organizations. O. Choe (2004) provides an excellent overview of how nested enterprises have successfully been used to overcome the weakness of relying only on large-scale or small-scale units to govern complex resource systems. We will return to this design principle in our discussion of polycentricity in the last section of this chapter.

Using the Design Principles in Practice

It is reassuring to review the research conducted on self-organized, common-pool resource governance systems since 1990 and find that many scholars have agreed with my earlier speculations about the design principles characterizing robust systems. Tucker (1999) uses the design principles to examine the evolution of a common-property forest owned by a community in Honduras. She finds that examining the congruence of this system with the design principles helps to identify underlying weaknesses in the regime that made this system more vulnerable to forest degradation stimulated by rapid economic development. Her findings are consistent with those of scholars who have identified multiple threats to the sustainability of self-organized governance systems over time—the topic of the next section of this chapter—but her analysis illustrates the connection between the lack of an adequate response to external threats and systems that are weak in regard to several of the design principles.

There is a danger, however, that project planners searching for the "right" design will try to build a one-size-fits-all project supposedly based on the design principles. Such an effort is entirely inconsistent with the theoretical argument presented in this book concerning the importance of matching the rules of a system to the underlying biophysical world and type of human community involved. The question is often raised, however: How can the design principles be used in practice in addition to their use in research?

At a recent colloquium where the design principles were discussed, Mike McGinnis made an interesting observation drawing broadly on the work of Herbert Simon. He noted that Simon has repeatedly stressed the complexity of designing humanly engineered systems whether they be computers, road networks, or institutional arrangements. In *The Sciences of the Artificial* (1981), Simon specially argues that no humanly designed, complex system can be fully planned to achieve optimal performance. Rather, he stressed that all complex systems must be built up from simpler components. Simon does point out that where one begins a search to improve the performance of a complex system, however, makes a substantial difference in the quality and speed of the search process (see also H. Simon, 1972, 1995, 1999).

My own conclusion related to the impossibility of doing a *complete* analysis of a complex, adaptive system is, of course, strongly influenced by the work of Simon, as well as our research on coupled social-ecological systems. So, one way of thinking about the practical implications of the design principles is as a beginning point for conducting a broad search for appropriate means of solving problems. One can translate the design principles into a series of questions that could be asked when thinking about improving the sustainability of a common-pool resource system. For local appropriators, a rough translation of the first six design principles into a set of initial questions would be:

1. How can we better define the boundaries of this resource, and of the individuals who are using it, so as to make clear who is authorized to harvest and where harvesting is authorized?

2. How can we clarify the relationship between the benefits received and the contributions to the costs of sustaining this system?

3. How can we enhance the participation of those involved in making key decisions about this system?

4. Who is monitoring this system and do they face appropriate incentives given the challenge of monitoring?

5. What are the sanctions we are authorizing and can they be adjusted so that someone who makes an error or a small rule infraction is sufficiently warned so as to ensure longer-term compliance without our trying to impose unrealistic sanctions?

6. What local and regional mechanisms exist to resolve conflicts arising over the use of this resource?

The seventh and eighth principles are targeted at a higher level of governance. They could be translated as:

7. Are there functional and creative efforts by local appropriators to craft effective stewardship mechanisms for local resources that should be recognized?

8. How do we create a multiple-layer, polycentric system that can be dynamic, adaptive, and effective over time?

These are not, of course, the only questions appropriators and officials should ask in an effective design process, but they can be thought of as a good beginning.

Threats to Robust Governance of Common-Pool Resources

No matter how well a governance system is initially designed, however, all humanly designed systems are vulnerable to threats. Self-organized, resource-governance regimes are no exception. Both exogenous and endogenous factors challenge their long-term viability. Robust institutions may survive many threats for long periods of time. New threats may, however, unravel systems that have survived for multiple generations.[5] Major migration (out of or into an area) is always a threat that may or may not be countered effectively (Baker 2005). Out-migration may simply change the economic viability of a regime due to loss of those who contribute needed resources. In-migration may bring new participants who do not trust others and do not rapidly learn social norms that have been established over a long period of time. Since collective action is largely based on mutual trust and reciprocity, some self-organized resource regimes that are in areas of rapid settlement have disintegrated within relatively short times (Baland and Platteau 1996).

Even institutions that are characterized by the design principles fail. Thus, we need to speculate about other threats to community governance that arise from observations in the field, theoretical conjectures, and empirical findings of scholars studying small-scale resource governance systems. Here is a list of five threats to sustainable community governance of small-scale resource governance systems that I have come across in different contexts:

1. rapid exogenous changes;
2. transmission failures from one generation to the next of the operational principles on which community governance is based;
3. programs relying on blueprint thinking and easy access to external funds;
4. corruption and other forms of opportunistic behavior; and
5. lack of large-scale institutional arrangements related to reliable information collection, aggregation, and dissemination; fair and low cost conflict-resolution mechanisms; educational and extension facilities; and facilities for helping when natural disasters or other major problems occur at a local level.

Let us briefly discuss each of these.

Rapid Exogenous Changes

All rapid changes in technology, in human, animal, or plant populations; in factor availability; in substitution of relative importance of monetary transactions in the national governance system; or in the heterogeneity of participants are a threat to the continuance of any self-organized system, whether it is a firm in a competitive market or a community-governed resource. Individuals who have adapted an effective way of coping with a particular technological, economic, or social environment may be able to adjust to slow changes in one or several variables if substantial feedback is provided about the consequences of these changes for the long-term sustainability of the resource and/or the set of institutions used for governing that resource (Gupta and Tiwari 2002). They may even be able to adjust to changes in these variables that occur at a moderate rate. The faster that key variables change and the more variables that change at the same time, the more demanding is the problem of adaptation to new circumstances. These kinds of threats are difficult for all organizations. Those that rely to a greater extent on quasi-voluntary compliance are, however, more threatened than those who are able to coerce contributions (Bromley and Chapagain 1984; Goodland, Ledec, and Webb 1989).

Ottar Brox (1990) provides a vivid illustration of what happened in the northern regions of Norway when technology, population density, and other factors changed rapidly. As he points out, traditional northern Norwegian fisheries were seasonal fisheries. "Large oceanic fish populations migrate during phases in their life or yearly cycles, and occur within reach of coastal fishermen only during short seasons" (231). Using traditional harvesting techniques, "coastal fishermen did not have the boats, gear and preservational techniques necessary to follow the fish populations continually" (231). This had the consequence that it was almost impossible to destroy the fishery.

Nor were the part-time farmers and part-time fishers able to reap most of the resource rent from fishing until the Norwegian Raw Fish Act of 1938, which empowered fishers with the right to negotiate legally enforceable landing prices. Fishers, who for many centuries could not themselves reap the rents from a migratory fishery, now could do so, and could do so in an era of fast-changing technology making it possible to capture and store ever-greater quantities of fish. Further, other fishermen from other countries after the Second World War had the technology and capital to substantially increase effort dramatically above that which could be devoted prior to this era. A fishery that had survived, and even flourished, during many centuries of part-time fishing rapidly changed to a threatened resource without adequate institutional means to respond to the new incentives facing the fishers.

Transmission Failures

Rapid change of population or culture may lead to a circumstance in which the general principles involved in the design of effective community-governed institutions are not transmitted from one generation to another. When individuals substitute rote reliance on formal rules for an understanding of *why* particular formal rules are used, they can argue for interpretations of the formal rules that undercut the viability of community organization. For example, the charter or constitution of a community organization may specify that simple majority rule will be used in making decisions about future projects and how the costs and benefits of these projects will be allocated. If the founders of such an organization recognize the importance of gaining general agreement, they will rarely push forward on a large project supported only by a minimal winning coalition. When there is a bare majority, almost as many community members oppose a project as those who support it. If over time, however, the principle of gaining general agreement to future projects is not conveyed and accepted by those who accept leadership responsibilities, then decisions barely receiving a majority may be pushed forward. Leaders of communities who rely for too many decisions on minimal winning coalitions may find themselves having to use patronage, coercion, and/ or corruption, rather than a foundation of general agreement, to keep themselves in power.

Similarly, if participants view their own rules as obstacles to be overcome, rather than as the written representation of general underlying principles of organization, they may push for interpretations of rules that lead to their general weakening. If each household tries to find every legal way to minimize the amount of labor contributed to the maintenance of a farmer-governed irrigation system, for example, eventually the cumulative effect is an insufficient maintenance effort and the unraveling of the contingent contributions of all. If one family tries to make a favorable interpretation of how much labor they should contribute, given the land they own, others come to know that this family is interpreting rules in a manner that is highly favorable to them. Others who would be favored by such an interpretation begin to use it as well. The total quantity of labor contributed declines. Unless there is a community discussion about the underlying principles that can be used in interpreting rules, practices may evolve that cannot be sustained over time. The danger exists that the unraveling continues unabated until the community organization falls apart.

If one family tries to make a favorable interpretation of how much labor they should contribute, given the land they own, others come to know that this family is interpreting rules in a manner that is highly favorable to them. Others, who would be favored by such an interpretation, begin to use it as well. The total quantity of labor contributed declines. Unless there is a community discussion about the underlying principles that can be used in interpreting rules, practices may evolve that cannot be sustained over time. Then, the danger exists that the unraveling continues unabated until the community organization falls apart.

Programs Relying on Blueprint Thinking and Easy Access to External Funds

Blueprint thinking occurs whenever policymakers, donors, citizens, or scholars propose uniform solutions to a wide variety of problems that are clustered under a single name based on one or more successful exemplars. David Korten (1980) called this the "blueprint approach" and made a devastating critique of its prevalence in development work at the end of the 1970s. Projects or programs rely on some formula—the design of another project, imposition of a particular voting rule in all settings, or the way the project is initiated—rather than learning the specifics of a particular setting and enabling participants to experiment and learn from their own experience and that of others.

Even with all of the lessons learned in the last three decades about the dangers of blueprint thinking, the temptation to fall into this trap continues unabated. Fabián Repetto (2002), for example, describes an ambitious, but failed, antipoverty program adopted in Argentina, the Plan Solidaridad, which was an imitation of the supposedly successful antipoverty program, Progresa, implemented in Mexico. Roconi (2002) describes another Argentine program that was modeled on a blueprint, Plan Trabajar, which also ended up stymied by clientelistic networks that resorted to rent seeking and other mutually beneficial actions that undermined the program. In searching for the "holy grail," efforts to design homegrown solutions to unique ecological conditions are stymied while policymakers switch policies rapidly trying to copy whatever is considered the latest and best (Mukand and Rodrik 2002; Acuna and Tommasi 2000). Pritchett and Woolcock (2003) bemoan the problem of trying to find solutions when "the" problem is actually the blueprint solution recommended by donors and national governments for solving a problem.

Tragically, advocates of community governance have sometimes fallen into this trap. A major program at the World Bank, Community Driven Development (CDD), sounds as if it should support effective local development. A requirement of this program is that the initial proposal for a World Bank project must come from local officials or communities. Many of the projects that are called "community driven," however, turn out to be quick investments in infrastructure such as local schools or roads. They are indeed recommended by local officials. What school principal would not actively lobby for a new school building once the possibility of gaining World Bank funds is announced? The principal only needs to make a good plea for the importance of a new school without any requirement for financing the repayment of the loan. One evaluation of such CDD projects found few other improvements beyond the infrastructure (e.g., few books in the new schools and little impact on children's educational achievement) (World Bank 2002). Negative evaluations have not, however, had much impact on the fervent advocates of CDD (Platteau 2004; Mansuri and Rao 2003). CDD projects at the Bank have increased from an annual expenditure of $325 million in 1996 to over $2 billion in 2003 (Mansuri and Rao 2003) based more on enthusiasm than on objective evaluations (Conning and Kevane 2002; Tendler 2000). Major risks of elite capture and fraud exist in such programs (Platteau and Gaspart 2003).

The availability of funds from donors or from national governmental budgets that make no requirements for contributions from recipients can also undermine local institutions.[6] This is particularly salient in regard to local infrastructure.[7] Monetary resources for constructing, operating, and maintaining infrastructure is frequently contributed by the taxpayers of the nation in which the infrastructure is located or the taxpayers of those nations providing economic assistance funds. When these external funds are used, the financial connection between supply and use is nonexistent. Whether the resources so mobilized are directly invested in the construction and operation of the infrastructure or are diverted for individual use by politicians or contractors depends on the professionalism of those involved and on active efforts to monitor and sanction diversions of resources and on the incentives built into the disbursement rules used (Platteau and Gaspart 2003). Consequently, a considerable portion of the mobilized resources is diverted to purposes other than those for which it was intended.

Further, the design of projects is oriented more toward capturing the approval of those who fund new construction than toward providing systems that solve the problems facing present and future users. To convince politicians that large chunks of a national budget should be devoted to the construction of local infrastructure, planners attempt to design projects that are "politically attractive." This means that politicians who support such expenditures can claim that the voters' funds are being used to invest in projects that will greatly expand the amount of food available and lower the cost of living. Development projects need to have considerable local involvement to be successful (Shivakumar 2005).

To convince external funding agencies that major infrastructure projects should be funded through loans or grants, the evaluative criteria used by these agencies in selecting projects has to play a prominent role in the design of projects (Gibson, Andersson, et al. 2005). Projects designed by engineers, who lack on-the-ground experience or training as institutional analysts, are frequently oriented toward winning political support or international funding. This orientation does not lead to the construction of projects that serve most users effectively or encourage the investment of users in their long-term sustenance. Inefficiencies occur at almost every stage. At the same time, this inefficient process leads to the construction of projects that generate substantial profits for large landholders and strong political support for a government.

Processes that encourage looking to external sources of funding make it difficult to build upon indigenous knowledge and institutions (Haller 2001, 2002). A central part of the message asking for external funds is that what has been accomplished locally has failed and massive external technical knowledge and funds are needed to achieve "development." In some cases, no recognition is made at all of prior institutional arrangements. This has three adverse consequences: (1) property rights that resource users had slowly achieved under earlier regimes are swept away and the poor lose substantial assets; (2) those who have lost prior investments are less willing to venture further investments; and (3) there is a general downgrading of the status of indigenous knowledge and institutions. In light of their own analysis of a failed effort to use external funds to create an effective community forestry project, Morrow and Hull (1996) provide a good summary of the problems resulting from externally driven funding and priorities: "This case, along with the experience of other community forestry enterprises in Latin America, suggests that donor-driven projects often fail to analyze in sufficient depth the factors outlined by the design principles, particularly the issues of institutional and technological appropriateness and the impact of the larger political economy" (1655).

Corruption and Rent-Seeking

All types of opportunistic behavior are encouraged, rather than discouraged, by the availability of massive funds to subsidize the construction and operation of large-scale infrastructure projects (Gibson, Andersson, et al., 2005). Corrupt exchanges between officials and private contractors are a notorious and widespread form of opportunism; corrupt payments by citizens to government officials are less publicized, but probably no less widespread. Free-riding on the part of those receiving benefits and the lack of trust between citizens and officials, as well as among citizens, are also endemic. Further, the potential rents that can be derived from free electricity and free water by large-scale landowners stimulate efforts to influence public decision making as to where projects should be located and how they should be financed. Politicians, for their part, win political support by strategic decisions concerning who will receive or continue to receive artificially created economic rents.

Robert Bates (1987, 128) explains many of the characteristics of African agricultural policies by arguing that major "inefficiencies persist because they are politically useful; economic inefficiencies afford governments means of retaining political power." Part of Bates's argument relates to the artificial control exercised over the prices paid for agricultural products, a topic that is not addressed in this study. The other part of Bates's argument relates to the artificial lowering of input prices.

> When they lower the price of inputs, private sources furnish lesser quantities, users demand greater quantities, and the result is excess demand. One consequence is that the inputs acquire new value; the administratively created short-

age creates an economic premium for those who acquire them. Another is that, at the mandated price, the market cannot allocate the inputs; they are in short supply. Rather than being allocated through a pricing system, they must be rationed. Those in charge of the regulated market thereby acquire the capacity to exercise discretion and to confer the resources upon those whose favor they desire. (128)

Public programs that distribute farm credit, tractor-hire services, seeds, and fertilizers, and which bestow access to government-managed irrigation schemes and public land, thus become instruments of political organization in the countryside of Africa (130).

There is an added dimension to rent seeking. The losses that the general consumer and taxpayer accrue from rent-seeking activities are one dimension. The second aspect of rent seeking in highly centralized economies is the acquisition of resources needed to accumulate and retain political power. All forms of opportunistic behavior, therefore, are exacerbated in an environment in which an abundance of funds are available for the construction of new and frequently large-scale infrastructure projects that provide subsidized electricity, local roads, schools, and water.

Lack of Large-Scale Supportive Institutions

While smaller-scale, community-governed resource institutions may be more effective than centralized government in achieving many aspects of sustainable development, the absence of supportive, large-scale institutional arrangements may be just as much a threat to long-term sustenance as the presence of preemptive large-scale governmental agencies. Obtaining reliable information about the effects of different uses of resource systems and resource conditions is an activity that is essential to long-term sustainability. If all local communities were to have to develop all of their own scientific information about the physical settings in which they were located, few would have the resources to accomplish this.

Let me use the example of the important role that the U.S. Geological Survey has played in the development of more effective local groundwater institutions in some parts of the United States. What is important to stress is that the Geological Survey does not construct engineering works or do anything other than obtain and disseminate accurate information about hydrologic and geologic structures within the United States. When a local set of water users wants to obtain better information about a local groundwater basin, they can contract with the Geological Survey to conduct an intensive study in their area. Water producers would pay a portion of the cost of such a survey. The Geological Survey would pay the other portion. The information contained in such a survey is then public information available to all interested parties. The Geological Survey employs a highly professional staff who rely on the most recent scientific techniques for determining the structure and condition of groundwater basins. Local water producers obtain the very best available information from an agency that is not trying to push any particular future project that the agency is interested in conducting. Many countries, such as India, that do have large and sometimes dominating state agencies do not have agencies that provide public access to high-quality information about resource conditions and consequences. Recent efforts to open up groundwater exploration in India may lead to the massive destruction of groundwater basins rather than a firm basis for long-term growth.

Similarly, the lack of a low-cost, fair method for resolving those conflicts that spill out beyond the bounds of a local community is also a threat to long-run sustainability. All groups face internal conflicts or intergroup conflicts that can destroy the fundamental trust and reciprocity on which so much effective governance is based. If the only kind of conflict-resolution mechanisms available are either so costly or so biased that most self-governed common-pool resources cannot make use of them, these conflicts can themselves destroy even very robust institutional arrangements.

Modest Coping Methods for Dealing with Threats to Sustainability

No surefire mechanisms exist for addressing all of the above threats. There are three modest methods that I would like to discuss here before turning to the concept of polycentricity—which is the major coping method discussed in the last section of this chapter. I do so because these methods are not frequently mentioned as being important ways of increasing the effectiveness of self-governed institutions. However, they frequently have high payoffs. They are: (1) the creation of associations of community-governed entities, (2) comparative institutional research that provides a more effective knowledge base about design and operating principles, and (3) the development of more effective high school and college courses on local governance.

Creating Associations of Community-Governance Entities

Those who think local participation is important in the process of developing sustainable resources and more effective governance of resources are frequently committed to doing a good deal of "community organization." All too frequently, this type of organization is conceptualized as fostering a large number of community groups at the same level. If community organization is fostered by nongovernmental organizations

(NGOs) who then provide staff assistance and some external resources, the organizations may flourish as long as the NGOs remain interested, but wither on the vine when the NGOs turn to other types of projects. A technique that draws on our knowledge of how self-governed institutions operate is helping to create associations of community organizations.

When community organizations are brought together in federations, they can provide one another some of the backup that NGOs may provide to single-layer community organizations. While no single community-governed organization may be able to fund information collection that is unbiased and of real value to the organization, a federation of such organizations may be able to amass the funds to do so. Simply having a newsletter that shares information about what has worked and why it has worked in some settings helps others learn from each other's trial-and-error methods. Having an annual meeting that brings people together to discuss their common problems and ways of tackling them greatly expands that repertoire of techniques for coping with threats that any one group can muster on its own.[8]

Rigorous Institutional Research

In addition to the type of exchange of information that those involved in self-governing entities can undertake on their own, it is important to find ways of undertaking rigorous, comparative research that controls for the many confounding variables that simultaneously affect performance (Hayes 2004; Gibson, Williams, and Ostrom 2005). In the field of medicine, folk medicine has frequently been based on unknown foundations that turned out to be relatively sound, but some folk medicine continued for centuries, doing more harm to patients than good. The commons that are governed by users and the institutions they use are complex and sometimes difficult to understand. It is important to blend knowledge and information obtained in many different ways as we try to build a more effective knowledge base about what works and why. The recent study of Theesfeld (2004) is an outstanding example of such a blend. It is a rigorous study drawing on theory, in-depth fieldwork, and quantitative survey research to understand the constraints facing Bulgarian farmers in their efforts to engage in collective action in the Bulgarian transitional economy.

Developing Better Curricula on Local Governance

Textbooks on governance used to focus as much on local as they did on national governance arrangements. During the past half-century, introductory textbooks on American government have moved from a fifty-fifty split between national and local government, to a ninety-five to five split.

The textbooks used in the West have strongly influenced the textbooks used in developing countries. Consequently, many public officials learn nothing in high school and college about how local communities can govern themselves effectively or about the threats to local self-governance. Instead, a presumption is made that governance is what is done in national capitals and what goes on in villages is outmoded if not completely useless.[9]

The Advantage and Limits of Polycentric Systems in Coping with Design and Long-Term Sustainability of Systems

The last major task to be undertaken in this chapter is to discuss why autonomous, self-organized resource governance systems may be more effective in learning from experimentation than a single central authority. I will first discuss the advantages and limits of a fully decentralized system where all responsibility for making decisions related to smaller-scale common-pool resources is localized. Then, I will discuss why a polycentric governance system involving higher levels of government as well as local systems is better able to cope more effectively with tragedies of the commons (V. Ostrom 1999).

Among the advantages of authorizing the users of smaller-scale common-pool resources to adopt policies regulating the use of these resources are:

- *Local knowledge.* Appropriators who have lived and appropriated from a resource system over a long period of time have developed relatively accurate mental models of how the biophysical system itself operates, since the very success of their appropriation efforts depends on such knowledge. They also know others living in the area well and what norms of behavior are considered appropriate.
- *Inclusion of trustworthy participants.* Appropriators can devise rules that increase the probability that others are trustworthy and will use reciprocity. This lowers the cost of relying entirely on formal sanctions and paying for extensive guarding.
- *Reliance on disaggregated knowledge.* Feedback about how the resource system responds to changes in actions of appropriators is provided in a disaggregated way. Fishers are quite aware, for example, if the size and species distribution of their catch is changing over time. Irrigators learn whether a particular rotation system allows most farmers to grow the crops they most prefer by examining the resulting productivity of specific fields.
- *Better adapted rules.* Given the above, appropriators are more likely to craft rules over time that are better adapted to each of the local common-pool resources than any general system of rules.

- *Lower enforcement costs.* Since local appropriators have to bear the cost of monitoring, they are apt to craft rules that make infractions highly obvious so that monitoring costs are lower. Further, by creating rules that are seen as legitimate, rule conformance will tend to be higher.
- *Parallel autonomous systems.* The probability of failure throughout a large region is greatly reduced by the establishment of parallel systems of rule making, interpretation, and enforcement.

There are, of course, limits to all ways of organizing the governance of common-pool resources. Among the limits of a highly decentralized system are:

- *Some appropriators will not organize.* While the evidence from the field is that many local appropriators do invest considerable time and energy into their own regulatory efforts, other groups of appropriators will not do so.
- *Some self-organized efforts will fail.* Given the complexity of the task involved in designing rules, some groups will select combinations of rules that generate failure instead of success. They may be unable to adapt rapidly enough to avoid the collapse of a resource system.
- *Local tyrannies.* Not all self-organized resource governance systems will be organized democratically or rely on the input of most appropriators. Some will be dominated by a local leader or a power elite who only change rules that they think will advantage them still further. This problem is accentuated in locations where the cost of exit is particularly high and reduced where appropriators can exercise choice over submitting to a local regime or not.
- *Stagnation.* Where local ecological systems are characterized by considerable variance, experimentation can produce severe and unexpected results leading appropriators to cling to systems that have worked relatively well in the past and to stop innovating.
- *Inappropriate discrimination.* The use of identity tags is frequently an essential method for increasing the level of trust and rule conformance. Tags based on ascribed characteristics that have nothing to do with their trustworthiness can, however, be the basis of excluding some individuals from access to sources of productive endeavor.
- *Limited access to scientific information.* While time and place information may be extensively developed and used, local groups may not have access to scientific knowledge concerning the type of resource system involved.
- *Conflict among appropriators.* Without access to an external set of conflict-resolution mechanisms, conflict within and across common-pool resource systems can escalate and provoke physical violence. Two or more groups may claim the same territory and may continue to make raids on one another over a very long period of time.
- *Inability to cope with larger-scale common-pool resources.* Without access to some larger-scale jurisdiction, local appropriators may have substantial

difficulties regulating only a part of a larger-scale common-pool resource. They may not be able to exclude others who refused to abide by the rules that a local group would prefer to use. Given this, local appropriators have no incentives to restrict their own use and watch others take away all of the valued resource units that they have not appropriated.

The Capabilities of Polycentric Systems in Coping with Tragedies of the Commons

Many of the capabilities of a parallel adaptive system can be retained in a polycentric governance system. By polycentric I mean a system where citizens are able to organize not just one but multiple governing authorities at differing scales (see V. Ostrom, Tiebout, and Warren 1961; V. Ostrom 1997, 1999). Each unit exercises considerable independence to make and enforce rules within a circumscribed domain of authority for a specified geographical area. In a polycentric system, some units are general-purpose governments while others may be highly specialized. Self-organized resource governance systems in such a system may be special districts, private associations, or parts of a local government. These are nested in several levels of general-purpose governments that also provide civil, equity, as well as criminal courts.[10]

In a polycentric system, the users of each common-pool resource would have some authority to make at least some of the rules related to how that particular resource will be utilized. Thus, they would achieve most of the advantages of utilizing local knowledge as well as the potential to learn from others who are also engaged in a similar trial-and-error learning process in parallel systems (Folke, Berkes, and Colding 1998). On the other hand, problems associated with local tyrannies and inappropriate discrimination can be addressed by larger, general-purpose governmental units who are responsible for protecting the rights of all citizens and for the oversight of appropriate exercises of authority within smaller units of government. It is also possible to make a more effective blend of scientific information with local knowledge where major universities and research stations are located in larger units but have a responsibility to relate recent scientific findings to multiple smaller units within their region. Because polycentric systems have overlapping units, information about what has worked well in one setting can be transmitted to others who may try it out in their settings. Associations of local resource governance units can be encouraged to speed up the exchange of information about relevant local conditions and about policy experiments that have proved particularly successful. And, when small systems fail, there are larger systems to call upon—and vice versa.

When there is only a single governing authority, policymakers have to experiment simultaneously with *all* of the common-pool resources within their jurisdiction with each policy change. And, once a major change has been made and implemented, further changes will not be made rapidly. The process of experimentation will usually be slow, and information about results may be contradictory and difficult to interpret. Thus, an experiment that is based on erroneous data about one key structural variable or one false assumption about how actors will react can lead to a very large disaster (see Wilson, Low, et al. 1999). In any design process where there is substantial probability of error, having redundant teams of designers has repeatedly been shown to have considerable advantage (see Landau 1969, 1973; Bendor 1985). The important point is: If the systems are relatively separable, allocating responsibility for experimenting with rules will not avoid failure, but will drastically reduce the probability of immense failures for an entire region.

While the theoretical argument in support of polycentric systems of governance to cope with multitier ecological systems is strong, the resistance to these forms of organization is also strong. As discussed in chapter 8, the very concept of organization is closely tied for many scholars to the presence of a central director who has designed a system to operate in a particular way. Consequently, the mechanisms used by polycentric systems are not well understood in many cases. Polycentric systems are themselves complex, adaptive systems without one central authority dominating all of the others. Thus, no guarantee exists that such systems will find the combination of rules at diverse levels that are optimal for any particular environment. In fact, one should expect that all governance systems will be operating at less than optimal levels given the immense difficulty of fine-tuning any complex, multitiered system.

Alcorn and Toledo (1998) stress the complementary institutional systems at the national level in Mexico, supportive of local communities, as generating a more sustainable governance system than exists in similar ecological conditions. In the United States, there are many examples of dynamic polycentric resource governance systems where there is strong evidence of high performance.

One example from the United States is the Maine lobster fishery. This system is noteworthy because of the long-term, complementary roles adopted by both local and state governance systems. Maine is organized into riparian territories along most of the coast. Boundary rules and many of the day-to-day fishing regulations are organized by harbor gangs (Acheson 1988, 2003).

> In order to go fishing at all, one must become a member of a "harbor gang,"
> the group of fishermen who go lobstering from a single harbor. Once one has

gained admittance into such a group, one can only set traps in the traditional territory of that particular harbor gang. Members of harbor gangs are expected to obey the rules of their gang concerning fishing practices, which vary somewhat from one part of the coast to another. In all areas a person who gains a reputation for molesting others' gear or for violating conservation laws will be severely sanctioned. Incursions into the territory of one gang by fishers from another are ordinarily punished by surreptitious destruction of lobster gear. There is strong statistical evidence that the territorial system, which operates to limit the number of fishers exploiting lobsters in each territory, helps to conserve the lobster resource. (Acheson, Wilson, and Steneck 1998, 400)

At the same time, the state of Maine has long established formal laws that protect the breeding stock and increase the likelihood that regeneration rates will be high. "At present, the most important conservation laws are minimum and maximum size measures, a prohibition against catching lobsters with eggs, and a law to prohibit the taking of lobsters which once had eggs and were marked—i.e. the 'V-notch' law" (Acheson, Wilson, and Steneck 1998, 400). Neither the state nor any of the harbor gangs has tried to limit the quantity of lobster captured. The state does not try to limit the number of lobster fishers, since this is already done at a local level. However, the state has been willing to intercede when issues exceed the scope of control of local groups. In the late 1920s, for example, when lobster stocks were at very low levels and many local areas appear to have had substantial compliance problems, the state took a number of steps— including threats to close the fishery—that supported informal local enforcement efforts. By the late 1930s, compliance problems were largely resolved and stocks had rebounded (although it can't be shown that these two results are related, just correlated).

Recently, in response to changes that were breaking down the informal harbor gang system, the state has formalized the system by dividing the state into zones with democratically elected councils. Each council has been given authority over rules that have principally local impacts—trap limits, days and times fished, and so forth. Interestingly, the formalization of local zones was followed almost immediately by the creation of an informal council of councils to address problems at a greater than local scale (J. Wilson 1997).

The system of comanagement of the Pacific salmon fisheries in the state of Washington is another noteworthy example of an evolving polycentric system that appears to be working much better than an earlier system that was dominated primarily by state and federal agencies (see Singleton 1998). The change in the system came as a result of a major court decision in the mid-1970s.[11] The court held that the twenty-one Indian tribes, who had signed treaties more than a century before, had protected rights to

50 percent of the fish that passed through the normal fishing areas of the tribes. The decision has required the state to develop a "comanagement" system that involves both the state of Washington and the twenty-one Indian tribes in diverse policy roles related to salmon. The salmon fisheries are a large, transboundary resource utilized by major commercial firms as well as by the Indian tribes. Having the state strongly involved means that it is "safe" for any local group to agree to follow strong conservation practices because they know that other local groups are also involved in the same conservation practices. At the same time, the earlier centrally regulated system had focused on the ocean fishery and spent little time on the fresh-water habitats that are essential to maintain the viability of salmon fisheries over the long term. Individual tribal authorities have concentrated their attention on the specific stocks and how to manage these better.

Polycentric systems can generate considerable conflict among the various units at multiple levels due to their interdependence. Conflicts that escalate from misunderstandings to ever more serious charges and countercharges that turn to violence are certainly negative processes. Conflict may, on the other hand, generate more information that is useful to participants in their efforts to solve challenging problems. Ebbin (2002, 2004) has traced the evolution of conflict in the comanaged salmon fisheries along the coast of Washington both as a fishery biologist working with several of the tribal organizations and as a researcher conducting extensive interviews with participants at all levels. While the early conflict was framed as a technical problem regarding the knowledge to be used in managing the system, later conflict "focused on questions of equity and conservation as well as authority and jurisdiction" (Ebbin 2004, 82). The redefinition of conflict in the court system and in other arenas helped to create new institutional mechanisms that "changed the rules of the game and the processes in which new conflicts are addressed" (82). After some experience with the new institutions, even the government officials recognized that new information was being generated that initially led to more conflict but eventually led to better management of the stock.[12]

Coping with potential tragedies of the commons is never easy and never finished. Now that we know that those dependent on these resources are not forever trapped in situations that will only get worse over time, we need to recognize that governance is frequently an adaptive process involving multiple actors at diverse levels. Such systems look terribly messy and hard to understand. The scholars' love of tidiness needs to be resisted. Instead, we need to develop better theories of complex adaptive systems focused on overcoming social dilemmas, particularly those that have proved themselves able to utilize renewable natural resources sustainably over time.

Conclusion

Contextual variables are essential for understanding the initial growth and sustainability of collective action as well as the challenges that long-surviving, self-organized regimes must try to overcome. Simply saying that "context matters" is not, however, a satisfactory theoretical approach. In particular, we need to address how context affects the recruitment of individuals who may become conditional cooperators and willing punishers into an ongoing system and the likelihood that the norms held by these participants are adopted and strengthened by others in a relevant population.

Trying to understand why so many diverse institutions are created in the first place, and then the consequences that are engendered in diverse ecological, social, and economic settings, is a big challenge. Considerable empirical and theoretical progress has been made and, I hope, adequately summarized in this volume.

Empirical and theoretical work in the future needs to ask how a large array of contextual variables affects the processes of teaching and evoking social norms, of informing participants about the behavior of others and their adherence to social norms, and of rewarding those who use social norms, such as reciprocity, trust, and fairness. We need to understand how institutional, cultural, and biophysical contexts affect the types of individuals who are recruited into and leave particular types of collective-action situations, the kind of information that is made available about past actions, and how individuals can themselves change structural variables so as to enhance the probabilities of norm-using types being involved and growing in strength over time.

Further developments along these lines are essential for the development of public policies that enhance socially beneficial, cooperative behavior based in part on social norms. It is possible that past policy initiatives that attempted to solve collective-action problems primarily by changing extrinsic payoff structures may have been misdirected. Imposing sanctions and inducements can crowd out the formation of social norms that can enhance cooperative behavior in their own way. Increasing the authority of individuals to devise their own rules may well result in processes that allow social norms to evolve and thereby increase the probability of individuals actually solving collective-action problems. There is a real role for legislators and government agency officials in solving problems at all levels but they need to follow Mark Moore's (1995, 20) advice to become "explorers who, with others, seek to discover, define, and produce public value."

Norms of reciprocity and trust are necessary for the long-term sustenance of self-governing regimes. Norms alone, however, are not sufficient to support individuals facing the temptations of social dilemmas. Rules that are fair, effective, and legitimate are necessary complements to shared norms for sustaining self-governing institutions over time. And, in turn, self-organizing arrangements enable people to learn more about one another's needs and the ecology around them. Learning problem-solving skills in a local context generates citizens with more general problem-solving skills that enables them to reach out and more effectively examine far-reaching problems that affect all peoples living on this earth.

Notes _____

Chapter One
Understanding the Diversity of Structured Human Interactions

1. The Workshop in Political Theory and Policy Analysis was established at Indiana University in the 1973–74 academic year. A central interest of all Workshop activities has always been understanding institutions at all scales. Early research focused on polycentric systems in metropolitan areas drawing on Vincent Ostrom's earlier work with Charles Tiebout and Robert Warren (1961), "The Organization of Government in Metropolitan Areas" (see E. Ostrom, Parks, and Whitaker 1974; McGinnis 1999b). Studies conducted at a macrolevel (see Kaminski 1992; V. Ostrom 1997; Loveman 1993; Sawyer 1992) have focused more on national-level constitutional and collective-choice decisions as these eventually impinge on the day-to-day decisions of citizens and/or subjects. Studies conducted at a microlevel (Firmin-Sellers 1996; Gibson 1999; Agrawal 1999; E. Ostrom, Gardner, and Walker 1994; E. Ostrom 1990) have tended to focus more on operational-level decisions as they are in turn affected by collective-choice and constitutional-choice rules—some of which have been crafted at the local level.

2. For earlier discussions see Kiser and Ostrom 1982; E. Ostrom 1986; Oakerson 1992; Gardner and Ostrom 1991; E. Ostrom, Gardner, and Walker 1994; Crawford and Ostrom 2000.

3. See Diermeier and Krehbiel (2003), who develop an institutional methodology using these four steps in an iterative process.

4. Elements of the framework have been used in teaching both graduate and undergraduate courses at Indiana University since the mid-1970s.

5. See Oakerson 1992; E. Ostrom 1986, 1999; and E. Ostrom, Gardner, and Walker 1994, chap. 2.

6. See discussion in chapter 5 on doing fieldwork related to studying rules and norms.

7. In an interesting paper, Ahn et al. (2004) examine the impact of an increase in the number of referees in the National Hockey League. Other studies had found that during the two seasons of a gradual transition from one to two referees, where part of the games were played with one referee, players derived more penalty minutes when two referees were on the ice. This is in contradiction to the economic theory of crime that predicts a deterrence effect. Ahn et al. found that over a period of seasons, a deterrence effect can be found at the team level since the composition of the team was adjusted. At the team level, the amount of penalty minutes dropped, and salaries of aggressive players, the "goons," decreased relative to the average.

8. In a sympathetic critique of E. Ostrom, Gardner, and Walker's (1994) use of the IAD framework, Jonathan Bendor (1995, 189) reflects on the confusion that exists regarding the concept of a framework. "Hard core social scientists, those believing that even frameworks must generate hypotheses if they are to have

any scientific value, might therefore dismiss the IAD approach as constituting a mere list of important variables." Bendor then argues that it would be premature to dismiss the IAD approach, but does worry about the problem of the number of possible rule configurations that it generates.

9. Chapter 2 of Thomas Dye's (1981) extensively used textbook, *Understanding Public Policy*, is devoted to "models of politics." Included among these "models" are organization charts (22), a framework for analyzing policy processes (24), group theory (26–28), elite theory (29–31), criteria for evaluating policy (31–35), incrementalism (36–37), game theory (36–40), and systems theory (41–43). No wonder students find it challenging to sort out the difference between frameworks, theories, and models.

10. As I have indicated elsewhere, I will forever be grateful to Larry Kiser and Sue Crawford for our long, long conversations, outlines, and rough drafts of chapters that were part of these earlier efforts and to Roger Parks for the many memos he has sent us to clarify key points and conversations we have had about these central issues. This book would not have been possible without those extensive efforts and many others by my wonderful Workshop colleagues.

Chapter Two
Zooming In and Linking Action Situations

1. When game theorists first formally describe the structure of a game, they make a distinction between the normal form and the extensive form. An n-player normal form game is usually specified as consisting of: (1) a set of *players* $i = 1, \ldots, n$; (2) a set S_i of *strategies* for player $i = 1, \ldots, n$. A strategy profile for the game would be: $s = (s_1, \ldots, s_n)$, where $s_i \in S_i$ for $i = 1, \ldots, n$; (3) function $\pi_i : S \rightarrow R$ for player $i = 1, \ldots, n$, where S is the set of strategy profiles, so $\pi_i (s)$ is player i's payoff when strategy profile s is chosen (Gintis 2000b, 12). A normal form game is usually represented in matrix format with the strategies represented by the rows and columns and the payoffs as the cells.

2. There are also major debates over whether Deep Blue is simply a *fast* processor or whether it represents a form of "real intelligence."

3. This game was inspired by a game of STEAL proposed by Plott and Meyer (1975).

4. Hamburger (1979) pointed out that participants in a two-person Prisoner's Dilemma are more likely to select cooperative strategies than those in a three-person PD Game.

5. Scharpf (1997) also examines two-level games.

6. Peter Hupe and Michael Hill (2004) develop a somewhat modified version of these three levels that they call constitutive, directive, and operation. They use these three levels to integrate many of the efforts in the policy science to lay out the stages of the policy process.

7. The four levels presented here are broadly similar to the four levels of social analysis presented by Oliver Williamson (2000). His top level is called the embedded level, where informal custom and tradition are located. The next level in his

system is "the institutional environment," where the formal rules establishing a judiciary, executive, etc., are found in his L2 (our constitutional-choice level). The governance level is his L3 (our collective-choice level), and resource allocation and employment is his L4 (our operational level).

8. Ciriacy-Wantrup and Bishop (1975) also recommended three levels when they described the nested multilevel aspect of rules within organizations. Their three levels of decision making were: (1) the "operating level," where decisions about daily activities were made; (2) the "institutional level," which regulates the decisions made at an operational level; and (3) the "policy level," which focuses on the structure of an organization by creating a charter that has standing with an external government.

9. It is important for the reader to recognize that not all constitutional rules are embodied in a written national constitution. Of course, the constitutions of some countries are not contained at all in a written constitution. Further, each house of a bicameral legislature will have its own rules related to the decision rules to be followed in making collective choices. Each private corporation will have a set of constitutional rules specifying the rights and duties of corporate officials in making policies for the firm. Every family will have made some basic rules for how future family policies will be made. These will rarely be made in a formal arena.

10. The decisions reached by members of a legislature will not be stable if opponents of these decisions are able (1) to win a majority of seats in future elections on promises made to the electorate that they will reverse the earlier decision or (2) to change the constitutions so as to make the decisions unconstitutional. The stability of decisions in complex modern institutions is dependent not only upon the preferences and procedures used to organize decision making in one arena, but upon the entire nested set of arenas (Shepsle 1989).

11. This problem is particularly acute if one were to adopt the "institutions-as-equilibria" approach described briefly in the first part of chapter 4. The complexity of the statements that would be required to specify an equilibrium if one took the institutions-as-equilibria approach are literally beyond comprehension.

12. As Hamilton wrote in *The Federalist*, no. 37: "All new laws though penned with the greatest technical skills and passed on the fullest and most mature deliberation, are considered as more or less obscure and equivocal, until their meaning be liquidated and ascertained by a series of particular discussions and adjudications."

Chapter Three
Studying Action Situations in the Lab

1. In some versions of this game, the Trustee also receives an endowment.

2. Another major effort to replicate experiments across cultures is the research conducted in fifteen small-scale and relatively isolated societies (see Henrich et al. 2004). In this case, the experiments included the Dictator and Ultimatum Games (and, in some locations, Public Good Games) where the predictions from traditional game theory using an assumption of selfish participants were very clear. No

cooperation should be seen in any of these experiments. The predictions, however, were not supported in this major effort. As one of the scholars responsible for organizing this study, Herbert Gintis (2004, 65) reports: "We found, first, that the self-interested actor model is not supported in any society studied. Second, there is considerably more behavioral variability across groups than had been found in previous cross-cultural research. . . . Third, group-level differences in the degree of cooperation in production and the extent of contact with market economies explain a substantial portion of the behavioral variations across societies."

3. Still further experiments with the basic Trust Game have been reported by Bolle (1998); Fehr, Gächter, and Kirchsteiger (1996); and Fehr and Gächter (forthcoming). Rieskamp and Gigerenzer (2003) report on a very interesting effort to program the heuristics that individuals tend to use when faced with situations involving the structure of the basic Trust Game. For an overview of this research tradition, see E. Ostrom and Walker 2003 and the special issue "Trust and Trustworthiness" edited by Bohnet and Croson 2004.

4. James Cox and colleagues at the University of Arizona have embarked on an ambitious and rigorous program to sort out behavior motivated by norms such as trust and reciprocity, as contrasted to other-regarding preferences. See Cox 2004; Cox and Deck in press; and Cox and Sadiraj 2004.

5. In the experiments reported herein, we used a return rate of 1 cent per unit.

6. Gürerk, Irlenbusch, and Rockenbach (2004) have examined cooperation levels in a public good experimental environment. They find cooperation reaches maximum levels when subjects can themselves adopt and use a costly sanctioning system. Not only is cooperation at a maximum; sanctioning costs are very low at the end of thirty periods. See also Maier-Rigaud and Apesteguia 2003.

7. Casari and Plott (2003) also changed the instructions given to players so as to make the differences between the three conditions very distinct. In general, the broad pattern of behavior in the base condition was very similar to our own earlier experiments.

8. A form of retribution, called a grim trigger strategy, was occasionally discussed in communication rounds but never deployed. Grim trigger strategies are those that cooperate until someone defects and then *never* cooperate again. They have been posited to be one of the strategies that, if known to be followed by some participants, will lead others to cooperate and thereby solve a social dilemma (see E. Ostrom, Gardner, and Walker 1994, chap. 7).

Chapter Four
Animating Institutional Analysis

1. It is also necessary to adopt a "solution concept," such as the core that is used in cooperative game theory (Shepsle 1975) or the Nash equilibrium that is used in noncooperative game theory (Calvert 1995). Both are used extensively in institutional theory to generate predictions (see Diermeier and Krehbiel 2003 for a comparison of these two solution concepts as used in institutional theories). Skyrms (1997) makes a powerful critique of how equilibrium concepts are casually used in the social sciences without positing a dynamic process that would lead

to a particular equilibrium. Animating institution theories, however, comes prior to choosing solution concepts.

2. Jerome Bruner (2004) provides an excellent overview of the diverse learning theories—molecular associationism, molar configurationism, associative bonds, conditioned reflex, gestalt theory, behavioralism, psycholoinquistics—of the last century and a half that have loosely led to a better understanding of how humans learn.

3. Mike McGinnis has pointed out to me that many of the situations that are modeled as if they were simple situations are actually very complex when one studies them in the field. Thus, the notion of a simple situation is one that we can use in analyzing models of a situation, but rarely in analyzing field settings. I deeply appreciate the exchange of memos and discussions I have had with Mike regarding this issue.

4. Classical utility theory did not make this assumption. In fact, little effort was devoted to where utility came from until researchers tried to test propositions derived from theory and have had to make a specific assumption as to the direct, monotonic linkage between external, objective payoffs and internal utility valuations (see V. Smith 1982). It is well known that without the second assumption, it is difficult to derive hypotheses about human behavior that can be empirically tested. In fact, it is impossible to test the proposition that individuals maximize utility without obtaining some objective measure of utility. A variety of recent theoretical efforts have explored different valuation assumptions by linking utility overtly to the distribution of objective payoffs to self and others (see Fehr and Gächter 1998, 2000a, for examples).

5. See Rabin 1998 and Kahneman and Tversky 2000 for recent reviews; Kahneman, Knetsch, and Thaler 1990 for a description of the endowment anomaly; and Grether and Plott 1979 for a discussion of the preference reversal anomaly. Hodgson 2004b also makes a cogent argument that the model of opportunistic behavior, which is an extension of the rational egoist to behavior within firms (Williamson 1985), places far too much emphasis on a single motivation as the primary source of contractual difficulties leading to the creation of firms.

6. In an ingenious experiment with monkeys as subjects, Sugrue, Corrado, and Newsome (2004) examined how the history of past choices and rewards affects the internal representation of the expected value of alternative potential moves. By training monkeys in a dynamic foraging environment, their eye movements and behavior provided a window into their subjective valuation. The researchers provided strong support that their subjects were using cognitive mechanisms leading them to match time spent in foraging at a particular site in proportion to the abundance of resources available at that site.

7. Thanks to John Schiemann for further clarification of this point via an e-mail communication.

8. In a thoughtful article on the development of shared norms in a community, Gibbard (1990, 798) places considerable emphasis on the importance of ritual as a vivid symbol. "A vivid symbol, after all, is a stimulus that commands attention and generalizes of itself. . . . Why are ritual and symbols so pervasive in human life? Perhaps because psychic mechanisms that respond to them stabilize cooperative arrangements and guard an individual's place in those arrangements."

9. Recent research using brain-imaging technology (Hasson et al. 2004; Pessoa 2004) investigated whether the brains of different subjects, who watched a vivid thirty-minute segment of the movie "The Good, the Bad, and the Ugly" had similar activation patterns. They found a relatively substantial correlation between the signals generated by one brain with those of another subject watching the same segment. Hasson et al. (2004) found that a major component of brain activation occurred when emotionally salient segments of the movie—e.g., scenes containing gunshots and explosions—occurred. They also recorded strong responses when subjects viewed faces. While Hasson et al. did find considerable evidence that regions of individual brains "ticked together," they also found that substantial portions of cortex activation could not be predicted from another subject's responses.

10. Vernon Smith (2001, 21) has reflected that we all function in at least two worlds: "one of personal exchange governed by self-policed norms of reciprocity (positive and negative) in which there is much *intentional* cooperation generating gains from such trade; another of impersonal exchange through markets governed by constantly evolving cultural rules invented by no one person, in which *unintentionally*, and without awareness, we cooperate by pursuing our own self-defined interests. Each world is a complex self-ordering system to which we, our parents, our parents' parents, etc., have adapted and contributed to its evolution."

11. Although the discussion in chapter 3 focused on the Trust Game and Commons Dilemma, the large number of experiments on the Ultimatum Game and the Dictator Game also challenge the predictions derived from using rational egoist assumptions about strategies and outcomes (Camerer 2003; Cox 2004).

12. Recent research by Brandts, Saijo, and Schram (2004) conduct the same experimental social dilemma (in this case, a linear, voluntary contribution, public goods game) in Japan, the Netherlands, Spain, and the United States. They found only minor differences in the level of cooperation in all four countries.

13. Cameron (1999), for example, conducted ultimatum experiments in Indonesia and was able to use sums that amount to three months' wages. In this extremely tempting situation, she still found that 56 percent of the Proposers allocated between 40 and 50 percent of this very substantial sum to the Responder.

14. See Rothstein 1998, 2005; Levi 1997a; Frohlich and Oppenheimer 1996. Many scholars are also engaged in serious theoretical efforts to try to understand how humans use norms (see, in particular, Falk, Fehr, and Fischbacher 2002; McCabe and Smith 2003; Frey 1997a; Ben-Ner and Putterman 2000a, 2000b; Casari and Plott 2003; Rothstein 2005).

15. Orbell and Dawes (1991) made a cogent theoretical argument that individuals project their own normative preferences onto others. Glaeser et al. (2000) observed a high correlation between those who *were* trustworthy in sequential trust settings and those who were also more likely to be trusting. Esarey and Ahn (2004) find that when no information is provided about the prior behavior of subjects in the second mover's position, that subjects who are themselves trustworthy tend to trust others at a significantly higher rate. Brosig (2002) finds that communication enables subjects to signal intentions accurately.

16. It is always a challenge to understand which heuristic is being used in a particular setting. Jager and Janssen (2003) assume that cognitive costs affect this

choice. In their analysis, an individual is likely to evaluate heuristics based on their satisfaction with outcomes achieved and the certainty with which a heuristic leads to satisfactory results.

17. The intrinsic cost or anguish that an individual suffers from failing to use a norm, such as telling the truth or keeping a promise, is usually referred to as guilt, if primarily self-inflicted, or as shame, when the knowledge of the failure is well known by others (Posner and Rasmusen 1999). While guilt may be self-inflicted, extensive research by psychologists have led to a recognition that it arises out of interpersonal transitions and varies by interpersonal context (Baumeister, Stillwell, and Heatherton 1994). The same action generates guilt in one situation (e.g., the immediate family), but not in another (e.g., the workplace) (Millar and Tesser 1988).

18. In chapter 5, where we define delta parameters in more detail, we make a further distinction between those parameters that are invoked by internal mechanisms (e.g., through guilt) and those that are invoked by external mechanisms (e.g., gossip leading to shame, etc.). For simplicity, I do not make a distinction here.

19. Gangs in urban areas can be thought of as a clique of participants who obtain positive rewards from doing acts that others think are prohibited. The positive internal reward is magnified by the increase in the esteem of other gang members for the perpetrator of these acts.

20. Riolo, Cohen, and Axelrod (2001) have shown how individuals who engage in image scoring (Nowak and Sigmund 1998) can contribute to others' welfare without any need for internal norms of reciprocity or even repeat encounters with the same individual. What is required is that all individuals carry arbitrary tags (Holland 1995), and that individuals at the beginning of an evolutionary process tend to donate resources to others who are "similar" to them—meaning they carry some or all of the same tags. They show that within a few hundred generations, a cluster of cooperative individuals reaching up to 80 percent of the population can emerge, be challenged by a new cluster who have inherited a different set of tags, and then be replaced by the new cluster as it grows to about 80 percent of the population (442). Such models are a useful starting point for thinking about competition and relative survival rates as among different strategies over a long time period.

21. An excellent example of the internal accounts that individuals develop without much self-conscious thought was conducted among a small group of sugarcane cultivators in Ecuador (Price, in press). The tradition in this region is to organize regular *mingas* where attendance is required and all are expected to work toward achieving a collective outcome such as clearing the weeds out of a sugarcane field with machetes. Since mingas were held once or twice a week, workers could become familiar with the effort that others regularly expended. Price asked a set of workers to rank the effort that others regularly expended and compared these individual perceptions with data obtained from systematic measurement of the same workers' effort in six observed mingas. Price found a high correlation between these perceptions of work effort and objective measures of effort.

22. The *Journal of Economic Theory* devoted a special issue in 2001 to the evolution of preferences (vol. 97, no. 2). See also Orbell et al. 2004 for a rigorous

and imaginative use of simulation of evolutionary processes to address how cooperative dispositions may have evolved. As Werner Güth had kindly pointed out to me in correspondence, preference evolution is only one of the possibilities open to models that use an indirect evolutionary approach. One can make other aspects of participant decision making endogenous as well, such as beliefs and timing of decisions.

23. Eshel, Samuelson, and Shaked (1998) develop a learning model where a population of Altruists who adopt a strategy of providing a local public good interacts in a local circular neighborhood with a population of Egoists who free ride. In this local interaction setting, Altruists' strategies are imitated sufficiently often in a Markovian learning process to become one of the absorbing states. Altruists interacting with Egoists in a larger environment are not so likely to survive.

24. This implies that in a game where players know only their own payoffs and not the payoffs of others, that they are more likely to behave like rational egoists. McCabe and Smith (2003) show that players tend to evolve toward the predicted, subgame perfect outcomes in experiments where they have only private information of their own payoffs and to cooperative outcomes when they have information about payoffs and the moves made by other players (see also McCabe, Rassenti, and Smith 1996).

25. Further, Kikuchi, Watanabe, and Yamagishi (1996) have found that those who express a high degree of trust are able to predict others' behavior more accurately than those with low levels of trust.

26. To examine the frequency of nonrational egoist preferences, a group of 181 undergraduates were given a questionnaire containing a similar payoff structure on the first day of classes at Indiana University in January 1999 (Ahn et al. 2003). They were asked to rank their preferences. In this nondecision setting, 52 percent reflected preferences that were not consistent with being rational egoists (27 percent ranked the outcome [C,C] over [D,C] and 25 percent were indifferent).

27. See also Esarey and Ahn (2004), who report on a critical experiment designed to test the capability of traditional game-theoretic predictions as contrasted to indirect evolutionary theory predictions for a repeated, sequential PD game. They found more cooperation than predicted by traditional game theory and that subjects enter the experiment with relatively stable preferences for reciprocity or being a rational egoist. The behavior of second movers was broadly consistent with the predictions of indirect evolutionary theory.

Chapter Five
A Grammar of Institutions

1. The grammar of institutions and much of the analysis in this chapter first appeared in print in a 1995 *American Political Science Review* article. This chapter builds on and adds to our *APSR* article. In particular, we add several figures that had to be cut from the original article due to space limitations and that existed in an appendix form until they were reprinted in Crawford and Ostrom 2000. In this chapter, we provide more information on how to use the grammar of institu-

tions, including new discussions of how the grammar relates to the other institutional analysis tools and frameworks described in this book. The grammar in this chapter retains the same logic and basic components as the grammar outlined in the 1995 article; however, we have refined the grammar a bit based on what we have learned from scholars using the grammar and what we learned as we worked through the grammar in the larger context of this book. We have tried in particular to improve the clarity of the distinction between rules and norms. To use a software analogy, this chapter is Institutional Grammar 2.0 with an expanded instruction book written specifically for institutional analysts.

2. All of these statements use the notion of a "holder"—a part of the rule that will be filled by concepts that are either defined in general everyday language, such as age, drive a car, or being in a particular location, or in legal documents, such as legislation, court decisions, administrative decisions. The fact that all of our rules involved "holders" is a recognition that ATTRIBUTES, AIMs, and CONDITIONS all refer to concepts that are either defined in everyday language or are created by a generative rule. The three deontic operators are defined in a formal language—deontic logic.

3. We can also compare our syntax with that of other scholars. The Dalhousie logic of rules, for example, uses a similar syntax without an OR ELSE and requires that prescriptive statements be recast to use the forbidden DEONTIC operator (see Braybrooke 1996).

4. Our concept of ATTRIBUTES is the same as the *wenn* component of the Dalhousie syntax (Braybrooke 1996).

5. The largest group to which a prescriptive statement could apply is the *folk* component in the Dalhousie system (Braybrooke 1996).

6. John R. Commons ([1924] 1968) stressed the correlative nature of rights. To state that someone has a right, someone must have a duty to observe that right. The person with the right, then, is permitted to do something, while those with the duty are forbidden or required to do something.

7. See V. Ostrom and E. Ostrom (1970) for further development of these ideas.

8. The deontic "may" is still meaningful in statements that do not contain an OR ELSE. Consider a legislative body that shares an institutional statement like the following: [All junior members] [P] [contest senior members] [in committee hearings]. This is the equivalent to: [All junior members] [~F] [contest senior members] [in committee hearings]. This prescription implies a prescription on senior members not to reprimand or castigate junior members who challenge them in committee hearings. Of course, the existence of such a norm does not ensure that senior members will follow it in all instances. However, there will be a shared notion that a rebuke based on seniority alone is inappropriate or unacceptable. If a senior member reprimands a junior member, then we might expect the junior member to use the grant of permission to defend against the senior member's actions. It means something for the junior member to say "everyone here knows that I am permitted to challenge senior members in committee hearings."

9. Societies undergoing substantial "liberalization" could be thought of as developing shared understandings that individuals who in earlier times had been forbidden to take certain actions are now permitted to do so. When the new norm is shared, individuals who still attempt to obstruct the previously restricted actors

now face a cost for breaking the norm. Thus, changes in norms over time will be reflected both in the particular deontic assigned to an action and potentially to whom a cost of breaking the norm is assigned.

10. Kreps et al. (1982, 247) do not assume that the basis for one actor playing tit-for-tat is necessarily the acceptance of a norm. They simply assume that either some players have available to them only a tit-for-tat strategy or that there is some probability that one player's payoffs are such that tit-for-tat is strongly dominant. The latter condition would be the case if some players in a population have some combination of delta parameters associated with playing tit-for-tat whose values are high enough to make tit-for-tat the dominant strategy for these players. Game theorists have frequently assumed that such players were somehow "irrational," but an institutional explanation would be that such players had accepted a norm that the obligatory way to play a repeated Prisoner's Dilemma game was to follow a tit-for-tat strategy.

11. We are, of course, aware that all actions have consequences as pointed out to us by many of our students—Ryan Adams, in particular. The difference that the OR ELSE makes is that the consequences specified by a rule would NOT have occurred without the rule being in place and being enforced. Thus, a specific rule adds further consequences to those that would occur as a result of individuals interacting in a situation without that specific rule.

12. Tsebelis (1989, 1991) argues that in a game with only mixed-strategy equilibria, increasing the size of the OR ELSE does not reduce the level of rule infraction but rather reduces the level of monitoring. Weissing and Ostrom (1991b) have shown that Tsebelis's results hold in many but not all cases.

13. Hans Albert (1986, 25) bemoaned the difficulty of making any universally binding demarcation between norms and rules of law. He opted to call prescriptions "law only where they meet certain minimum requirements such as the existence of secondary rules that regulate the identification, modification and adjudication of the various primary rules in a society" (see also Hart 1961).

14. Or, as we indicated above, the rule or norm backing a rule may reward the sanctioner for taking positive actions rather than punishing the sanctioner for shirking.

15. It would, of course, be possible to include discount rates in the analysis, but we assume they are zero here to keep the focus on other questions and not those related to the size of the discount rate. For a discussion of the importance of discount rates in the analysis of cooperation see Axelrod 1981, 1986.

16. A mixed strategy is a probability distribution over the pure strategies for a player. In a static game, one may view the mixed strategy as the probability of choosing one of the other pure strategies. One can also interpret mixed strategies as behavioral tendencies in a repeated context where the probability of choosing a pure strategy, say C, is viewed as a cooperation rate.

17. In many farmer-governed irrigation systems, for example, farmers devise simple rules that are easy to monitor themselves and do not employ any formal guards. In others, where a guard is employed by the farmers, a frequent payment to the guard is in a proportion of the yield obtained by the irrigators. Thus, the guard participates in the increased productivity of a system that reduces the rate

of stealing water or free-riding on the provision of needed resource inputs to maintain the system (see E. Ostrom 1992a).

18. The delta parameters for player 4 could be disaggregated into their internal and external components for an analysis that wished to focus on questions that distinguished between internal and external sources of normative constraints related to the Sanctioner.

19. One could argue that when prescriptions are rules, individuals will place higher values on the deltas than when the prescriptions are norms (see Braybrooke 1987). If one assumes that the presence of rules influences the internal deltas, that δ^{oi} are higher in the Rules Game (figure 5.6) than in the Norms Game (figure 5.4), then the rule would influence the structure of the game even when the Monitor fails.

20. In this game, player 3 always correctly detects whether defection has occurred and player 4 only has the option of sanctioning players who have defected. If players 1 and 2 cooperate, player 4 does not have a choice of whether or not to sanction. This eliminates issues of false detection and corrupt sanctioners from the current analysis but not from future efforts that assumed only a probability of correct detection and honest sanctioning.

21. Offe and Wiesenthal 1980; Hirschman 1985; Etzioni 1988; Coleman 1988; Ellickson 1991; Elster 1989b; Knack 1992; Udéhn 1993; Margolis 1991; E. Ostrom 1990; V. Ostrom 1997; Mansbridge 1990, 1994; Schmid 2004.

22. See E. Ostrom 1986 for a discussion of the configurational aspect of rules.

23. This logic of the delta parameter is similar to Etzioni's (1988) discussion of deontology.

Chapter Six
Why Classify Generic Rules?

1. And, it turns out, for other evolving sciences as well. Grimm and Wissel (1997) note a babbling equilibrium problem in ecology, for example, when they identify 163 definitions of "stability" in the ecological literature.

2. The latter problem assumed a substantial urgency during the summer of 2001 as I was writing an early draft of this chapter. I had taken a new laptop computer to our Canadian writing cabin on the Manitoulin Island and had not used the new computer with the old printer that I have used there for years. When I first started to print, out came gibberish that occasionally had a recognizable word but was generally a mess. After many hours of trying to fix this myself, I took it to the island's "Computer Doc," Roland Panamick. He had to work through a dozen hypotheses as to what was the problem. The first was a mechanical problem—the printer might have needed to be cleaned. This was eminently reasonable, given that I had used it for some time without a cleaning. However, in this case, cleaning was not the source of the problem. After that, he began working on the various levels of software that drive a computer. It turned out that there was a major conflict occurring in the Windows software commands for a printer and the software needed to run my old-fashioned dot matrix printer. After digging down layer after layer of software commands, he was finally able to make my printer work. If he had not understood which software commands did what and

how they fit (or did not fit) together, he could not have fixed this system for me. I will always remember the several hours I spent in his shop, both for the terror in my heart that he would not be able to fix it (meaning I would be stuck without a printer for several more weeks) and for the lesson he gave me in the importance of understanding the multiple languages that create the structure that I use all the time and take pretty much for granted.

3. See, for example, the seven market rules that Gode and Sunder (1997) use in their analysis "What Makes Markets Allocationally Efficient?" and the fifteen types of rules that Libecap (1996, 44) examines to understand the evolution of mining law in the American West.

4. Readers who would like to pursue the impact of the "lack of agreement" in these earlier studies are invited to look at E. Ostrom 1986, where I do discuss the impact of these rules in some depth. It has also been reprinted in McGinnis 2000, chap. 3.

Chapter Seven
Classifying Rules

1. See Benda-Beckmann 2000 for critique of the simple dichotomy of public versus private as an adequate conceptual foundation for comparative legal research. Schmid (1999) makes a strong critique of the tendency to talk about government versus markets.

2. Since strategies and norms also have AIMs, we could also use the same way of classifying them. Given the focus of this volume, however, we are most interested in understanding the prescriptions that create the structure of an action situation and will not focus here on the way that individuals adopt normative values (internal delta components) in relation to actions they feel that must, must not, or may take or outcomes to which similar prescriptions have been attached.

3. The classes of rules proposed in this chapter are somewhat similar to the five "dimensions" of rules that Koremenos, Lipson, and Snidal (2001, 763) propose as being basis for the rational design of institutional institutions:

Membership rules (MEMBERSHIP)
Scope of issues covered (SCOPE)
Centralization of tasks (CENTRALIZATION)
Rules for controlling the institution (CONTROL)
Flexibility of arrangements (FLEXIBILITY)

The classification used in this chapter does have a distinct theoretical foundation—that rules do directly, and indirectly, affect the elements of an action situation, and thus we focus first on the seven rules that have this direct impact.

4. Anthony Giddens (1979, 65) expressed the configural nature of rules when he stated: "There is not a singular relation between 'an activity' and 'a rule,' as is sometimes suggested or implied by statements like 'the rule governing the Queen's move' in chess. Activities or practices are brought into being in the context of overlapping and connected sets of rules, given coherence by their involvement in the constitution of social systems in the movement of time."

5. Anthony Giddens (1979, 117) defined a position in a similar manner, as "a social identity that carries with it a certain range . . . of prerogatives and obligations that an actor who is accorded that identity (or is an 'incumbent' of that position) may activate or carry out: these prerogatives and obligations constitute the role-prescriptions associated with that position."

6. When some persons can be forced into a decision situation, unscrupulous participants may initiate formal actions in order to obtain illegal payoffs to let the person withdraw. Whenever formal rules are written in an overly strict, unenforceable manner, they can be used by street-level bureaucrats to force a shakedown. The New York "bite" occurs when residents pay building inspectors not to enforce overly strict building codes. Hobbes characterized bad laws as "traps for money."

7. The four sets of position rules are similar to a set of rules used by Shepsle (1979b) to define a committee system in a legislature. However, the form of the statements differs. Shepsle's formulations state the result of the operation of the rule in a situation. Shepsle shows that equilibria can be structurally induced by a particular combination of rules when the distribution of preferences and a simple majority-rule institution could not lead to an equilibrium.

8. In earlier papers, this type of rule has been called "authority rule." Since all rules assign some form of authority to some participant in regard to one of the components of an action situation, we thought it would be clearer to use the term "choice" for this kind of rule.

9. Lack of agreement rules strongly affects the bargaining strength and strategies adopted in labor management disputes. For an interesting empirical study of the effect of three different rules specifying what actions can be taken by either labor or management, see Dannin and Singh forthcoming.

10. President Clinton issued Executive Order No. 12866, which was retained by President Bush. The order directs regulatory agencies to specify performance objectives whenever possible in new regulations rather than requiring the acts that must, or must not, be done.

11. The use of scope rules do date back, however, to one of the earliest-known government codes—the Hammurabi Code (at <http://www.yale.edu/lawweb/avalon/medieval/hammenu.htm/>). See Foliente 2000 for a discussion of this code, as well as recent efforts to devise building codes relying more on scope rules.

12. This is a modified version originally presented in Gardner and Ostrom 1991.

13. Gode and Sunder (1997, 610–11) analyze the set of rules that they posit is needed to transform a simple market into an efficient market even with "zero intelligence traders." They specify the following seven rules as needed to accomplish this task:

1. Voluntary trading rule: traders are free to accept or reject offers.

2. Binding contract rule: bids and asks are binding, i.e., buyers must pay what they bid; and sellers must sell at what they ask.

3. Price priority rule: higher bids dominate lower bids, and lower asks dominate higher asks.

4. Accumulation rule: the highest bid (and the lowest ask if it is a double auction) are picked only after all bids (and tasks) have been collected.

5. Double auction rule: buyers can bid as well as sellers can ask.

6. Multiple rounds rule: multiple rounds of bids and asks are allowed; i.e., if the highest bid is less than the lowest ask, then there are further rounds of bids and asks.

7. Public bids and asks with bid-ask improvement rule: a bid must be greater than previous bids, and an ask must be less than previous asks.

One would also need a judge or some other enforcer to ensure these rules are followed.

14. As we discuss in chapters 2 and 5, rules at one level are operational only when these rules are backed by monitoring and sanctioning rules (or norms) at another level. To undertake analysis at one level, one may assume that the rules needed to change a situation at that level will be monitored and enforced. This helps to simplify the analysis, but the assumption must be thoroughly examined when doing applied work. All too many formal laws have been passed to change behavior at an operational level without asking how the police and judges at that level will themselves be monitored and sanctioned if they do not apply the rules appropriately.

15. The extensive historical and analytical review of Greif, Milgrom, and Weingast (1994) of the history of merchant guilds in the medieval era demonstrate that local rulers frequently did renege on their promises and either let local merchants steal the goods of an alien trader or confiscated their goods for themselves. Greif, Milgrom, and Weingast argue that to obtain stable, long-term commitment from rulers required that the merchants themselves organize so as to be able to threaten (and enforce the threat so it was credible) a boycott of all merchants from the organizing city or region if rulers did not keep their pledges. Such an organization—a merchant guild—could coordinate the actions of its own members so that rulers who failed to keep their commitments would face serious expected costs. "To permit an efficient expansion of trade in the medieval environment, there was a need for an organization that would supplement the operation of a multilateral reputation mechanism by *coordinating* the responses of a large fraction of the merchants. Only when a coordinating organization exists can the multilateral reputation mechanism potential overcome the commitment problem" (753). To implement such a system would require still a further set of rules beyond those specified above.

Chapter Eight
Using Rules as Tools to Cope with the Commons

1. McCay and Acheson 1987; Fortmann and Bruce 1988; Berkes 1989; Berkes et al. 2001; V. Ostrom, Feeny, and Picht 1993; Netting 1993; Bromley et al. 1992; National Research Council 2002.

2. On the other hand, one can use simplified models of a policy process as useful benchmarks to examine deviations observed in the field (see Scharpf 1997). One can then ask: What is it about a setting that leads officials and/or appropriators to deviate a little or a lot from a presumed solution?

3. Boundary rules are also important in more urban and industrial settings. In a recent study of the biophysical, social, and institutional factors associated with the establishment of conjunctive surface and groundwater arrangements, Heikkila (2004) randomly selected seventy groundwater basins in California. Her statistical analysis demonstrated that "institutional settings devised around the boundaries of the resource, which allow water providers to control the resource through basin adjudication or special groundwater management districts, can facilitate conjunctive water management" (111).

4. Faysse (2003) provides a good analysis of these types of rules on the efficiency of the allocation process.

5. Lobe and Berkes (2004) provide a detailed study of the *padu* fishing system on an island off the coast of the state of Kerala in India. Each local shrimp fishery governance system creates a set of fishing locations. All of these systems "attempt to redistribute the catch fairly among the fishers by rotating access to the fishing location" (276). They rotate according to a lottery system run each year that assures an equal opportunity to fish in the best locations.

6. The water-holding capacity of paddy fields in Chitwan is also considerably better than the sloped terraces that characterize Tanahun and other districts in the middle hills (Shivakoti personal communication).

7. As a field researcher, I have witnessed a wide variety of systems that change their rule structure regularly during a year depending on the seasons. Many such systems have been developed locally and without knowledge of what others have done. When I visited several sites in Tarija, Bolivia (near Cochabamba), for example, in the mid-1990s, the local officials proudly told me that they had developed a complex system of land allocation that existed nowhere else on earth! They then described their system of small plots of land allocated as private property during the good agricultural season of the year. All of the land in the valley was then converted to a common-property system during the dry period of each year. This enabled all of the local farmers to graze animals on the stubble of their agricultural fields without concern for who owned which plot. It was indeed an ingenious system well tailored to the local environment. It was, however, not unique given the long history of the "open field system" of Europe (see Dahlman 1980; de Moor, Shaw-Taylor, and Warde 2002).

8. See, for example, Weimer and Vining 1992. Other, more critical approaches taken to the study of policy include scholars' focus on the deliberative processes involved in efforts to solve problems. See, for example, Dryzek 2000; Elster 1998; Habermas 1996; Rawls 1971; and Fisher 2003.

9. Plott and Porter (1996) undertook a similar analysis including experiments examining diverse ways of pricing the use of space stations. They point out the importance of using lab experiments as a method for avoiding some of the costs of experimenting later in the world using only models as a basis for choosing policies.

10. See McKean 1992, 2000; Wade 1994; Schlager 1990; Baland and Platteau 1996; Tang 1992; E. Ostrom 1990, 1992b; E. Ostrom, Gardner, and Walker 1994; Meinzen-Dick, Raju, and Gulati 2002. In addition, see Agrawal 2002 for an excellent discussion of the over thirty variables that one or more scholar has speculated affect the likelihood of collective action being undertaken.

11. Theesfeld (2004) provides an analysis of these calculations in regard to irrigation in a transitional economy—Bulgaria.

12. See Feeny, Hanna, and McEvoy 1996 for a discussion of these issues related to the collapse of the California sardine industry.

13. See Libecap 1995 for a discussion of the efforts to use the courts to challenge the validity of de facto governance of inshore fisheries in the U.S.; see also P. Alexander (1982).

Chapter Nine
Robust Resource Governance in Polycentric Institutions

1. As Jared Diamond (2005) illustrates so dramatically, some ecological disasters might have been avoided if those making major decisions were not isolated from the impact of their own decisions.

2. On the other hand, this also means that corrupt leaders searching for rules that will maximize the returns they obtain over time are not fully able to do a complete analysis either. Firmin-Sellers (1996) provides a well-documented study of the failed effort of a strong African leader to gain the benefits he predicted would come his way when the constitution he strongly supported for the Gold Coast was approved and put into operation.

3. Recently, considerable attention has also been devoted to the relevance of these principles for the governance of digital resources (Mueller 2002; Schweik and Semenov 2003; Schweik, Evans, and Grove forthcoming; Hess and Ostrom 2003; Van Wendel de Joode 2004; Less 2002).

4. Four levels of monitoring were recorded: never, occasionally, seasonally, or year-round. We dichotomized this variable and recoded seasonal or year-round monitoring as "regular" and never or sporadic monitoring as "sporadic."

5. Lansing (1991) graphically describes how changes in agricultural practices induced by external agencies supposedly to help farmers in Bali increase their productivity almost destroyed irrigation systems that had flourished for centuries.

6. The problem of local units becoming dependent on external funding is not limited to the funding provided by international aid agencies. Two decades ago, Sieber (1981) reviewed some of the reverse effects created by domestic U.S. policy. The supposed aim of Nixon's "New Federalism" reform was to increase the autonomy of local units and strengthen the overall federal system. A study by Hudson (1980) revealed that the policy has an opposite effect in some cities such as El Paso. "El Paso is now more dependent, politically and economically, on federal grants than it was prior to the New Federalism and local autonomy is significantly reduced" (Hudson 1980, 900, quoted in Sieber 1981, 186).

7. Douglas Vermillion (2001) provides a cogent story about this process. In discussing the Small-Scale Irrigation Turnover Program in Indonesia, he heard about an earlier effort to increase "farmer participation" in the project. A member of the project staff

informed farmers in a small scheme located in a hilly area of West Sumatra that a certain, but undisclosed amount of funds were available to make small repairs to their scheme before full management responsibility would be turned over to them. Farmers were invited to make a list of priorities for repairs. This was seen as a form of farmer participation. The farmers responded by generating a long wish list. High on the list was a curious request for the government to raise the masonry embankment along a 300-meter reach of the upper main canal by about 25 cms. When asked why they requested this, some farmer representatives answered that about 11 years before, the government had first installed the masonry embankment. By now the calan had accumulated about 20 cms of silt. They said that if the government raised the embankment another 25 cms they would probably not have to do any desiltation for another 11 years! (187)

8. See Yoder 1991, Pradhan and Yoder 1989, and Water and Energy Commission Secretariat 1990 for descriptions of a highly innovative and successful program of assisting farmers to design their *own* institutional rules rather than imposing a set of model bylaws on them.

9. For a refreshing and different view of the importance of village governance, see Ayo 2002.

10. See Blomquist, Schlager, and Heikkila 2004 for an insightful study of polycentric institutions in the American West. Wagner (in press) provides an excellent overview of the study of polycentricity. Hong and Page (2004) provide strong evidence of the superiority of having *diverse* problem solvers involved in making decisions about complex systems. While their study focuses on individual decision makers rather than on the diversity of decision-making units in a polycentric system, the core point of their study is that diversity of skills and backgrounds enhance decision-making performance. This provides another foundation for why polycentric systems that draw on diversely organized units will outperform single-layer systems solving the same set of problems over time.

11. This decision was rendered by Judge Boldt of the Western District Court in 1974 and upheld in 1979 by the Supreme Court (443 U.S. 658 1979).

12. For good analyses of other "co-management" systems on the Pacific Coast of North America, see Pinkerton 1989 and Poffenberger and McGean 1996. Wilson, Nielsen, and Degnbol (2003) provide an excellent collection of empirical studies focusing on relative successes and failures of systems that are called "co-management," in many parts of the world. Unfortunately, some such systems have fallen into the trap of "blueprint" thinking described above and have lost the vitality of evolving polycentric systems, while others have continued to adapt and develop productive institutional structures.

References

Abernathy, Charles L., and Hilmy Sally. 2000. "Experiments of Some Government-Sponsored Organizations of Irrigators in Niger and Burkina Faso, West Africa." *Journal of Applied Irrigation Studies* 35(2):177–205.

Acheson, James M. 1988. *The Lobster Gangs of Maine*. Hanover, NH: University Press of New England.

———. 2003. *Capturing the Commons: Devising Institutions to Manage the Maine Lobster Industry*. Hanover, NH: University Press of New England.

Acheson, James M., James A. Wilson, and Robert S. Steneck. 1998. "Managing Chaotic Fisheries." In *Linking Social and Ecological Systems: Management Practices and Social Mechanisms for Building Resilience*, ed. Fikret Berkes and Carl Folke, 390–413. New York: Cambridge University Press.

Acuna, Carlos H., and Mariano Tommasi. 2000. "Some Reflections on the Institutional Reforms Required for Latin America." In *Institutional Reforms, Growth and Human Development in Latin America*, 357–400. New Haven: Yale Center for International and Area Studies.

Aggarwal, Vinod K., and Cédric Dupont. 1999. "Goods, Games, and Institutions." *International Political Science Review* 20(4):393–409.

Agrawal, Arun. 1994. "Rules, Rule Making, and Rule Breaking: Examining the Fit between Rule Systems and Resource Use." In *Rules, Games, and Common-Pool Resources*, ed. Elinor Ostrom, Roy Gardner, and James Walker, 267–82. Ann Arbor: University of Michigan Press.

———. 1999. *Greener Pastures: Politics, Markets, and Community among a Migrant Pastoral People*. Durham, NC: Duke University Press.

———. 2000. "Small Is Beautiful, but Is Larger Better? Forest-Management Institutions in the Kumaon Himalaya, India." In *People and Forests: Communities, Institutions, and Governance*, ed. Clark Gibson, Margaret McKean, and Elinor Ostrom, 57–85. Cambridge: MIT Press.

———. 2002. "Common Resources and Institutional Sustainability." In *The Drama of the Commons*, National Research Council, Committee on the Human Dimensions of Global Change, ed. Elinor Ostrom, Thomas Dietz, Nives Dolšak, Paul C. Stern, Susan Stonich, and Elke Weber, 41–85. Washington, DC: National Academy Press.

———. 2005. *Environmentality: Technologies of Government and the Making of Subjects*. Durham, NC: Duke University Press.

Agrawal, Arun, and Clark Gibson, eds. 2001. *Communities and the Environment: Ethnicity, Gender, and the State in Community-Based Conservation*. New Brunswick, NJ: Rutgers University Press.

Agrawal Arun, and Sanjeev Goyal. 2001. "Group Size and Collective Action: Third-Party Monitoring in Common-Pool Resources." *Comparative Political Studies* 34(1):63–93.

Agrawal, Arun, and Gautam N. Yadama. 1997. "How Do Local Institutions Mediate Market and Population Pressures on Resources? Forest *Panchayats* in Kumaon, India." *Development and Change* 28(3):435–65.

Ahn, T. K., Marco A. Janssen, Derek S. Reiners, and Jeffrey E. Stake. 2004. "Learning to Play Nice: Strategy Evolution in the National Hockey League." Working Paper. Bloomington: Indiana University, Workshop in Political Theory and Policy Analysis.

Ahn, T. K., Elinor Ostrom, David Schmidt, and James Walker. 2003. "Trust in Two-Person Games: Game Structures and Linkages." In *Trust and Reciprocity: Interdisciplinary Lessons from Experimental Research*, ed. Elinor Ostrom and James Walker, 323–51. New York: Russell Sage Foundation.

Ahn, T. K., Elinor Ostrom, and James Walker. 2003. "Heterogeneous Preferences and Collective Action." *Public Choice* 117(3–4) (December): 295–314.

Alba, Joseph W., and Howard Marmorstein. 1987. "The Effects of Frequency Knowledge on Consumer Decision Making." *Journal of Consumer Research* 14 (June): 14–25.

Albert, Hans. 1986. "Law as an Instrument of Rational Practice." In *Contract and Organization: Legal Analysis in the Light of Economic and Social Theory*, ed. Terence Daintith and Gunther Teubner, 25–51. Berlin: Walter de Gruyter.

Alchian, Armen A. 1950. "Uncertainty, Evolution, and Economic Theory." *Journal of Political Economy* 58(3):211–21.

Alcorn, Janis B., and Victor Toledo. 1998. "Resilient Resource Management in Mexico's Forest Ecosystems: The Contribution of Property Rights." In *Linking Social and Ecological Systems: Management Practices and Social Mechanisms for Building Resilience*, ed. Fikret Berkes and Carl Folke, 216–49. New York: Cambridge University Press.

Aldrich, John. 1995. *Why Parties?* Chicago: University of Chicago Press.

Alexander, Christopher. 1964. *Notes on the Synthesis of Form*. Cambridge: Harvard University Press.

Alexander, Paul. 1982. *Sri Lankan Fishermen: Rural Capitalism and Peasant Society*. Canberra: Australian National University.

Allen, Barbara. 2005. *Tocqueville, Covenant, and the Democratic Revolution: Harmonizing Earth with Heaven*. Lanham, MD: Lexington Books.

Allport, Floyd H. 1962. "A Structuronomic Conception of Behavior: Individual and Collective." *Journal of Abnormal and Social Psychology* 64:3–30.

Amaro de Matos, João, and Pedro P. Barros. 2004. "Social Norms and the Paradox of Elections' Turnout." *Public Choice* 121(1–2):239–55.

Anderies, John M., Marco A. Janssen, and Elinor Ostrom. 2004. "A Framework to Analyze the Robustness of Social-Ecological Systems from an Institutional Perspective." *Ecology and Society* 9(1):18. <http://www.ecologyandsociety.org/vol9/iss1/art18>

Anderson, John R. 1991. "Is Human Cognition Adaptive?" *Behavioural and Brain Sciences* 14(3):471–517.

Anderson, Lee G. 1986. *The Economics of Fisheries Management*. Rev. ed. Baltimore: Johns Hopkins University Press.

———. 1995. "Privatizing Open Access Fisheries: Individual Transferable Quotas." In *The Handbook of Environmental Economics*, ed. Daniel W. Bromley, 453–74. Oxford: Blackwell.

Andersson, Krister P. 2002. "Can Decentralization Save Bolivia's Forests? An Institutional Analysis of Municipal Forest Governance." Ph.D. diss., Indiana University.

———. 2004. "Who Talks with Whom? The Role of Repeated Interactions in Decentralized Forest Governance." *World Development* 32(2):233–49.

Andreoni, James. 1988. "Why Free Ride? Strategies and Learning in Public Goods Experiments." *Journal of Public Economics* 37 (December): 291–304.

———. 1989. "Giving with Impure Altruism: Applications to Charity and Ricardian Equivalence." *Journal of Political Economy* 97:1447–58.

Appleyard, Roger. 1987. "Events and Acts: The Structure of their Effects." *Behavioral Science* 32:92–105.

Arnason, Ragnar, and Hannes H. Gissurarson, eds. 1999. *Individual Transferable Quotas in Theory and Practice*. Reykjavik: University of Iceland Press.

Arnold, J. E. M. 1998. *Managing Forests as Common Property*. FAO Forestry paper no. 136. Rome, Italy: Food and Agriculture Organization of the United Nations.

Arnold, J. E. M., and J. Gabriel Campbell. 1986. "Collective Management of Hill Forests in Nepal: The Community Forestry Development Project." In *Proceedings of the Conference on Common Property Resource Management*, National Research Council, 425–54. Washington, DC: National Academy Press.

Arnold, J. E. M., and William C. Stewart. 1991. *Common Property Resource Management in India*. Tropical Forestry papers no. 24. Oxford: Oxford Forestry Institute.

Arrow, Kenneth J. 1951. *Social Choice and Individual Values*. 2d ed. New York: Wiley.

———. 1963. "Uncertainty and the Welfare Economics of Medical Care." *American Economic Review* 53:91–6.

———. 1974. *The Limits of Organization*. New York: W. W. Norton.

Ascher, William. 1995. *Communities and Sustainable Forestry in Developing Countries*. San Francisco: ICS Press.

Axelrod, Robert. 1981. "The Emergence of Cooperation among Egoists." *American Political Science Review* 75:306–18.

———. 1984. *The Evolution of Cooperation*. New York: Basic Books.

———. 1986. "An Evolutionary Approach to Norms." *American Political Science Review* 80:1095–111.

———. 1997. *The Complexity of Cooperation: Agent-Based Models of Competition and Collaboration*. Princeton: Princeton University Press.

Ayers, Ian, and John Braithwaite. 1992. *Responsive Regulation: Transcending the Regulation Debate*. Oxford: Oxford University Press.

Ayo, S. Bamidele. 2002. *Public Administration and the Conduct of Community Affairs among the Yoruba in Nigeria*. Oakland, CA: ICS Press.

Azar, Ofer H. 2004. "What Sustains Social Norms and How They Evolve? The Case of Tipping." *Journal of Economic Behavior and Organization* 54(1):49–64.

Bacharach, Michael, and Diego Gambetta. 2001. "Trust in Signs." In *Trust in Society*, ed. Karen S. Cook, 148–84. New York: Russell Sage Foundation.

Baker, Mark. 2005. *The Kuhls of Kangra: Community Managed Irrigation in the Western Himalaya*. Seattle: University of Washington Press.

Baland, Jean-Marie, and Jean-Phillipe Platteau. 1996. *Halting Degradation of Natural Resources: Is There a Role for Rural Communities?* Oxford: Clarendon Press.

Banana, Abwoli Y., and William Gombya-Ssembajjwe. 2000. "Successful Forest Management: The Importance of Security of Tenure and Rule Enforcement in Ugandan Forests." In *People and Forests: Communities, Institutions, and Governance*, ed. Clark Gibson, Margaret McKean, and Elinor Ostrom, 87–98. Cambridge: MIT Press.

Bardhan, Pranab K. 2000. "Irrigation and Cooperation: An Empirical Analysis of Forty-eight Irrigation Communities in South India." *Economic Development and Cultural Change* 48:847–65.

Bardhan, Pranab K., and Jeff Dayton-Johnson. 2002. "Unequal Irrigators: Heterogeneity and Commons Management in Large-Scale Multivariate Research." In *The Drama of the Commons*, National Research Council, Committee on the Human Dimensions of Global Change, ed. Elinor Ostrom, Thomas Dietz, Nives Dolšak, Paul Stern, Susan Stonich, and Elke Weber, 87–112. Washington, DC: National Academy Press.

Barker, Randolph, E. Walter Coward, Jr., Gilbert Levine, and Leslie E. Small. 1984. *Irrigation Development in Asia: Past Trends and Future Directions.* Ithaca: Cornell University Press.

Barkow, Jerome H., Leda Cosmides, and John Tooby, eds. 1992. *The Adapted Mind: Evolutionary Psychology and the Generation of Culture.* Oxford: Oxford University Press.

Barnard, Chester. 1938. *The Functions of the Executive.* Cambridge: Harvard University Press.

Barry, Brian, and Russell Hardin. 1982. *Rational Man and Irrational Society? An Introduction and Sourcebook.* Beverly Hills, CA: Sage.

Barwise, Jon, and John Perry. 1983. *Situations and Attitudes.* Cambridge: MIT Press.

Bates, Robert H. 1987. *Essays on the Political Economy of Rural Africa.* Berkeley and Los Angeles: University of California Press.

Bates, Robert H., Avner Greif, Margaret Levi, Jean-Laurent Rosenthal, and Barry Weingast. 1998. *Analytical Narratives.* Princeton: Princeton University Press.

———. 2000. "The Analytic Narrative Project." *American Political Science Review* 94 (September): 696–702.

Batistella, Mateus. 2001. "Landscape Change and Land-Use/Land-Cover Dynamics in Rondônia, Brazilian Amazon." Ph.D. diss., Indiana University.

Baumeister, Roy F., Arlene M. Stillwell, and Todd F. Heatherton. 1994. "Guilt: An Interpersonal Approach." *Psychological Bulletin* 115(2):243–67.

Becker, C. Dustin. 2003. "Grassroots to Grassroots: Why Forest Preservation Was Rapid at Loma Alta, Ecuador." *World Development* 31(1):163–76.

Benda-Beckmann, Franz von. 1995. "Anthropological Approaches to Property Law and Economics." *European Journal of Law and Economics* 2:309–36.

———. 1997. "Citizens, Strangers and Indigenous Peoples: Conceptual Politics and Legal Pluralism." *Law and Anthropology* 9:1–42.

———. 2000. "Relative Publics and Property Rights: A Cross-Cultural Perspective." In *Property and Values: Alternatives to Public and Private Ownership*, ed. Charles Geisler and Gail Daneker, 151–74. Washington, DC: Island Press.

———. 2001. "Between Free Riders and Free Raiders: Property Rights and Soil Degradation in Context." In *Economic Policy and Sustainable Land Use*, ed. Nico Heerink, Herman van Keulen, and Marijke Kuiper, 293–316. New York: Physica-Verlag.

Bendor, Jonathan. 1985. *Parallel Systems: Redundancy in Government*. Berkeley and Los Angeles: University of California Press.

———. 1995. "Book Review of *Rules, Games, and Common-Pool Resources*." *American Political Science Review* 89(1) (March): 188–89.

Bendor, Jonathan, and Dilip Mookherjee. 1990. "Norms, Third-Party Sanctions, and Cooperation." *Journal of Law, Economics, and Organization* 6:33–63.

Benedict, Ruth. 1934. *Patterns of Culture*. Boston: Houghton Mifflin.

Ben-Ner, Avner, and Louis Putterman. 2000a. "On Some Implications of Evolutionary Psychology for the Study of Preferences and Institutions." *Journal of Economic Behavior and Organization* 43(1):91–99.

———. 2000b. "Values Matter." *World Economics* 1(1):39–60.

Benz, Matthias, and Alois Stutzer. 2004. "Are Voters Better Informed When They Have a Larger Say in Politics? Evidence for the European Union and Switzerland." *Public Choice* 119(1–2):31–59.

Berg, Joyce, John Dickhaut, and Kevin McCabe. 1995. "Trust, Reciprocity, and Social History." *Games and Economic Behavior* 10(1):122–42.

Berkes, Fikret. 1985. "Fishermen and 'The Tragedy of the Commons.' " *Environmental Conservation* 12:199–206.

———. 1987. "Common Property Resource Management and Cree Indian Fisheries in Subarctic Canada." In *The Question of the Commons: The Culture and Ecology of Communal Resources*, ed. Bonnie J. McCay and James Acheson, 66–91. Tucson: University of Arizona Press.

———, ed. 1989. *Common Property Resources: Ecology and Community-Based Sustainable Development*. London: Belhaven Press.

Berkes, Fikret, Robin Mahon, Patrick McConney, Richard Pollnac, and Robert Pomeroy. 2001. *Managing Small-Scale Fisheries: Alternative Directions and Methods*. Ottawa: International Development Research Centre.

Bicchieri, Cristina. 1997. "Learning to Cooperate." In *The Dynamics of Norms*, ed. Cristina Bicchieri, Richard Jeffrey, and Brian Skyrms, 17–46. Cambridge: Cambridge University Press.

Bickers, Kenneth N., and John T. Williams. 2001. *Public Policy Analysis: A Political Economy Approach*. Boston: Houghton Mifflin.

Black, Max. 1962. *Models and Metaphors*. Ithaca: Cornell University Press.

Blomquist, William. 1992. *Dividing the Waters: Governing Groundwater in Southern California*. Oakland, CA: ICS Press.

———. 1994. "Changing Rules, Changing Games: Evidence from Groundwater Systems in Southern California." In *Rules, Games, and Common-Pool Resources*, ed. Elinor Ostrom, Roy Gardner, and James Walker, 283–300. Ann Arbor: University of Michigan Press.

Blomquist, William, and Helen M. Ingram. 2003. "Boundaries Seen and Unseen: Resolving Transboundary Groundwater Problems." *Water International* 28(2):162–69.

Blomquist, William, Edella Schlager, and Tanya Heikkila. 2004. *Common Waters, Diverging Streams: Linking Institutions and Water Management in Arizona, California, and Colorado*. Washington, DC: Resources for the Future.

Bloom, Paul. 2000. *How Children Learn the Meanings of Words*. Cambridge: MIT Press.

Bohnet, Iris, and Rachel Croson. 2004. "Introduction to Special Issue on Trust and Trustworthiness." *Journal of Economic Behavior and Organization* 55(4):443–45.

Bohnet, Iris, and Bruno S. Frey. 1999. "The Sound of Silence in Prisoner's Dilemma and Dictator Games." *Journal of Economic Behavior and Organization* 38(1) (January): 43–58.

Bolle, Friedel. 1998. "Rewarding Trust: An Experimental Study." *Theory and Decision* 45(1):83–98.

Bolton, Gary E., and Axel Ockenfels. 2000. "ERC: A Theory of Equity, Reciprocity, and Competition." *American Economic Review* 90:166–93.

Börgers, Tilman, and Rajiv Sarin. 1997. "Learning through Reinforcement and Replicator Dynamics." *Journal of Economic Theory* 77:1–14.

Boulding, Kenneth E. 1963. "Towards a Pure Theory of Threat Systems." *American Economic Review* 53:424–34.

Bourdieu, Pierre. 1977. *Outline of a Theory of Practice*. New York: Cambridge University Press.

Bowles, Samuel. 1998. "Endogenous Preferences: The Cultural Consequences of Markets and Other Institutions." *Journal of Economic Literature* 36 (March): 75–111.

Bowles, Samuel, and Herbert Gintis. 2004. "The Evolution of Strong Reciprocity: Cooperation in Heterogeneous Populations." *Theoretical Population Biology* 65(1):17–28.

Boyd, Robert, Herbert Gintis, Samuel Bowles, and Peter J. Richerson. 2003. "The Evolution of Altruistic Punishment." *Proceedings of the National Academy of Science* 100:3531–35.

Boyd, Robert, and Peter J. Richerson. 1985. *Culture and the Evolutionary Process*. Chicago: University of Chicago Press.

Brander, James A., and M. Scott Taylor. 1998. "The Simple Economics of Easter Island: A Recardo-Malthus Model of Renewable Resource Use." *American Economic Review* 88(1):119–38.

Brandts, Jordi, Tatsuyoshi Saijo, and Arthur Schram. 2004. "How Universal Is Behavior? A Four Country Comparison of Spite and Cooperation in Voluntary Contribution Mechanisms." *Public Choice* 119(3–4):381–424.

Braybrooke, David. 1987. *Philosophy of Social Science*. Englewood Cliffs, NJ: Prentice Hall.

———. 1996. "The Representation of Rules in Logic and Their Definition." In *Social Rules: Origin; Character; Logic; Change*, ed. David Braybrooke. Boulder, CO: Westview Press.

Brennan, Geoffrey, and James Buchanan. 1985. *The Reason of Rules: Constitutional Political Economy.* New York: Cambridge University Press.

Bromley, Daniel W. 1982. *Improving Irrigated Agriculture: Institutional Reform and the Small Farmer.* Working Paper no. 531. Washington, DC: World Bank.

Bromley, Daniel W., and Devendra P. Chapagain. 1984. "The Village against the Center: Resource Depletion in South Asia." *American Journal of Agricultural Economics* 66:868–73.

Bromley, Daniel W., David Feeny, Margaret McKean, Pauline Peters, Jere Gilles, Ronald Oakerson, C. Ford Runge, and James Thomson, eds. 1992. *Making the Commons Work: Theory, Practice, and Policy.* San Francisco: ICS Press.

Brosig, Jeannette. 2002. "Identifying Cooperative Behavior." *Journal of Economic Behavior and Organization* 47(3):275–90.

Brown, William M., and Christopher Moore. 2002. "Smile Asymmetries and Reputation as Reliable Indicators of Likelihood to Cooperate: An Evolutionary Analysis." In *Advances in Psychology Research*, ed. Serge Shohov, 59–78. Huntington, NY: Nova Science Publishers.

Brox, Ottar. 1990. "The Common Property Theory: Epistemological Status and Analytical Utility." *Human Organization* 49(3):227–35.

Bruner, Aaron, Raymond Gullison, Richard Rice, and Gustavo da Fonseca. 2001. "Effectiveness of Parks in Protecting Tropical Biodiversity." *Science* 291(5501):125–29.

Bruner, Jerome. 2004. "The Psychology of Learning: A Short History." *Daedalus* 133(1):13–20.

Buchan, Nancy R., Rachel T. Croson, and Eric J. Johnson. 1999. "Getting to Know You: An International Experiment of the Influence of Culture, Communication, and Social Distance on Trust and Reciprocation." Wharton School Working Paper no. 98–03–05. Philadelphia: University of Pennsylvania.

Buchanan, James M., and Alberto di Pierro. 1980. "Cognition, Choice, and Entrepreneurship." *Southern Economic Journal* 46(3):693–701.

Buchanan, James M., and Gordon Tullock. 1962. *The Calculus of Consent.* Ann Arbor: University of Michigan Press.

Burns, James MacGregor. 1963. *The Deadlock of Democracy: Four-Party Politics in America.* Englewood Cliffs, NJ: Prentice Hall.

Burns, Tom R., and Tom Dietz. 1991. "Institutional Dynamics: An Evolutionary Perspective." Paper presented at the Fifteenth World Congress of the International Political Science Association, Buenos Aires, Argentina, July 21–25.

Burns, Tom R., and Helena Flam. 1987. *The Shaping of Social Organization: Social Rule System Theory with Applications.* Beverly Hills, CA: Sage.

Burns, Tom R., and Anna Gomolińska. 1998. "Modelling Social Game Systems by Rule Complexes." In *Rough Sets and Current Trends in Computing: Proceedings of the First International Conference, Warsaw, Poland*, ed. Lech Polkowski and Andrzej Skowron, 581–84. Berlin/Heidelberg: Springer-Verlag.

Busemeyer, Jerome R., and In Jae Myung. 1992. "An Adaptive Approach to Human Decision Making: Learning Theory, Decision Theory, and Human Performance." *Journal of Experimental Psychology: General* 121(2):177–94.

Bushouse, Brenda K. 1999. "The Mixed Economy of Child Care: An Institutional Analysis of Nonprofit, For-Profit, and Public Enterprises." Ph.D. diss., Indiana University.

Cain, Michael. 1998. "An Experimental Investigation of Motives and Information in the Prisoner's Dilemma Game." *Advances in Group Processes* 15:133–60.

Calvert, Randall L. 1992. "Rational Actors, Equilibrium, and Social Institutions." Paper presented at the Public Choice Meetings, New Orleans, LA, March.

———. 1995. "The Rational Choice Theory of Social Institutions: Cooperation, Coordination, and Communication." In *Modern Political Economy: Old Topics, New Directions*, ed. Jeffrey Banks and Eric Hanushek, 216–18. New York: Cambridge University Press.

Camerer, Colin F. 2003. *Behavioral Game Theory: Experiments in Strategic Interaction*. Princeton: Princeton University Press.

Cameron, Lisa A. 1999. "Raising the Stakes in the Ultimatum Game: Experimental Evidence from Indonesia." *Economic Inquiry* 37(1):47–59.

Campbell, Donald T. 1969. "Reforms as Experiments." *American Psychologist* 24(4):409–29.

———. 1975. "On the Conflicts between Biological and Social Evolution and between Psychology and Moral Tradition." *American Psychologist* 30(11):1103–26.

Cardenas, Juan-Camilo. 2000. "How Do Groups Solve Local Commons Dilemmas? Lessons from Experimental Economics in the Field." *Environment, Development and Sustainability* 2:305–22.

———. 2003. "Real Wealth and Experimental Cooperation: Evidence from Field Experiments." *Journal of Development Economics* 70:263–89.

Cardenas, Juan-Camilo, John K. Stranlund, and Cleve E. Willis. 2000. "Local Environmental Control and Institutional Crowding-Out." *World Development* 28(10):1719–33.

Carlson, Jean M., and John Doyle. 2002. "Complexity and Robustness." *Proceedings of the National Academy of Sciences* 9 (suppl. 1) (February 19): 2499–545.

Carr, Jered, and Richard Feiock. 2004. *City-County Consolidation and Its Alternatives: Reshaping the Local Governing Landscape*. Armonk, NY: M. E. Sharpe.

Carson, Richard T., Nadja Marinova, and David Zilberman. 1999. "Smoothing the Waters: The Jordan Rift." Policy Brief 11–1. San Diego: University of California, Institute on Global Conflict and Cooperation.

Casari, Marco, and Charles R. Plott. 2003. "Decentralized Management of Common Property Resources: Experiments with a Centuries-Old Institution." *Journal of Economic Behavior and Organization* 51:217–47.

Cashdan, Elizabeth. 1990. *Risk and Uncertainty in Tribal and Peasant Economies*. Boulder, CO: Westview Press.

Cernea, Michael M. 1989. *User Groups as Producers in Participatory Afforestation Strategies*. World Bank Discussion Papers no. 70. Washington, DC: World Bank.

Chakraborty, Rabindra N. 2004. "Sharing Rules and the Commons: Evidence from Ha'apai, Tonga." *Environment and Development Economics* 9:455–72.

Chamberlin, John. 1974. "Provision of Collective Goods as a Function of Group Size." *American Political Science Review* 68(2) (June): 707–16.

Chan, Kenneth S., Rob Godby, Stuart Mestelman, and R. Andrew Muller. 1997. "Equity Theory and the Voluntary Provision of Public Goods." *Journal of Economic Behavior and Organization* 32:349–64.

Charness, Gary, and Matthew Rabin. 2003. "Understanding Social Preferences with Simple Tests." *Quarterly Journal of Economics* 117:817–69.

Choe, Jaesong. 1992. "The Organization of Urban Common-Property Institutions: The Case of Apartment Communities in Seoul." Ph.D. diss., Indiana University.

Choe, Olivia S. 2004. "Appurtenancy Reconceptualized: Managing Water in an Era of Scarcity." *Yale Law Journal* 113 (June): 1909–53.

Ciriacy-Wantrup, Siegfried V., and Richard C. Bishop. 1975. " 'Common Property' as a Concept in Natural Resource Policy." *Natural Resources Journal* 15(4):713–27.

Clark, Andy, and Annette Karmiloff-Smith. 1991. "The Cognizer's Innards: A Psychological and Philosophical Perspective on the Development of Thought." *Mind and Language* 8(4) (Winter): 487–519.

Coase, Ronald H. 1937. "The Nature of the Firm." *Economica* 4:386–405.

Coglianese, Cary, Jennifer Nash, and Todd Olmstead. 2003. "Performance-Based Regulation: Prospects and Limitations in Health, Safety, and Environmental Protection." *Administrative Law Review* 55(4):705–29.

Coleman, James S. 1964. *Introduction to Mathematical Sociology.* New York: Free Press.

———. 1973. *The Mathematics of Collective Action.* Chicago: Aldine.

———. 1987. "Norms as Social Capital." In *Economic Imperialism,* ed. Gerard Radnitzky and Peter Bernholz, 133–55. New York: Paragon.

———. 1988. "Free Riders and Zealots: The Role of Social Networks." *Sociological Theory* 6 (Spring): 52–7.

Commons, John R. [1924] 1968. *Legal Foundations of Capitalism.* Madison: University of Wisconsin Press.

Conning, Jonathan, and Michael Kevane. 2002. "Community Based Targeting Mechanisms for Social Safety Nets: A Critical Review." *World Development* 30(3):375–94.

Cook, Karen S., and Robin M. Cooper. 2003. "Experimental Studies of Cooperation, Trust, and Social Exchange." In *Trust and Reciprocity: Interdisciplinary Lessons from Experimental Research,* ed. Elinor Ostrom and James Walker, 209–44. New York: Russell Sage Foundation.

Cooter, Robert D. 1994. "Structural Adjudication and the New Law Merchant: A Model of Decentralized Law." *International Review of Law and Economics* 14:215–31.

Cooter, Robert D., and Thomas S. Ulen. 1996. *Law and Economics.* 2d ed. Reading, MA: Addison-Wesley.

Copes, Parzival. 1986. "A Critical Review of the Individual Quota as a Device in Fisheries Management." *Land Economics* 62(3):278–91.

Cordell, John C., and Margaret McKean. 1992. "Sea Tenure in Bahia, Brazil." In *Making the Commons Work: Theory, Practice, and Policy*, ed. Daniel W. Bromley et al., 183–205. San Francisco: ICS Press.

Corson, Trevor. 2002. "Stalking the American Lobster." *Atlantic Monthly* (April): 62–81.

Cox, James C. 2004. "How to Identify Trust and Reciprocity." *Games and Economic Behavior* 46:260–81.

Cox, James C., and Cary Deck. In press. "On the Nature of Reciprocal Motives." *Economic Inquiry* 43(3).

Cox, James C., Daniel Friedman, and Steven Gjerstad. 2004. "A Tractable Model of Reciprocity and Fairness." Working Paper. Tucson: University of Arizona, Department of Economics.

Cox, James C., and Vjollca Sadiraj. 2004. "Direct Tests of Models of Social Preferences and a New Model." Economics Lab Working Paper. Tucson: University of Arizona.

Crawford, Sue E. S., and Elinor Ostrom. 2000. "A Grammar of Institutions." Reprinted in *Polycentric Games and Institutions: Readings from the Workshop in Political Theory and Policy Analysis*, ed. Michael McGinnis, 114–55. Ann Arbor: University of Michigan Press. Originally published in *American Political Science Review* 89(3) (September 1995): 582–600.

Crawford, Vincent P., and Joel Sobel. 1982. "Strategic Information Transmission." *Econometrica* 50:1431–51.

Crook, Darren S., and Anne M. Jones. 1999. "Design Principles from Traditional Mountain Irrigation Systems (Bisses) in the Valais, Switzerland." *Mountain Research and Development* 19(2):79–122.

Crutchfield, James P., and Peter Schuster. 2003. *Evolutionary Dynamics: Exploring the Interplay of Selection, Accident, Neutrality, and Function*. Oxford: Oxford University Press.

Cruz, Wilfrido D. 1986. "Overfishing and Conflict in a Traditional Fishery: San Miguel Bay, Philippines." In *Proceedings of the Conference on Common Property Resource Management*, National Research Council, 115–35. Washington, DC: National Academy Press.

Cummins, Denise D. 1996. "Evidence of Deontic Reasoning in Three- and Four-Year-Old Children." *Memory and Cognition* 24(6):823–29.

Dahlman, Carl J. 1980. *The Open Field System and Beyond: A Property Rights Analysis of an Economic Institution*. New York: Cambridge University Press.

Dana, David. 2001. "Rethinking the Puzzle of Escalating Penalties for Repeat Offenders." *Yale Law Journal* 110 (March): 733–83.

Dannin, Ellen, and Gangaram Singh. Forthcoming. "Creating a Law Reform Laboratory: Empirical Research and Labor Law Reform." *Wayne Law Review* 50.

Dasgupta, Partha. 1982. *The Control of Resources*. Cambridge: Harvard University Press.

Dawes, Robyn M. 1988. *Rational Choice in an Uncertain World*. Chicago: Harcourt Brace Jovanovich.

Deadman, Peter. 1997. "Modeling Individual Behavior in Common Pool Resource Management Experiments with Autonomous Agents." Ph.D. diss., University of Arizona, Tucson.

de Castro, Fabio. 2000. "Fishing Accords: The Political Ecology of Fishing Intensification in the Amazon." Ph.D. diss., Indiana University.

Deci, Edward L. 1975. *Intrinsic Motivation*. New York: Plenum Press.

Deci, Edward L., Richard Koestner, and Richard M. Ryan. 1999. "A Meta-Analytic Review of Experiments Examining the Effects of Extrinsic Rewards on Intrinsic Motivation." *Psychological Bulletin* 125(6):627–68.

Deci, Edward L., and Richard M. Ryan. 1985. *Intrinsic Motivation and Self-Determination in Human Behavior*. New York: Plenum Press.

Decker, Christopher S., and Rafael Reuveny. 2005. "Endogenous Technological Progress and the Malthusian Trap: Could Simon and Boserup Have Saved Easter Island?" *Human Ecology* 33(1):119–40.

Delhey, Jan, and Ken Newton. 2003. "Who Trusts? The Origins of Social Trust in Seven Societies." *European Societies* 5:93–137.

de los Reyes, Romana P. 1980. *Managing Communal Gravity Systems: Farmers' Approaches and Implications for Program Planning*. Quezon City, Philippines: Ateneo de Manila University, Institute of Philippine Culture.

de Moor, Martina, Leigh Shaw-Taylor, and Paul Warde. 2002. *The Management of Common Land in North West Europe, c. 1500–1850*. Turnhout, Belgium: Brepols Publishers.

Demsetz, Harold. 1967. "Toward a Theory of Property Rights." *American Economic Review* 57 (May): 347–59.

Denzau, Arthur T., and Douglass C. North. 2000. "Shared Mental Models: Ideologies and Institutions." In *Elements of Reason—Cognition, Choice, and the Bounds of Rationality*, ed. Arthur Lupia, Mathew D. McCubbins, and Samuel L. Popkin, 23–46. Cambridge: Cambridge University Press.

de Soto, Hernando. 2000. *The Mystery of Capital: Why Capitalism Triumphs in the West and Fails Everywhere Else*. New York: Basic Books.

Diamond, Jared. 2005. *Collapse: How Societies Choose to Fail or Succeed*. New York: Viking.

Dickhaut, John, John Hubbard, Kevin McCabe, and Vernon Smith. 1997. "Trust, Reciprocity, and Interpersonal History: Fool Me Once, Shame on You, Fool Me Twice, Shame on Me." Working Paper. Tucson: University of Arizona.

Diermeier, Daniel, and Keith Krehbiel. 2003. "Institutionalism as a Methodology." *Journal of Theoretical Politics* 15(2):123–44.

Dietz, Thomas, Elinor Ostrom, and Paul Stern. 2003. "The Struggle to Govern the Commons." *Science* 302 (December 12): 1907–12.

DiMaggio, Paul J., and Walter W. Powell. 1991. Introduction to *The New Institutionalism in Organizational Analysis*, ed. Walter W. Powell and Paul J. DiMaggio, 1–34. Chicago: University of Chicago Press.

Dixit, Avinash K., and Susan Skeath. 1999. *Games of Strategy*. New York: W. W. Norton.

Dolšak, Nives. 2000. "Marketable Permits: Managing Local, Regional, and Global Commons." Ph.D. diss., Indiana University.

Dougherty, Keith. 2001. *Collective Action under the Articles of Confederation*. Cambridge: Cambridge University Press.

Downs, Anthony. 1957. *An Economic Theory of Democracy*. New York: Harper and Row.

Dryzek, John S. 2000. *Deliberative Democracy and Beyond: Liberals, Critics, Contestations*. Oxford: Oxford University Press.

Dye, Thomas R. 1981. *Understanding Public Policy*. 4th ed. Englewood Cliffs, NJ: Prentice Hall.

Ebbin, Syma A. 2002. "Enhanced Fit through Institutional Interplay in the Pacific Northwest Salmon Co-management Regime." *Marine Policy* 26:253–59.

———. 2004. "The Anatomy of Conflict and the Politics of Identity in Two Co-operative Salmon Management Regimes." *Policy Sciences* 37(1):71–87.

Eggertsson, Thráinn. 2005. *Imperfect Institutions: Possibilities and Limits of Reform*. Ann Arbor: University of Michigan Press.

Ellickson, Robert C. 1991. *Order without Law: How Neighbors Settle Disputes*. Cambridge: Harvard University Press.

Elster, Jon. 1979. *Ulysses and the Sirens: Studies in Rationality and Irrationality*. Cambridge: Cambridge University Press.

———. 1989a. *The Cement of Society: A Study of Social Order*. Cambridge: Cambridge University Press.

———. 1989b. *Solomonic Judgements: Studies in the Limitations of Rationality*. Cambridge: Cambridge University Press.

———, ed. 1998. *Deliberative Democracy*. New York: Cambridge University Press.

Ensminger, Jean. 1990. "Co-opting the Elders: The Political Economy of State Incorporation in Africa." *American Anthropologist* 92:662–75.

———. 2000. "Experimental Economics in the Bush: Why Institutions Matter." In *Institutions, Contracts, and Organizations*, ed. Claude Menard, 158–71. London: Edward Elgar.

———. 2001. "Reputations, Trust, and the Principal Agent Problem." In *Trust in Society*, ed. Karen S. Cook, 185–201. New York: Russell Sage Foundation.

Ensminger, Jean, and Jack Knight. 1997. "Changing Social Norms: Common Property, Bridewealth, and Clan Exogamy." *Current Anthropology* 38(1): 1–24.

Epstein, Joshua M. 2001. "Learning to Be Thoughtless: Social Norms and Individual Computation." *Computational Economics* 18(1):9–24.

Esarey, Justin, and T. K. Ahn. 2004. "Strategic and Norm-Based Behavior in a Laboratory Experiment." Paper presented at the American Political Science Annual Meeting, Chicago.

Eshel, Ilan, Larry Samuelson, and Avner Shaked. 1998. "Altruists, Egoists, and Hooligans in a Local Interaction Model." *American Economic Review* 88(1) (March): 157–79.

Etzioni, Amitai. 1988. *The Moral Dimension: Toward a New Economics*. New York: Free Press.

Falk, Armin, Ernst Fehr, and Urs Fischbacher. 2002. "Appropriating the Commons: A Theoretical Explanation." In *The Drama of the Commons*, National Research Council, Committee on the Human Dimensions of Global Change, ed. Elinor Ostrom, Thomas Dietz, Nives Dolšak, Paul C. Stern, Susan Stonich, and Elke Weber, 157–92. Washington, DC: National Academy Press.

Farr, James. 1985. "Situational Analysis: Explanation in Political Science." *Journal of Politics* 47(4) (November): 1085–107.

Farrell, James. 1993. "Meaning and Credibility in Cheap-Talk Games." *Games and Economic Behavior* 5:514–31.

Faysse, Nicolas. 2003. "Allocating Irrigation Water: The Impact of Strategic Interactions on the Efficiency of Rules." *European Review of Agricultural Economics* 30(3):305–32.

Feeny, David. 1988. "Agricultural Expansion and Forest Depletion in Thailand, 1900–1975." In *World Deforestation in the Twentieth Century*, ed. John F. Richards and Richard P. Tucker, 112–43. Durham, NC: Duke University Press.

Feeny, David, Susan Hanna, and Arthur F. McEvoy. 1996. "Questioning the Assumptions of the 'Tragedy of the Commons' Model of Fisheries." *Land Economics* 72(2) (May): 187–205.

Fehr, Ernst, and Armin Falk. 1999. "Wage Rigidity in a Competitive Incomplete Contract Market." *Journal of Political Economy* 107:106–34.

Fehr, Ernst, and Simon Gächter. 1998. "Reciprocity and Economics: The Economic Implications of *Homo Reciprocans*." *European Economic Review* 42(3–5):845–59.

———. 2000a. "Cooperation and Punishment in Public Goods Experiments." *American Economic Review* 90(4):980–94.

———. 2000b. "Fairness and Retaliation: The Economics of Reciprocity." *Journal of Economic Perspectives* 14(3):159–81.

———. Forthcoming. "Do Incentive Contracts Undermine Voluntary Cooperation?" *Review of Economic Studies*.

Fehr, Ernst, Simon Gächter, and Georg Kirchsteiger. 1996. "Reciprocal Fairness and Non-compensating Wage Differentials." *Journal of Institutional and Theoretical Economics* 152(4):608–40.

Fehr, Ernst, Georg Kirchsteiger, and Arno Riedl. 1993. "Does Fairness Prevent Market Clearing? An Experimental Investigation." *Quarterly Journal of Economics* 108(2):437–60.

Fehr, Ernst, and Bettina Rockenbach. 2003. "Detrimental Effects of Sanctions on Human Altruism." *Nature* 422 (March 13): 137–40.

Fehr, Ernst, and Klaus Schmidt. 1999. "A Theory of Fairness, Competition, and Cooperation." *Quarterly Journal of Economics* 114(3):817–68.

Finlayson, A. Christopher, and Bonnie J. McCay. 1998. "Crossing the Threshold of Ecosystem Resilience: The Commercial Extinction of Northern Cod." In *Linking Social and Ecological Systems: Management Practices and Social Mechanisms for Building Resilience*, ed. Fikret Berkes and Carl Folke, 311–38. New York: Cambridge University Press.

Firmin-Sellers, Kathryn. 1996. *The Transformation of Property Rights in the Gold Coast: An Empirical Study Applying Rational Choice Theory*. New York: Cambridge University Press.

Fishburn, Peter C. 1974. "Lexicographic Orders, Utilities, and Decision Rules: A Survey." *Management Science* 20:1442–71.

Fisher, Frank. 2003. *Reframing Public Policy: Discursive Politics and Deliberative Practices*. Oxford: Oxford University Press.

Foliente, Greg C. 2000. "Developments in Performance-Based Building Codes and Standards." *Forest Products Journal* 50(7–8):12–21.

Folke, Carl, Fikret Berkes, and Johan Colding. 1998. "Ecological Practices and Social Mechanisms for Building Resilience and Sustainability." In *Linking Social and Ecological Systems: Management Practices and Social Mechanisms for Building Resilience*, ed. Fikres Berkes and Carl Folke, 414–36. New York: Cambridge University Press.

Fortmann, Louise, and John W. Bruce. 1988. *Whose Trees? Proprietary Dimensions of Forestry.* Boulder, CO: Westview Press.

Frank, Robert. 1988. *Passions within Reason: The Strategic Role of the Emotions.* New York: W. W. Norton.

Frey, Bruno S. 1994. "How Intrinsic Motivation Is Crowded Out and In." *Rationality and Society* 6:334–52.

———. 1997a. *Not Just for the Money: An Economic Theory of Personal Motivation.* Cheltenham, England: Edward Elgar.

———. 1997b. "A Constitution for Knaves Crowds out Civic Virtue." *Economic Journal* 107:1043–53.

Frey, Bruno S., Matthias Benz, and Alois Stutzer. 2004. "Introducing Procedural Utility: Not Only What, but also How Matters." *Journal of Institutional and Theoretical Economics* 160(3):377–401.

Frey, Bruno S., and Reto Jegen. 2001. "Motivation Crowding Theory: A Survey of Empirical Evidence." *Journal of Economic Surveys* 15(5):589–611.

Frohlich, Norman, and Joe A. Oppenheimer. 1996. "Experiencing Impartiality to Invoke Fairness in the n-PD: Some Experimental Results." *Public Choice* 86(1–2):117–35.

———. 2001. "Choosing: A Cognitive Model of Economic and Political Choice." Working Paper. Winnipeg: University of Manitoba, Faculty of Management.

Frohlich, Norman, Joe A. Oppenheimer, and Cheryl Eavey. 1987. "Choices of Principles of Distributive Justice in Experimental Groups." *American Journal of Political Science* 31(3):606–36.

Frohlich, Norman, Joe Oppenheimer, and Anja Kurki. 2004. "Modeling Other-Regarding Preferences and an Experimental Test." *Public Choice* 119(1–2): 91–117.

Fudenberg, Drew, Bengt Holmström, and Paul Milgrom. 1990. "Short-Term Contracts and Long-Term Agency Relationship." *Journal of Economic Theory* 51:1–31.

Futemma, Celia. 2000. "Collective Action and Assurance of Property Rights to Natural Resources: A Case Study from the Lower Amazon Region, Santarem, Brazil." Ph.D. diss., Indiana University.

Gadgil, Madhav, Natabar Shyam Hemam, and B. Mohan Reddy. 1998. "People, Refugia, and Resilience." In *Linking Social and Ecological Systems: Management Practices and Social Mechanisms for Building Resilience*, ed. Fikret Berkes and Carl Folke, 30–47. New York: Cambridge University Press.

Gadgil, Madhav, and Prema Iyer. 1989. "On the Diversification of Common-Property Resource Use by Indian Society." In *Common Property Resources: Ecology and Community-Based Sustainable Development*, ed. Fikret Berkes, 240–72. London: Belhaven Press.

Gambetta, Diego, ed. 1988. *Trust: Making and Breaking Cooperative Relations.* Oxford: Oxford University Press.

Ganz, Joan S. 1971. *Rules: A Systematic Study*. Paris: Mouton.

Gardner, Roy. 2003. *Games for Business and Economics*. 2d ed. New York: Wiley.

Gardner, Roy, and Elinor Ostrom. 1991. "Rules and Games." *Public Choice* 70(2) (May): 121–49.

Gavrilets, Sergey. 2003. "Evolution and Speciation in a Hyperspace: The Roles of Neutrality, Selection, Mutation, and Random Drift." In *Evolutionary Dynamics: Exploring the Interplay of Selection, Accident, Neutrality, and Function*, ed. James P. Crutchfield and Peter Schuster, 135–62. Oxford: Oxford University Press.

Gellar, Sheldon. 2005. *Democracy in Senegal: Tocquevillian Analytics in Africa*. New York: Palgrave Macmillan.

Ghate, Rucha. 2000. "The Role of Autonomy in Self-Organizing Processes: A Case Study of Local Forest Management in India." Paper presented at the Workshop in Political Theory and Policy Analysis miniconference, Indiana University, Bloomington.

———. 2003. "Global Gains at Local Costs: Imposing Protected Areas; Evidence from Central India." *International Journal of Sustainable Development and World Ecology* 10(4):377–89.

Gibbard, Allan. 1990. "Norms, Discussion, and Ritual: Evolutionary Puzzles." *Ethics* 100 (July): 787–802.

Gibson, Clark. 1999. *Politicians and Poachers: The Political Economy of Wildlife Policy in Africa*. New York: Cambridge University Press.

———. 2001. "Forest Resources: Institutions for Local Governance in Guatemala." In *Protecting the Commons: A Framework for Resource Management in the Americas*, ed. Joanna Burger, Elinor Ostrom, Richard B. Norgaard, David Policansky, and Bernard D. Goldstein, 71–89. Washington, DC: Island Press.

Gibson, Clark, Krister Andersson, Elinor Ostrom, and Sujai Shivakumar. 2005. *The Samaritan's Dilemma: The Political Economy of Development Aid*. Oxford: Oxford University Press.

Gibson, Clark, and C. Dustin Becker. 2000. "A Lack of Institutional Demand: Why a Strong Local Community in Western Ecuador Fails to Protect Its Forest." In *People and Forests: Communities, Institutions, and Governance*, ed. Clark Gibson, Margaret McKean, and Elinor Ostrom, 135–61. Cambridge: MIT Press.

Gibson, Clark, Margaret McKean, and Elinor Ostrom, eds. 2000. *People and Forests: Communities, Institutions, and Governance*. Cambridge: MIT Press.

Gibson, Clark, John Williams, and Elinor Ostrom. 2005. "Local Enforcement and Better Forests." *World Development* 33(2):273–84.

Giddens, Anthony. 1979. *Central Problems in Social Theory: Action, Structure, and Contradiction in Social Analysis*. Berkeley and Los Angeles: University of California Press.

Gigerenzer, Gerd, and Daniel G. Goldstein. 1996. "Reasoning the Fast and Frugal Way: Models of Bounded Rationality." *Psychological Review* 103(4):650–69.

Gigerenzer, Gerd, and Reinhard Selten, eds. 2001. *Bounded Rationality: The Adaptive Toolbox*. Cambridge: MIT Press.

Gigerenzer, Gerd, Peter M. Todd, and the ABC Research Group. 1999. *Simple Heuristics that Make Us Smart*. Oxford: Oxford University Press.

Gilles, Jere L., and Keith Jamtgaard. 1981. "Overgrazing in Pastoral Areas: The Commons Reconsidered." *Sociologia Ruralis* 21:129–41.

Gintis, Herbert. 2000a. "Beyond *Homo Economicus*: Evidence from Experimental Economics." *Ecological Economics* 35(3):311–22.

———. 2000b. *Game Theory Evolving: A Problem-Centered Introduction to Modeling Strategic Interaction*. Princeton: Princeton University Press.

———. 2004. "The Genetic Side of Gene-Culture Coevolution: Internalization of Norms and Prosocial Emotions." *Journal of Economic Behavior and Organization* 53(1):57–67.

Glaeser, Edward, David Labson, Jose Scheinkman, and Christine Soutter. 2000. "Measuring Trust." *Quarterly Journal of Economics* 115(3):811–46.

Gode, Dhananjay K., and Shyam Sunder. 1997. "What Makes Markets Allocationally Efficient?" *Quarterly Journal of Economics* 112(2) (May): 603–30.

Goffman, Irving. 1974. *Frame Analysis: An Essay on the Organization of Experience*. Cambridge: Harvard University Press.

Gombya-Ssembajjwe, William. 1995. "Sacred Forests in Modern Ganda Society." *Uganda Journal* 42:32–44.

Goodland, Robert, George Ledec, and Maryla Webb. 1989. "Meeting Environmental Concerns Caused by Common-Property Mismanagement in Economic Development Projects." In *Common Property Resources: Ecology and Community-Based Sustainable Development*, ed. Fikret Berkes, 148–63. London: Belhaven Press.

Gopnik, Alison. 2004. "Finding Our Inner Scientist." *Daedalus* 133(1):21–28.

Gordillo, Gustavo, and Krister Andersson. 2004. "From Policy Lessons to Policy Actions: Motivation to Take Evaluation Seriously." *Public Administration and Development* 24:305–20.

Gordon, H. Scott. 1954. "The Economic Theory of a Common Property Resource: The Fishery." *Journal of Political Economy* 62:124–42.

Grafton, R. Quentin. 2000. "Governance of the Commons: A Role for the State." *Land Economics* 76(4):504–17.

Grainger, Alan. 1993. *Controlling Tropical Deforestation*. London: Earthscan Publications.

Granovetter, Mark. 1978. "Threshold Models of Collective Behavior." *American Journal of Sociology* 83:1420–43.

Greif, Avner, Paul Milgrom, and Barry R. Weingast. 1994. "Coordination, Commitment, and Enforcement: The Case of the Merchant Guild." *Journal of Political Economy* 102:745–77.

Grether, David M., R. Mark Isaac, and Charles R. Plott. 1979. "Alternative Methods of Allocating Airport Slots: Performance and Evaluation." Report prepared for the Civil Aeronautics Board and Federal Aviation Administration, Polinomics Research Laboratories, Inc., Pasadena, California.

———. 1981. "The Allocation of Landing Rights by Unanimity among Competitors." *American Economic Review* 71(2):166–71.

Grether, David M., and Charles R. Plott. 1979. "Economic Theory of Choice and the Preference Phenomenon." *American Economic Review* 69 (September): 623–38.

Greve, Michael S. 2001. "Affirmative Action Is on the Rocks, Thanks to College Leaders." *Chronicle of Higher Education*, April 20, 2001.

Grimm, Volker, and Christian Wissel. 1997. "Babel, or the Ecological Stability Discussions: An Inventory and Analysis of Terminology and a Guide for Avoiding Confusion." *Oecologia* 109:323–34.

Guillet, David W. 1992a. "Comparative Irrigation Studies: The Órbigo Valley of Spain and the Colca Valley of Perú." *Polígonos* 2:141–50.

——. 1992b. *Covering Ground: Communal Water Management and the State in the Peruvian Highlands*. Ann Arbor: University of Michigan Press.

Gunderson, Lance H., and Crawford S. Holling, eds. 2001. *Panarchy: Understanding Transformations in Human and Natural Systems*. Washington, DC: Island Press.

Gunderson, Lance H., and Lowell Pritchard, Jr., eds. 2002. *Resilience and the Behavior of Large-Scale Systems*. Washington, DC: Island Press.

Gupta, Radhika, and Sunandan Tiwari. 2002. "At the Crossroads: Continuity and Change in the Traditional Irrigation Practices of Ladakh." Paper presented at "The Commons in an Age of Globalization," the Ninth Conference of the International Association for the Study of Common Property, Victoria Falls, Zimbabwe.

Gürerk, Özgür, Bernd Irlenbusch, and Bettina Rockenbach. 2004. "On the Evolvement of Institutions in Social Dilemmas." Working Paper. Erfurt, Germany: University of Erfurt, Laboratory for Experimental Economics.

Güth, Werner. 1988. "On the Behavioral Approach to Distributive Justice—A Theoretical and Experimental Investigation." In *Applied Behavioral Economics*, vol. 2, ed. Shlomo Maital, 703–17. New York: New York University Press.

——. 1995. "An Evolutionary Approach to Explaining Cooperative Behavior by Reciprocal Incentives." *International Journal of Game Theory* 24:323–44.

Güth, Werner, and Hartmut Kliemt. 1998. "The Indirect Evolutionary Approach: Bridging the Gap between Rationality and Adaptation." *Rationality and Society* 10(3) (August): 377–99.

Güth, Werner, and Wilhelm Neuefeind. 2001. "Heuristics as Decision Rules—Part 1: The Single Consumer." Discussion paper. Berlin: Humboldt University.

Güth, Werner, Peter Ockenfels, and Markus Wendel. 1997. "Cooperation Based on Trust: An Experimental Investigation." *Journal of Economic Psychology* 18(1):15–43.

Güth, Werner, and Menahem Yaari. 1992. "An Evolutionary Approach to Explaining Reciprocal Behavior in a Simple Strategic Game." In *Explaining Process and Change: Approaches to Evolutionary Economics*, ed. Ulrich Witt, 23–34. Ann Arbor: University of Michigan Press.

Habermas, Jürgen. 1996. *Between Facts and Norms: Contributions to a Discourse Theory of Law and Democracy*. Cambridge: MIT Press.

Hackett, Steven. 1992. "Heterogeneity and the Provision of Governance for Common-Pool Resources." *Journal of Theoretical Politics* 4 (July): 325–42.

Hackett, Steven, Edella Schlager, and James Walker. 1994. "The Role of Communication in Resolving Commons Dilemmas: Experimental Evidence with Heterogeneous Appropriators." *Journal of Environmental Economics and Management* 27:99–126.

Haley, Sharman. 2002. "Sustainable Development and Oil: Lessons from the Ecuadorian Amazon." *Cultural Survival Quarterly* 26:65–68.

Haller, Tobias. 2001. "Rules Which Pay Are Going to Stay: Indigenous Institutions, Sustainable Resouerce Use and Land Tenure among the Ouldem and Paltha, Mandara Mountains, Northern Cameroon." In *Everyday Governance of Land in Africa*, ed. Pierre-Yyes Le Meur and Christian Lund, 117–32. New Brunswick, NJ: Transaction Publishers.

———. 2002. "Common Property Resource Management, Institutional Change, and Conflict in African Floodplain Wetlands." *African Anthropologist* 9(1):25–35.

Hamburger, Henry. 1979. *Games as Models of Social Phenomena*. San Francisco: W. H. Freeman.

Hammerstein, Peter, ed. 2003. *Genetic and Cultural Evolution of Cooperation*. Cambridge: MIT Press.

Hammond, Thomas H., and Christopher K. Butler. 2003. "Some Complex Answers to the Simple Question 'Do Institutions Matter?': Policy Choice and Policy Change in Presidential and Parliamentary Systems." *Journal of Theoretical Politics* 15(2):145–200.

Hardin, Garrett. 1968. "The Tragedy of the Commons." *Science* 162:1243–48.

Hardin, Russell. 1982. *Collective Action*. Baltimore: Johns Hopkins University Press.

Harré, Rom. 1974. "Some Remarks on 'Rule' as a Scientific Concept." In *Understanding Other Persons*, ed. Theodore Mischel, 143–84. Oxford: Basil Blackwell.

Harsanyi, John C. 1955. "Cardinal Welfare, Individual Ethics, and Interpersonal Comparison of Utility." *Journal of Political Economy* 63(4):309–21.

———. 1967–68. "Games with Incomplete Information Played by 'Bayesian' Players." *Management Science* 14:159–82, 320–34, 486–502.

Hart, Herbert L. A. 1961. *The Concept of Law*. Oxford: Clarendon Press.

Hasson, Uri, Yuval Nir, Ifat Levy, Galit Fuhrmann, and Rafael Malach. 2004. "Intersubject Synchronization of Cortical Activity during Natural Vision." *Science* 303 (March 12): 1634–40.

Hawkes, Kristen, James F. O'Connell, and Nicholas G. Blurton Jones. 2001. "Hadza Meat Sharing." *Evolution and Human Behavior* 22:113–42.

Hawley, Amos, and Basil G. Zimmer. 1970. *The Metropolitan Community: Its People and Government*. Beverly Hills, CA: Sage.

Hayes, Tanya. 2004. "Parks, People, and Forest Protection: An Institutional Assessment of the Effectiveness of Protected Areas." Working Paper. Bloomington: Indiana University, Center for the Study of Institutions, Population, and Environmental Change (CIPEC).

Heal, Geoffrey M. 1998. *Valuing the Future: Economic Theory and Sustainability*. New York: Colombia University Press.

Hechter, Michael, and Karl-Dieter Opp, eds. 2001. *Social Norms*. New York: Russell Sage Foundation.

Heikkila, Tanya. 2004. "Institutional Boundaries and Common-Pool Resource Management: A Comparative Analysis of Water Management Programs in California." *Journal of Policy Analysis and Management* 23(1) (Winter): 97–117.

Heiner, Ronald A. 1983. "The Origin of Predictable Behavior." *American Economic Review* 73(4):560–95.

———. 1990. "Rule-Governed Behavior in Evolution and Human Society." *Constitutional Political Economy* 1:19–46.

Heise, David R. 1979. *Understanding Events: Affect and the Construction of Social Action.* New York: Cambridge University Press.

Henrich, Joseph. 2004. "Cultural Group Selection, Coevolutionary Processes and Large-Scale Cooperation." *Journal of Economic Behavior and Organization* 53(1):3–35.

Henrich, Joseph, Robert Boyd, Samuel Bowles, Colin Camerer, Ernst Fehr, and Herbert Gintis, eds. 2004. *Foundations of Human Sociality: Economic Experiments and Ethnographic Evidence from Fifteen Small-Scale Societies.* Oxford: Oxford University Press.

Herzberg, Roberta, and Vincent Ostrom. 2000. "Votes and Vetoes." Reprinted in *Polycentric Games and Institutions: Readings from the Workshop in Political Theory and Policy Analysis*, ed. Michael McGinnis, 168–83. Ann Arbor: University of Michigan Press. Originally published in *Guidance, Control, and Evaluation in the Public Sector*, ed. Franz-Xaver Kaufmann, Giandomenico Majone, and Vincent Ostrom, 431–43 (Berlin and New York: Walter de Gruyter, 1986).

Hess, Charlotte. 1999. *A Comprehensive Bibliography of Common Pool Resources.* (CD-ROM) Bloomington: Indiana University, Workshop in Political Theory and Policy Analysis.

Hess, Charlotte, and Elinor Ostrom. 2003. "Ideas, Artifacts, and Facilities: Information as a Common-Pool Research." *Law and Contemporary Problems* 66(1 & 2):111–45.

Higgs, Robert. 1996. "Legally Induced Technical Regress in the Washington Salmon Fishery." In *Empirical Studies in Institutional Change*, ed. Lee J. Alston, Thráinn Eggertsson, and Douglass C. North, 247–79. New York: Cambridge University Press.

Hilpinen, Risto, ed. 1971. *Deontic Logic: Introductory and Systematic Readings.* Dordrecht, Holland: D. Reidel.

———, ed. 1981. *New Studies in Deontic Logic: Norms, Actions, and the Foundations of Ethics.* Dordrecht, Holland: D. Reidel.

Hilton, Rita. 1992. "Institutional Incentives for Resource Mobilization: An Analysis of Irrigation Schemes in Nepal." *Journal of Theoretical Politics* 4(3):283–308.

Hirschman, Albert O. 1985. "Against Parsimony: Three Easy Ways of Complicating Some Categories of Economic Discourse." *Economics and Philosophy* 1 (April): 16–19.

Hockings, Marc, and Adrian Phillips. 1999. "How Well Are We Doing? Some Thoughts on the Effectiveness of Protected Areas." *Parks* 9(2):5–16.

Hodgson, Geoffrey M. 2004a. *The Evolution of Institutional Economics: Agency, Structure, and Darwinism in American Institutionalism.* London: Routledge.

———. 2004b. "Opportunism Is Not the Only Reason Why Firms Exist: Why an Explanatory Emphasis on Opportunism May Mislead Management Strategy." *Industrial and Corporate Change* 13(2):401–18.

Hodgson, Geoffrey M., and Thorbjørn Knudsen. 2004. "The Complex Evolution of a Simple Traffic Convention: The Functions and Implications of Habit." *Journal of Economic Behavior and Organization* 54:19–47.

Hofstadter, Douglas R. 1979. ". . . Ant Fugue." In *Gödel, Escher, Bach: An Eternal Golden Braid*, ed. Douglas R. Hofstadter, 310–36. New York: Basic Books.

Hohfeld, Wesley N. 1964. *Fundamental Legal Conceptions*. New Haven: Yale University Press.

Holland, John H. 1995. *Hidden Order: How Adaptation Builds Complexity*. Reading, MA: Addison-Wesley.

Holland, John H., Keith J. Holyoak, Richard E. Nisbett, and Paul R. Thagard. 1986. *Induction: Processes of Inference, Learning, and Discovery*. Cambridge: MIT Press.

Holling, Crawford S. 1973. "Resilience and Stability of Ecological Systems." *Annual Review of Ecology and Systematics* 4:2–23.

Holling, Crawford S., Lance H. Gunderson, and Donald Ludwig. 2001. "In Quest of a Theory of Adaptive Change." In *Panarchy: Understanding Transformations in Human and Natural Systems*, ed. Lance Gunderson and Crawford S. Holling, 3–24. Washington, DC: Island Press.

Hong, Lu, and Scott E. Page. 2004. "Groups of Diverse Problem Solvers Can Outperform Groups of High-Ability Problem Solvers." *Proceedings of the National Academy of Science* 101(46):16385–89.

Huber, Oswald. 1980. "The Influence of Some Task Variables on Cognitive Operations in an Information-Processing Decision Model." *Acta Psychologica* 45:187–96.

Hudson, William E. 1980. "The New Federalism Paradox." *Policy Studies Journal* 8:900–6.

Hupe, Peter, and Michael Hill. 2004. "The Three Action Levels of Governance: Reframing the Policy Process beyond the Stages Model." Working Paper. Rotterdam, the Netherlands: Erasmus University, Department of Public Administration.

Hurwicz, Leonid. 1994. "Institutional Change and the Theory of Mechanism Design." *Academia Economic Papers* 22:1–26.

Igoe, Jim. 2004. *Conservation and Globalization: A Study of National Parks and Indigenous Communities from East Africa to South Dakota*. Belmont, CA: Wadsworth Thompson Learning.

Isaac, R. Mark, and James Walker. 1988a. "Communication and Free-Riding Behavior: The Voluntary Contribution Mechanism." *Economic Inquiry* 26(4):585–608.

———. 1988b. "Group Size Effects in Public Goods Provision: The Voluntary Contributions Mechanism." *Quarterly Journal of Economics* 103:179–99.

Isaac, R. Mark, James Walker, and Arlington W. Williams. 1994. "Group Size and the Voluntary Provision of Public Goods: Experimental Evidence Utilizing Large Groups." *Journal of Public Economics* 54(1) (May): 1–36.

Ito, Masaru, Tatsuyoshi Saijo, and Masashi Une. 1995. "The Tragedy of the Commons Revisited: Identifying Behavioral Principles." *Journal of Economic Behavior and Organization* 28(3):311–35.

Ives, Anthony R., Jennifer L. Klug, and Kevin Goss. 2000. "Stability and Species Richness in Complex Communities." *Ecology Letters* 3:399–411.

Jacob, Francois. 1977. "Evolution and Tinkering." *Science* 196 (4295) (June 10): 1161–66.

Jager, Wander, and Marco A. Janssen. 2003. "Using Artificial Agents to Understand Laboratory Experiments of Common-Pool Resources with Real Agents." In *Complexity and Ecosystem Management: The Theory and Practice of Multi-Agent Systems*, ed. Marco A. Janssen, 75–102. Cheltenham, UK/Northampton, MA: Edward Elgar.

Jager, Wander, Marco A. Janssen, and Charles A. J. Viek. 2001. "Experimentation with Household Dynamics: The Consumat Approach." *International Journal of Sustainable Development* 4(1):90–100.

Janssen, Marco A., ed. 2003. *Complexity and Ecosystem Management: The Theory and Practice of Multi-agent Systems*. Northampton, MA: Edward Elgar.

———. 2004. "Evolution of Cooperation When Feedback to Reputation Scores Is Voluntary." Working Paper. Bloomington: Indiana University, Center for the Study of Institutions, Population, and Environmental Change (CIPEC).

Janssen, Marco A., and T. K. Ahn. 2003. "Adaptation vs. Anticipation in Linear Public Good Games." Paper presented at the first conference of the European Social Simulation Association, Groningen University, Groningen, the Netherlands, September 18–21.

Janssen, Marco, and Elinor Ostrom. Forthcoming a. "Governing Social-Ecological Systems." In *Handbook of Computational Economics II: Agent-Based Computational Economics*, ed. Kenneth L. Judd and Leigh Tesfatsion. Amsterdam: Elsevier.

Janssen, Marco, and Elinor Ostrom. Forthcoming b. "Adoption of a New Regulation for the Governance of Common-Pool Resources by a Heterogeneous Population." In *Inequality, Cooperation, and Environmental Sustainability*, ed. Jean-Marie Baland, Pranab Bardhan, and Samuel Bowles. Princeton: Princeton University Press.

Jodha, Narpat S. 1990. "Depletion of Common Property Resources in India: Micro-Level Evidence." In *Rural Development and Population: Institutions and Policy*, ed. Geoffrey McNicoll and Mead Cain, 261–83. Oxford: Oxford University Press.

———. 1996. "Property Rights and Development." In *Rights to Nature*, ed. Susan Hanna, Carl Folke, and Karl-Goran Mäler, 205–22. Washington, DC: Island Press.

Johnson, Craig, and Timothy Forsyth. 2002. "In the Eyes of the State: Negotiating a 'Rights-Based Approach' to Forest Conservation in Thailand." *World Development* 30(9):1591–605.

Johnson, Ronald N., and Gary D. Libecap. 1982. "Contracting Problems and Regulation: The Case of the Fishery." *American Economic Review* 72(5): 1005–23.

Jones, Bryan D. 2001. *Politics and the Architecture of Choice: Bounded Rationality and Governance*. Chicago: University of Chicago Press.

Jones, Bryan D., Frank R. Baumgartner, and James L. True. 1996. "The Shape of Change: Punctuations and Stability in U.S. Budgeting, 1947–1994." Paper presented at the Annual Meeting of the Midwest Political Science Association, Chicago.

Jones, Eric C. 2003. "Building on Ostrom's 'The Rudiments of a Theory of the Origins, Survival and Performance of Common-Property Institutions.' " *Journal of Ecological Anthropology* 7:65–72.

Joshi, Neeraj N., Elinor Ostrom, Ganesh Shivakoti, and Wai Fung Lam. 2000. "Institutional Opportunities and Constraints in the Performance of Farmer-Managed Irrigation Systems in Nepal." *Asia-Pacific Journal of Rural Development* 10(2) (December): 67–92.

Kagel, John, and Alvin Roth, eds. 1995. *The Handbook of Experimental Economics*. Princeton: Princeton University Press.

Kahneman, Daniel, and Amos Tversky, eds. 2000. *Choice, Values, and Frames.* Cambridge: Cambridge University Press.

Kahneman, Daniel, Jack Knetsch, and Richard Thaler. 1990. "Experimental Tests of the Endowment Effect and the Coase Theorem." *Journal of Political Economy* 98(6):1325–48.

Kameda, Tatsuya, Masanori Takezawa, and Reid Hastie. 2003. "The Logic of Social Sharing: An Evolutionary Game Analysis of Adaptive Norm Development." *Personality and Social Psychology Review* 7(1):2–19.

Kaminski, Antoni. 1992. *An Institutional Theory of Communist Regimes: Design, Function, and Breakdown.* Oakland, CA: ICS Press.

Kaminski, Juliane, Josep Call, and Julia Fischer. 2004. "Word Learning in a Domestic Dog: Evidence for 'Fast Mapping.' " *Science* 304 (June 11): 1682–83.

Kaplan, Hillard, Kim Hill, and A. Magdalena Hurtado. 1990. "Risk, Foraging, and Food Sharing among the Ache." In *Risk and Uncertainty in Tribal and Peasant Economies*, ed. Elizabeth Cashdan, 107–44. Boulder, CO: Westview Press.

Karkkainen, Bradley. 2001/2. "Collaborative Ecosystem Governance: Scale, Complexity, and Dynamism." *Virginia Environmental Law Journal* 21: 189–243.

Karotkin, Drora, and Jacob Paroush. 1994. "Variability of Decisional Ability and the Essential Order of Decision Rules." *Journal of Economic Behavior and Organization* 23:343–54.

Kikuchi, Masao, Masako Fujita, Esther Marciano, and Yujiro Hayami. 1998. "State and Community in the Deterioration of a National Irrigation System." Paper presented at the World Bank-EDI Conference "Norms and Evolution in the Grassroots of Asia," Stanford University, Stanford, CA, February 6–7.

Kikuchi, Masao, Yoriko Watanabe, and Toshio Yamagishi. 1996. "Accuracy in the Prediction of Others' Trustworthiness and General Trust: An Experimental Study." *Japanese Journal of Experimental Social Psychology* 37(1):23–36.

Kirchler, Erich, Ernst Fehr, and Robert Evans. 1996. "Social Exchange in the Labor Market: Reciprocity and Trust versus Egoistic Money Maximization." *Journal of Economic Psychology* 17:313–41.

Kiser, Larry L., and Elinor Ostrom. 1982. "The Three Worlds of Action: A Meta-theoretical Synthesis of Institutional Approaches." In *Strategies of Political Inquiry*, ed. Elinor Ostrom, 179–222. Beverly Hills, CA: Sage.

Knack, Stephen. 1992. "Civic Norms, Social Sanctions, and Voter Turnout." *Rationality and Society* 4:133–56.

Knight, Frank H. 1921. *Risk, Uncertainty, and Profit*. Boston: Houghton Mifflin.

———. 1965. *Freedom and Reform: Essays in Economics and Social Philosophy*. New York: Harper and Row.

Knight, Jack. 1992. *Institutions and Social Conflict*. New York: Cambridge University Press.

Knox, Anna, and Ruth Meinzen-Dick. 2001. "Collective Action, Property Rights, and Devolution of Forest and Protected Area Management." In *Collective Action, Property Rights, and Devolution of Natural Resource Management*, ed. Ruth Meinzen-Dick, Anna Knox, and Monica DiGregorio, 41–74. Feldafing, Germany: Deutsche Stiftung für internationale Entwicklung.

Koestler, Arthur. 1973. "The Tree and the Candle." In *Unity through Diversity*, pt I, ed. William Gray and Nicholas D. Rizzo, 287–314. New York: Gordon and Breach Science Publishers.

Koford, Kenneth. 2003. "Experiments on Trust and Bargaining in Bulgaria: The Effects of Institutions and Culture." Prepared for presentation at the International Society of New Institutional Economics 7th Annual Meeting, Budapest, September 11–13.

Koford, Kenneth, and Jeffrey B. Miller. 1995. "Contracts in Bulgaria: How Firms Cope When Property Rights Are Incomplete." Working Paper. Newark: University of Delaware.

Koremenos, Barbara, Charles Lipson, and Duncan Snidal. 2001. "The Rational Design of International Institutions." *International Organization* 55(4) (Autumn): 761–99.

Korten, David C. 1980. "Community Organization and Rural Development: A Learning Process Approach." *Public Administration Review* 40(5):480–511.

Kreps, David M. 1990. "Corporate Culture and Economic Theory." In *Perspectives on Positive Political Economy*, ed. James Alt and Kenneth Shepsle, 90–143. New York: Cambridge University Press.

Kreps, David M., Paul Milgrom, John Roberts, and Robert Wilson. 1982. "Rational Cooperation in the Finitely Repeated Prisoners' Dilemma." *Journal of Economic Theory* 27:245–52.

Kuran, Timur. 1989. "Sparks and Prairie Fires: A Theory of Unanticipated Political Revolution." *Public Choice* 61:41–74.

Kurzban, Robert. 2003. "Biological Foundations of Reciprocity." In *Trust and Reciprocity: Interdisciplinary Lessons from Experimental Research*, ed. Elinor Ostrom and James Walker, 105–27. New York: Russell Sage Foundation.

Laffont, Jean-Jacques, and David Martimort. 2002. *The Theory of Incentives: The Principal-Agent Model*. Princeton: Princeton University Press.

Laland, Kevin N., John Odling-Smee, and Marcus W. Feldman. 2000. "Niche Construction, Biological Evolution, and Cultural Change." *Behavioral and Brain Sciences* 23:131–75.

Lam, Wai Fung. 1998. *Governing Irrigation Systems in Nepal: Institutions, Infrastructure, and Collective Action.* Oakland, CA: ICS Press.

Landau, Martin. 1969. "Redundancy, Rationality, and the Problem of Duplication and Overlap." *Public Administration Review* 29(4):346–58.

———. 1973. "Federalism, Redundancy, and System Reliability." *Publius* 3(2):173–96.

Lansing, J. Stephen. 1991. *Priests and Programmers: Technologies of Power in the Engineered Landscape of Bali.* Princeton: Princeton University Press.

Lasswell, Harold, and Abraham Kaplan. 1950. *Power and Society: A Framework for Political Inquiry.* New Haven: Yale University Press.

Lawry, Steven W. 1990. "Tenure Policy toward Common Property Natural Resources in Sub-Saharan Africa." *Natural Resources Journal* 30:403–22.

Lederman, Leandra. 2003. "The Interplay between Norms and Enforcement in Tax Compliance." *Ohio State Law Journal* 64(6):1453–514.

Ledyard, John. 1995. "Public Goods: A Survey of Experimental Research." In *The Handbook of Experimental Economics*, ed. John Kagel and Alvin Roth, 111–94. Princeton: Princeton University Press.

Less, Hangwoo. 2002. "'No Artificial Death, Only Natural Death': The Dynamics of Centralization and Decentralization of Usenet Newsgroups." *Information Society* 18(5):361–70.

Levi, Margaret. 1988. *Of Rule and Revenue.* Berkeley and Los Angeles: University of California Press.

———. 1990. "A Logic of Institutional Change." In *The Limits of Rationality,* ed. Karen S. Cook and Margaret Levi, 403–18. Chicago: Chicago University Press.

———. 1997a. *Consent, Dissent, and Patriotism.* New York: Cambridge University Press.

———. 1997b. "A Model, a Method, and a Map: Rational Choice in Comparative and Historical Analysis." In *Comparative Politics: Rationality, Culture, and Structure*, ed. Mark Irving Lichbach and Alan S. Zuckerman, 19–42. Cambridge: Cambridge University Press.

Levin, Jonathan, and Barry Nalebuff. 1995. "An Introduction to Vote-Counting Schemes." *Journal of Economic Perspectives* 9(1):3–26.

Levin, Simon A. 1992. "The Problem of Pattern and Scale in Ecology." *Ecology* 73(6) (December): 1943–67.

———. 1998. "Ecosystems and the Biosphere as Complex Adaptive Systems." *Ecosystems* 1:431–36.

Levine, Gilbert. 1980. "The Relationship of Design, Operation, and Management." In *Irrigation and Agricultural Development in Asia*, ed. E. Walter Coward, 51–64. Ithaca: Cornell University Press.

Lewis, David K. 1969. *Convention: A Philosophical Study.* Cambridge: Harvard University Press.

Lian, Peng, and Charles R. Plott. 1998. "General Equilibrium, Markets, Macroeconomics, and Money in a Laboratory Experimental Environment." *Economic Theory* 12(1):21–75.

Libecap, Gary D. 1989. *Contracting for Property Rights.* New York: Cambridge University Press.

———. 1995. "The Conditions for Successful Collective Action." In *Local Commons and Global Interdependence: Heterogeneity and Cooperation in Two Domains*, ed. Robert O. Keohane and Elinor Ostrom, 161–90. London: Sage.

———. 1996. "Economic Variables and the Development of the Law: The Case of Western Mineral Rights." In *Empirical Studies in Institutional Change*, ed. Lee Alston, Thráinn Eggertsson, and Douglass North, 34–58. New York: Cambridge University Press.

Libecap, Gary D., and Steven N. Wiggins. 1984. "Contractual Responses to the Common Pool: Prorationing of Crude Oil Production." *American Economic Review* 74:87–98.

———. 1985. "The Influence of Private Contractual Failure on Regulation: The Case of Oil Field Unitization." *Journal of Political Economy* 93:690–714.

Lobe, Kenton, and Fikret Berkes. 2004. "The *Padu* System of Community-Based Fisheries Management: Change and Local Institutional Innovation in South India." *Marine Policy* 28:271–81.

Loveman, Brian. 1993. *The Constitution of Tyranny: Regimes of Exception in Spanish America*. Pittsburgh: University of Pittsburgh Press.

Low, Bobbi S. 1989. "Cross-Cultural Patterns in the Training of Children: An Evolutionary Perspective." *Journal of Comparative Psychology* 103:311–19.

———. 1990. "Human Responses to Environmental Extremeness and Uncertainty: A Cross-Cultural Perspective." In *Risk and Uncertainty in Tribal and Peasant Economies*, ed. Elizabeth Cashdan, 229–56. Boulder, CO: Westview Press.

Low, Bobbi S., Elinor Ostrom, Carl Simon, and James Wilson. 2003. "Redundancy and Diversity: Do They Influence Optimal Management?" In *Navigating Social-Ecological Systems: Building Resilience for Complexity and Change*, ed. Fikret Berkes, Johan Colding, and Carl Folke, 83–114. New York: Cambridge University Press.

Luce, R. Duncan. 1956. "Semiorders and a Theory of Utility Discrimination." *Econometrica* 24:178–91.

Maass, Arthur, and Raymond L. Anderson. 1986. *. . . and the Desert Shall Rejoice: Conflict, Growth, and Justice in Arid Environments*. Malabar, FL: R. E. Krieger.

Maier-Rigaud, Frank P., and José Apesteguia. 2003. "The Role of Choice in Social Dilemma Experiments." Working Paper no. 2003/7. Bonn, Germany: Max Planck Institute for Human Development.

Manktelow, Ken I., and David E. Over. 1991. "Social Roles and Utilities in Reasoning with Deontic Conditionals." *Cognition* 39:85–105.

Mansbridge, Jane. 1990. "On the Relation of Altruism and Self-Interest." In *Beyond Self-Interest*, ed. Jane Mansbridge, 133–43. Chicago: University of Chicago Press.

———. 1994. "Public Spirit in Political Systems." In *Values and Public Policy*, ed. Henry J. Aaron, Thomas E. Mann, and Timothy Taylor, 146–72. Washington, DC: Brookings Institution.

Mansuri, Ghazala, and Vijayendra Rao. 2003. "Evaluating Community Driven Development: A Review of the Evidence." Washington, DC: World Bank, Development Research Group.

Mantzavinos, Chris, Douglass C. North, and Syed Shariq. 2004. "Learning, Institutions, and Economic Performance." *Perspectives on Politics* 2(1):75–84.

March, James G., and Johan P. Olsen. 1989. *Rediscovering Institutions: The Organizational Basis of Politics*. New York: Free Press.

Marcus, Gary. 2004. *The Birth of the Mind: How a Tiny Number of Genes Creates the Complexities of Human Thought*. New York: Basic Books.

Margolis, Howard. 1991. "Self-Interest and Social Motivation." In *Individuality and Cooperative Action*, ed. Joseph E. Earley, 129–36. Washington, DC: Georgetown University Press.

Marwell, Gerald, and Pamela Oliver. 1993. *The Critical Mass in Collective Action*. Cambridge: Cambridge University Press.

Maynard Smith, John, and David Harper. 2003. *Animal Signals*. Oxford: Oxford University Press.

Maynard Smith, John, and Eörs Szathmáry. 1997. *The Major Transitions in Evolution*. Oxford: Oxford University Press.

Mayntz, Renate, and Fritz W. Scharpf. 1995. *Steuerung and Selbstorganisation in Staatsnahen Sektoren*. Frankfurt am Main: Campus-Verlag.

McAdams, Richard H. 2001. "Conventions and Norms: Philosophical Aspects." In *International Encyclopedia of the Social and Behavioral Sciences*, ed. Neil Smelser and Paul Baltes, 2735–41. Oxford: Pergamon.

McAdams, Richard H., and Eric Rasmusen. Forthcoming. "Norms in Law and Economics." In *Handbook of Law and Economics*, ed. A. Mitchell Polinsky and Steven Shavell. Amsterdam: Elsevier.

McCabe, Kevin A. 2003. "A Cognitive Theory of Reciprocal Exchange." In *Trust and Reciprocity: Interdisciplinary Lessons from Experimental Research*, ed. Elinor Ostrom and James Walker, 147–69. New York: Russell Sage Foundation.

McCabe, Kevin A., Stephen J. Rassenti, and Vernon L. Smith. 1996. "Game Theory and Reciprocity in Some Extensive Form Experimental Games." *Proceedings of the National Academy of Sciences* 93 (November): 13421–428.

McCabe, Kevin A., and Vernon Smith. 2003. "Strategic Analysis in Games: What Information Do Players Use?" In *Trust and Reciprocity: Interdisciplinary Lessons from Experimental Research*, ed. Elinor Ostrom and James Walker, 275–301. New York: Russell Sage Foundation.

McCay, Bonnie J., and James M. Acheson. 1987. *The Question of the Commons: The Culture and Ecology of Communal Resources*. Tucson: University of Arizona Press.

McDermott, Rose. 2001. "The Psychological Ideas of Amos Tversky and Their Relevance for Political Science." *Journal of Theoretical Politics* 13(1):5–33.

McGinnis, Michael, ed. 1999a. *Polycentric Governance and Development: Readings from the Workshop in Political Theory and Policy Analysis*. Ann Arbor: University of Michigan Press.

———, ed. 1999b. *Polycentricity and Local Public Economies: Readings from the Workshop in Political Theory and Policy Analysis*. Ann Arbor: University of Michigan Press.

————, ed. 2000. *Polycentric Games and Institutions: Readings from the Workshop in Political Theory and Policy Analysis.* Ann Arbor: University of Michigan Press.

————. Forthcoming. *Dilemmas of Global Response to Conflict: Lessons from the Horn of Africa.* Bloomington: Indiana University, Workshop in Political Theory and Policy Analysis.

McGinnis, Michael, and John T. Williams. 1989. "Change and Stability in Superpower Rivalry." *American Political Science Review* 83(4) (December): 1101–23.

————. 2001. *Compound Dilemmas: Democracy, Collective Action, and Superpower Rivalry.* Ann Arbor: University of Michigan Press.

McKean, Margaret A. 1992. "Management of Traditional Common Lands (*Iriaichi*) in Japan." In *Making the Commons Work: Theory, Practice, and Policy,* ed. Daniel W. Bromley et al., 63–98. San Francisco: ICS Press.

————. 2000. "Common Property: What Is It, What Is It Good For, and What Makes It Work?" In *People and Forests: Communities, Institutions, and Governance,* ed. Clark Gibson, Margaret McKean, and Elinor Ostrom, 27–55. Cambridge: MIT Press.

Medard, Modesta, and Kim Geheb. 2001. *Fisheries Co-management in the Tanzanian Sector of Lake Victoria.* Mwanza, Tanzania: Tanzania Fisheries Research Institute.

Mehra, Shakuntla. 1981. *Instability in Indian Agriculture in the Context of the New Technology.* Research Report no. 25. Washington, DC: International Food Policy Research Institute.

Meinzen-Dick, Ruth, K. Vengamma Raju, and Ashok Gulati. 2002. "What Affects Organization and Collective Action for Managing Resources? Evidence from Canal Irrigation Systems in India." *World Development* 30(4): 649–66.

Merrey, Douglas J. 1996. "Institutional Design Principles for Accountability on Large Irrigation Systems." Research Report no. 8. Colombo, Sri Lanka: International Irrigation Management Institute.

Messner, Matthias, and Mattias K. Polborn. 2004. "Voting on Majority Rules." *Review of Economic Studies* 71(1):115–32.

Meyer, John W., and Brian Rowan. 1991. "Institutionalized Organizations: Formal Structure as Myth and Ceremony." In *The New Institutionalism in Organizational Analysis,* ed. Walter W. Powell and Paul J. DiMaggio, 41–62. Chicago: University of Chicago Press.

Milgrom, Paul R., Douglass C. North, and Barry R. Weingast. 1990. "The Role of Institutions in the Revival of Trade: The Law Merchant, Private Judges, and the Champagne Fairs." *Economics and Politics* 2(1) (March): 1–23.

Milgrom, Paul R., and John Roberts. 1992. *Economics, Organization, and Management.* Englewood Cliffs, NJ: Prentice Hall.

Millar, Karen U., and Abraham Tesser. 1988. "Deceptive Behavior in Social Relationships: A Consequence of Violated Expectations." *Journal of Psychology* 122:263–73.

Miller, Gary J. 2001. "Why Is Trust Necessary in Organizations? The Moral Hazard of Profit Maximization." In *Trust in Society*, ed. Karen S. Cook, 307–31. New York: Russell Sage Foundation.

Monroe, Burt. Forthcoming. *Electoral Systems in Theory and Practice: Toward an Empirically Relevant Theory of Social Choice*. Ann Arbor: University of Michigan Press.

Moore, Mark H. 1995. *Creating Public Value: Strategic Management in Government*. Cambridge: Harvard University Press.

Moran, Emilio, and Elinor Ostrom, eds. 2005. *Seeing the Forest and the Trees: Human-Environment Interactions in Forest Ecosystems*. Cambridge: MIT Press.

Morrow, Christopher E., and Rebecca Watts Hull. 1996. "Donor-Initiated Common Pool Resource Institutions: The Case of the Yanesha Forestry Cooperative." *World Development* 24(10):1641–57.

Moxnes, Erling. 1996. "Mismanagement of Fish Resources." Working Paper no. 1. Bergen, Norway: SNF.

———. 1998. "Not Only the Tragedy of the Commons: Misperceptions of Bioeconomics." *Management Science* 44(9):1234–48.

Mueller, Milton L. 2002. *Ruling the Roots*. Cambridge: MIT Press.

Mueller, Ulrich O., Benzion Chanowitz, and Ellen Langer. 1983. "The Rationality of the Free Ride." Paper presented at the Annual Meetings of the Public Choice Society, Savannah, Georgia, March 24–26.

Mukand, Sharun, and Dani Rodrik. 2002. "In Search of the Holy Grail: Policy Convergence, Experimentation, and Economic Performance." Mimeo. Cambridge, MA: National Bureau of Economic Research.

Mwangi, Esther. 2003. "Institutional Change and Politics: The Transformation of Property Rights in Kenya's Maasailand." Ph.D. diss., Indiana University.

Myers, Ransom A., and Boris Worm. 2003. "Rapid Worldwide Depletion of Predatory Fish Communities." *Nature* 423 (May 15): 280–83.

Myerson, Roger B. 1991. *Game Theory: Analysis of Conflict*. Cambridge: Harvard University Press.

Nardulli, Peter. 1995. "The Concept of a Critical Realignment, Electoral Behaviors, and Political Change." *American Political Science Review* 89:10–22.

National Research Council. 2002. *Drama of the Commons*. Committee on the Human Dimensions of Global Change, ed. Elinor Ostrom, Thomas Dietz, Nives Dolšak, Paul C. Stern, Susan Stonich, and Elke Weber. Washington, DC: National Academy Press.

Nemarundwe, Nontokozo, and Witness Kozanayi. 2003. "Institutional Arrangements for Water Resource Use: A Case Study from Southern Zimbabwe." *Journal of Southern African Studies* 29(1):193–206.

Netting, Robert McC. 1972. "Of Men and Meadows: Strategies of Alpine Land Use." *Anthropological Quarterly* 45:132–44.

———. 1974. "The System Nobody Knows: Village Irrigation in the Swiss Alps." In *Irrigation's Impact on Society*, ed. Theodore E. Downing and McGuire Gibson, 67–75. Tucson: University of Arizona Press.

———. 1993. *Smallholders, Householders: Farm Families and the Ecology of Intensive, Sustainable Agriculture*. Stanford, CA: Stanford University Press.

Niskanen, William A. 1971. *Bureaucracy and Representative Government.* Chicago: Aldine Atherton.

North, Douglass C. 1981. *Structure and Change in Economic History.* New York: W. W. Norton.

———. 1986. "The New Institutional Economics." *Journal of Institutional and Theoretical Economics* 142:230–37.

———. 1990. *Institutions, Institutional Change, and Economic Performance.* New York: Cambridge University Press.

———. 2005. *Understanding the Process of Institutional Change.* Princeton: Princeton University Press.

Noussair, Charles N., Charles R. Plott, and Raymond G. Reizman. 1995. "An Experimental Investigation of the Patterns of International Trade." *American Economic Review* 85(3) (June): 462–91.

Nowak, Martin A., and Karl Sigmund. 1998. "Evolution of Indirect Reciprocity by Image Scoring." *Nature* 393(6685):573–77.

Oakerson, Ronald J. 1981. "Erosion of Public Goods: The Case of Coal-Haul Roads in Eastern Kentucky." *Research in Public Policy Analysis and Management* 2:73–102.

———. 1992. "Analyzing the Commons: A Framework." In *Making the Commons Work: Theory, Practice, and Policy,* ed. Daniel W. Bromley et al., 41–59. Oakland, CA: ICS Press.

———. 1994. "The Logic of Multi-level Institutional Analysis." Paper presented at the "Workshop on the Workshop" conference, Workshop in Political Theory and Policy Analysis, Indiana University, Bloomington, June 15–19.

Oaksford, Mike, and Nick Chater. 1994. "A Rational Analysis of the Selection Task as Optimal Data Selection." *Psychological Review* 101(4):608–31.

Offe, Claus, and Helmut Wiesenthal. 1980. "Two Logics of Collective Action: Theoretical Notes on Social Class and Organizational Form." *Political Power and Social Theory* 1:67–115.

O'Leary, Brendan, Ian S. Lustick, and Thomas Callaghy. 2001. *Right-Sizing the State: The Politics of Moving Borders.* Oxford: Oxford University Press.

Olson, Mancur. 1965. *The Logic of Collective Action: Public Goods and the Theory of Groups.* Cambridge: Harvard University Press.

———. 1991. "The Role of Morals and Incentives in Society." In *Individuality and Cooperative Action,* ed. Joseph E. Earley, 117–28. Washington, DC: Georgetown University Press.

Opp, Karl-Dieter. 1982. "The Evolutionary Emergence of Norms." *British Journal of Social Psychology* 21:139–49.

Orbell, John M., and Robyn M. Dawes. 1991. "A 'Cognitive Miser' Theory of Cooperators' Advantage." *American Political Science Review* 85(2):515–28.

———. 1993. "Social Welfare, Cooperators' Advantage, and the Option of Not Playing the Game." *American Sociological Review* 58(6) (December): 787–800.

Orbell, John M., Tomonori Morikawa, Jason Hartwig, James Hanley, and Nicholas Allen. 2004. " 'Machiavellian' Intelligence as a Basis for the Evolution of Cooperative Dispositions." *American Political Science Review* 98(1):1–15.

Orbell, John M., Perry Schwarz-Shea, and Randy T. Simmons. 1984. "Do Cooperators Exit More Readily Than Defectors?" *American Political Science Review* 78:147–62.

Orbell, John M., Alphons J. van de Kragt, and Robyn M. Dawes. 1991. "Covenants without the Sword: The Role of Promises in Social Dilemma Circumstances." In *Social Norms and Economic Institutions*, ed. Kenneth J. Koford and Jeffrey B. Miller, 117–34. Ann Arbor: University of Michigan Press.

Osterloh, Margit, and Bruno S. Frey. 2000. "Motivation, Knowledge Transfer, and Organizational Forms." *Organization Science* 11(5) (September–October): 538–50.

Ostrom, Elinor. 1986. "An Agenda for the Study of Institutions." *Public Choice* 48:3–25.

———. 1990. *Governing the Commons: The Evolution of Institutions for Collective Action*. New York: Cambridge University Press.

———. 1992a. *Crafting Institutions for Self-Governing Irrigation Systems*. San Francisco, CA: ICS Press.

———. 1992b. "The Rudiments of a Theory of the Origins, Survival, and Performance of Common-Property Institutions." In *Making the Commons Work: Theory, Practice, and Policy*, ed. Daniel W. Bromley et al., 41–59. Oakland, CA: ICS Press.

———. 1996. "Incentives, Rules of the Game, and Development." In *Proceedings of the Annual World Bank Conference on Development Economics 1995*, 207–34. Washington, DC: World Bank.

———. 1998. "A Behavioral Approach to the Rational Choice Theory of Collective Action." *American Political Science Review* 92(1) (March): 1–22.

———. 1999. "Institutional Rational Choice: An Assessment of the Institutional Analysis and Development Framework." In *Theories of the Policy Process*, ed. Paul A. Sabatier, 35–71. Boulder, CO: Westview Press.

———. 2001. "Reformulating the Commons." In *Protecting the Commons: A Framework for Resource Management in the Americas*, ed. Joanna Burger, Elinor Ostrom, Richard B. Norgaard, David Policansky, and Bernard D. Goldstein, 17–41. Washington, DC: Island Press.

Ostrom, Elinor, Arun Agrawal, William Blomquist, Edella Schlager, Shui Yan Tang, et al. 1989. *CPR Coding Manual*. Bloomington: Indiana University, Workshop in Political Theory and Policy Analysis.

Ostrom, Elinor, and T. K. Ahn, eds. 2003. *Foundations of Social Capital*. Cheltenham, UK: Edward Elgar.

Ostrom, Elinor, Joanna Burger, Christopher Field, Richard B. Norgaard, and David Policansky. 1999. "Revisiting the Commons: Local Lessons, Global Challenges." *Science* 284(5412) (April 9): 278–82.

Ostrom, Elinor, Roy Gardner, and James Walker. 1994. *Rules, Games, and Common-Pool Resources*. Ann Arbor: University of Michigan Press.

Ostrom, Elinor, Roger B. Parks, and Gordon P. Whitaker. 1974. "Defining and Measuring Structural Variations in Interorganizational Arrangements." *Publius* 4(4) (Fall): 87–108.

Ostrom, Elinor, Larry Schroeder, and Susan Wynne. 1993. *Institutional Incentives and Sustainable Development: Infrastructure Policies in Perspective*. Boulder, CO: Westview Press.

Ostrom, Elinor, and James Walker. 1991. "Communication in a Commons: Cooperation without External Enforcement." In *Laboratory Research in Political Economy*, ed. Thomas R. Palfrey, 287–322. Ann Arbor: University of Michigan Press.

———, eds. 2003. *Trust and Reciprocity: Interdisciplinary Lessons from Experimental Research*. New York: Russell Sage Foundation.

Ostrom, Elinor, James Walker, and Roy Gardner. 1992. "Covenants with and without a Sword: Self-Governance Is Possible." *American Political Science Review* 86(2) (June): 404–17.

Ostrom, Vincent. 1980. "Artisanship and Artifact." *Public Administration Review* 40(4) (July/August): 309–17.

———. 1986. "A Fallabilist's Approach to Norms and Criteria of Choice." In *Guidance, Control, and Evaluation in the Public Sector*, ed. Franz K. Kaufmann, Giandomenico Majone, and Vincent Ostrom, 229–44. Berlin: Walter de Gruyter.

———. 1987. *The Political Theory of a Compound Republic: Designing the American Experiment*. 2d rev. ed. San Francisco, CA: ICS Press.

———. 1991. *The Meaning of American Federalism: Constituting a Self-Governing Society*. Oakland, CA: ICS Press.

———. 1993. "Epistemic Choice and Public Choice." *Public Choice* 77(1) (September): 163–76.

———. 1996. "Faustian Bargains." *Constitutional Political Economy* 7:303–8.

———. 1997. *The Meaning of Democracy and the Vulnerability of Democracies: A Response to Tocqueville's Challenge*. Ann Arbor: University of Michigan Press.

———. 1999. "Polycentricity (Parts 1 and 2)." In *Polycentricity and Local Public Economies: Readings from the Workshop in Political Theory and Policy Analysis*, ed. Michael McGinnis, 52–74, 119–38. Ann Arbor: University of Michigan Press.

Ostrom, Vincent, David Feeny, and Hartmut Picht, eds. 1993. *Rethinking Institutional Analysis and Development: Issues, Alternatives, and Choices*. 2d ed. Oakland, CA: ICS Press.

Ostrom, Vincent, and Elinor Ostrom. 1970. "Conditions of Legal and Political Feasibility." In *Natural Resource System Models in Decision Making*, Proceedings of a 1969 Water Resources Seminar, ed. Gerrit H. Toebes. Lafayette, IN: Purdue University, Water Resources Research Center.

———. 1977. "Public Goods and Public Choices." In *Alternatives for Delivering Public Services: Toward Improved Performance*, ed. E. S. Savas, 7–49. Boulder, CO: Westview Press.

———. 1999. "Legal and Political Conditions of Water Resource Development." Reprinted in *Polycentric Governance and Development: Readings from the Workshop in Political Theory and Policy Analysis*, ed. Michael McGinnis, 42–

59. Ann Arbor: University of Michigan Press. Originally published in *Land Economics* 48(1) (February 1972): 1–14.

Ostrom, Vincent, Charles M. Tiebout, and Robert Warren. 1961. "The Organization of Government in Metropolitan Areas: A Theoretical Inquiry." *American Political Science Review* 55(4) (December): 831–42.

Palanisami, K. 1982. *Managing Tank Irrigation Systems: Basic Issues and Implications for Improvement.* Presented at the workshop "Tank Irrigation: Problems and Prospects." Bogor, Indonesia: CIFOR.

Pant, Takur Nath, and Jyoti Lohani. 1983. "Some Observations on Irrigation Development of Nepal." In *Water Management in Nepal: Proceedings of the Seminar on Water Management Issues, held in Kathmandu, 31 July–2 August,* ed. Edward Martin and Robert Yoder, 3–46. Kathmandu: Ministry of Food and Agriculture, Agricultural Projects Services Centre, Agricultural Development Council.

Parker, Dawn C., Steven M. Manson, Marco A. Janssen, Mathew J. Hoffmann, and Peter Deadman. 2003. "Multi-agent Systems for the Simulation of Land-Use and Land-Cover Change: A Review." *Annals of the Association of American Geographers* 93(2):314–37.

Pessoa, Luiz. 2004. "Seeing the World in the Same Way." *Science* 3003 (March 12): 1617–18.

Pickett, Steward T. A., and Mary L. Cadenasso. 1995. "Landscape Ecology: Spatial Heterogeneity in Ecological Systems." *Science* 269 (July 21): 331–34.

Pinker, Steven. 1994. *The Language Instinct.* New York: W. Morrow.

Pinkerton, Evelyn, ed. 1989. *Co-operative Management of Local Fisheries: New Directions for Improved Management and Community Development.* Vancouver: University of British Columbia Press.

Platteau, Jean-Philippe. 2003. "Community Based Development in the Context of Within Group Heterogeneity. " Paper presented at the Annual Bank Conference on Development Economics, Bangalore, India.

———. 2004. "Monitoring Elite Capture in Community-Driven Development." *Development and Change* 35(2):223–46.

Platteau, Jean-Philippe, and Frederic Gaspart. 2003. "The Risk of Resource Misappropriation in Community-Driven Development." *World Development* 31(10):1687–1703.

Plott, Charles R. 1996. "Rational Individual Behaviour in Markets and Social Choice Processes: The Discovered Preference Hypothesis." In *The Rational Foundations of Economic Behaviour,* ed. Kenneth Arrow, Enrico Colombatto, Mark Perlman, and Christian Schmidt, 225–50. New York: St. Martin's Press.

Plott, Charles R., and Michael E. Levine. 1978. "A Model of Agenda Influence on Committee Decisions." *American Economic Review* 68:146–60.

Plott, Charles R., and Robert A. Meyer. 1975. "The Technology of Public Goods, Externalities, and the Exclusion Principle." In *Economic Analysis of Environmental Problems,* ed. Edwin S. Mills, 65–94. New York: Columbia University Press.

Plott, Charles R., and David P. Porter. 1996. "Market Architectures and Institutional Testbedding: An Experiment with Space Station Pricing Policies." *Journal of Economic Behavior and Organization* 31(2):237–72.

Poffenberger, Mark, and Betsy McGean. 1996. *Village Voices, Forest Choices: Joint Forest Management in India.* New Delhi: Oxford University Press.

Polski, Margaret M. 2003. *The Invisible Hands of U.S. Commercial Banking Reform: Private Action and Public Guarantees.* Boston: Kluwer.

Popper, Karl. 1961. *The Poverty of Historicism.* New York: Harper and Row.

———. 1976. "The Logic of the Social Sciences." In *The Positivist Dispute in German Sociology,* ed. Theodore W. Adorno, 87–104. New York: Harper and Row.

Posner, Richard A., and Eric Rasmusen. 1999. "Creating and Enforcing Norms, with Special Reference to Sanctions." *International Review of Law and Economics* 19(3) (September): 369–82.

Poteete, Amy, and Elinor Ostrom. 2004. "Heterogeneity, Group Size, and Collective Action: The Role of Institutions in Forest Management." *Development and Change* 35(3):435–61.

Poudel, Rabi, Kala N. Pandit, Keshav Adhikari, S. M. Shakya, D. N. Yadav, and Neeraj R. Joshi. 1994. *Inventory and Need Assessment of Irrigation Systems in North-Eastern Tanahu. (Vol. I).* Chitwan, Rampur, Nepal: Institute of Agriculture and Animal Science, Irrigation Management Systems Study Group.

Pradhan, Naresh C., and Robert Yoder. 1989. "Improving Irrigation System Management through Farmer-to-Farmer Training: Examples from Nepal." IIMI Working Paper no. 12. Colombo, Sri Lanka: International Irrigation Management Institute.

Pradhan, Prachanda. 1989. "Patterns of Irrigation Organization in Nepal: A Comparative Study of 21 Farmer-Managed Irrigation Systems." Kathmandu, Nepal: International Irrigation Management Institute.

Price, Michael E. In press. "Monitoring, Reputation and 'Greenbeard' Reciprocity in a Shuar Work Team." *Journal of Organizational Behavior.*

Pritchett, Lant, and Michael Woolcock. 2003. "Solutions When the Solution Is the Problem: Arraying the Disarray in Development." *World Development* 35(3):435–61.

Rabin, Matthew. 1993. "Incorporating Fairness in Game Theory and Economics." *American Economic Review* 83:1281–302.

———. 1998. "Psychology and Economics." *Journal of Economic Literature* 36 (March): 11–46.

Raiffa, Howard. 1982. *The Art and Science of Negotiation.* Cambridge: Harvard University Press.

Rapoport, Anatol. 1966. *Two-Person Game Theory: The Essential Ideas.* Ann Arbor: University of Michigan Press.

Rappaport, Roy A. 1979. *Ecology, Meaning, and Religion.* Richmond, CA: North Atlantic Books.

Rasmusen, Eric. 1989. *Games and Information: An Introduction to Game Theory.* Oxford: Basil Blackwell.

Raub, Werner, and Thomas Voss. 1986. "Conditions for Cooperation in Problematic Social Situations." In *Paradoxical Effects of Social Behavior: Essays in Honor of Anatol Rapoport,* ed. Andreas Diekmann and Peter Mitter, 85–104. Heidelberg: Physica-Verlag.

Rawls, John. 1971. *A Theory of Justice.* Cambridge: Harvard University Press.

Ray, Isha, and Jeffrey Williams. 1999. "Evaluation of Price Policy in the Presence of Water Theft." *American Journal of Agricultural Economics* 81(4):928–41.

Repetto, Fabián. 2002. "Plan Solidaridad: Notas Sobre la Incapacidad del Estado Nacional para Gerenciar un Programa Complejo." Working Paper no. 64. Buenos Aires, Argentina: Fundación Gobierno y Sociedad, Centro de Estudios para el Desarrollo Institucional (CEDI).

Repetto, Robert. 1986. *Skimming the Water: Rent-Seeking and the Performance of Public Irrigation Systems.* Research report no. 4. Washington, DC: World Resources Institute.

Reuveny, Rafael, and John Maxwell. 2001. "Conflict and Renewable Resources." *Journal of Conflict Resolution* 45:719–42.

Reynolds, Andrew. 2002. *The Architecture of Democracy: Constitutional Design, Conflict Management, and Democracy.* Oxford: Oxford University Press.

Richerson, Peter J., and Robert Boyd. 2002. "Culture Is Part of Human Biology." In *Probing Human Origins*, ed. Morris Goodman and Anne Simon Moffat, 59–86. Cambridge, MA: American Academy of Arts and Sciences.

Richerson, Peter J., Robert Boyd, and Brian Paciotti. 2002. "An Evolutionary Theory of Commons Management." In *The Drama of the Commons*, National Research Council, Committee on the Human Dimensions of Global Change, ed. Elinor Ostrom, Thomas Dietz, Nives Dolšak, Paul C. Stern, Susan Stonich, and Elke Weber, 403–42. Washington, DC: National Academy Press.

Rieskamp, Jörg, and Gerd Gigerenzer. 2003. "Heuristics for Social Interactions: How to Generate Trust and Fairness." Working Paper. Berlin: Max Planck Institute for Human Development.

Rieskamp, Jörg, and Ulrich Hoffrage. 2003. "The Use of Simple Heuristics: Inferences and Preferences under Time Pressure." Working Paper. Berlin: Max Planck Institute for Human Development.

Riker, William H. 1962. *The Theory of Political Coalitions.* New Haven: Yale University Press.

Rilling, James K., David A. Gutman, Thorsten R. Zeh, Giuseppe Pagnoni, Gregory S. Berns, and Clinton D. Kilts. 2002. "A Neural Basis for Social Cooperation." *Neuron* 35(2) (July): 395–405.

Riolo, Rick, Michael Cohen, and Robert Axelrod. 2001. "Evolution of Cooperation without Reciprocity." *Nature* 414 (November): 441–43.

Rocco, Elena, and Massimo Warglien. 1995. "Computer Mediated Communication and the Emergence of 'Electronic Opportunism.' " Venice, Italy: University of Venice, Department of Economics, Laboratory of Experimental Economics.

Roconi, Lucas. 2002. "El Programa TRABAJAR." Working Paper no. 63. Buenos Aires, Argentina: Fundación Gobierno y Sociedad, Centro de Estudios para el Desarrollo Institucional (CEDI).

Rolett, Barry, and Jared Diamond. 2004. "Environmental Predictors of Pre-European Deforestation on Pacific Islands." *Nature* 431 (September 23): 443–46.

Romer, Thomas, and Howard Rosenthal. 1978. "Political Resource Allocation, Controlled Agendas, and the Status Quo." *Public Choice* 33(4):27–43.

Rose, Carol. 2002. "Common Property, Regulatory Property, and Environmental Protection: Comparing Community-Based Management to Tradable Environmental Allowances." In *The Drama of the Commons*, National Research Council, Committee on the Human Dimensions of Global Change, ed. Elinor Ostrom, Thomas Dietz, Nives Dolšak, Paul C. Stern, Susan Stonich, and Elke Weber, 233–57. Washington, DC: National Academy Press.

Rothstein, Bo. 1998. *Just Institutions Matter: The Moral and Political Logic of the Universal Welfare State*. Cambridge: Cambridge University Press.

———. 2005. "Is Political Science Producing Technically Competent Barbarians?" *European Political Science* 4:3–13.

———. 2005. *Social Traps and the Problem of Trust*. Cambridge: Cambridge University Press.

Rowe, Nicholas. 1989. *Rules and Institutions*. Ann Arbor: University of Michigan Press.

Sally, David. 1995. "Conversation and Cooperation in Social Dilemmas: A Meta-analysis of Experiments from 1958 to 1992." *Rationality and Society* 7:58–92.

Sawyer, Amos. 1992. *The Emergence of Autocracy in Liberia: Tragedy and Challenge*. Oakland, CA: ICS Press.

———. 2005. *Beyond Plunder: Toward Democratic Governance in Liberia*. Boulder, CO: Lynne Rienner Publishers.

Schaaf, Jeanne. 1989. "Governing a Monopoly Market under Siege: Using Institutional Analysis to Understand Competitive Entry into Telecommunications Markets, 1944–1982." Ph.D. diss., Indiana University.

Schank, Roger C., and Robert P. Abelson. 1977. *Scripts, Plans, Goals, and Understanding: An Inquiry in Human Knowledge Structures*. Hillsdale, NJ: Lawrence Erlbaum Associates.

Scharpf, Fritz W. 1997. *Games Real Actors Play: Actor-Centered Institutionalism in Policy Research*. Boulder, CO: Westview Press.

Schelling, Thomas C. 1978. *Micromotives and Macrobehavior*. New York: W. W. Norton.

Schiemann, John W. 2002. "History and Emotions, Beliefs and Mental Models: Toward a Hermeneutics of Rational Choice." Paper presented at the American Political Science Association meeting, Boston, 29 August–1 September.

Schlager, Edella. 1990. "Model Specification and Policy Analysis: The Governance of Coastal Fisheries." Ph.D. diss., Indiana University.

———. 1994. "Fishers' Institutional Responses to Common-Pool Resource Dilemmas." In *Rules, Games, and Common-Pool Resources*, ed. Elinor Ostrom, Roy Gardner, and James Walker, 247–66. Ann Arbor: University of Michigan Press.

———. 1999. "A Comparison of Frameworks, Theories, and Models of Policy Processes." In *Theories of the Policy Process*, ed. Paul A. Sabatier, 233–60. Boulder, CO: Westview Press.

———. 2004. "Common-Pool Resource Theory." In *Environmental Governance Reconsidered: Challenges, Choices, and Opportunities*, ed. Robert Durant, Daniel Fiorino, and Rosemary O'Leary, 145–75. Cambridge: MIT Press.

Schlager, Edella, William Blomquist, and Shui Yan Tang. 1994. "Mobile Flows, Storage, and Self-Organized Institutions for Governing Common-Pool Resources." *Land Economics* 70(3) (August): 294–317.

Schlager, Edella, and Elinor Ostrom. 1992. "Property-Rights Regimes and Natural Resources: A Conceptual Analysis." *Land Economics* 68(3) (August): 249–62.

———. 1993. "Property-Rights Regimes and Coastal Fisheries: An Empirical Analysis." In *The Political Economy of Customs and Culture: Informal Solutions to the Commons Problem*, ed. Terry L. Anderson and Randy T. Simmons, 13–41. Lanham, MD: Rowman and Littlefield.

Schmid, Allan. 1999. "Government, Property, Markets . . . In That Order . . . Not Government versus Markets." In *The Fundamental Interrelationships between Government and Property*, ed. Nicholas Mercuro and Warren Samuels, 233–37. Stamford, CT: JAI Press.

———. 2004. *Conflict and Cooperation: Institutional and Behavioral Economics*. Malden, MA: Blackwell.

Schmitt, Pamela, Kurtis Swope, and James Walker. 2000. "Collective Action with Incomplete Commitment: Experimental Evidence." *Southern Economic Journal* 66(4):829–54.

Schotter, Andrew. 1981. *The Economic Theory of Social Institutions*. Cambridge: Cambridge University Press.

Schuessler, Rudolf. 1989. "Exit Threats and Cooperation under Anonymity." *Journal of Conflict Resolution* 33(4):728–49.

Schweik, Charles M. 2000. "Optimal Foraging, Institutions, and Forest Change: A Case from Nepal." In *People and Forests: Communities, Institutions, and Governance*, ed. Clark Gibson, Margaret McKean, and Elinor Ostrom, 57–85. Cambridge: MIT Press.

Schweik, Charles M., Tom Evans, and J. Morgan Grove. Forthcoming. "Open Source and Open Content: A Framework for the Development of Socio-Ecological Research." *Ecology and Society*.

Schweik, Charles M., and Andrei Semenov. 2003. "The Institutional Design of 'Open Source' Programming: Implications for Addressing Complex Public Policy and Management Problems." *First Monday* 8(1). <http://www.first monday.org/issues/issue8_1/schweik/>

Scott, Anthony D. 1955. "The Fishery: The Objectives of Sole Ownership." *Journal of Political Economy* 63:116–24.

———. 1993. "Obstacles to Fishery Self-Government." *Marine Resource Economics* 8:187–99.

———. Forthcoming. *The Evolution of Resource Rights*. Oxford: Oxford University Press.

Seabright, Paul. 1993. "Managing Local Commons: Theoretical Issues in Incentive Design." *Journal of Economic Perspectives* 7(4):113–34.

Searle, John. 1969. *Speech Acts: An Essay in the Philosophy of Language*. New York: Cambridge University Press.

Seixas, Cristiana, and Fikret Berkes. 2003. "Dynamics of Social-Ecological Changes in a Lagoon Fishery in Southern Brazil." In *Navigating Social-Ecological Systems*, ed. Fikret Berkes, Johan Colding, and Carl Folke, 271–98. Cambridge: Cambridge University Press.

Sekher, Madhushree. 2000. "Local Organisations and Participatory CPR Management: Some Reflections." Working Paper no. 61. Bangalore, India: Institute for Social and Economic Change.

Selten, Reinhard. 1998. "Features of Experimentally Observed Bounded Rationality." *European Economic Review* 42:413–36.

Selten, Reinhard, Klaus Abbink, and Ricarda Cox. 2001. "Learning Direction Theory and the Winners Curse." Discussion paper no. 10/2001. Bonn, Germany: University of Bonn, Department of Economics.

Sen, Amartya K. 1977. "Rational Fools: A Critique of the Behavioral Foundations of Economic Theory." *Philosophy and Public Affairs* 6(4):317–44.

Sengupta, Nirmal. 1991. *Managing Common Property: Irrigation in India and the Philippines.* New Delhi: Sage.

Sethi, Rajiv. 1996. "Evolutionary Stability and Social Norms." *Journal of Economic Behavior and Organization* 29(1):113–40.

Shepherd, Gill. 1992. *Managing Africa's Tropical Dry Forests: A Review of Indigenous Methods.* London: Overseas Development Institute.

Shepsle, Kenneth A. 1975. "Congressional Committee Assignments: An Optimization Model with Institutional Constraints." *Public Choice* 22:55–78.

———. 1979a. "Institutional Arrangements and Equilibrium in Multidimensional Voting Models." *American Journal of Political Science* 23:27–59.

———. 1979b. "The Role of Institutional Structure in the Creation of Policy Equilibrium." In *Public Policy and Public Choice,* ed. Douglas W. Rae and Theodore J. Eismeier, 249–83. Sage Yearbooks in Politics and Public Policy, vol. 6. Beverly Hills, CA: Sage.

———. 1989. "Studying Institutions: Some Lessons from the Rational Choice Approach." *Journal of Theoretical Politics* 1(2) (April): 131–47.

Shepsle, Kenneth A., and Barry R. Weingast. 1984. "When Do Rules of Procedure Matter?" *Journal of Politics* 46:206–21.

———. 1987. "The Institutional Foundations of Committee Power." *American Political Science Review* 81 (March): 85–104.

Sherman, K., and T. Laughlin, eds. 1992. *NOAA Technical Memorandum NMFS-F/NEC 91. The Large Marine Ecosystem (LME) Concept and Its Application to Regional Marine Resource Management.* Woods Hole, MA: Northeast Fisheries Science Center.

Shimanoff, Susan B. 1980. *Communication Rules: Theory and Research.* Beverly Hills, CA: Sage.

Shivakoti, Ganesh, and Elinor Ostrom, eds. 2002. *Improving Irrigation Governance and Management in Nepal.* Oakland, CA: ICS Press.

Shivakumar, Sujai J. 2005. *The Constitution of Development: Crafting Capabilities for Self-Governance.* New York: Palgrave Macmillan.

Shubik, Martin. 1986. "The Games within the Game: Modeling Politico-Economic Structures." In *Guidance, Control, and Evaluation in the Public Sector,* ed. Franz-Xaver Kaufmann, Giandomenico Majone, and Vincent Ostrom, 571–91. Berlin and New York: Walter de Gruyter.

Shukla, Ashutosh K. 2002. "Policies, Processes, and Performance of Management: Turnover and Agency-Initiated Interventions." In *Improving Irrigation*

Governance and Management in Nepal, ed. Ganesh Shivakoti and Elinor Ostrom, 71–102. Oakland, CA: ICS Press.

Shukla, Ashutosh K., Kishor Gajurel, Ganesh Shivakoti, Rabi Poudel, Kala N. Pandit, Keshav R. Adhikari, Tej Thapa, S. M. Shakya, D. N. Yadav, Neeraj R. Joshi, and A. P. Shrestha. 1993. *Irrigation Resource Inventory of East Chitwan.* Rampur, Chitwan, Nepal: Institute of Agriculture and Animal Science, Irrigation Management Systems Study Group.

Sieber, Sam D. 1981. *Fatal Remedies: The Ironies of Social Intervention.* New York: Plenum Press.

Simon, Adam, and Heather Gorgura. 2003. "Say the Magic Word: Effective Communication in Social Dilemmas." Working Paper. Seattle: University of Washington, Department of Political Science.

Simon, Herbert A. 1955. "A Behavioural Model of Rational Choice." *Quarterly Journal of Economics* 69:99–188.

———. 1957. *Models of Man.* New York: Wiley.

———. 1972. "Theories of Bounded Rationality." In *Decision and Organization: A Volume in Honor of Jacob Marschak*, ed. C. B. McGuire and Roy Radner, 161–76. Amsterdam: North Holland.

———. 1981. *The Sciences of the Artificial.* 2d ed. Cambridge: MIT Press.

———. 1995. "Near Decomposability and Complexity: How a Mind Resides in a Brain." In *The Mind, the Brain, and Complex Adaptive Systems*, ed. Harold J. Morowitz and Jerome L. Singer, 25–44. Reading, MA: Addison-Wesley.

———. 1999. "The Potlatch between Political Science and Economics." In *Competition and Cooperation: Conversations with Nobelists about Economics and Political Science*, ed. James Alt, Margaret Levi, and Elinor Ostrom, 112–9. New York: Russell Sage Foundation.

Singleton, Sara. 1998. *Constructing Cooperation: The Evolution of Institutions of Comanagement in Pacific Northwest Salmon Fisheries.* Ann Arbor: University of Michigan Press.

Singleton, Sara, and Michael Taylor. 1992. "Common Property Economics: A General Theory and Land Use Applications." *Journal of Theoretical Politics* 4(3):309–24.

Skyrms, Brian. 1997. "Chaos and the Explanatory Significance of Equilibrium: Strange Attractors in Evolutionary Game Dynamics." In *The Dynamics of Norms*, ed. Cristina Bicchieri, Richard Jeffrey, and Brian Skyrms, 199–222. Cambridge: Cambridge University Press.

Smith, Robert J. 1981. "Resolving the Tragedy of the Commons by Creating Private Property Rights in Wildlife." *CATO Journal* 1:439–68.

Smith, Vernon L. 1982. "Microeconomic Systems as an Experimental Science." *American Economic Review* 72 (December): 923–55.

———. 1991. *Papers in Experimental Economics.* New York: Cambridge University Press.

———. 2000. *Essays in Experimental Economics.* New York: Cambridge University Press.

———. 2001. "Mind, Reciprocity, and Markets in the Laboratory." *Wirtschaft* (August 10): 21 (English version of German translation).

Spooner, Brian. 1974. "Irrigation and Society: The Iranian Plateau." In *Irrigation's Impact on Society*, ed. Theodore E. Downing and McGuire Gibson, 43–57. Tucson: University of Arizona Press.

Sproule-Jones, Mark. 1993. *Governments at Work: Canadian Parliamentary Federalism and Its Public Policy Effects*. Toronto: University of Toronto Press.

Stevens, Stan. 1997. "New Alliances for Conservation." In *Conservation through Cultural Survival: Indigenous Peoples and Protected Areas*, ed. Stan Stevens, 33–62. Washington, DC: Island Press.

Straffin, Philip D. 1977. "Majority Rule and General Decision Rules." *Theory and Decision* 8:351–60. Reprinted in *Rational Man and Irrational Society?: An Introduction and Sourcebook*, ed. Brian Barry and Russell Hardin, 316–24. Beverly Hills, CA: Sage, 1982.

Sugden, Robert. 1986. *The Economics of Rights, Co-operation and Welfare*. Oxford: Basil Blackwell.

Sugrue, Leo P., Greg S. Corrado, and William T. Newsome. 2004. "Matching Behavior and the Representation of Value in the Parietal Cortex." *Science* 304 (June 18): 1782–87.

Sundquist, James L. 1968. *Politics and Policy: The Eisenhower, Kennedy, and Johnson Years*. Washington, DC: Brookings Institution.

Sussman, Robert W., and Audrey R. Chapman, eds. 2004. *The Origins and Nature of Sociality*. New York: Walter de Gruyter.

Tang, Shui Yan. 1992. *Institutions and Collective Action: Self-Governance in Irrigation*. Oakland, CA: ICS Press.

———. 1994. "Institutions and Performance in Irrigation Systems." In *Rules, Games, and Common-Pool Resources*, ed. Elinor Ostrom, Roy Gardner, and James Walker, 225–45. Ann Arbor: University of Michigan Press.

Taylor, Michael. 1982. *Community, Anarchy, and Liberty*. New York: Cambridge University Press.

———. 1987. *The Possibility of Cooperation*. New York: Cambridge University Press.

Tendler, Judith. 2000. "Why Are Social Funds So Popular?" In *Local Dynamics in an Era of Globalization: 21st-Century Catalysts for Development*, ed. Shahid Yusuf, Weiping Wu, and Simon Evenett, 114–29. Oxford: Oxford University Press.

Tesfatsion, Leigh. 2002. "Agent-Based Computational Economics: Growing Economies from the Bottom Up." ISU Economics Working Paper no. 1. Ames: Iowa State University.

Theesfeld, Insa. 2004. "Constraints on Collective Action in a Transitional Economy: The Case of Bulgaria's Irrigation Sector." *World Development* 32(2):251–71.

Thompson, Leigh L., Elizabeth A. Mannix, and Max H. Bazerman. 1988. "Group Negotiation: Effects of Decision Rule, Agenda, and Aspiration." *Journal of Personality and Social Psychology* 54(1):86–95.

Thomson, James T. 1977. "Ecological Deterioration: Local-Level Rule Making and Enforcement Problems in Niger." In *Desertification: Environmental Degradation in and around Arid Lands*, ed. Michael H. Glantz, 57–79. Boulder, CO: Westview Press.

Thomson, James T., David Feeny, and Ronald J. Oakerson. 1992. "Institutional Dynamics: The Evolution and Dissolution of Common-Property Resource Management." In *Making the Commons Work: Theory, Practice, and Policy*, ed. Daniel W. Bromley et al., 129–60. Oakland, CA: ICS Press.

Tietenberg, Tom. 2002. "The Tradable Permits Approach to Protecting the Commons: What Have We Learned?" In *The Drama of the Commons*, National Research Council, Committee on the Human Dimensions of Global Change, ed. Elinor Ostrom, Thomas Dietz, Nives Dolšak, Paul C. Stern, Susan Stonich, and Elke Weber, 197–232. Washington, DC: National Academy Press.

Tilman, David. 1999. "The Ecological Consequences of Changes in Biodiversity: A Search for General Principles." *Ecology* 80:1455–74.

Tilman, David, Clarence L. Lehman, and Charles E. Bristow. 1998. "Diversity-Stability Relationships: Statistical Inevitability or Ecological Consequences?" *American Naturalist* 151:277–82.

Tomasello, Michael. 2004. "Learning through Others." *Daedalus* 133(1):51–58.

Toulmin, Stephen. 1974. "Rules and Their Relevance for Understanding Human Behavior." In *Understanding Other Persons*, ed. Theodore Mischel, 185–215. Oxford: Basil Blackwell.

Trawick, Paul B. 2001. "Successfully Governing the Commons: Principles of Social Organization in an Andean Irrigation System." *Human Ecology* 29(1):1–25.

Trosper, Ronald L. 2002. "Northwest Coast Indigenous Institutions That Supported Resilience and Sustainability." *Ecological Economics* 41(2):329–44.

Tsebelis, George. 1989. "The Abuse of Probability in Political Analysis: The Robinson Crusoe Fallacy." *American Political Science Review* 83:77–91.

———. 1991. "The Effect of Fines on Regulated Industries: Game Theory versus Decision Theory." *Journal of Theoretical Politics* 3(1):81–101.

———. 2002. *Veto Players: How Political Institutions Work*. Princeton: Princeton University Press.

Tucker, Catherine M. 1999. "Common Property Design Principles and Development in a Honduran Community." *Praxis: The Fletcher Journal of Development Studies* 15:47–76.

Tversky, Amos. 1972. "Elimination by Aspects: A Theory of Choice." *Psychological Review* 79:281–99.

Tyler, Tom R. 1990. *Why People Obey the Law*. New Haven: Yale University Press.

Udéhn, Lars. 1993. "Twenty-five Years with *The Logic of Collective Action*." *Acta Sociologica* 36:239–61.

Ullmann-Margalit, Edna. 1977. *The Emergence of Norms*. Oxford: Oxford University Press.

Uphoff, Norman T. 1986. *Getting the Process Right: Improving Irrigation Water Management with Farmer Participation*. Boulder, CO: Westview Press.

Valenzuela, Arturo. 1993. "Latin America: Presidentialism in Crisis." *Journal of Democracy* 4:3–16.

Vanberg, Viktor J. 2002. "Rational Choice versus Program-Based Behavior: Alternative Theoretical Approaches and Their Relevance for the Study of Institutions." *Rationality and Society* 14(1):7–54.

Vanberg, Viktor J., and Roger D. Congleton. 1992. "Rationality, Morality, and Exit." *American Political Science Review* 82(2):418–31.

Van Vugt, Mark, Mark Snyder, Tom R. Tyler, and Anders Biel, eds. 2000. *Cooperation in Modern Society: Promoting the Welfare of Communities, Organizations, and States*. London: Routledge.

Van Wendel de Joode, Ruben. 2004. "Continuity of the Commons in Open Source Communities." Paper presented at the Symposium of Santa Caterina on Challenges in the Internet and Interdisciplinary Research, Amalfi, Italy.

Varughese, George. 2000. "Population and Forest Dynamics in the Hills of Nepal: Institutional Remedies by Rural Communities." In *People and Forests: Communities, Institutions, and Governance*, ed. Clark Gibson, Margaret McKean, and Elinor Ostrom, 193–226. Cambridge: MIT Press.

Varughese, George, and Elinor Ostrom. 2001. "The Contested Role of Heterogeneity in Collective Action: Some Evidence from Community Forestry in Nepal." *World Development* 29(5) (May): 747–65.

Vermillion, Douglas. 2001. "Property Rights and Collective Action in the Devolution of Irrigation System Management." In *Collective Action, Property Rights, and Devolution of Natural Resource Management*, ed. Ruth Meinzen-Dick, Anna Knox, and Monica DiGregorio, 183–220. Feldafing, Germany: Deutsche Stiftung für internationale Entwicklung.

Vogt, Nathan, Abwoli Banana, William Gombya-Ssembajjwe, and Joseph Bahati. 2005. "Understanding the Long Term Stability of the West Mengo Forest Reserve Boundaries." Working paper. Bloomington: Indiana University, Center for the Study of Institutions, Population, and Environmental Change (CIPEC).

von Wright, Georg Henrik. 1951. "Deontic Logic." *Mind* 60:1–15.

———. 1966. "The Logic of Action: A Sketch." In *The Logic of Decision and Action*, ed. Nicholas Rescher, 121–36. Pittsburgh, PA: University of Pittsburgh Press.

———. 1968. "The Logic of Practical Discourse." In *Contemporary Philosophy*, ed. Raymond Klikensky, 141–67. Italy: La Nuava Italia Editrice.

Wade, Robert. 1994. *Village Republics: Economic Conditions for Collective Action in South India*. San Francisco: ICS Press.

Wagner, Richard E. In press. "Self-Governance, Polycentrism, and Federalism: Recurring Themes in Vincent Ostrom's Scholarly Oeuvre." *Journal of Economic Behavior and Organization* 57(2).

Walker, S. Tjip. 1998. "Both Pretense and Promise: The Political Economy of Privatization in Africa." Ph.D. diss., Indiana University.

Water and Energy Commission Secretariat, Nepal, and International Irrigation Management Institute. 1990. *Assistance to Farmer-Managed Irrigation Systems: Results, Lessons, and Recommendations from an Action-Research Project*. Colombo, Sri Lanka: IIMI.

Weber, Max. 1947. *The Theory of Social and Economic Organization*. Translated by A. M. Henderson and Talcott Parsons. New York: Free Press.

Weimer, David L., and Aidan R. Vining. 1992. *Policy Analysis: Concepts and Practice*. 2d ed. Englewood Cliffs, NJ: Prentice Hall.

Weingast, Barry R. 1989. "Floor Behavior in the U.S. Congress: Committee Power under the Open Rule." *American Political Science Review* 78:417–34.

Weinstein, Martin S. 2000. "Pieces of the Puzzle: Solutions for Community-Based Fisheries Management from Native Canadians, Japanese Cooperatives, and Common Property Researchers." *Georgetown International Environmental Law Review* 12(2):375–412.

Weissing, Franz J., and Elinor Ostrom. 1991a. "Irrigation Institutions and the Games Irrigators Play: Rule Enforcement without Guards." In *Game Equilibrium Models II: Methods, Morals, and Markets*, ed. Reinhard Selten, 188–262. Berlin: Springer-Verlag.

——. 1991b. "Crime and Punishment." *Journal of Theoretical Politics* 3(3):343–9.

——. 1993. "Irrigation Institutions and the Games Irrigators Play: Rule Enforcement on Government- and Farmer-Managed Systems." In *Games in Hierarchies and Networks: Analytical and Empirical Approaches to the Study of Governance Institutions*, ed. Fritz W. Scharpf, 387–428. Frankfurt am Main: Campus Verlag; Boulder, CO: Westview Press.

Wells, Michael, and Katrina Brandon. 1992. *People and Parks: Linking Protected Area Management with Local Communities*. Washington, DC: World Bank.

Wiggins, Steven N., and Gary D. Libecap. 1987. "Firm Heterogeneities and Cartelization Efforts in Domestic Crude Oil." *Journal of Law, Economics, and Organization* 3:1–25.

Williamson, Oliver E. 1975. *Markets and Hierarchies: Analysis and Antitrust Implications*. New York: Free Press.

——. 1985. *The Economic Institutions of Capitalism*. New York: Free Press.

——. 2000. "The New Institutional Economics: Take Stock, Looking Ahead." *Journal of Economic Literature* 38 (September): 593–613.

Wilson, Douglas, Jesper Nielsen, and Poul Degnbol, eds. 2003. *The Fisheries Co-management Experience: Accomplishments, Challenges, and Prospects*. Dordrecht, the Netherlands: Kluwer.

Wilson, James A. 1990. "Fishing for Knowledge." *Land Economics* 66:12–29.

——. 1997. "Maine Fisheries Management Initiative." In *The Social Impacts of Individual Transferable Quotas*, ed. Gisli Palsson, 335–53. Copenhagen: TemaNord.

——. 2002. "Scientific Uncertainty, Complex Systems, and the Design of Common-Pool Institutions." In *The Drama of the Commons*, National Research Council, Committee on the Human Dimensions of Global Change, ed. Elinor Ostrom, Thomas Dietz, Nives Dolšak, Paul C. Stern, Susan Stonich, and Elke Weber, 327–59. Washington, DC: National Academy Press.

Wilson, James A., James M. Acheson, Mark Metcalfe, and Peter Kleban. 1994. "Chaos, Complexity, and Community Management of Fisheries." *Marine Policy* 18:291–305.

Wilson, James A., Bobbi Low, Robert Costanza, and Elinor Ostrom. 1999. "Scale Misperceptions and the Spatial Dynamics of a Social-Ecological System." *Ecological Economics* 31(2) (November): 243–57.

Wilson, Paul N., and Gary D. Thompson. 1993. "Common Property and Uncertainty: Compensating Coalitions by Mexico's Pastoral *Ejidatorios*." *Economic Development and Cultural Change* 41(2):299–318.

World Bank. 2002. *Social Funds—Assessing Effectiveness*. Washington, DC: World Bank Operations Evaluation Department (OED).

Wynne, Susan G. 1989. "The Land Boards of Botswana: A Problem in Institutional Design." Ph.D. diss., Indiana University.

Yandle, Tracy. 2001. "Market-Based Natural Resource Management: An Institutional Analysis of Individual Tradable Quotas in New Zealand's Commercial Fisheries." Ph.D. diss., Indiana University.

Yandle, Tracy, and Christopher Dewees. 2003. "Privatizing the Commons . . . Twelve Years Later: Fishers' Experiences with New Zealand's Market-Based Fisheries Management." In *The Commons in the New Millennium: Challenges and Adaptations*, ed. Nives Dolšak and Elinor Ostrom, 101–27. Cambridge: MIT Press.

Yoder, Robert D. 1991. "Peer Training as a Way to Motivate Institutional Change in Farmer-Managed Irrigation Systems." In *Proceedings of the Workshop on Democracy and Governance*. Decentralization: Finance and Management Project Report, 53–67. Burlington, VT: Associates in Rural Development.

———. 1994. *Locally Managed Irrigation Systems*. Colombo, Sri Lanka: International Irrigation Management Institute.

Young, H. Peyton. 1998. *Individual Strategy and Social Structure: An Evolutionary Theory of Institutions*. Princeton: Princeton University Press.

Young, Oran R. 1997. *Global Governance: Drawing Insights from the Environmental Experience*. Cambridge: MIT Press.

———. 2002. *The Institutional Dimensions of Environmental Change: Fit, Interplay, and Scale*. Cambridge: MIT Press.

Index